ENCYCLOPEDIA OF
JEWISH HUMOR

ENCYCLOPEDIA
of
JEWISH HUMOR

From Biblical Times to the Modern Age

Compiled and Edited by
HENRY D. SPALDING

With a Glossary by
DOROTHY H. ROCHMIS

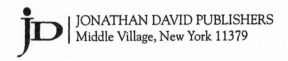

JONATHAN DAVID PUBLISHERS
Middle Village, New York 11379

ENCYCLOPEDIA OF JEWISH HUMOR

Copyright © 2001
by
Henry D. Spalding

No part of this book may be reproduced
in any manner without written
permission from the publisher.

Address all inquiries to:

JONATHAN DAVID PUBLISHERS, INC.
68-22 Eliot Avenue
Middle Village, NY 11379

www.jdbooks.com

2 4 6 8 10 9 7 5 3 1

Library of Congress Cataloging-in-Publication Data

Encyclopedia of Jewish humor : from Biblical times to the modern age /
compiled and edited by Henry D. Spalding ; with a glossary by Dorothy H.
Rochmis.
    p. cm.
Originally published: New York : J. David, 1969.
ISBN 0-8246-0439-3 (CL) – ISBN 0-8246-0437-7 (PB)
1. Jewish wit and humor. I. Spalding, Henry D.
PN6231.J5 S67 2001
808.87'0089'924–dc21   CIP
                                                    00-050895

Printed in the United States of America

Acknowledgements

Grateful acknowledgment is made to the lovely and scholarly Dorothy H. Rochmis for the brilliant (and often humorous) glossary appended to this anthology, and for her long-suffering patience as I struggled with the correct grammatical usage of the Yiddish, Hebrew, Russian and Polish words and phrases used throughout. If there are any errors in the text, the reader may be sure they are mine, not Dorothy's. May she marry a Rothschild and live to a hundred and twenty!

My deep appreciation is extended to Samuel B. Gach, publisher of *The California Jewish Voice*, whose fine journal provided so many anecdotes; Julie H. Collen, Jewish-Russian-Hebrew historian, transliterationist and writer, for her dedicated research in the interests of factual accuracy; Rabbi Montague Isaacs, Los Angeles spiritual leader of Congregation Tifereth Jacob, for his counsel and suggested stories so freely given; David Schwartz, syndicated columnist for *The Jewish Telegraphic Agency*, for his kind permission to quote from his witty dispatches; Yetta Koffman, my dear cousin, and her sons, Bill and George, for their many contributions; Sam and Bella Monoson, my uncle and aunt, for their delightful remembrances which you will read in these pages. . . .

And to the many others whose encouragement, suggestions and wealth of stories and witticisms helped bring this encyclopedia to fruition—

My profound thanks.

H. D. S.

To Danny, Randy, Susie and Laurie, all four of whom are undoubtedly convinced they can tell a funny story better than their

DAD

Contents

CONTENTS *(continued)*

CONTENTS *(continued)*

CONTENTS *(continued)*

Preface

The surest way to destroy the humor of a funny story is to analyze it. Except for the professional entertainer, and perhaps the psychiatrist, the components are seldom as interesting as the composite: it is the denouement that evokes our merriment, and that should be the only criterion. After all, to make a big *megillah* out of a brief witticism nobody needs. Yet, our intellect tells us there must be underlying reasons why Jewish wit and humor have endured for some thirty-five centuries—the oldest recorded humor known to man.

Before we define the Jewish joke, let us first ask ourselves "What is a Jew?" That question has been intermittently propounded by the sages of the House of Israel ever since Shem, Ham (you should pardon the expression), and Japheth indignantly demanded of Papa Noah what was the big idea of bringing two pigs aboard the Ark. Even for the contemporary American, the statement, "I am a Jew because I am a Jew" is often met with skepticism, as witnessed the old woman who approached a blonde, blue-eyed man. "Excuse me, Mister," she began tentatively, "but you're a Jewish boy?" He regarded her disdainfully for a moment and then replied, "No, madam, I am not." Still uncertain, she repeated her question. Irritated, he answered icily, "I told you, I am not a Jew!" But she was a persistent soul and she put the question to him for the third time: "You're sure you're not Jewish?" The old lady's determination finally broke down his defenses. "Yes," he confessed, "I'm Jewish." To which she replied, "That's funny, you don't *look* Jewish!"

What, then, is a Jew? In selecting, editing and rewriting the varied source material in this anthology I have considered Jews to be members of an ethnic group who, to a greater or lesser extent, share a common religion, a community of ideals embodied in their spiritual and traditional teachings, a fierce dedication to the principles of democracy, and who enjoy a secondary, but important, relationship to each other in their personal and collective outlook. This is an oversimplification, to be sure, but for the purposes of this book it is, I hope, sufficient.

As a general rule, the Jewish joke revolves around those objects, ideas and situations which are familiar to Jews everywhere, geography notwithstanding. The Jew, dwelling in an obscure *shtetl* in Galicia, immediately grasps the point of a traditional joke as quickly as his more sophisticated co-religionist in Staten Island, and he responds in much the same way; with an appreciative grin, a delighted chuckle, or a *poopik*-busting howl of laughter. One such traditional joke is the yarn about Job's trials and tribulations which stresses the biblical figure's intense piety, his fervent worship, and the poignancy of his almost hourly prayers. One day, in despair, Job lifts his voice to the heavens and wails, "God, why do You permit me to suffer like this when I spend all my time in prayerful devotion?" And a wrathful voice booms down from the sky: "Because you *nudgehd* me!"

Why is it that the untutored Jew of eastern Europe reacts to an institutionalized or ritualized "inside" story in the same way as his more urbane American *mishpoche*? The answer, I believe, is that both listen to the joke with a third ear or read it with a third eye. Even if only subconsciously, they experience an awareness of fraternity, a sharing of latent emotion, a recognition of oneness evolved over a span of 3500 years, and perhaps most important, an innate *need* for such identity.

The true Jewish joke mirrors the history of the Jewish people. It is a reflection of their joy and anguish, their aspirations and discouragements, their all too brief periods of social and economic well-being. It expresses their ages-old yearning for a world in which justice, mercy, understanding and equality will prevail—not only for themselves but for all people. It portrays their quest for eternal truths.

Unlike the progress of science, Jewish humor did not advance in a straight line from primitive to modern times, but rather developed in concentric circles, sometimes expanding, at others contracting, which illuminated the mores of the day. The Jews were a humorous people even in biblical times, and the Torah abounds in every form of witticism, humor, riddle and practical joke. When David caused the death of Uriah in order to marry his beautiful wife, the prophet Nathan moved him to repentance by the parable of the rich man who robbed a poor man of his only lamb in order to entertain his guest.

Some well-known scholars claim that true Jewish humor did not flower until after the Emancipation. These otherwise knowledgeable scholars should know better—and so should their publishers. Take *Isaiah*, for example. Its pages bristle with humor, parody and biting wit. ("Woe unto them that are mighty to drink wine.") We also find sarcasm in the earlier prophets. When Achish, King of Gath, looked at David who was simulating insanity, he exclaimed, "Have I need of madmen that you have brought this fellow to play the madman?" Then there is the withering sarcasm of Elijah when he taunts the prophets of Baal: "Cry aloud, for he is a god; either he is talking, or he is pursuing, or he is on a journey, or peradventure he sleepeth and must be awakened."

With the destruction of the Second Temple and the Dispersion, Jewish humor entered a broader plane. The people's contacts with other cultures, the persecutions and indignities that followed, forced them to create allegories by which they expressed their protests against their tormentors. We find much of this allegorical humor in the Talmud. Indeed, the ancient rabbis were masters of repartee and the shattering retort, but they differed from the biblical sages in that they were far more subtle. The rabbinic story is calculated to evoke a smile and make one think, but rarely to cause hilarious laughter. Some talmudic witticisms, of course, had no other purpose than to amuse, such as the humorous observation by a third-century rabbi who claimed that the sea was salty because so many salt herrings lived in it.

It is probably true that the modern Jewish joke came into being just prior to the 20th century. For this we owe a debt of gratitude to pre-Soviet Russia—a pox on its head!! Just as the Czarist regime brought about its own downfall by refusing admittance in the imperial universities to young intellectuals (thus forcing them to enter Western European centers of learning where they discovered and then brought back Marxian philosophy), the government, also unwittingly, stimulated the resurgence of Jewish humor by permitting, however reluctantly, foreign students to attend talmudic academies in Russia.

The students made the *yeshivah* their home. They ate there and slept there. Late of a winter evening after school hours, the *bachurim* gathered around the large warm brick stove and swapped stories. As with youths the world over—and never mind their race or religion—their opening stories were about girls. But once the sex jokes expected of virile young men were told and re-told, they exchanged folk tales current among the masses. Other anecdotes were the ingenious creations of the narrators in which they wove their hopes for the future as well as their pride in the past. Returning to their native countries, cities and villages, the talmudic students recounted their droll stories and bon mots to their friends and relatives. Thus, the stories gained in popularity and took on the flavor of the approaching and more enlightened 20th century.

The typical old-time Jewish joke was often a sardonic, even merciless self-derogation that bordered on the masochistic. Dr. Sigmund Freud, in his *Wit and Its Relation to the Unconscious,* published in 1905, attributes this phenomenon to an innate self-hatred of the Jew's own Jewishness. Perhaps!—but I offer another explanation. It seems to me that the reason is plain enough: the narrator recognizes himself for what he is—a simple human being, subject to all the foibles of mortal mind and frailties of the flesh. And because he has the moral and intellectual courage to recognize and then ridicule his own weaknesses, he sees no reason to spare the sensibilities of his adversaries for their own deficiencies.

Therein lies the key to the difference between the Jewish and the anti-Semitic joke: the latter emphasizes the faults but never the virtues of the Jew. Nor should we forget that the target of the true Jewish joke is not necessarily an anti-Semite, as many believe, nor even a despotic government. Derision is more often directed at another Jew, as I shall point out in a moment.

Where the Jewish quip is aimed at a nation, rather than an individual, it is always sharp, penetrating and informative, e.g., "The trouble with eating a German meal is that you are quickly hungry again—for power!"

One would think that the scripturally-termed "stiff-necked" Jews would react harshly to the motley transgressors, fools and sharpies among them. But here we are confronted with an anomaly: it is just as likely that the opposite is true. Once again we return to that inner identity which permits the Jew to regard his *landsleit* with amused toleration. He can smile at the *shlemiel* who testifies as a minor witness in court at his friend's trial and winds up as the convicted party; the *shlimazl*, Jewry's original Hard Luck Harry, whose pants fall down during his wedding ceremony; the convert to Christianity who now insists on his right to eat ham—but on matzoh; the rabbi who demands a mink *yarmulkeh*; the cantor who fancies himself as a reincarnated Caruso; the fancy *mohel* on Park Avenue who insists on using pinking shears for circumcisions; the *nouveau riche*, the parvenu, the status-seeker, the chronic imbiber, the atheist, the thief and the inveterate liar. And the merriment they evoke is tolerant rather than overly critical, because in many of them the Jewish listener recognizes a little *eppes* of himself.

There is another unique element which Jews employ in their humor: a propensity to hurl honey-coated barbs at those nearest and dearest to their hearts. They scoff at their loved ones, their religion, the very ideals and institutions which exalt and enrich their souls. The singularity of this banter lies in the fact that it radiates affection—a kiss with salt on the lips, but a kiss nevertheless. What other people joke about their mothers, for example, as do the Jews? The Yiddishe Mama has become a stereotype, but what lovely expressions of tenderness those waggish stories convey! Among them is the following World War II joke:

Mama's three sons are in the Army, her daughter is serving in the Navy as a WAVE, and her husband works in a munitions plant. So she decides that she too will do her bit to defend freedom. She applies to the chief supervisor of nurses at Montefiore Hospital as a first-aid helper. The supervisor asks, "What would you do if suddenly the bombs fell here in New York and the dead and horribly injured were strewn all over the streets?" Mama replies, "First I would sit down in a chair, then I'd bend forward till my head touched my knees—and that would keep me from fainting."

Another:

At a banquet for a famous Zionist, a half-dozen speakers rose to eulogize the guest of honor, stressing his integrity, his honesty, his sense of duty and his contributions to charity. Puzzled, Mama turned to her husband and whispered, *sotto voce*, "What's the matter such a prominent man needs so many character witnesses?"

The idiom, indeed the very flow and cadence of most European jokes that revolve around religion (and that includes biblical characters, rabbis, apostates and references to God), often assumes the quality of a *krechtz*, or groan. Not so in America. Here, religious raillery has attained a high degree of sophistication. Dorothy H. Rochmis, the gifted lexicographer who prepared the glossary for this anthology, offers the following illustration of contemporary Jewish-American satire:

The Exodus had just begun. Moses stood on the shore of the Red Sea and, with a despairing heart, gazed upon the vast expanse of ocean that barred the avenue of escape for his people. Not far behind, the Egyptians were in hot pursuit of the fleeing Israelites, bent on returning them to bondage. Moses turned to his public relations man for guidance but the PR man's expression was blank. Suddenly Moses' face brightened. "Say, I have a terrific idea!" he exclaimed. "Just suppose I were to raise my left hand and immediately the waters of the Red Sea parted and allowed us to pass through. And then suppose that after our people had crossed over safely to the other side, I were to raise my right hand and close the parted waters, drowning the Egyptian soldiers who are chasing us! How would you like that?" The public relations man saw the possibilities at once. "Listen, Moe," he replied enthusiastically, "you pull a miracle like that and I can guarantee you ten whole pages in the Bible!"

Now let us focus our attention on the difference between those jokes told by Jews but which are not necessarily Jewish, and those that unquestionably retain the flavor of *schmaltz* and *gribbn*. Harry Hershfield provides an illustration of the former:

A professor of anatomy, addressing his students, holds up a live frog and says, "I am about to prove an important theory." He places the frog on his desk and cries "Jump!" It makes a great leap. The professor then cuts off all four of its legs. "Now I am about to demonstrate my thesis," he announces. Again he puts the frog down on the desk and commands, "Jump!" The poor frog, of course, makes no move. Again he shouts, "Jump!" No response from the frog. "I have just proved my point," the professor concludes. "If you cut off a frog's legs it can't hear."

Hershfield's story is a funny one, but the characters could just as well be gentile as Jewish, nor does he pretend to label this as a Jewish story. Now let us look at another type of joke in which Jewish characters are used, but in which the effect would have remained equally humorous had the subjects been gentile.

An El Al jetliner takes off from the Tel Aviv airport, bound for New York. On the plane an elderly man is sitting next to a proud young mother whose infant is cradled in her arms. The man peers into the folds of the baby's blanket, takes one look at its face and exclaims, *"Oy vay!* What a monstrosity! Never in my life did I see such an ugly baby!" The mother is outraged. "How dare you!" she shrieks. The stewardess, hearing the commotion, hurries over to the quarreling pair. "I'm Mrs. Litvak, your friendly shtudess," she announces, "and on my plane I don't need there should be any fighting or I'll call my son, the captain." The young lady sobs, "He insulted me." The man heatedly denies the accusation. Mrs. Litvak then attempts to placate them both, "Look, mister, you go sit someplace else and stop insulting the passengers." Now she turns to the mother and says consolingly, "For you I'll bring a nice glass hot tea with lemon—and I'll also bring a banana for your monkey."

Contrast the above two illustrations with one that is truly Jewish in characterization and thought. Here we find a typical Jewish mother confronted with her daughter's sudden elopement, religious and racial problems, unemployment and a housing shortage. One almost anticipates the mother's solution:

Rosie telephones her house with some breath-taking news:

"Mama, I got married."

"*Mazel Tov!*"

"I might as well tell you, he's a *goy*."

"So he's a *goy!* I'm prejudiced?"

"But, Mama, he's also a Negro."

"All right, he's a *schvartzeh*. By me everybody should be tolerant."

"Well, frankly, Mama, he's unemployed."

"*Nu*, so you'll support him. A wife she should help her husband."

"But, Mama, we have no place to live."

"Don't worry, Rosie darling. You'll stay right here in our house."

"But you only have one bedroom."

"That's all right. You and your new husband can sleep in the bedroom and Papa can sleep on the sofa in the living room."

"Yes, but, Mama, where will you sleep?"

"Rosie dear, about me you got nothing to worry. The minute I'm hanging up I'll drop dead!"

Mama's reaction mirrors the concern of a people whose ranks, depleted by the Nazis, are being further reduced through intermarriage and conversion. Apostasy is usually viewed with suspicion—as though the convert had some ulterior motive for adopting another religion. "Once a Jew, always a Jew" seems to be the underlying belief. There are a number of such jokes in this anthology, of which this one is representative: For the past five years Max has been a Christian Scientist. One Sunday morning, as he is leaving the house to go to church, his wife seizes his arm. "What's the matter with you?" she cries. "You're wearing a *yarmulkeh!*" Startled, Max groans, "*Oy*, I forgot! It's my *goyisheh kop*."

The reader will notice that I have included several stories in which Negroes are mentioned. There is an affinity between these two peoples. Both have known slavery, deprivation and social ostracism. Today's American Jew has, for the most part, escaped from the anti-Semitism of earlier times, but his memories are still too acute to be easily forgotten; thus his compassion for his fellow man. The word *schvartzeh*, in this case, is not used in a pejorative sense any more than is the use of the word *goy*, which simply means "gentile." We can therefore laugh unselfconsciously at the story of the little colored boy, Abraham Lincoln Goldstein. At the end of the first day of school, the teacher calls him aside and says, "Abe, your last name interests me. Are you Jewish?" And little Abraham answers, "No ma'am. I got enough *tsorres* being a *schvartzeh!*"

The difference between the Jewish jokes of old Europe and modern America is seen in the easy flow of the latter—especially in the delightful non sequiturs. Consider the tale of six-year-old Sammy who was taken to see Santa Claus at Macy's Department Store. The reluctant boy was pushed into the long line of other waiting children eager to tell Santa their Christmas wishes. But when little Sammy's turn came he sullenly refused to sit on Santa's knee.

"What would you like for Christmas, young man?" asked the white-bearded old gentleman.

"Nuttin'!" Sammy muttered.

"Don't you believe in Christmas?"

"Nahhh!"

"Don't you believe in anything?"

"Yeah," answered Sammy. "Chanukah."

Santa grinned broadly, patted the boy's head, and crooned, *"A leben of dein shein keppele."*

Where to begin reading this anthology! In the unlikely event that I am consulted, I would suggest that you choose your subject at random. Chapter 38, *Only in America,* may, for some, be the funniest part of the book, but don't overlook the earnest rabbi, Jewry's most predominant personality who, for many centuries, was the legal as well as the spiritual leader of his community; the *schnorrer*—that gay rogue who scorned honest toil and lived by his wits—Jewry's original con man; yesterday's *shadchan,* whose chase after the marriage broker's fee induced him to make the grossest exaggerations, but who invariably stressed the ideals of womanly virtue and integrity rather than transient physical beauty. You may want to open these pages to, not that darling Jewish mother of whom we have grown so fond, but to the *Yiddishe* papa, as he instructs little Mortie in the ways of the birds and the bees. Surely he has been as neglected as Whistler's father.

There are, in this collection, thirty-nine chapters in which the colorful characters of Jewish folklore march hand in hand through the centuries. But I confess that I have granted myself wide latitude in the classifications selected for the subjects. Often it was the merest nuance that decided whether an anecdote would be included in the Science or Education chapters, the Dirty Crooks or Legal chapters, and so on. If my categories are not as sharply defined as they should be, do me something! I am not a statistician all of a sudden.

In the very first line of this preface, I said, "The surest way to destroy the humor of a funny story is to analyze it." So what did I do? I did what any other perverse, self-respecting Jew would do: I analyzed it. Now I am done with explanations.

Read a little something.

H. D. S.

Chapter One

Merry Mishmash from Old Europe

Once upon a time there lived a man whose name was Saul the Dreamer. Saul was a man of roving and adventurous disposition, always ready to travel and explore. One day, an itinerant *maggid* told him about a far-away country where onions were unknown.

"No onions!" mused the Dreamer. "Now what kind of pleasure can they derive from their food without onions? I'll go there and introduce this delicious vegetable."

Without any further delay he acquired a wagon-load of onions and started out for that country. It was a distant land and the journey took many months.

Immediately upon his arrival he went directly to the royal court and asked for an audience with the emperor.

"Your Highness, I bring you a new vegetable that possesses the unique quality of improving all food," began Saul. "Even by itself it is a gourmet's delight. I urge you to try it."

"Very well," agreed the monarch. "But if this strange vegetable should prove injurious you will forfeit your head."

The dinner at which the onions were to be served was a formal one. All the ministers of state, the nobles and high priests of the mighty realm were invited. The dishes which contained the onions were tasted first by Saul the Dreamer, then by the slaves, and then, in turn, by the potentates and prelates. Finally the king tasted the new vegetable. The reaction among all was one of great enthusiasm. Serf and sovereign alike pronounced it most excellent in flavor and succulence.

The monarch appropriated the wagon-load of onions for his court and gave Saul their weight in gold.

When the adventurer returned home, a committee of prominent citizens gathered to congratulate him on his good fortune. For hours he told his curious *landsleit* of the splendor and magnificence he had witnessed in that distant and mysterious country where gold was cheaper than onions.

Fired by these tales, one enterprising individual, Kolboynik by name, conceived a plan by which he was certain to make even a bigger fortune

1

than had Saul the Dreamer. Garlic, he figured, is not only more expensive than onions but infinitely more fragrant. So why not take a few sacks of that delicacy to the far-away land? Surely, if they would exchange gold for onions, they would give him the equivalent weight in diamonds! Whereupon he set out for that mystic country with a cargo of five bags of garlic.

As did Saul the Dreamer, he succeeded in inducing the king to give his innovation a trial. And, just as he had foretold, the garlic was relished much more than the onions. The monarch held a consultation with his ministers as to the form of recompense to be paid to this noble visitor. Gold, they unanimously decided (and as Kolboynik had guessed), would not be an adequate remuneration for such delectable food in which even God and the angels might take delight. Therefore, they decided to reward him with the most precious commodity in all their kingdom.

Kolboynik returned home with his reward—five sacks of onions!

✓ ✓ ✓

There is a difference between being able and being willing, as this century-old message conveys.

Reba, the wife of Yankel the poet, sent her husband to market to buy a cow. Before long, Yankel returned with the animal and brought it into the barn.

Reba, looking through the window, grabbed a pail and hurried out to the barn to milk the new cow, but a few minutes later she stormed into the house, blazing with fury.

"*Shlemiel!*" she screeched. "How could you pay good money for such a useless animal?"

"Why, what's the matter with her?" asked Yankel.

"You ask yet? I'll tell you. Your expensive cow doesn't want to give one drop of milk!"

"Maybe you don't know how. Let me try."

So Yankel took the pail and went to the barn to woo the moo. Within a few minutes, he too returned with an empty pail.

"Reba, hereafter I must caution you to watch your sentence structure," said the poet-husband sternly.

"Wh-what!"

"You made a grievous error, semantically speaking. How could you say the cow doesn't *want* to give any milk, when the simple truth is that she wants to, but, the poor thing, she *can't!*"

✓ ✓ ✓

Two woebegone talmudic students came to their rabbi and made a shamefaced confession. "Rabbi, we've committed a sin."

"A sin? What kind of a sin?"

"We looked with lust upon a woman."

"May God forgive you!" cried the holy man. "That is indeed a serious transgression."

"Rabbi," said the students, humbly, "what can we do to atone?"

"Well, if you sincerely seek penance, I order you to put peas into your shoes and walk about that way for ten days. Perhaps that will teach you not to sin again."

The two young men went home and did as the rabbi had ordered them. A few days later the penitents met on the street. One was hobbling painfully, but the other walked easily, his manner calm and contented.

"Is this the way to obey the rabbi?" asked the first student reproachfully: "I see you ignored his injunction to put peas into your shoes."

"I didn't ignore him at all," said the other cheerfully. "I just cooked them first."

✔   ✔   ✔

Two Jewish knights of the road were trudging wearily to the next town where they hoped to *shnorr* something to eat, when suddenly they came upon a loaf of fresh bread. Apparently it had dropped from a baker's wagon only a short time before.

The starved pilgrims pounced on the precious bread like two birds of prey.

"Break it in half and let's start eating," said the first impatiently.

The other, however, was something of a philosopher, and being of an aesthetic turn of mind, he protested vigorously against the unseemly haste of his colleague.

"How can you be so greedy?" he scolded. "Before we consume this heaven-sent loaf, let us feast our eyes upon it and gratify our visual and spiritual senses. Let us take note of its beauty and revel in its fragrance."

"Bread is bread," grumbled the pragmatic partner. "Let's eat. I'm famished!"

"Ah, but bread is not simply bread, my uncouth friend," replied the other. "Every object in this great universe is not single, but double."

"What's double about this bread?"

"It has a spiritual and a material element; a tangible and intangible aspect; the precept and the concept. So you see, we have found not one, but two loaves of bread."

"Well, if you're through with your speech," the other said curtly, "let's eat."

"Eat your share now, if you wish," suggested the aesthete, "but first I'll take a short nap. When I've rested, I will then ask God's blessing and enjoy my food like a civilized man."

But when the philosopher awoke he was astounded to find not a single remaining crumb.

"Where is my portion of the bread?" cried the good man indignantly.

"Oh it's around somewhere," answered the other, waving his hand airily. "You said that the bread was double, so I ate mine and left the other one for you!"

✔   ✔   ✔

A noted theologian and historian was given the important assignment of translating the Dead Sea Scrolls into simple, everyday language. He was to deliver the finished manuscript to The Amsterdam Jewish Committee and Historical Society.

For two years and eleven months he labored mightily, around the clock, to finish the valuable reference work on time. On the very last day, his wife, seeing her husband on the verge of physical exhaustion, persuaded him to eat a sandwich and take a short nap. "You can return to your last chapter when you awaken," she reminded him.

Two hours later, refreshed and alert, he returned to his study to write the last few pages. But to his horror, there was not a sign of his manuscript and voluminous notes.

"Hilda," he shrieked at his wife, "what happened to all my papers?"

"I don't know," answered Hilda. "There was no one in your study but the maid. I asked her to tidy up a little while you slept."

The maid was immediately summoned. "What have you done with my papers?" he ranted, almost incoherent with worry.

"Everything is fine, Sir," the maid assured him brightly. "I only burned the papers that were already written on. The nice clean sheets I put in your desk drawer."

✓ ✓ ✓

The rabbi of Odessa was reproaching his *chazan*. "You should be ashamed of yourself—a cantor, of all people!"

"Why, what did I do?" asked the suprised *chazan*.

"Not you, your children. The way they run after the town lunatic and torment him is perfectly disgraceful. I want it stopped at once."

"But they don't tease him because of his mental condition," protested the cantor. "It is only because he is also the garbage collector and smells so horrible. I assure you, Rabbi, that if you were the village idiot you would be gratified with the respect my children would have for you."

✓ ✓ ✓

It was in the dead of winter when a young Polish Jew crossed the border into Russia, seeking asylum from one of the many pogroms in that area. The thermometer read twenty below zero, and he was looking for a place to warm his bones when he was attacked by a huge Russian wolfhound. He stopped to grab a stick with which to defend himself. But it was frozen solid in the ground.

"What kind of a stupid country is this!" he cried. "Instead of tying up the dogs they tie down the sticks!"

✓ ✓ ✓

Of all the Jews in the world, perhaps the least advanced were the Yemenites, isolated from the mainstream of civilization until their mass emigration to Israel a few years ago.

MERRY MISHMASH FROM OLD EUROPE

In one remote section of Yemen lived a young married couple who had never ventured beyond the confines of their tiny settlement and were in complete ignorance of even the most commonplace utilities of modern society.

One day the husband was sent by the villagers to the city on a matter of taxes. His loving wife kissed him goodbye and then shyly asked that he bring her a gift from the big, mysterious city.

"What would you like?" he smiled.

"Oh, anything at all, just so it is pretty. As pretty as the moon."

When the young man had accomplished his mission and had his fill of wonderment at the sights of the great metropolis, he remembered his wife's request, so he went to a large store. At first the complexity and variety of merchandise bewildered him, but he finally found just the thing; a round mirror, shaped like the moon.

On his return to the distant village, he presented the gift to his wife. She unwrapped it carefully, saving the fancy paper and string, and then examined the mirror curiously. Suddenly, to her complete astonishment, she saw the image of a lovely maiden in the glass. For a moment she stared at the face in dumb-struck silence, and then, frantic with worry, she ran to her mother.

"Mama! Mama! My husband doesn't love me anymore. He brought home a beautiful girl from the city!"

"Where? Where?" cried the old woman, looking about.

"Right here," sobbed the wife. "Look for yourself."

The mother took the looking glass and peered into it. When she too had recovered from her surprise, she handed the mirror back to her daughter and cackled: "Believe me, you have nothing to worry about. No man in his right mind would ever leave a beauty like you for that ugly old crone."

✔ ✔ ✔

The *shammes* was boasting that he owned the most dependable watch on earth.

"No matter what time it is—4 o'clock in Moscow, 3 o'clock in Warsaw, 2 o'clock in Berlin, you can depend on it that on my watch it's exactly seven-thirty."

✔ ✔ ✔

"Ask a foolish question and you get a foolish answer" is an ancient Jewish axiom that is universally quoted today. This story, "Napoleon and the Jewish Tailor," translated and adapted from *Royte Pomerantsen*,* is a classic illustration.

During the Emperor Napoleon's retreat from Russia, he passed through

---

* *Royte Pomerantsen,* a collection of Jewish folk humor by Immanuel Olsvanger, published by Schocken Books, New York.

5

a Jewish community. The enemy was close upon his heels and he feared for his life. Looking about for a refuge, he dashed into a house in which lived a Jewish tailor.

In a tremulous voice Napoleon pleaded with the tailor, "Hide me, quick! If the Russians find me they'll kill me!"

Although the little tailor had no idea who the stranger was, he was moved to pity for a fellow human being. So he said to the emperor, "Get under the featherbed and lie still."

Napoleon got into bed and the tailor piled on him one featherbed, and another, and then still another. It wasn't long before the door burst open and two Russian soldiers, armed with spears, rushed into the house.

"Is anybody hiding in here?" they demanded roughly.

"Who would be foolish enough to hide in my house?" asked the tailor, falling back on the traditional Jewish manner of answering a question with a question.

The soldiers pried into every corner but found no one. As they were leaving, just for good measure, they stuck their spears several times through the featherbeds.

When the door had finally closed on them, Napoleon crawled out from under the pile of featherbeds, deathly pale and covered with perspiration, but safe. Turning to the tailor, he said, "I want you to know that I am the Emperor Napoleon. Because you have saved me from certain death you can ask me three favors. No matter what they are I will grant them to you."

The little tailor thought for awhile, then he said, "Your Majesty, the roof of my house is leaking, but I do not have the money to repair it. Would you be so kind and have it fixed for me?"

"Blockhead!" exclaimed Napoleon impatiently. "Is that the greatest favor you can ask of an emperor? But never mind—I'll see that your roof is fixed. Now you can make your second wish, but be sure this time that it is something substantial."

The humble tailor scratched his head, utterly perplexed. What on earth could he ask for? His face suddenly brightened.

"Some months ago, Your Majesty," he began, "another tailor opened his shop across the way and he is ruining my business. Would it be too much trouble for you to ask him to find another location?"

"What a fool!" cried Napoleon disdainfully. "Very well, my friend, I'll ask your competitor to go to the devil. Now you must try and think of something that is *really* important. Bear in mind, though, that this is positively the last favor I'll grant you."

The tailor knitted his brow and thought and thought. Suddenly an impish look came into his eyes.

"Begging your pardon, Emperor," he asked with burning curiosity, "but I'd very much like to know how you felt while the Russian soldiers were poking their spears through the featherbed."

"Imbecile!" cried Napoleon, beside himself with rage. "How dare you put such a question to an emperor? For your insolence I'll have you shot at dawn!"

So said, so done. He called in three French soldiers who placed the little tailor in irons and led him away to the guardhouse.

That night the tailor could not sleep. He wept and quaked, quaked and wept. Then he recited the prayer of confession and made his peace with God.

Promptly at dawn he was taken out of his cell and tied to a tree. A firing squad drew up opposite and aimed their muskets at him. Nearby stood an officer with watch in hand, waiting to give the signal to fire. He lifted his hand and began to count: "One - two - thr—" But before he could complete the word, the Emperor's aide-de-camp dashed up on horseback, crying "Stop! Don't Shoot!"

The courier then went up to the tailor and said to him, "His Majesty, the Emperor, gives you his gracious pardon. He also asked me to give you this note."

The tailor heaved a deep sigh and began to read, "You wanted to know," wrote Napoleon, "how I felt under the featherbed in your house. Well, now you know!"

✦ ✦ ✦

A gentile landlord was approached by the town rabbi for a donation for the poor.

"Why should I give to a Jew?" argued the landlord. "If my religion does not suit you then neither should my money."

"Sir," the rabbi answered gently, "the people who farm your lands are all Jews; it is they who provide you with your wealth. As to your religion, let me answer it this way: We may not eat pork, but there is nothing in the Scriptures that forbids us to wear pigskin shoes."

✦ ✦ ✦

Sokolov and Hirshkovitch, strangers to each other, met in a train compartment on their way to Yekaterinoslav. Soon they struck up a conversation.

"Do you know a man in Yekaterinoslav named Chaim Lubetski?" asked Sokolov.

"Lubetski the grocer? I know him like I know myself."

"What kind of person is he?" Sokolov wanted to know.

"I'll tell you what kind of person Lubetski is! He has a temper like an old goat. Dishonest? Believe me, the scales in his store are fixed so that one pound comes out two pounds. His poor wife—he beats her black and blue. He's disrespectful to the rabbi and I know for a fact he eats on Yom Kippur."

"But how can you be so sure of all these dreadful things?"

"What do you mean, how can I be so sure?" demanded Hirshkovitch

7

indignantly. "Who else should know better? Lubetski is my very best friend!"

✔ ✔ ✔

The mental gymnastics in which bigots indulge in order to justify their warped prejudices is illustrated in this story, adapted from the Midrash.

One of the Caesars was being carried through the streets of Rome when a Jew passed by.

"Blessings upon you, O Emperor!" greeted the Jew, bowing low.

"And who may you be?" demanded Caesar.

"A humble Jew, Sire. One of your loyal subjects."

"What! A Jew greeting me!" the emperor raged. "The impudence of you Jews!" He turned to his bodyguards. "Off with his head!"

The Nubian slaves then lifted the litter and continued the procession through the streets. But they had only journeyed a few yards when they passed another Jew. This one, however, had seen what happens when the emperor is greeted by an Israelite, so he remained prudently silent.

Caesar leaned from his seat and called out, "Who are you?"

"A Jew, Sire!"

"What! A Jew passing by me, the emperor, without a greeting?" Again he turned to his bodyguards. "Chop his head off!"

Now Caesar's chief minister approached him.

"O Great and Mighty Emperor, teach me your wise ways. I understand your reason for having the first Jew decapitated because he had the temerity to greet you without being addressed, but why did you have the other Jew's head chopped off?"

The Emperor glared balefully at his minister and growled: "Are you insinuating that I don't know how to keep the peace with my enemies?"

✔ ✔ ✔

The recurrent pogroms against the Jews of Czarist Russia taught them to be extremely cautious about their personal and community activities. Whenever a problem concerning communal matters arose, for example, the proceedings were kept from government officials who often used any innocent act as a pretext for further persecutions. So allright already with the history—here's the story:

It so happened that the Jews of a small Russian town had among them an informer. For their own safety, they found it necessary to bribe him before any meetings were held, so that he would not report their affairs to the authorities. One day, a matter of considerable importance was discussed and the informer demanded 300 rubles as his price for silence.

The Council of Elders called the rabbi and implored him to do something about the grasping *moser*. The rabbi, widely known for his good judgment, agreed to put a stop to the problem once and for all. He summoned the spy to his house.

"I insist on 300 rubles," the informer snarled. "That, or else I tell."

"You are a worthless pig!" the rabbi cried, his face aflame with anger. "I am offering you fifty rubles, and I assure you that if you don't accept we can always get another informer who will spy on us for only twenty-five!"

✓ ✓ ✓

There were two carriage-drivers of Poland who were in constant rivalry for passengers. One was Ivan and the other Mikhail. One day, as Ivan was driving from Warsaw, and the other was approaching Warsaw from the opposite direction, they met on the road, several miles from the city.

When they recognized each other, they drew up their horses and exchanged chilly greetings.

"I see, Mikhail, that you have that crook, Yussel the Jew, as a passenger," Ivan called, his voice dripping with sarcasm.

"What do you mean, 'crook'!" Mikhail shouted back. "My Jew is ten times more honest than that Jewish money-lender you have as your own passenger."

"Now hold on there!" Ivan roared. "You can't insult my Jew like that and get away with it."

"I'll insult him all I like! My Jew is better than your Jew, and I'm warning you, pig, one more word out of you and I'll punch your Jew in the nose."

"Oh yeah! Well you just try it and see what happens!"

Good as his word, Mikhail climbed down from his wagon, crossed over to Ivan's cart and let fly a stinging blow to the Jewish passenger's nose.

When Ivan saw that his passenger's nose was bleeding profusely, he was beside himself with rage.

"Son of a horse-fly!" he yelled. "How dare you bloody my Jew's nose? If you think I'm going to let you get away with that you are sadly mistaken!" With that, he ran over to Mikhail's wagon and hit his passenger in the eye with all his might. "You hit my Jew, I hit your Jew," he shrilled angrily.

Mikhail was now almost hysterical in his fury. "I swear by the Czar and with God as my witness, you provoked me into this. Remember, I warned you!" And with that, he fell upon Ivan's passenger and pummeled him unmercifully.

"Don't worry," Mikhail called to his nearly unconscious passenger, "I'll take care of that dirty dog. Believe me, I'll give him something to remember me by for the rest of his life!" So saying, he grabbed Ivan's passenger by the throat and almost choked him to death, meanwhile pounding his head against a rock.

Then, glaring at each other out of hate-filled eyes, Ivan and Mikhail mounted their respective coaches and drove on their way.

"That will teach Ivan a little respect for the Jews," muttered Mikhail to himself.

"That will teach Mikhail a little respect for the Jews," muttered Ivan to himself.

*   *   *

One pleasant morning in June, a rabbi decided to take advantage of the lovely summer weather. He summoned a carriage and ordered the driver to take him for a leisurely ride through the town.

Suddenly the town lunatic leaped into the carriage and sat down beside the rabbi, nor would he leave under any circumstances.

"Tell me, why are you so determined to ride with me?" inquired the holy man.

"Because insane people always follow a rabbi. On the other hand, sane people are always following me about."

"*Nu?*"

"Well, just think, rabbi. Together, the whole world is following us."

*   *   *

Columnist David Schwartz, writing in the California *Jewish Voice*, made this contribution to Jewish folklore:

Population explosions are not always bad. The wealth and power of the Rothschilds stemmed from the numerous Rothschild progeny. With a Rothschild in the capital city of each leading nation, they were able to forge a kind of international league of finance.

Once, a *shnorrer* who was soliciting Baron Rothschild for a handout expressed displeasure with the sum he had been given. "Your son gave me twice as much," complained the beggar.

"Well, my son can afford to," said Baron Rothschild. "He has a rich father."

*   *   *

It is not surprising that old jokes seldom lose their flavor, but are repeated generation after generation. What tickled the *kishkes* centuries ago can still elicit an appreciative chuckle. Perhaps the oldest joke in Judaica, if not in the literature of all other cultures, was reputedly told at the time when Pharaoh once again broke his promise to Moses, refusing to release the children of Israel from bondage.

Aaron, Moses' brother, was discussing the problem with his wife. "This Pharaoh—he's a first-class *momzer!*" he spat.

"Aaron, you mustn't talk like that," reproved his wife. "We are children of God. After all, every living person is descended from Adam and Eve. We're all one family—even Pharaoh."

"That I can't deny," retorted Aaron, "but Pharaoh, he must come from *your* side of the family!"

*   *   *

10

MERRY MISHMASH FROM OLD EUROPE

Another ancient and hallowed tale goes back to about 100 B.C.E., when Jerusalem was held captive by the mighty Roman Empire:

Eleazer Bokar appeared at the gates of Heaven and knocked for admittance. The great doors slowly swung open and the patriarch Abraham stepped out, blowing his golden trumpet. When he finished the welcoming concerto, he addressed Eleazer:

"Greetings, blood of my blood and flesh of my flesh. Jehovah awaits you."

Eleazer, naturally enough, was overawed by the splendor of this welcome, but he quickly gathered his wits. "Father Abraham," he said boldly, "I am ready to meet our God."

Eleazer stepped forward to enter the celestial portals, but patriarch Abraham halted him with an imperious, upflung palm. "Wait, my brother! Before you enter Jehovah's kingdom, you must be worthy of the honor."

"How can I prove my worthiness?"

"You must show that, at least once in your mortal life, you displayed outstanding courage. Can you recall one unquestionably brave deed?"

Eleazer's face brightened. "Yes, I can. I remember once I went to the Roman Consul's palace and I met him face to face. He was surrounded by dozens of legionnaires, all of them armed to the teeth, but I simply ignored them. I told him that he was a camel's behind, a vulture feeding on the bones of Jerusalem's oppressed people, a persecutor of Jews. Then I spat in his face."

Abraham was immensely impressed. "I must agree, that was an extremely brave thing to do—considering all the armed guards who were present, and knowing of the Roman Consul's hatred for the Jews. Yes, my brother, you certainly have earned admittance into Paradise, but tell me, when did all this happen?"

"Oh," replied Eleazer casually, "about three or four minutes ago."

ⅎ　　ⅎ　　ⅎ

During the last days of the reign of cruel Czar Nicholas, a Jew fell into the Moskva River and was in imminent danger of drowning.

"Help! Help! I can't swim!" screamed the terror-stricken Jew.

A squad of the Czar's soldiers, loitering on the bank, laughed derisively, making no move to help the doomed man.

"Save me!" bellowed the poor soul again. But the soldiers only laughed louder.

"Down with the Czar—up with the revolution!" screamed the nimble-witted Jew hoarsely as he was going under for the third time.

The soldiers immediately jumped into the river and dragged the man to safety.

"We'll teach you to defame the sacred name of the Czar," they roared as they hauled the grinning Jew to jail.

ⅎ　　ⅎ　　ⅎ

A certain rabbi of Vienna was so enamored of his own importance and infallibility that, in his own eyes, he could do no wrong. Any pronouncements or advice he offered were, to him, as immutable as the law of gravity.

One day a *chassid* came to his house and beseeched him to pray for his wife who was critically ill.

"Don't worry about a thing," the rabbi declared with an exalted smile. "Just go home. I have taken care of her at this moment."

The next day, however, the *chassid* returned, his eyes red-rimmed from weeping. "Rabbi—my poor wife—my *liebeh*—she died last night!"

"But that's impossible!" the rabbi retorted with unswerving conviction in his own powers.

"But it's true, Rabbi. She's dead!" cried the heartbroken husband.

"How can that be?" demanded the rabbi. "I personally grappled with the Angel of Death—I even wrested the dagger from his hand."

"You don't seem to understand, Rabbi," wept the bereaved man. "I tell you she's dead!"

"Well, if that's the case," retorted the rabbi, "the only logical answer is that the Angel of Death, finding himself without the knife which I tore from his hands, went ahead and strangled her."

✦ ✦ ✦

It isn't generally known, but the Jews are the discoverers of perpetual motion. Here is a hundred-year-old story that proves the point.

Two poverty-stricken Jews of Alsace-Lorraine were discussing the marvelous lives led by the wealthy.

"Did you know that Herrmann, the jeweler, puts on a clean white shirt every *shabbes* before he goes to synagogue?" asked one.

"That's nothing," said the other. "Miller, the contractor, puts on a clean white shirt twice a week!"

"And the emperor?"

"Listen, the emperor changes shirts at least every day!"

"It is hard to believe," sighed the other. "If he changes every day, then what about the great Baron Rothschild, the richest man in the world?"

"Ah, Rothschild! Even an emperor cannot compare to him. Rothschild puts on a shirt and immediately takes it off; he puts on another and immediately takes that one off; he puts on one, takes it off; then another and another and another—all day and all night—he puts on, he takes off, he puts on, he takes off, he puts on . . ."

✦ ✦ ✦

An old Yiddish folk legend tells of an emperor who had heard of the superior intelligence of his Jewish subjects. A vain and cruel ruler, he at once issued a decree that the Jews within his domain were to select one of their number to debate with him.* But, said the monarch, not a single word was to be uttered during the dialogue. Instead they were to communicate through hand gestures. In the event that the Jew failed to comprehend the imperial hand-signs he was to receive a hundred lashes. If no one appeared to debate with the king, every Jew in the realm would be tortured or put to death, at His Majesty's whim.

The members of the unhappy race were in deep despair. Not one among them was anxious to participate in the hazardous debate, but just when it seemed that they would all be punished, a poor cobbler volunteered to save his people by meeting the king in silent controversy.

The debate attracted wide attention; wealthy and poor, master and serf, men, women and children flocked from all corners of the realm to the palace courtyard where the event was to take place.

As the emperor ascended the platform where his humble opponent waited, trembling, he gazed with scorn upon his lowly adversary. His shabby clothes, worn boots and coarse, work-calloused hands formed a striking contrast to the glittering and gaudy appearance of his royal antagonist.

Now the contest began. The sovereign raised his forefinger. The brave Israelite, in reply, pointed his finger toward the ground. Surprised with this quick response, the emperor then held out two fingers, and to his further astonishment, his humble subject immediately thrust out one finger. Now the monarch dramatically stretched forth his hand, with fingers spread, and the poor cobbler clenched a fist in his regal opponent's face. The emperor next produced a bottle of red wine, whereupon the cobbler brought forth a large cheese.

The emperor smiled and arose. "Reward this man," he said to his ministers. "He has done well."

But the chief minister could not contain his curiosity. "Tell us, Your Highness, what were the meanings of those mystic signs you both exchanged?"

"Very well, I will interpret for you. My first gesture meant 'You Jews are as numerous as the stars in Heaven,' which I indicated by pointing my finger toward the sky. The contention of my worthy opponent was, 'No, they are like the sands of the earth, everybody treading on them,' which he signified by pointing a finger toward the ground.

"By showing two fingers," the emperor continued, "I meant to assert that there were two gods; one of good and the other of evil. But my antagonist contested by exhibiting one finger, symbolizing one God.

" 'You are not a nation,' I further argued, by stretching out my hand with fingers spread apart, illustrating how the Jews were scattered all over

---

* This legend is symbolic of the forced debates instituted by the Roman Catholic Church during the Crusades, and later during the Inquisition, in which Jews were forced to debate with Catholic prelates. Jews who presented an argument considered "detrimental to the Church" were tortured on the rack or put to death for heresy.

the world. 'But we are united,' countered my invincible foe by making a fist.

" 'Your sins are as red as wine,' I reproached by producing a bottle of vintage. 'They are as white as cheese,' refuted the Jewish champion of his people, by flaunting his cheese for all to see."

But when the cobbler returned to his village and was asked by the elders for his interpretation, the questions and answers bore little resemblance to the emperor's version.

"The emperor hinted with an upward movement of his finger that he was going to string me up; so, in return, I sent him to hell. The *momzer* then threatened to gouge out my eyes, which he expressed by showing me two fingers, and I simply told him that it would be an eye for an eye, which I made quite clear by pushing one finger toward his ugly countenance.

"Then His Majesty expressed a desire to slap my face by stretching forth his hand with fingers spread, ready for action. So I put forward my fist to let him know I'd break his nose if he tried it.

"Finally, when His Highness saw that I intended to stand my ground, he realized it would be wiser to offer me a friendly drink of wine. So what else could I do? I offered him a piece of my cheese."

✓ ✓ ✓

The German-Jewish philosopher, Moses Mendelssohn, was an intimate friend of Frederick the Great.

Once, while strolling aimlessly on Unter den Linden, the chief thoroughfare of Berlin, the king met his learned friend. After saluting each other in an amiable fashion, the monarch asked his Jewish subject where he was going.

"I don't know," Mendelssohn replied quite truthfully.

The eyes of the mighty ruler flashed with quick anger. Friend or not, this man could not trifle with His Majesty. "I will ask you just once more," he growled ominously. "Where are you going?"

"I'm sorry, Your Highness, but I don't know."

The king at once ordered his guards to arrest the "insolent" man, but before the day was over he relented. He visited the eminent philosopher in his cell.

"Look here, Mendelssohn," he scolded, "what was the idea of trifling with your king in such a frivolous manner?"

"I didn't mean to trifle with you, Your Majesty," explained the scholar ruefully. "I really did not know where I was going. It certainly must be clear to you by this time. Earlier today I set out for a simple stroll and I landed in jail. What more proof do you need?"

✓ ✓ ✓

A wealthy merchant ordered a pair of new pants from the local tailor, with the stipulation that the work be finished within a week.

"Remember," said the merchant, "I must leave town next week and I will be away for six weeks on an extended buying trip. And I want those trousers for the journey."

But the tailor, an unreliable fellow, did not have the pants ready on time, and the merchant was compelled to leave without them.

Immediately upon his return he went to the tailor shop and was greeted warmly. "Here are your new pants," the tailor said proudly, holding them aloft for the customer to admire. "I just finished them."

"You just finished?" gasped the merchant. "Look, I want to ask you a question."

"*Nu*, ask!"

"Why is it that God Almighty was able to create the world—this whole universe—in only six days, but it takes you six weeks to make a simple pair of pants?"

"What kind of comparison is that?" snorted the tailor. "Just look at the mess God made, and then look at this gorgeous pair of pants *I* made!"

✓ ✓ ✓

Although it is the writer who transcribes the accumulated wisdom of the past, couples it with the knowledge of the present, and hands it down to the next generation so that the culture of a civilized people might endure, he has traditionally been poorly paid for his labors. This ancient anecdote well illustrates the thesis.

An exceptionally bright young scholar, barely out of his teens, completed a brilliant manuscript in which he explored the obscure laws and morals of Jewish folklore. To help make his book more saleable he went to Rabbi Elijah, the *Gaon* of Vilna, and begged him to write a preface.

The rabbi, a gentle soul, poured tea for both, and as they were sipping, he spoke kindly to the young man.

"My son, the time of youth is one of ideals, passions, dreams and hopes. And that is as it should be. But life also has its cold realities. If you have decided to dedicate yourself to writing, you must expect to suffer privation and hunger. And there will be loneliness, too, for writing is the loneliest labor of all. But if you must write, then resign yourself to poverty at least until you are fifty."

"And when I'm fifty, what then?" the young would-be writer asked hopefully.

The rabbi smiled gently. "Why then you'll be used to it!"

✓ ✓ ✓

Just before the turn of the century, there lived in Lithuania a poor tailor named Mottel. But though Mottel mended, patched and pressed garments for everyone in town, he himself walked about in tatters. He would even appear in the synagogue dressed like a scarecrow, to the mortification of the rabbi and the congregants.

"Mottel," commented one of his customers, a Polish nobleman, "it's disgraceful that you, a tailor, should go around in rags. Why don't you repair your own clothes?"

"What can I do, Your Excellency?" whined the tailor. "I'm a poor man and I can only find the time to do work for which I am paid."

The nobleman, a kindly man, pondered the tailor's explanation for a few moments and then his face brightened. "I have an idea," he said. "I want you to consider me as a new customer." Now he handed the tailor a ruble. "I am paying you to repair your own shabby suit. Just remember, you are doing it for a paying customer."

The following week, the Polish gentleman returned to the shop, only to find that the tailor was still wearing the same torn and tattered clothing.

"Now see here," cried the nobleman indignantly, "there is no excuse for you to be dressed like a beggar. Didn't I pay you a ruble to fix your suit? Look at you—your clothes haven't even been touched!"

"Sir, I'm afraid I must return your money," said Mottel gravely.

"Why, for heaven's sake?"

"Well, Your Excellency, after you left I examined my suit very carefully. Frankly, sir, considering the awful condition it is in, I realized that for only one ruble I'd be losing money on the job."

✓ ✓ ✓

Fire insurance was unknown in the small Jewish communities of Czarist Russia. When a poor man lost his home because of a fire the local rabbi would give him a *ksav,* or document, attesting to the fact that he was a *nisraf,* a fire victim, and therefore in need of funds to rebuild. And as might be surmised, there were the usual number of *shnorrers,* and ne'er-do-wells who traveled from town to town, with or without documents, collecting money far in excess of their needs. It was a good racket while it lasted.

One day, exactly as it happened in the Chicago fire, Mrs. Chernov's cow kicked over the lantern as she was doing her evening milking. Soon the whole village went up in flames. House after house was reduced to ashes as the people milled about helplessly, wringing their hands and wailing.

The next morning, the rabbi called a meeting of the village Council of Elders and they quickly agreed to open the communal treasury to give immediate emergency financial aid to the victims. Later on they could use their rabbinical documents to solicit rebuilding funds from more fortunate townspeople.

Among those who came to the village elders for assistance was the inevitable gypster whose house had only been slightly scorched.

"What are you doing here?" asked the rabbi sternly. "I gave you no *ksav* attesting that you are among the *nisrafim.* Do you mean to tell me that you suffered from the fire?"

"*Oy*, Rabbi, did I suffer!" groaned the man. "As God is my witness, I was frightened out of my wits the whole time."

✓   ✓   ✓

Yankel was afraid to return home without a *kopek* to his name. His shrewish wife, he knew, would din a never-ending tirade into his ears until they ached. She had cautioned him against leaving their small town to seek his fortune in Moscow, but would he listen? No, not he! He had to be the big fortune-seeker with the big ideas!

Now, after spending a year in the metropolis, he realized that she had been right; he never should have left. Misfortune had confronted him on all sides, and at year's end, he was left with only one problem—how to save face before his wife.

"How can I return home without bringing any money at all?" pondered Yankel. "I must think of a logical excuse or I will never hear the end of it."

Just then he hit upon a brilliant idea. Reaching into his pocket he withdrew a large red handkerchief and tied it across his face so that only his eyes were visible.

The moment he opened the door to his house, his wife screamed: "*Oy gevald!* What happened to your face?"

"It was terrible!" moaned Yankel quite convincingly. "Just before I reached town I was held up by a band of Cossacks who ordered me to give them all my money or they would cut off my nose."

"*Shlemiel!*" wailed his wife. "What kind of life will you have without a nose! Why didn't you give them your money?"

"*Sha! Sha!* Don't carry on so," grinned Yankel, snatching off the red handkerchief. "That's exactly what I did!"

✓   ✓   ✓

The immensely wealthy Russian landowner summoned Malbim, his Jewish business agent, and said to him, "Here are twenty-five rubles; I want you to buy me a dachshund."

"May it please Your Excellency," answered Malbim promptly, "but you cannot possibly obtain a first-class dachshund for so small a sum. I would have to pay twice as much as that. Take my advice; give me fifty rubles and I'll buy you a dachshund you can really be proud of."

"Very well," agreed the nobleman. "Here are twenty-five more rubles. But remember, it must be the best in all the land, as befits my station in life."

"Your worries are over, Excellency," Malbim assured him confidently. "Just leave everything to me."

Malbim turned to leave, when a sudden thought occurred to him. He hesitated, and then asked apologetically:

"A thousand pardons, Your Excellency, but tell me, what is a dachshund?"

17

Chapter Two

Logic and Deduction

(The origin of this illustration of pseudo-talmudic deduction has long been lost in the mists of antiquity. Various versions are still told in the Jewish communities of Russia, Poland, Hungary and other eastern European areas.)

Reb Berel Charif interrupted his study of the Talmud to get a glass of tea, and upon returning to his books could not remember where he had placed his eye-glasses. Now it was the sage's customary practice to place his spectacles atop whatever book he was reading so that he always knew where to look for them when he resumed his studies. This time, however, he had absent-mindedly pushed them up from the bridge of his nose to his forehead. It was only natural, therefore, that he was unable to find them on his book as usual. He searched everywhere; underneath the furniture, among the books and papers that cluttered the room, even in the tea cannister, but they were nowhere to be found.

The venerable scholar took a firm grip on himself, steeling his mind against panic. "I will apply my knowledge of talmudic reasoning," he said to himself, stroking his long, patriarchal beard.

So he began:

"First, who would have profited by stealing my glasses?—if indeed they were stolen at all. Let us assume that they were taken by someone who needs eyeglasses. On the other hand, though, a man who needs glasses undoubtedly has a pair of his own, so why steal mine? We must therefore eliminate him as a suspect.

"But suppose they were taken by a man who does *not* need glasses! No, that is unlikely! If he has no use for them he would have no reason to steal mine. Of course, he might sell them to a man who needs glasses, but if the man who needs glasses already has glasses, then why would he pay good money for my glasses? And if the thief derives no benefit from the spectacles, it is illogical to think that he would expose himself to arrest.

"Yet, logic compels us to deduce that the glasses were stolen, and if that is the case, they must have been taken by someone who both needs

18

and already has glasses. Now why would such a person steal someone else's? Simple deduction indicates that such a person lost his own. But if he were a scrupulously careful person, as are most spectacle-owners, it is unlikely that he would lose them. So, with this premise established, we can only assume that he absent-mindedly pushed them up on his forehead and promptly forgot about them.

"So far, so good! Now that we have reached this hypothesis, why not personalize the problem and say that I myself might well have done the very same thing?"

Having reached this conclusion, Reb Berel touched his hand to his forehead and, lo and behold!—there was his property.

"Praise the Lord for having given to our people the power of talmudic analysis," he said fervently, pleased with his successful application of the formula. "Had it not been for our rabbinical reasoning, I would have had to wait until the end of eternity when the Messiah would have had to find my glasses for me."

↑ ↑ ↑

A shy, unlettered peasant knocked on his rabbi's door one day, and when he was made welcome he explained, somewhat bashfully, that he had always wanted to understand the Talmud but, until now, had never found the courage to ask for instructions. "Please, Rabbi," he implored, "teach me what is Talmud."

"Explain the Talmud?" The rabbi smiled patiently. "Even many of the most learned of our scholars do not fully comprehend it. How can an uneducated peasant grasp its complex laws and subtle shades of meaning?"

The peasant insisted, and the rabbi, seeing his earnestness, resignedly agreed.

"Now follow every word carefully. If two burglars break into a house through the chimney, and once inside they find that one has a dirty face and the other a clean face, which one will wash?"

"That's easy," answered the peasant. "The one with the dirty face, of course."

The rabbi shook his head. "That's what I meant about illiterate peasants trying to master the Talmud. If you will think a moment, my friend, you will perceive that the one with the clean face looked at the other with the dirty face and, assuming his own face was also dirty, he washed it. The one whose face was really dirty, seeing the clean face of the other burglar, naturally assumed that his own face was clean, so, of course, he did not wash it."

The peasant mulled over the explanation, his forehead creased in thought. Finally he grinned and nodded. "Rabbi, how can I thank you? Now, at last, I understand Talmud."

"Ah, my friend, you have a long way to go," the rabbi answered sadly.

"How could you possibly believe that when two burglars crawl down a chimney, only one will have a dirty face?"

✓   ✓   ✓

Certain jokes just cannot start out with "Two Christians met on the street," because the content of the story is too typically Jewish to be transposed into the general idiom. This anecdote is representative. It deals with the traditional expression "Till a hundred and twenty," meaning that the person should live to the same age as did Moses.

Two immigrants, a young man and an aged woman, were in line at the customs office on Ellis Island. The old lady's turn came and the officer asked her name. She told him.

"And how old are you?" was the next question.

"Seventy-five, till a hundred and twenty," she replied.

The customs official stared. "I beg your pardon—how old?"

"Seventy-five, till a hundred and twenty."

"Madam, I just don't understand. Surely you can tell me your age in simple numbers."

"I told you. Seventy-five, till a hundred and twenty."

The youth, who was waiting in line behind her, tapped the woman on the shoulder.

"*Tanteh*," he asked, "till a hundred and twenty, how old are you?"

"Seventy-five," she answered promptly.

✓   ✓   ✓

A young man boarded a train bound for Odessa and sat down beside a prosperous-looking passenger.

"Can you tell me the time, sir?" the young man asked, attempting to strike up a conversation.

The stranger glanced at him contemptuously. "Drop dead!!" he snapped.

"What the devil is wrong with you!" the young man exploded indignantly. "I ask you like a gentleman, 'what time is it' and you answer so rudely. What's the idea?"

The older passenger made as if to ignore him, then, sighing, he turned and said, "All right, so I'll tell you. First you ask a question and I'm supposed to answer, yes? Okay, so I tell you the time. Then you start up with discussions about the weather, about politics, about the war, about business—soon we discover that we're both Jews. So what happens? I live in Odessa but you're a stranger there so I must extend Jewish hospitality and invite you to my home. You meet Sophie, my beautiful daughter, and after a few more visits you both fall in love—after all, I admit you are a rather handsome young fellow. Finally you ask my blessing so that you and Sophie can get married. So why not avoid this big *megillah*? I can tell you right now, young man, I positively refuse to let my daughter marry anyone who can't even afford to own a watch!"

✓   ✓   ✓

LOGIC AND DEDUCTION

Rabbi Scharf was in the Budapest railway terminal, waiting in line to buy a return ticket to his remote little village some 60 miles distant. In front of him was an imposing, well-dressed gentleman who also purchased a ticket for the same destination. Aboard the train they both settled themselves in the same compartment.

Ordinarily, the monotonous clickety-clack of steel wheels on rails would have made the good rabbi drowsy, but this time all his senses were alert. "Who is this man?" he wondered, "and what business can such a fine gentleman have in our little village?"

One does not boldly inquire into a stranger's private affairs, of course, so Rabbi Scharf decided to find out by applying the talmudic process of elimination.

"Judging from his tailored clothes and expensive luggage he must be a professional man. Hmmm. A doctor perhaps? Yes, that might be it! Yoshilov is sick. But then again, Yoshilov is only a poor water-carrier. How could he afford a big-city specialist? Let me see. There's Sarah, Meyer the dairyman's wife. She seems to be filling out of late. She could be pregnant again. But even so, Sarah's other two children were delivered by Malka, the midwife. Why should Meyer pay out his hard-earned money for an expensive doctor from Budapest?

"Maybe he's not a doctor after all. What else, then? An engineer? But who needs a fancy engineer in our little village? Nobody! That's out! It could be he's a lawyer, but I myself adjudicate all local cases, so that can't be right either.

"Wait a minute! Perhaps he is coming to visit a relative. Now let me think. Nobody has left our village for thirty years, but . . . say, didn't Feivel the waggoner have a brother who went to live with an uncle in Budapest thirty-three years ago? Of course, that's who he is! Feivel Cohen's brother, Jacob!

"But why should Jacob be returning after so many years? Feivel seems to be in perfect health—except for an occasional toothache. Aha—now I have it! Jacob is a dentist and he is coming to fix his brother's teeth. That means he's a doctor after all.

"But whoever heard of a big-city dentist named Jacob Cohen? No, he must have changed his name to something similar in Hungarian. Hmmm. Jacob. That would now be John. Yes, John Cohen! No! He would have Hungarianized his last name too. Cohen— Cohen— Cohen—! Ah, I have it—Kovac!"

Now the rabbi smiled and turned to his traveling companion. "Doctor John Kovac, I believe. Permit me to introduce myself. I am Rabbi Scharf."

The stranger was somewhat taken aback. "How did you know I was Doctor Kovac?"

Replied the rabbi, "It was obvious."

✓   ✓   ✓

In the city of Prague there once lived two brothers. One was a highly respected professor at the university; the other was a thief.

The professor, understandably, had little use for his brother and avoided him like the plague. One day, however, as the professor was strolling on the avenue, whom should he almost bump into but his no-goodnik of a brother. He averted his eyes, deliberately snubbing him.

"Just a minute there!" snapped the outraged sibling. "What makes you so high and mighty? If I were stuck up at least I'd have an excuse—after all, my brother is a college professor. But your brother is nothing but a common thief, so what right have you to put on such airs?"

✓   ✓   ✓

Feld and Bein met on the street.

"*Sholom aleichem*," said Feld politely.

"Go to hell!" said Bein.

"Look," complained Feld, "I speak to you nicely and you tell me to go to hell. Is this a gentleman by you? What's the big idea?"

"I'll tell you," explained Bein. "If I answered you politely you would ask me where I am going and I would tell you I'm going to the 8th Street baths.

"You would tell me I'm crazy, the Avenue A baths are better, and I would say you're the one that's crazy, the 8th Street baths are better, and you would call me a damn fool and I would tell you to go to hell.

"This way it's simpler. You say '*Sholom aleichem*,' and I say 'go to hell,' and it's finished!"

✓   ✓   ✓

The *yeshivah* instructor was lecturing on the necessity for original thinking.

"Man's problem," he said, "is that he does not apply objective thought to even the most elemental of subjects. Let me give you an illustration. Consider three wagons filled with hay, and drawn by three horses, one directly behind the other. As they trudge along the road, in single file, two horses eat the hay from the wagons in front of their own. Now which horse would you say is more fortunate than the others?"

"W-e-l-lll," stammered one student, "surely not the first horse. He was unable to eat while pulling his load."

Another student commented, "Since the first horse cannot eat, then the other two must be equally fortunate because they are both eating hay."

"That's what I mean about not thinking things through," sighed the teacher. "If you reason it out, you will agree that the center horse is luckiest. Not only does he get to eat, but he is the only one whose load becomes lighter."

✓   ✓   ✓

A recent arrival to these shores was trying to orient himself to his new land. "Tell me something," he asked a friend, "how far is it from New York to Philadelphia?"

LOGIC AND DEDUCTION

"About a hundred miles," answered the friend.

"And from Philadelphia to New York?"

"Why, it's the same distance, naturally."

"What's so natural?" retorted the immigrant. "Backwards and forwards is not necessarily the same distance. For example, from *Purim* to *Pesach* is one month. But from *Pesach* to *Purim* isn't it eleven months?"

✓ ✓ ✓

Two *chassidim* were ruminating about the persecutions suffered by their people when the older *chassid* shocked his friend by declaring that the Jew-haters were not always to blame in their anti-Semitic accusations.

"That's a terrible thing to say—especially for a pious man like you!" exclaimed the other indignantly.

"But it's true!" insisted the older man. "Take for example the charge that we are internationalists."

"You mean Zionism?"

"No, not that; I'm speaking personally. In my own family, when my son needed help to start a little business here in town I got him a loan from the American Joint Committee. My rent was paid by my other son who is in Argentina; my taxes were supplied by a brother-in-law who lives in Canada; coal was sent to me by the Polish-Jewish Relief Committee in London. My sister in Paris forwarded potatoes, and the price of shoes came from the Helping Hand of Johannesburg. Now I ask you, how international can you get?"

✓ ✓ ✓

A blind peddler and his seeing friend bought a basket of cherries and agreed, as gentlemen, to take turns in eating one cherry at a time.

They sampled the cherries for a few minutes when suddenly the blind man struck out wildly, his blow landing on the seeing man's nose.

"What's the matter with you?" cried the surprised friend. "What did I do?"

"You are a cheat—a *paskudniak* of the lowest order!" rasped the blind one. "Here I am taking two cherries at a time and you don't say a word. So it figures—you must be taking three or four at a time or you would have complained; you lowlife you!"

✓ ✓ ✓

Zussman lived in a tiny, remote village fifty miles from Odessa. But he had never been to the big city and was ignorant of even the most prosaic innovations to which city folk are accustomed.

One day, the rabbi returned from Odessa and brought with him a newspaper, the first that Zussman had ever seen. His curiosity was so great that the rabbi gave him the paper.

"Gittele," cried Zussman to his wife, "'see what I have brought home!"

Together they pored over the newspaper, but what intrigued Zussman

23

most was an advertisement with the picture of a man wearing a straw hat and gloves.

"This is very strange," remarked Zussman after studying the picture at length. "If the season of the year is winter, then why is he wearing a straw hat? And if it is summer, why is he wearing gloves?"

"I don't know," confessed Gittele. "It is one of the mysteries of the big city."

But Zussman was not to be put off so easily. He pondered the strange picture, cudgeling his mind as to its deeper meaning. Finally he smiled and nodded to his wife.

"Ah, Gittele, I have it now! It's summer time. That accounts for the straw hat. And he's wearing gloves because he is going out to pick berries among the thorns."

1   *1*   *1*

An exceptionally pious *chassid* of Drozhen was accustomed to a serving of chopped eggs as an appetizer for his *shabbes* supper. But there came the inevitable time when his favorite dish was missing. He asked his wife the reason.

"It is the end of the summer and the hens are laying very few eggs," she explained. "Now they're very expensive. Earlier in the season the price of a single egg was one *groschen*, but today it is three *groschen*."

"Praise be the Lord!" exclaimed the holy man. "We can only marvel at His exalted logic. He gives intelligence even to the lowly chicken so that she stops laying eggs at one *groschen* and starts in again when the price goes up to three *groschen*. Gittele, what a būsinessman God would make!"

1   *1*   *1*

The law of compensation was known to the ancient Israelites centuries before the advent of the Common Era, as this perky little tale shows:

Two patriarchs, in their flowing priestly robes, sat on a hillside observing the scurrying toilers who labored by the thousands in King Solomon's mines.

"Great is the wisdom of Solomon," remarked one of the sages. "This great mine will compensate for any calamity should the crops fail. For then we will have the *shekels* to buy food from neighboring countries."

"Yes, Solomon is wise," agreed the other, "but wisdom must be tempered with mercy, and there is no wise mercy in all the earth that compares with Jehovah's."

"I do not understand."

"Consider the man who is blind in one eye. Does not the Lord make his other eye especially keen?"

"Yes, that is divine compensation for a loss."

"And if a man be deaf in one ear, does not our God make his other ear more acute?"

"That too is true."

"And if a man has one leg that is a little too short, does not our Lord make the other one a little extra long?"

✓ ✓ ✓

The customer in the fish market was displeased with her purchase. "Mister," she complained bitterly, "not only is this carp too small for the money, but it smells bad."

"Lady, take my word for it—be happy with what you got," responded the store owner. "It's a question of simple logic. If I gave you twice as much for your money, I'm asking you, wouldn't the fish smell twice as bad?"

✓ ✓ ✓

Teenage Izzy felt that fifty cents a week was not enough for a boy his age, so he asked his father for an increase in his allowance.

The father sipped his tea and thought for a moment or two before he answered. "And if you get an increase, so what?"

"I'll save my money until I have enough to buy a car."

"And if you buy a car, so what?"

"I'd learn all about how a car works and become a mechanic."

"So you're a mechanic, so what?"

"Why, when business improved I could open up my own garage."

"*Nu*, so you have a garage, so what?"

"Well, with the profits I could open my own automobile dealership, with branches all over the country. I'd be rich."

"All right, you're rich, so what?"

"Then I could afford to marry a beautiful girl from a fine family."

"And if you get married, so what?"

"Gee, Pop, then I'd be happy!"

"Eh-heh, you're happy. So what?"

✓ ✓ ✓

The story is told of a rabbi at one of the larger *yeshivas* who was famed for his orderly thinking processes and facile wit. One day, during philosophy class, a grinning student asked, "Rabbi, would you rather have five daughters or five thousand dollars?"

"Five daughters," answered the rabbi instantly.

"But that is based on emotion, not cold reason," protested the youth.

"My preference is based on pure logic," the rabbi said evenly. "First, human nature being what it is, if I had five thousand dollars I would undoubtedly want more. As a pious man I cannot condone greed, even in myself. You will agree that this cannot possibly apply to five daughters. Secondly, should I desire to have five thousand dollars it would not happen anyway; simple desire without practical application does not produce money. So why make a fool of myself? Thirdly, young man, I would rather have five daughters because I actually have eight!"

✓ ✓ ✓

A *chassidic* rabbi was asked to explain the difference between the righteous and the wicked individual. The sage replied:

"The truth of the matter (and don't bother to look for it in the Torah or Talmud) is that both the righteous and the wicked constantly commit sins, but with this difference: As long as the righteous lives he knows he is sinning, but as long as the wicked sins he knows he's really living!"

✓ ✓ ✓

A Jewish farmer who had three sons made out a will which stipulated that one-half of his cows should go to the oldest son, one-third to the second son, and one-ninth to the youngest. After the farmer's death it was discovered that he had seventeen cows, and no matter how the sons tried they could not divide them according to their father's last wishes. So they brought their problem to the rabbi.

The rabbi wrestled with the awkward situation for some time until, after much deep thought, he solved the problem by adding his own cow. This made the division easy. He gave the oldest son one-half, or nine cows; to the second son he gave six cows, or one-third; and to the youngest son he gave two cows, or one-ninth.

This left one undistributed cow—the rabbi's—so he took it home; what else?

Chapter Three

Shnorrers

Chutzpah—monumental gall—was one of the trade-marks of the professional *shnorrer*. He needed it in order to survive. But with that impudence often went a razor-sharp tongue and a quick, perceptive mind that was sarcastic perhaps, but witty.

One such *shnorrer* was Lomitski of Prague, a man of powerful build.

"My family is starving," he began with his carefully rehearsed whine. "I beg you, give me alms."

"Give you alms!" the rich householder snorted. "What nerve! A muscular man like you with the body of a Samson has no business begging. Just look at those mighty arms of yours!"

"*Nu*, what do you expect me to do?" retorted the bold *shnorrer*, "Cut off my arms for the miserable kopek you might give me?"

✓   ✓   ✓

There may have been more successful beggers in Kiev, but none were so imaginative in their *shnorring* as Max Bender. Indeed, there were a few rich men who actually enjoyed his visits. He seldom asked for much and his lively imagination was more than recompense for the sums they handed him.

So it was that Simon the landlord smiled when he opened the door to find Max Bender waiting to see him.

"I am not here only for money," said Bender quickly. "It is a matter of life or death."

"Whose, yours or mine?" grinned Simon.

"Yours!"

"Then you had better tell me about it. We'll have a little *shnapps* while you explain."

Drinks were served and Bender launched into the details.

"Last night the rabbi told us that when the Judgment Day arrives, two bridges will be created across the Great Sea. One will be made of iron, the other of paper. The sinful ones will take the iron bridge but it will collapse and they will all fall into the sea and drown. But the righteous ones will take the paper bridge and they will cross over safely to Paradise. That, Simon, is what the rabbi said in his sermon."

The landlord nodded. "I have heard all this many times before. What about it?"

"This about it! I have given the matter deep thought and I finally came to the conclusion that at the end of time the tensile strengths of iron and paper will be exactly as they are today. Therefore the rabbi's prophecy must be incorrect. So I implore you, Simon, when the Messiah comes, for God's sake, *take the iron bridge*; do you hear?—*the iron bridge!*"

✓ ✓ ✓

A beggar who was not averse to petty thievery when he thought he could steal without detection, knocked on a door and pleaded for something to eat. The compassionate housewife set the table for him and served a hearty meal.

The scoundrel, however, instead of feeling gratitude, pocketed a silver spoon and left.

The housewife missed the spoon almost at once. She flew through the kitchen door and ran down the street shouting, "Mister, wait a minute! I want to talk to you!"

A police officer was on the corner, just ahead of the beggar, so he thought it more prudent to halt.

"What is it?" he asked fearfully, one eye on the curious policeman.

"That spoon you took," the woman gasped, out of breath. "Remember, it's *milchik!*"

✓ ✓ ✓

A *shnorrer* went to the house of the wealthiest but most miserly man in town.

"Sir," he said to the old skinflint, "I have sought charity from you before but never have you parted with so much as a penny. This time, however, my need is more serious than at any previous time. My family is hungry and Passover is nearly here."

But this pathetic appeal failed to move the rich miser. He argued fiercely with the caller and then ordered him out of the house.

"Very well, I'll leave," said the *shnorrer*, "but first let me recite a short parable."

"Go ahead and recite it, but you won't get a cent!"

"Ever since the beginning of time no one has ever figured out why a dog grabs a pig by the ear when he catches it. According to the Talmud there is no man as poor as a dog nor is there any man as rich as a pig. So it must be clear to you, sir, that the dog secretly whispers into the pig's ear, "If you are so rich then why are you such a pig?"

✓ ✓ ✓

Chernov, the *shnorrer* of Petrograd, had a very wealthy patron who, for some obscure reason, had taken a liking to the nervy little beggar.

Each year he would give Chernov a handsome stipend—never less than 500 rubles.

One year, however, the rich man gave him only 250 rubles.

"What is the meaning of this?" demanded the insolent *shnorrer*. "This is only half of what you have been giving me!"

"I'm sorry, Chernov, but I must cut my expenses this year," apologized the wealthy man. "My son married an actress and I am paying all the bills."

"Well, of all the *chutzpah*!" roared Chernov, hopping mad. "If your son wants to support an actress that's his business. But how dare he do it with my money!"

1 1 1

The itinerant *shnorrer* arrived in the small Lithuanian community late Friday afternoon and was told by the local *parnes* that his chances of being billeted for the Sabbath were very poor. Everyone, it seemed, had already taken in a poor man for *shabbes*.

"You mean there's no one who will give me a place to sleep and something to eat?" asked the *shnorrer* bitterly.

"Well," acknowledged the *parnes*, "there's a man here named Landau, the magnate of the town. Nobody has been assigned to him yet. But Landau is the worst miser in town. He would never welcome a stranger to his home."

"Just tell me where he lives," said the beggar confidently. "I know how to deal with his type."

Within a few minutes he was knocking boldly on the rich man's door. A servant came out and offered him a copper.

"I want no charity," declared the *shnorrer* loftily. "I came to see Reb Landau on business."

The servant quickly ushered him into the rich man's presence. "What can I do for you?" he asked politely.

"Reb Landau, what could you offer me for a flawless diamond as big as an egg?"

"I can't say offhand," replied the wealthy tightwad with a show of studied casualness, though his eyes were bulging with greed. "Stay with me over Saturday, rest up a little, and then we'll talk business."

"I hate to impose on you, but since you insist . . ."

All that Saturday the stranger was royally entertained. The host saw to it that his guest did not leave the house even for a minute, fearing that he might be approached by someone else. When the Sabbath had finally passed, the host broached the subject that had been uppermost in his mind.

"Now, let's see the diamond."

"Diamond? What diamond?" asked the *shnorrer* innocently, as he rose to leave the premises.

29

"You said you had a diamond as big as an egg," snapped Landau, a dawning suspicion bringing a flush to his face.

"My dear man, I said no such thing!" the *shnorrer* reminded him. "All I asked was how much would you offer if I had one. Can't a man ask an academic question?"

✓   ✓   ✓

A Jewish mendicant implored the lady of the house for a morsel of food. Pitying him, she invited him to her table and placed before him a generous serving of *gefilteh fish* and a plate heaped high with black bread and *chaleh*.

The *chaleh* was almost twice as expensive as the black bread but the beggar did not touch the cheaper variety. Instead, he gorged himself on the *chaleh*.

The housewife, growing more irritated by the minute, finally asked, "Did it ever occur to you that the *chaleh* costs twice as much as the black bread?"

"I thought of it many times," the beggar answered agreeably, "and believe me, Madam, it's worth every cent!"

✓   ✓   ✓

A *shammes* happened to be looking out of the synagogue's open door when he saw a familiar face. All at once it dawned on him where he had seen the man before. He rushed out and collared the passerby.

"Swindler! Thief!" the *shammes* yelled. "Only yesterday I saw you begging in front of a Catholic church. Today you're begging at the entrance to a synagogue. What are you, Catholic or Jew?"

"A Jew," the beggar gulped. "But in these hard times, who can make a living from only one religion?"

✓   ✓   ✓

Aaron Laibovitch was determined to extract a healthy sum from Baron de Rothschild, but the servants threw him out every time he tried to gain entrance to the banker's mansion.

Now there is one technique many *shnorrers* use to gain their ends when all other means have failed—create a tumult.

So this time, the *shnorrer* opened the door without bothering to knock, pushed boldly past the startled servants and created a wild commotion in the foyer, screaming for the Baron at the top of his lungs.

Upstairs, the Baron held his hands over his ears in a vain attempt to shut out the intruder's din, but finally, nearly driven to distraction, he came downstairs and confronted the trouble-maker.

"My wife and children are in rags; we haven't eaten in three days," the *shnorrer* bellowed, inwardly praying that God would not punish him too severely for the exaggerations.

"All right, you win," Rothschild shrugged wearily. "Here are twenty thalers. But let me give you a piece of good advice. If you hadn't made such a damned nuisance of yourself I'd have given you twice as much."

"Baron de Rothschild," the *shnorrer* replied, drawing himself up proudly, "you are a financier, no? But do I give you financial advice? Well, I'm a professional *shnorrer,* so please don't give me *shnorring* advice!"

✔ ✔ ✔

"I am no run-of-the-mill beggar," said the poorly dressed man to the fabulously wealthy but very charitable Baron de Rothschild. "In fact I'm a musician—one of the best. For more than ten years I played in the Vienna Philharmonic, but after the symphony was disbanded I simply could not find any more work. Believe me, Baron, ever since then I have had nothing but bad luck."

"What instrument do you play?" asked Rothschild sympathetically.

"The bassoon."

"Oh, really? Why, that's my favorite instrument! I just love the dulcet tones of a bassoon! In fact I have one right here in the house. My friend, I will help you, but first come into the music room and play something for me."

The *shnorrer* paled and then buried his face in his hands. *"Oy vay!"* he moaned. "I *told* you I have nothing but bad luck. Of all the thousands of instruments in the world, I had to go and pick the bassoon!"

✔ ✔ ✔

Two brothers, Ganseh and Mishpocheh, who could not or would not work for their daily bread, were regular callers at the Rothschild residence where, once a month, they were given 100 marks each.

It happened that Ganseh died, so Mishpocheh made the usual call alone. The family treasurer who disbursed funds to the poor handed him the usual 100 marks.

"Just a chicken-pluckin' minute!" Mishpocheh protested. "What's with this hundred mark business? I'm entitled to two hundred, and when a man is entitled he's entitled, so hand it over!"

"Entitled nothing!" retorted the treasurer. "Your brother, Ganseh, is dead. His hundred marks is withdrawn."

"What do you mean, withdrawn?" the *shnorrer* said icily, "Who is my brother's heir—me or Rothschild?"

✔ ✔ ✔

Then there's the story of the *shnorrer* who made a nuisance of himself by calling at the home of a rich merchant every evening, just in time for dinner.

The merchant was a kind man, but his patience was growing thin. Yet, what could he do? Jewish tradition requires that those who have must share with those who have not.

One evening, when the rich man was entertaining a lady of whom he was quite fond, who should knock on the door but Reb Nuisance himself—the star boarder.

"Look," hissed the merchant fiercely through the slightly opened door, "if you don't mind, I'm entertaining a lady friend."

"I don't mind at all," said the nervy *schnorrer*. "I'll eat in the kitchen."

"Then tell me, do you like cold chicken?"

"Oh, I just love cold chicken—I wouldn't have it any other way," said the beggar enthusiastically.

"That's just fine!" snapped the merchant. "Come back tomorrow night. The chicken is piping hot right now!"

1   1   1

There were two men in the town whom no one had ever been able to outwit: Eisinger the rich miser, and Fenster the *shnorrer*. Neither had ever tested his mettle against the other but the day of reckoning inevitably came.

Fenster, the crafty beggar, decided to challenge Eisinger, the cunning skinflint, to a duel of wits. He went to the miser's house and, after a lengthy argument, persuaded him to lend a silver cup.

On the following day, Fenster not only returned the cup but he also gave Eisinger a little cup.

"What's the extra cup for?" asked the wealthy man suspiciously.

"Take it and have no fears, it rightfully belongs to you. You see, last night your large cup gave birth to this little one, so I thought it no more than right to give it to you."

"A regular *shlemiel*," thought the miser. "Very well," he said aloud, scarcely able to conceal his glee, "as long as you are honest enough to admit it, I'll be honest enough to accept it."

"Thank you," said Fenster. "And now I'd like to borrow a silver candelabra for the weekend. I'm expecting an important guest and I want to make a good impression."

The old tightwad was impressed, not only with the *shnorrer's* honesty but also with his apparent stupidity. "Sure, take it!" he said.

On the following Monday, bright and early, Fenster returned the candelabra, together with a separate candlestick.

"Your candelabra gave birth to this candlestick," explained the *shnorrer*.

Eisinger was too crafty a man to question Fenster about the absurdity of an inanimate object bearing offspring. "Anytime I can be of service in the future just call on me," he said pleasantly as he accepted the newborn gift.

"Well, there's something I can use right now," said Fenster. "I am expecting my brother-in-law tomorrow, and just to create a show, I'd like to borrow your diamond-studded gold watch."

The rich man immediately conjured up visions of an immaculate conception whose progeny would be a "baby" watch of comparable value to the "parent." He promptly handed over the watch, on the assurance that it would be returned the following evening. "What an ignorant fool!" he thought contemptuously.

But Fenster did not return the expensive watch the next evening, nor the next week, nor the following month. So the miser went to the *shnorrer's* humble dwelling to demand the return of his property.

"Where's my gold watch?" Eisinger asked.

"It grieves me to tell you this," explained Fenster, "but your watch took sick and died."

"Died? That's ridiculous!"

"Why is it ridiculous?" asked the *shnorrer* calmly. "If a silver cup and a candelabra can bear children, as you yourself agreed, then why can't a watch pass away?"

✓　　✓　　✓

Harry Houdini, the late and legendary magician, had a cousin who was a first-class *shlepper*—he dragged away everything and anything for which he did not have to pay.

One day he visited the famous Harry and because he was, after all, a first cousin, he was accorded the red-carpet treatment. But no matter what gifts and money Harry gave him, he always managed to wheedle a little extra. A week later he left, with five suitcases bulging with presents and a wallet stuffed with large denomination greenbacks.

But the very next day he was back.

"What in the world are you doing here?" asked the surprised Harry Houdini. "I thought you were on your way home."

"Harry, I had the feeling that you would have a big celebration when I left," explained the shrewd cousin. "So what kind of relative would I be if I didn't show up at my own cousin's party?"

✓　　✓　　✓

Mendel the beggar was pleading with Winograd the furrier for a few pennies to buy food. "I swear to the God of Israel that I haven't had so much as a crust of bread in two days," the *shnorrer* bleated piously, beating his breast. So Winograd gave him five dollars, being a generous man.

That afternoon, the furrier was walking down Eighth Avenue when he passed an exclusive restaurant. And whom should he see inside but the very same *shnorrer*, his plate piled high with *gefilteh fish* and *chaleh*. Boiling with indignation, he rushed inside.

"How dare you come to my house and beg when you actually eat better than I do?" demanded Winograd harshly. "I give you five dollars and what do you do—eat expensive *gefilteh fish* and the highest priced bread! What kind of starvation do you call that?"

"What are you hollering on me?" retorted the beggar, equally offended. "Before you gave me the five dollars I couldn't afford to eat like a *mensch*. Now, according to you, I'm not allowed. So tell me, just when am I supposed to eat *gefilteh fish* and *chaleh?*"

🕯 🕯 🕯

There are many wondrous tales about *shnorrers*, but this seems to be the only one about a *shnorrer-in-law*.

For many years a certain *shnorrer* had made it a practice to appear at a rich man's house on Friday evenings—at exactly the time when the host was sitting down to dinner.

One evening, however, he was accompanied by a young stranger.

The householder was understandably irritated at this display of rudeness. "What is this? You're now inviting guests to my table?"

"Not quite," the *shnorrer* answered pleasantly. "This is my new son-in-law. I promised him free board for the first year!"

🕯 🕯 🕯

Yossel the *shnorrer* had only been in the little town for a few hours when he realized that he would starve to death if he did not find some other way to earn his bread and butter. The two *shnorrers* who were natives of the town had a closed monopoly on begging and they did not take kindly to the possibility of sharing their benefactors with the interloper.

In the midst of his despair, Yossel hit upon a brilliant idea. From one end of the town to the other, approaching every person on the street, young, middle-aged and old, he announced to them that next Friday morning he would walk across the river on a wire, stretched high above the water, from one bank to the other. The charge for his daring performance would be only two kopeks.

At the appointed time the whole town was on hand. Sure enough, there was the newcomer, and wonder of wonders, there was the wire attached to either bank! Now even the last few cynics in the festive crowd paid the two kopeks admission fee.

The *shnorrer* walked up to the wire and then raised his hand to quiet the excited throng. "Good people," he cried, "I am not a tightrope walker. I never performed on a high-wire in my life. If I attempt this trick I will undoubtedly fall into the river and drown. However, I am not only a reasonable but an honest man. If you are willing to see a poor Jew go to his death for just two miserable kopeks I shall go ahead with the trick; but remember—my blood will be on your hands!"

🕯 🕯 🕯

A *shnorrer* called at the house of a rich man, only to learn from the butler that the master had gone to the hot springs for his arthritis.

"Hot springs!" spat the furious little beggar. "How dare he go to an expensive health resort on my money!"

🕯 🕯 🕯

SHNORRERS

The town banker was awakened at six o'clock in the morning by a furious pounding on his front door. Sure that it must be a dire emergency to summon him at that unearthly hour, he ran quickly to the door, but when he opened it there stood a *shnorrer* seeking a handout.

"What is the meaning of this outrage!" cried the banker. "Don't you realize what time it is?"

"Look, Mister, do I tell you what time you should report to your bank?" retorted the beggar. "Then don't tell me what time *I* should start work!"

✔   ✔   ✔

A traveling *schnorrer*, a bum who had never worked a day in his life and had no intention of doing so, stopped at a poor farmer's house for a night's lodging. He was welcomed with traditional Jewish hospitality, given a substantial hot supper and a comfortable bed.

The following morning, after a robust breakfast, he burped contentedly and said, "You people have been so good to me, I am wondering whether I might impose on you for just one more day. I give you my word, I'll leave tomorrow for sure."

The farmer and his wife exchanged uneasy glances, but after a momentary hesitation, they nodded.

On the second day the farmer's wife prepared a much simpler meal, although still wholesome. Poor people themselves, it was all they could afford.

Still the *shnorrer* found excuses to remain. By the fifth day all the farmer's wife could offer was a piece of black bread and a glass of weak tea.

"What kind of a meal do you call this?" asked the "guest." "Are you people trying to starve me to death?"

"I'm sorry; truly sorry," answered the impoverished farmer, "but this is all we have left. After this we won't have anything to eat ourselves."

"In that case I'll leave the first thing in the morning. I can't very well stay here and die of hunger."

Bright and early the next morning, the farmer awoke him. "Time to rise," he said, gently shaking the man. "The cock has already crowed."

"What! You mean to say you still have a chicken?" the *shnorrer* cried. "Listen, would it bother you if I stayed for just one more day?"

✔   ✔   ✔

A sad-faced little man, wearing dark glasses and holding a battered tin cup in his hand, poked his way along the street, whining piteously; "Help the blind! Help the blind!"

An elderly *rebbetzn* passed by. "Ahh, you poor man! What a pity!" she commiserated, dropping two nickels into his cup.

"Lady," said the beggar gratefully, "the minute I took a look at you I knew you had a kind heart!"

✔   ✔   ✔

Aaron Lomitski, Warsaw's wiliest *shnorrer*, went to see Baron de Rothschild for his usual stipend. The servant, however, informed him that the Baron was gravely ill and not expected to live.

"Tell him that I can cure him," the beggar said promptly. "Without a doubt!"

He was quickly ushered into Rothschild's bedroom.

"You have a cure for me?" asked the Baron hopefully.

"Yes, but it will cost you."

"Never mind the cost. What must I do?"

"Listen carefully. Do you know the ghetto settlement on the other side of the garbage dump by the river? The place where all the city's rats and roaches breed? Where the streets are slippery with rotting, slimy garbage that the people throw out of the windows?"

Baron de Rothschild shuddered in disgust. "Yes, I know the section."

"Well, that's where I live."

"But what has that to do with my illness?"

"Move in with me, Baron. In all our history, no rich man has ever died in our part of the ghetto!"

✓ ✓ ✓

Spiegel was making his usual rounds, extracting nickels and dimes from his regular "customers." But when he reached the house of Mrs. Hurwitz he was told, "Come back tomorrow; I haven't any spare cash right now."

"I'm sorry, Madam," said Spiegel firmly, "but you'll have to give me something now. I don't do business on credit!"

✓ ✓ ✓

The small-town *shnorrer* had walked all night and most of the next day to be on hand when Baron de Rothschild handed out his annual largesse to the hordes of alms-seekers. It had been raining ever since the mendicant started out, but having sloshed through the rain and along the muddy roads, he arrived on time. He knocked on the door of Rothschild's mansion and a butler ushered him inside. But when he strode across the Oriental rug the butler was infuriated to see that the *shnorrer* had left muddy tracks on the priceless carpeting.

"Haven't you the common decency to wipe the mud off your shoes?" he yelled.

The *shnorrer* stared at the butler in amazement. "Shoes?" he echoed blankly. "*What* shoes?"

✓ ✓ ✓

Sidney, not long in this country, received a Christmas card from his employer. He took the card to a friend.

"Moishe," he asked, "what means this 'Yuletide Greetings'?"

SHNORRERS

"That's easy," replied the friend. "It means, if you'll lend me a little something until payday, *you'll tide* me over!"

↑ ↑ ↑

A *shnorrer*, one of the cleverest in all of Eastern Europe, emigrated to America, but he hadn't been here more than a few days when he realized that his ignorance of the English language precluded any possibility of making a livelihood in the same profession. But this *shnorrer* had no intention of earning his bread by the sweat of his brow, so he conceived an idea that would make him a fortune in the antique business.

He went into Rosenthal's Antique Shoppe, on Park Avenue, and offered for sale an old silk shirt which, he claimed, was worn by the Czar of all the Russias at his coronation.

"I will have to consult with my expert," said Mr. Rosenthal. "Oh Mr. Montgomery, will you please come over here and evaluate this merchandise?"

Mr. Montgomery shuffled forward, adjusted his eyeglasses, and peered at the shirt. "It's the Czar's, no question about it," he said, "but we already have nine shirts worn by the Czar in his last few days of life."

So the *shnorrer* left without a sale, but with his mind ever alert. On the next day he returned to the antique shop and confronted Mr. Rosenthal. "Here is a page from the original manuscript of the Jerusalem Talmud, going all the way back to the fourth century. It's very valuable but I'm a reasonable man—what do you offer?"

Once more Rosenthal said, "I will have to ask my expert." He called out, "Oh Mr. Montgomery, that man is here again."

Montgomery peered closely at the page which looked suspiciously new and which bore a photo-offset picture. He handed the page back to the *shnorrer*. "It's authentic," he agreed as before, "but we have the complete manuscript in our storeroom. Sorry."

This time the *shnorrer* waited several days. When he felt that he had concocted the perfect deal he went back to the store, his head swathed in bandages. "Rosenthal, have I got a scarce item for you!"

"What is it this time?"

"You heard of the great painter Van Gogh? Well, I got one of his ears. How's that for a real prize?"

Rosenthal turned to call his expert, but the *shnorrer* grasped his sleeve. "Just a minute," he interrupted. "There's no use calling Montgomery because there's nothing in your storeroom. I found Van Gogh's other ear too!"

↑ ↑ ↑

Shnorrers may be a cynical lot but sometimes they meet their match. Consider the beggar who used the "charity" approach.

"Mister," he said to a likely looking prospect, "will you give a little something to help the Old Ladies Home?"

"Yeah," replied the man, "if you'll tell me how they got out in the first place."

✓ ✓ ✓

It was a balmy morning in June. A cool breeze was blowing in from the ocean, the birds were singing and the flowers blooming. Leonard was walking along the street when he was buttonholed by a well-known *shnorrer*.

"I'm looking for someone to lend me twenty dollars," said the conniver.

"Well," said Leonard, "I must say you picked a nice day for it."

✓ ✓ ✓

A beggar knocked on the door but as soon as the lady of the house opened it she let fly with a scathing denunciation. "Go away, you bum, you loafer, you big mouth!"

"Why, what did I do?"

"You know very well what you did! Last week you were here and I gave you some of my home made *chaleh*, and *gefilteh fish* I made with my own hands. So what do you do? You send all your no-good friends here ever since."

"Lady," sighed the beggar, remembering her cooking, "they weren't my friends. They were my enemies!"

✓ ✓ ✓

Despite the *shnorrer's* entreaties the wealthy miser refused to change his lifelong policy of refusing to give alms. "I don't give to a soul and I have no intention of making an exception in your case," he said.

"Well then," replied the *shnorrer*, "even though you will not help a poor man I'll leave you with a prayer—that God will treat you as he did our patriarchs, Abraham, Isaac and Jacob."

The astonished skinflint started to answer but, instead he reached into his purse and gave the visitor a handsome donation. "Tell me," he said when he finally could speak, "why did you bless me when I was mean to you?"

"Bless you? Who blessed you?" retorted the *shnorrer*. "I was only hoping you would be a wanderer like Abraham, blind like Isaac and, like Jacob, you should break a leg!"

✓ ✓ ✓

Meyer Amschel Rothschild of Frankfurt, popularly known as Reb Amschel, was enjoying a leisurely stroll one day when he came upon a beggar with a Yiddish sign suspended from his neck: "Help A Poor Man." But what struck his fancy was the fellow's cheerful demeanor, his smiling acknowledgment whenever someone dropped a coin in his cup or greeted him by name.

Reb Amschel walked over to the mendicant and gave him a gold coin. "Tell me something, my friend," he began conversationally, "have you no family?"

"Of course I have a family," replied the beggar.

"Children?"

"Five—all grown up and well to do."

"And they won't support you?"

"They would if I let them."

"Why don't you?"

"What," cried the beggar indignantly, "and lose my independence?"

Chapter Four

Tightskates and Cheapwads

Teivel, a rich silversmith of Minsk, and his wife Malke found it necessary to journey to Pinsk at once. Because of a heavy snowfall the night before, the only train was indefinitely delayed.

What to do? Teivel had an inspiring thought: "Moishe, the driver, will take us to Pinsk in his wagon."

But Moishe was anything but willing to make the trip. "The roads are covered with ice," he complained. "In some places the snow is banked in ten-foot drifts. It is bitter cold. My horses might slip and break a leg—and what would happen to my livelihood?" His objections shot out like bullets from a machine gun.

But Teivel, meanwhile, had conceived an idea. After all, he had not grown rich because he was a fool. "I'll tell you what, Moishe," he said craftily, "if you get us from Minsk to Pinsk on time I'll pay you double the regular fare."

"Double? You'll pay me twenty rubles?"

"Yes, but on one condition."

"I thought there was a catch. So what's the condition?"

"This: If I utter just one sound—even the slightest noise—during the whole trip then I'll pay twice the fare—twenty rubles. But if I remain absolutely silent then I owe you nothing."

Moishe scratched his head, turning the proposition over in his mind. "Hmmm-m-m," was his only audible reaction.

"*Nu*, is it a deal?" asked the impatient Teivel.

Finally Moishe nodded, the trace of a cunning grin at the corners of his mouth. "Double fare if he makes a single sound, eh?" he laughed to himself. "He'll make a sound—he'll holler at the top of his lungs!"

As soon as Moishe and his passengers had left the outskirts of Minsk and were on the open road, Moishe urged his two horses into a wild gallop, reining them from one side of the road to the other, causing the wagon to careen wildly. Over the icy roads they flew, mile after mile, at breakneck speed. They hit every rock, every rut and hole, rounding sharp turns at full gallop, the wheels skidding crazily on the ice.

But not a sound was heard from Teivel or Malke. Desperately, Moishe raced the horses at the very edge of the road where the slightest mishap would have sent them plunging down the steep embankment. He did everything he could think of to frighten his passengers into making just one tiny sound, but they remained as silent as a grave.

Finally, the perilous journey reached its end, and Moishe pulled his horses to a halt in Pinsk. He alighted and helped Teivel down from his seat.

"You win," said the driver ruefully. "You never made a single sound."

Teivel, still pale and shaken, managed to gulp, "Just between you and me, Moishe, I want to confess something. Back there at that last wild turn when the carriage nearly turned over, you almost won your bet. That's where my wife fell out!"

✓ ✓ ✓

The richest bachelor in town, and unquestionably the stingiest, hovered between life and death. A doctor was summoned to the bedside of the critically ill man, and when he had completed his diagnosis he declared that the patient's only hope for survival was to perspire. In vain, the doctor tried every method known to medical science to induce sweating, but the old miser would not perspire. Finally, a rabbi was called to hear the sick man's last testament.

"My friend," the rabbi said, "since you are unable to perspire I suggest that you give your possessions to charity, now while you are alive, as a *mitzvah* for the hereafter. Surely, you of all people, need a blessing."

The sick man nodded weakly. "My box of gold," he whispered feebly, "I leave to the Jewish Home for the Aged."

The rabbi wrote it down. "How about your real estate?" he asked.

"My two houses I leave to the synagogue to be used as places of study." The rabbi wrote that down also. "And the farmlands?" he asked gently.

"The farmlands I donate to . . ." Suddenly the patient sat up, his eyes wide and bright. Frantically he clutched at the sheet of paper on which the rabbi had been writing.

"Give it back!" he shouted hoarsely. "I'm sweating! I'm sweating!"

✓ ✓ ✓

Beggar: "Believe me, if I don't eat soon I'll die."
Miser: "How long has it been since you had anything to eat?"
Beggar: "A week."
Miser: (sympathetically) "Sometimes you have to force yourself!"

✓ ✓ ✓

A rich, penny-pinching landlord passed a beggar on the street and reached into his pocket. "I'd like to give you ten cents," he said, "but all I have with me is a quarter. Take it and give me fifteen cents change."

"Fifteen cents! Who has fifteen cents?" demanded the beggar. "What am I, a banker?"

"All right, don't get fresh. Take the quarter and I'll walk along with you until you beg enough to give me the change."

"This is very generous of you," said the beggar, his voice oozing sarcasm. "Walk with me then, and for your kindness you should stay in good health—at least until you get your fifteen cents change!"

✓   ✓   ✓

A group of *yeshivah* students were on their way home from classes one evening, when they passed the house of one of their professors, a penurious rich man with a disposition that could curdle vinegar and a tongue that could clip a hedge. To their surprise, the front door which was always tightly shut was now ajar. On impulse, the young students trooped into the house.

The professor was at dinner, and having no alternative, he told his wife to set places at the table for all of them. She, unlike her husband, was a generous person, and she set a bounteous repast before them. The youths devoured it to the last savory morsel.

After dinner, one of the students undertook to thank the professor for his amazing hospitality. "And to think that we arrived unexpectedly," the lad enthused. "Just imagine the kind of reception we would have had if you expected us!"

"My dear young man," the professor replied icily, "if I had expected you, the door would have been securely bolted!"

✓   ✓   ✓

In all of Lithuania there was no *Litvak* more selfish or greedy than Kirschmeyer. For that reason, most of the poor didn't even ask him to contribute to the needy. It was simply a waste of time. But one year, when the harvest was meager, the merchants had a poor season, and the need among the townspeople was greater than ever, the rabbi decided to ask a donation of the old skinflint.

"Kirschmeyer," the rabbi began, "you are seldom asked to give to charity because of your well-known reluctance to part with your money. But this time our people are in desperate circumstances. *Pesach* is only a few days off and many poor families have nothing set aside for the holiday. I beseech you to help."

The iron-hearted miser stared at the rabbi out of eyes that were as cold and unresponsive as a lizard's. "Rabbi," he snapped, "I cannot give you a single penny for the simple reason that I have a very poor brother and sister."

The rabbi departed without a contribution, well aware of the injunction that a brother and sister must take preference over others. But on Passover eve, who should appear at the synagogue seeking alms but the rich man's brother and sister.

"What are you doing here?" demanded the rabbi brusquely. "Your wealthy brother takes care of you."

"But he never gives us a penny," they cried. "We're destitute!"

The rabbi's face darkened in anger. He rushed to Kirschmeyer's mansion and confronted him with the story. "Is this true?" he demanded.

"Yes, it is," the miser agreed calmly. "I give nothing to either my brother or my sister."

"Then how dare you tell me about them in the first place?"

"All I meant was that if I won't give a penny to my own brother and sister, why should you expect me to give anything to a bunch of total strangers?"

✔ ✔ ✔

A miser who owned vast farmlands, dairy herds and wholesale grain warehouses, became gravely ill. When his temperature rose to 105° his frightened wife sent for the doctor.

"I'm sorry, Madam," the doctor said after he examined the patient, "but your husband has no chance. All I can suggest now is prayer."

With his last remaining ounce of strength, the husband raised his head from the pillow and weakly implored his wife to go to the synagogue, make a contribution, and pray that his life be spared. So she went to the synagogue, donated fifty dollars, and prayed fervently and tearfully that God spare her husband's life.

As though God had answered her supplications, the rich miser miraculously became well, but when he learned that his wife had given fifty dollars, his face purpled with rage.

"But you yourself told me to give the money," his wife reminded him.

"So what?" he roared. "You couldn't see I was delirious?"

✔ ✔ ✔

A stingy farmer grew resentful of the cost of feeding his plow horse. "Every day he consumes precious oats and hay. Starting tomorrow," he promised his wife, "I'll eliminate the oats."

A month later, satisfied with the savings on oats, the thought occurred to him that he could easily accustom the horse to even less food by gradually decreasing the quantity of hay.

Each day, thereafter, he reduced the portion of fodder he had been giving to the horse until, three months later, the now-emaciated animal was receiving only a few wisps a day.

"Look," he cried excitedly to his wife, "all we have to do now is to cut out his hay entirely and in no time at all it won't cost us a penny to keep him."

But the horse soon died.

"*Oy, vay, iz mir!*" he wept. "Of all the rotten luck! Here I had that horse accustomed to going without any food at all, and it had to go and die!"

✔ ✔ ✔

43

"Mr. Kantor," said a rabbi to a wealthy merchant, "I would like a loan of a few hundred dollars. I can repay the loan within six months."

The merchant, a member of the rabbi's congregation, looked up craftily. "I don't want to throw this up to you, rabbi, but didn't I myself hear you say yesterday in your sermon that to lend money on interest is the same as killing the borrower?"

"Interest!" exclaimed the surprised rabbi, "I am not here to borrow on interest. I merely want a loan."

"*Oy*, that's even worse!" groaned the miser. "In that case I'd be killing myself!"

✓ ✓ ✓

A lady who owned a boarding house was such a penny-pincher that she even skimped on the cheapest of food. Her specialty was a thin, watery soup.

One evening, when she had just served noodle soup, one of the boarders, a young student with a healthy appetite, bent his head low over the table and put his ear to the plate.

"What are you doing?" asked the woman suspiciously.

"I hear a noodle talking," he said.

"You don't mean it!" she exclaimed, surprise written all over her face. "What is it saying?"

"It's saying," the young man responded, "Gee, I'm lonesome! I wish there were another noodle to keep me company!"

✓ ✓ ✓

Itzig went to the mansion of the richest banker in all of Hungary and described his plight in tones of utter dejection.

"For five days my wife and I have had nothing to eat," he wept. "My dear little children, all five of them, are actually starving to death. The landlord is about to throw us out into the street because we cannot pay the rent. We're all sick but no doctor will treat us because we have no money. On top of all that, *Pesach* will soon be here and we haven't a drop of wine, a morsel of meat or a piece of *matzoh* for the holiday."

The rich banker was profoundly shaken by this tale of woe. He immediately rang for the butler.

"Throw this man out!" he cried. "He's breaking my heart!"

✓ ✓ ✓

The ailing skinflint needed the aid of a specialist, but the fees appalled him: $25 for a first visit and $10 for subsequent visits. Still, it was a matter of life or death, and besides, he had an idea!

As he entered the doctor's office, the miser said cordially, "Well, Doctor, here I am—*again!*"

But the doctor had met this type before. He made a great show of examining the patient with minute thoroughness, then said, "Just continue the same treatment as before!"

✓　　✓　　✓

In an obscure *shtetl* in the Pale of Settlement lived a granite-hearted money-grubber who took a sadistic delight in tantalizing dinner guests and sending them to bed hungry. He would set a bountiful table and then, his eyes gleaming wickedly, he would ply his guest with endless irrelevant questions so that the poor visitor was too occupied with his answers to taste a morsel of food. Meanwhile, the conniving host would gorge himself until the serving plates were empty. Everyone knew of his niggardly character and evil ways so the old skinflint could only entice an occasional traveler who happened to be passing through town.

Now it so happened that Herschel Ostropolier, one of Judaism's greatest wits, chanced to arrive in this *shtetl*. Hearing of the miser's unkind treatment of innocent and hungry sojourners, he decided to teach the man a lesson. Through the good offices of the local rabbi he managed an invitation to the rich man's house, and so it was that the two sat down to *shabbes* dinner together. Chortling inwardly at the entertainment that awaited him, the host commanded his servant to bring in the food: a tureen of fish, mounds of mashed potatoes and gravy, pieces of succulent chicken, thick slices of rare roast beef, wine and honey cakes. The sight and aroma of the feast made Herschel's mouth water. As expected, the miser reached for the serving plate of chicken, placed a fat piece on his plate and then, instead of passing the dish to his guest, he began the inquisition:

"Tell me, have you traveled far?" he asked.

"All the way from Berditchev," echoed Herschel, waiting like a bloodhound sniffing a scent.

"Berditchev? Then you must know my cousin Aaron Goddesov."

"Which Goddesov?"

"Aaron—the wine maker."

"Oh, you mean Aaron Goddesov the wine maker," responded Herschel. "He's dead."

The miser's eyes bulged at the unexpected news, and for once he was speechless. In the dead silence, Herschel reached over and helped himself to the choicest chicken parts and poured himself a full tumbler of wine.

The host, recovering his composure, moaned: "I invested a thousand rubles in that wine business. Did his brother take over the firm?"

"Which brother?" answered Herschel innocently.

"What do you mean, which brother? Mendel, of course."

"Naturally—Aaron's brother Mendel. Of course."

"Well, he's an honest man. He'll pay me back."

"Sorry," said Herschel, "but he died."

The skinflint clapped both palms to his forehead. "Mendel died? But how about his son, Avrum? Surely he is in charge now."

Herschel shook his head. "He died too."

As the completely unnerved host set down his fork and gasped, Herschel speared a large portion of fish, helped himself to the roast beef, mashed potatoes and another glass of wine. He ate slowly, savoring the flavor with every bite.

When the host was finally able to speak, he asked, "Do you know Leibel, the lawyer of Berditchev?"

"You mean Leibel, the lawyer of Berditchev?"

"Yes."

"Poor man!"

"Wh-wh-what do you mean, poor man?"

"Dead also."

"Vay iz mir!" wailed the host. "Now who will take care of my investment? I know what! I'll send my wife to Berditchev. She'll recover my money."

Herschel helped himself to some stuffed *helzel* and another piece of fish. "Sorry, but she too is dead."

The miser's face turned red, then green, then yellow, then ghostly white. "Are you insane?" he shrieked. "She just finished preparing this meal. How can she be dead?"

Herschel, having devoured everything in sight, burped contentedly and leaned back in his chair. "Very simple," he drawled. "As far as I'm concerned, everyone is dead when I'm eating."

"Why, you dirty . . . !"

"I must say," interrupted the grinning Herschel, "you set a fine table, and my compliments to your wife on her excellent cooking. But look here, you've been so busy talking you forgot to eat!"

✓   ✓   ✓

There was a wealthy cloak-and-suiter who lived in Scarsdale with his wife and children, but who also kept one of his models in a fancy apartment on Riverside Drive. Occasionally he would visit Las Vegas to gamble, and he frequently imbibed more freely than was good for him.

One day the rabbi came to see him for a donation to a charity.

"I'm sorry," said the cloak-and-suiter, "but I already gave. You see, I always donate secretly."

The rabbi looked him squarely in the eye. "Isn't it strange," he asked, "how you can sin in secret and all of New York knows about it, but not a living soul ever hears about the charity you give secretly?"

✓   ✓   ✓

Jake Levine, president of Jacques LaVine Paris Creations, was usually a pleasant sort of fellow, but this morning he was glum and irritable.

"What's with you?" asked the bookkeeper. "You got troubles?"

"It's my wife," complained Levine. "She's driving me crazy with her constant demands for money. Last week she asked me for $150. Yesterday she insisted on $100, and only today she wanted $75."

"What in the world does she need all that money for?" asked the bookkeeper.

"Who knows?" answered Levine. "So far I haven't given her a dime!"

✓ ✓ ✓

A couple of businessmen were talking about a mutual acquaintance.

"I put him on his feet," boasted the first.

"You did?" exclaimed the other. "Why, you have a reputation as the most hard-hearted man in town! Why would you put him on his feet?"

"Because he couldn't keep up with his payments. I repossessed his car!"

✓ ✓ ✓

A *shnorrer*, new to the city, called on a wealthy banker for some money. To his surprise, the man shook his hand warmly. "Welcome to our city," he said genially.

The beggar was taken aback. "Sir, I thank you for your welcome, but how did you know I was a stranger here?"

"Easy," replied the miserly banker. "There isn't a soul in town who would waste his time asking me for charity!"

✓ ✓ ✓

Morty, who would walk a mile for a caramel if it would save him a penny, took his best girl to a restaurant.

"Marry me, darling, and I'll buy you the sun, the moon and the stars," he crooned. *"Separate checks, Waiter!"*

✓ ✓ ✓

A prosperous, aging furrier, now that death was not too far in the future, decided to get on the good side of God. So he went to the local rabbi and insisted that he had finally bowed to religion.

The dubious rabbi, after questioning the furrier at length, asked, "Are you going to repay all your debts and forgive those who are indebted to you?"

"Just a minute, Rabbi," protested the other, "you aren't talking religion now—you're talking business!"

✓ ✓ ✓

The little old man approached his boss timidly. "Mr. Shlepper, can I have tomorrow off? It's my golden anniversary."

"By God!" snarled Shlepper, "will I have to put up with this *chutzpah* every fifty years?"

✓ ✓ ✓

It was the slow season in heaven, so the Admitting Angel was having a friendly little game of pinochle with Father Abraham, the Recording

Angel. Suddenly there sounded a loud rapping on the Heavenly Portal and when they opened the gates in walked arrogant Harry Sperling, the most notorious miser in all New York.

"All right, let's get the preliminaries over with!" ordered Harry. "Sign me up and then assign me to an exclusive neighborhood up here. I don't want to mix with the *yentehs*."

"Abe, look up this guy's history," said the Admitting Angel to the Recording Angel. The latter found Harry's dossier and handed it over.

"Ah yes, you died an hour ago," said the Admitting Angel. "Tell me, what kind of work did you do?"

Harry drew himself proudly. "Whaddyamean, *work*! I'll have you know I was the biggest dress goods manufacturer in the business. I had two thousand employees to do my work for me!"

The Recording Angel checked the record and nodded. "That's correct," he said.

"Now then, what good deeds have you done to merit a place in heaven?" asked the Admitting Angel.

"Wel-l-l, let's see now. Hmmm! Oh yes, once I gave fifteen cents to a starving widow and her children. I'd have given more, ya unnerstand, but it doesn't pay to spoil these people."

"Any other magnificent works of charity?" asked the Admitting Angel sarcastically.

"Yeah, as long as you ask. I don't wanna brag, but once I found a dog lying in the street. It was terribly skinny and near death from hunger. Know what I did? I put a nickel on its half-frozen, emaciated body, figuring that somebody would pass by sooner or later and buy it something to eat."

The Admitting Angel turned to the Recording Angel. "Abe," he asked, "what shall we do with this character?"

"I know exactly," said Father Abraham. "Give him back his twenty cents and tell him to go to hell!"

✓   ✓   ✓

"What do you mean, I should help you out? I have nothing—and very little of that!"

✓   ✓   ✓

"Are you sure you actually need this nickel?" asked the penny-pincher.

"No, not really!" retorted the *shnorrer*. "I have all the money I'll ever need for as long as I live—provided I drop dead this instant!"

✓   ✓   ✓

A penurious young man heard that a lady friend was ill, so he called on her and presented her with a gift—a box of cough drops.

"Well!" she snapped, "I hope this didn't set you back too much! Couldn't you at least have brought flowers?"

"I suppose so," he answered, "but I heard you had a cold, not that you were dead."

𝆑 𝆑 𝆑

You heard, maybe, about the fellow who took a girl home in a taxi? She was so lovely he could hardly take his eyes off the meter.

𝆑 𝆑 𝆑

Mannie, who still had the first penny he ever earned, went into the Last National Bank of New York and asked for a one-year loan of a dollar.

"Do you have any collateral?" queried the bank clerk.

"Yeah," answered Mannie, producing a bulky envelope, "stocks and bonds with a value of $50,000."

"That's fine," said the clerk. "At the end of the year you will owe us 6% interest on your dollar loan, and your security will be returned to you."

The president of the bank, sitting at his desk a few feet away, heard every word of the discussion and could not contain his curiosity. As Mannie was leaving with his dollar, the official approached him.

"Mister," he asked, "why does anybody with $50,000 in stocks and bonds want to borrow a dollar?"

"Because," answered Mannie, "I don't know any other way to get a safety deposit box for six cents a year!"

𝆑 𝆑 𝆑

The bus was crossing the Brooklyn Bridge when the motorman noticed that the bearded man sitting a few rows back had not paid his fare. "Hey, buddy," he called out, "you owe me a dime!"

"A nickel I'll pay, not a penny more," snapped the oldster.

"Look, Mac, the fare's a dime. Don't gimme no arguments."

"Last year it was a nickel!"

Enraged, the short-tempered driver slammed on the brakes and brought the bus to a screeching stop in the middle of the bridge. He went back to where the bearded gentleman was sitting and jabbed his forefinger into the other's chest. "Okay, Buster, pay your dime. I already told you the fare went up."

"A nickel!"

"A dime!"

"A nickel—no more!"

The bus driver grabbed the old man's suitcase and thrust it halfway out of the open window. "All right, I've had it!" he snarled. "Either pay the ten cents fare or I'll throw your suitcase into the damn river!"

"*Oy gevald!*" screamed the old man, "isn't it enough you're trying to overcharge me, you have to drown my innocent little grandson?"

𝆑 𝆑 𝆑

Papa kissed his wife, as was his custom before leaving for the shop every morning, and then he patted his little boy on the head. "Goodbye, Sollie," he said, "and don't forget to take your glasses off when you're not looking at anything important!"

✔   ✔   ✔

Cousin Yankel had to make a selling trip, so he went into a store to buy a satchel. He picked one whose price and appearance were suitable.

"Shall I wrap the suitcase for you, sir?" asked the clerk.

"Never mind," answered Cousin Yankel. "Just put the wrapping paper and cord inside the satchel."

✔   ✔   ✔

The rabbi needed funds with which to purchase supplies for the synagogue so he called a meeting, but prudently avoided mentioning that he intended to ask for money. Among those who attended were Moishe and Mendel, two of the most notorious tightwads in the city. Even the good rabbi was curious to see how they would respond.

The rabbi got right down to business and explained the purpose of the gathering. He then announced that a collection would be taken.

Upon hearing this unpleasant news Moishe promptly fainted, and Mendel carried him outside.

Chapter Five

Shlemiels and Shlimazls

Once upon a time there were two brothers, Zelig and Leo. Zelig was a clever and alert young fellow, but Leo was a dolt—a first class *shnook*! Zelig, as might be expected, was welcomed wherever he went. He could tell witty stories and fascinating parables with intelligence and high humor. But poor Leo was never invited anywhere, for obvious reasons.

Now the boys' mother was very unhappy about Leo's plight, so she pleaded with Zelig to teach him how to become popular.

"Tell him some of the riddles, the stories and funny anecdotes you know so well. Teach him something, so that people will at least listen to him and maybe even pay him a compliment."

"All right, Mama, I'll teach him," sighed Zelig. So he took his brother aside and said, "Listen to me carefully, Leo. I am going to teach you a riddle. Tomorrow night at the meeting house you are to stand up and say 'What am I?' Some will answer 'You are a fool!' Others will reply 'You are an idiot!' To each one you are to answer 'Wrong—guess again!' Finally, when they have all given up, you are to answer the riddle by saying 'I am hungry!' Isn't that clever, Leo?"

"Wonderful! Wonderful!" enthused Leo, doubling up with laughter.

All that day and the next he practiced the riddle, rehearsing every word Zelig had taught him. In the evening he went to the meeting house which was packed with the townspeople. He stood up and called loudly for silence. When the hubbub subsided, he shouted, "A riddle! What am I?"

As Zelig had foretold, everybody laughed. "A fool!" cried the tailor.

"Wrong! Guess again!" answered Leo gleefully.

"An idiot!" yelled the grocer.

"Wrong! Guess again!"

"All right, we give up," they acknowledged. "Tell us, what are you?"

"Let's eat!" hollered Leo proudly.

✦   ✦   ✦

A farmer was driving along the road one torrid summer day when he came upon an undersized old peddler with a heavy load of merchandise

51

on his back. The poor little man appeared to be utterly exhausted as he trudged on.

The kindhearted farmer pulled his horse to a halt and offered the weary traveler a ride to the city.

They had been riding together for several minutes when the farmer noticed that his new companion was still holding the heavy burden on his back.

"My friend," he said, "why not set your pack down in the wagon and make yourself comfortable?"

"Sir, you are a kind man and I don't want to take advantage of your goodness," answered the humble peddler. "It is enough that you are taking me to the city, and for that I thank you—but you don't have to carry my pack too!"

✓ ✓ ✓

Seymour Kaplan, a pants-maker in New York, saved up enough money to justify a visit to the town of his birth in Russia. Having no passport, and ignorant of the procedure necessary to obtain one, he bought a passport for $15 from a local *ganeff* who specialized in such matters.

"All you need to remember is that your name is now Isaac Leibovitch," cautioned the *ganeff*. "Just forget your own name and you won't get into trouble."

Seymour repeated the new name over and over again, committing it to memory so that he would not be found out. When he arrived at the Russian border his passport was taken from him and the imperious customs official examined the picture on the document and then scrutinized Seymour's face. There was a slight resemblance, but the officer wanted to make sure. He snapped several questions at the trembling little man who was beginning to sweat. Finally he asked, "What is your name?"

By this time, Seymour was so flustered and frightened that his mind was a blank. "My name—my name is—well, I—I . . ."

"Come, come!" rapped out the official curtly. "Surely you know your own name!"

"Look, mister," he pleaded, "call me anything you want, but for Heaven's sake, don't call me Seymour Kaplan!"

✓ ✓ ✓

A salesman who was traveling to Petrograd was unable to continue his journey because of a severe snowstorm. The stationmaster told him that the trains would surely be running again at six o'clock the next morning, as the tracks would be cleared by that hour. The traveler had no alternative but to go to the local hotel.

By the time he arrived at the small-town hostelry all the rooms had been taken by the other passengers of the delayed train. However the desk clerk was a kindly soul who could not bear to put a weary stranger out in such a blizzard, and he hit upon an idea.

"Listen, my friend, all of the rooms here have a single bed each, so I can't very well ask the occupants to put you up for the night. But there is one room here with two beds in it."

"Thank God!" breathed the salesman. "I was afraid I might have to sleep out in the cold tonight."

"Wait a minute, I must tell you something," said the clerk hurriedly. "The guest in that room is a General in the Czar's army. But I'll ask him if he will share his room with you."

"Don't bother," sighed the other resignedly. "A General would never share his room with a Jew." He thought about it for a moment and then his face brightened. "Look, I have an idea!" he said excitedly. "Maybe I can sleep in that extra bed after all. It is very late now, so the General must be fast asleep. Tomorrow I must rise early to catch the six o'clock train. At that hour of the morning he'll still be sound asleep, and he'll never know that I was in the other bed. Just be sure to wake me up on time."

The hotel clerk agreed. Quietly the traveler tip-toed into the room of the Czarist officer, and without a sound—almost afraid to breathe—the intruder undressed and went to sleep. In the morning the clerk awakened the General's clandestine roommate at the appointed hour.

But in the predawn darkness the Jewish guest unwittingly donned the General's uniform and hurried off to meet his train. On the way, he could not help but notice that everyone he met bowed and greeted him in a most respectful manner.

"How do they know that I shared the same room with a General?" he wondered.

He met a Captain and then a Major, and both saluted him smartly. At the ticket office the agent handed him a first-class ticket and assigned him to a private compartment.

"How is it that a Jew is treated so magnificently?" he asked himself, bewildered by the unaccustomed courtesy.

Inside the compartment he speculated on the probability that his single night's association with a great Czarist officer might have given him a kind of aristocratic aura—one of reflected glory. He stood before a mirror and stared at his reflection and examined his features for any possible change in his appearance, and as he did, a look of utter shock spread over his face as he recognized the General's uniform.

"*Oy vay!*" he groaned. "That *shlemiel* of a desk clerk! I ask him to wake me up and instead he wakes up the General. Now, how will I ever catch this six o'clock train when I'm still sleeping back at the hotel?"

✓   ✓   ✓

Not all *shlemiels* are Jewish, as this bit of whimsy suggests.

Motke Kesslov, well known for his nimble wit, was walking along the street in Petrograd, his mind preoccupied with the *seder* over which he was to preside that evening, when he accidentally brushed against the shoulder of a *mujik*. Snarling, the burly peasant spun around and crashed his fist into Motke's face.

But when Motke picked himself up from the gutter, instead of showing anger, he smiled affably and handed the astonished peasant a crisp ruble bill.

"Why are you giving me money?" asked the *mujik*.

"Because it is the custom among our people," explained the wily Motke. "Today is *Pesach*—our Passover—and it is written that an orthodox Jew must pay a gentile who strikes him on this holy day."

"Well, in that case I'll hit you again!" said the *mujik*, raising his huge fist.

"That won't be necessary. I am a poor man and I can't afford to pay you again. But if you go to the mansion of Yudel Opotow, the banker, and hit him as hard as you did me, he may give you as much as a hundred rubles."

The simple-minded peasant grinned. 'What a race of fools these Jews are!' he thought contemptuously. Straightaway, he made for the wealthy Opotow's luxurious home, and when the banker opened the door the peasant gave him a smashing blow to the jaw. Opotow fell to the floor, howling and screeching for his servants and bodyguards. In a moment the peasant was surrounded by the banker's retainers who knocked him down, loosened his teeth, blackened his eyes, broke several ribs, and then threw him half-unconscious into the street.

Painfully dragging himself to his feet, he muttered, "That damned *Zhid* had a lot of nerve sending me to a house where they don't even keep their most important holiday!"

*   *   *

Although Herman was twenty-three years old, he had never been alone with a girl, nor had he even so much as talked to one for more than a few minutes. So when the *shadchen* brought a proposal of marriage, Herman's father, a man of the world, decided to coach him in the intricacies of winning a lady's heart and hand. Realizing that his son's IQ was nothing to rave about, he made an attempt to simplify his instructions.

"A woman's life is wrapped up in a need for security," the father began, "and a woman is secure only when she has a husband with these three qualities: an affectionate nature, a love of family, and a good mind."

Herman looked blankly at his father.

"Listen carefully," continued the older man. "To convince her you have those qualities, all you need do is remember three steps. First, start talking about love. That takes care of your affectionate nature. Next mention family. That will show her you are not anti-social. Third, to prove you have a good mind, you can touch on a little philosophy."

On the appointed evening of their first meeting, the intended bride welcomed Herman and set out honeycakes and tea. At first he was tongue-tied, but then he remembered his father's advice. "Tell me," he suddenly asked, "do you love *knaidlach*?"

"Well," she answered, surprise and hesitancy in her voice, "I suppose so."

After a few minutes of painful silence he went to the second phase of his courtship. "Do you have a brother?"

The girl shook her head. "No, I have no brother."

Herman congratulated himself, pleased that he had surmounted the first two obstacles—love and family. Now for the philosophy!

"Tell me something," he asked, knitting his brow as he had seen his scholarly father do, "if you *had* a brother, would he have loved *knaidlach*?"

✓   ✓   ✓

Why such a *shlimazl* as Joe ever decided to become a private detective no one will ever know. Nothing he ever did came out right. Once, he received a call from a jeweler who had been robbed three times and, in each case, the thief had escaped scot-free.

Joe decided to catch the burglar red-handed. He rigged up a camera so that the robber would snap his own picture in the act of burglarizing the store. As bait, he put a tray of cheap watches and some inexpensive costume jewelry in front of the camera.

So what happened? On his next visit, the thief ignored the cheap jewelry and watches, and disappeared in the night with Joe's $250 camera.

✓   ✓   ✓

A Jew had been cheated by a local *yishuvnik*, and the difference of opinion soon resulted in a heated argument in which they hurled insults at each other.

"You aren't fit to sleep with pigs!" spat the Jew.

"I am so!" retorted the peasant defensively.

✓   ✓   ✓

Duvid had failed in every business venture he ever attempted, so this time he started a marriage-brokerage venture, the only enterprise he could launch without capital. Soon he compiled a list of the most eligible bachelors and single girls available, and if prospects were realities, Duvid would have been the most successful *shadchen* in all the Russias.

In fact, for his very first proposition, it seemed that he would make a fortune. He made a deal with two of the richest families in the country in which he suggested that a merger by marriage would benefit each. The proposal was met with deep satisfaction by both sides, and the next day Duvid brought the lovely daughter of one of the wealthy families to the home of the other.

But once again, his *mazel* was all bad. The other family also had a daughter!

✓   ✓   ✓

A *shlimazl* whose lifelong misfortunes were overwhelming, went to his brother-in-law to borrow some money. The relative, knowing the other's propensity for losing, refused.

"But you *must* give me a loan," insisted the *shlimazl.*

"I must? Why *must* I?"

"Because if you don't, I'll—I'll go into the hat business!"

"So what?"

"What do you mean, 'so what?' If a man with my bad luck ever goes into the hat business, every baby in this country will be born without a head!"

✔   ✔   ✔

Valid or not, the assertion "Once a *shlemiel* always a *shlemiel*" is well known to Jews everywhere. In this tale, *circa* 1600, we find that a university degree is not necessarily equated with innate *saichel.*

A fabulously wealthy merchant of Kiev, renowned for his business acumen as well as for his vast properties, broached a subject to his wife—a subject that had long concerned him.

"*Liebeh*," he said, "I am nearing my alotted span of three-score-and-ten, and it will not be long before I must pass on to my reward. But I am worried. How can I possibly leave my business holdings to our only son? In the hands of such a *shlemiel* the family fortune would be dissipated within a year or two."

They discussed the problem at length, and then the merchant's good wife smiled broadly. "I know the answer," she cried. "Send him to the great university in Moscow. There he will gain wisdom and learning from the finest professors in all Europe."

So it was done. The merchant sent his son to Moscow where for four years he applied all his energies to the study of the arts and sciences, theology and philosophy, agriculture, mining and general business. Now the youth was convinced that he had learned all that the illustrious professors had to teach. In the beginning of the fifth year he returned to Kiev, sure of his ability to carry on his father's business enterprises.

The reunion was a joyous one, the mother having prepared a sumptuous repast. When they had dined heartily and were finishing their *compote,* the father thought it time to test his son's newly acquired wisdom.

"Tell me, my son, how deep is the ocean?"

"From the surface of the water to the bottom," was the prompt answer.

The merchant was truly startled at this display of wisdom. "Another question: why does a centipede have a hundred legs—fifty on one side and fifty on the other?"

"Because if it had fifty on one side and only forty-nine on the other it would be a cripple."

This time the mother joined her husband in pleased smiles at their son and heir's profundity.

56

"A final test," said the father, surreptitiously slipping a ring from his finger and enclosing it in his clenched fist. "Tell me, what am I holding in my palm?"

The youth studied his father's hand for several moments and then spoke. "According to the laws of physics, algebra, calculus and anatomy— all of which I have thoroughly mastered—it is apparent to me that you are holding a round object, and furthermore, that object has a hole in the center."

The merchant and his wife were thrilled with this display of brilliance. But before they could congratulate him, the son went on, "I cannot tell precisely what the object is that you are holding in your fist, but judging from my long years of study, I would say it is a wagon wheel."

✓ ✓ ✓

Yussel Magila had once prospered as a wholesale grain dealer but he had fallen on sad days. It started with a crop failure, then a prolonged drought, and finally utter ruin. Life, for him, was at its lowest ebb, when he remembered his old friend, Brodsky, whom he had helped years before when he had been the city's biggest dealer in wheat and corn. So he went to Brodsky's mansion to ask for a loan.

"When I was rich and you were poor I advanced you two thousand rubles so you could get started in the lumber business," reminded Yussel.

"Yes, you did, and I will always be grateful to you for the help you offered when I needed it," affirmed Brodsky.

"Then here's your chance. I haven't a ruble to my name and I'd appreciate a loan so I can get back into business."

"Sure," agreed Brodsky. "Whatever you need."

Yussel accepted the money, went back into the grain business, but was unable to buck the stiff competition of the younger competitors who had grabbed all his old accounts. In short order he was broke again.

He returned to Brodsky for another loan and again was given a large sum of money. Once more Yussel went into business, this time in another field, and again he lost every ruble. Brodsky gave him still another loan, and then another and another—and each time Yussel failed in his new venture.

But the last time Yussel's business failed he did not return to his benefactor for another loan, and Brodsky, that kind-hearted man, began to worry about his old friend. The rich man went to Yussel's house.

"Yussel, my old friend, why haven't you come to me for another loan?" asked Brodsky. "I'd be glad to do you another favor."

"Favor! You call that a favor?" Yussel barked.

"Wh-what?"

"You heard me! I figured it all out. The reason I keep failing in business is that you're bad luck. Get out of here, you bum!"

✓ ✓ ✓

Rabbi Montague Isaacs, spiritual leader of Congregation Tifereth Jacob, in Los Angeles, contributes the following gem:

Count Esterhazy was organizing an expedition to the Near East and beyond. He had engaged most of the helpers but he needed a general factotum for the long journey.

Knowing the position was hard to fill he advertised for a seasoned traveler who spoke the languages of the Near East, a fearless swordsman, an intrepid rider, and so forth. The advertisement was worded to attract only the right man—and there were no applicants. After a week, the butler announced that a small and shabby looking fellow had come in response to the ad.

"He doesn't sound very promising," said the Count, "but show him in."

The man proved to be even less prepossessing than the butler's description. But clothes do not always make the man, and the Count began by asking, "You like to travel?"

"No!" said the little man. "I hate traveling. Boats make me seasick. And trains are worse."

"But you are a linguist," continued the Count. "I presume you speak Arabic, Persian, Turkish, Hindustani . . ."

"Who, me?" gasped the candidate. "I talk nothing but Yiddish."

"Your swordsmanship?" inquired the Count.

"What do you mean, swordsmanship? What should I do with a sword?"

"And as a horseman?"

"I hate horses. I wouldn't go near one."

"But," said the Count, "what did you come here for?"

"I saw your ad," said the man. "And I just came to tell you that on me you shouldn't depend!"

Chapter Six

Atheists, Agnostics and Converts

Morris Levy knelt at the altar of Calvary Lutheran Church.

"In the name of the Father, the Son and the Holy Ghost, I now baptise you and welcome you into the Kingdom of Christ," intoned the minister, sprinkling the new convert with water.

Levy arose and the preacher shook his hand. "Now that you have been baptised you may choose a Christian name if you wish," he said. "Have you given any thought to the matter?"

"Yes, Reverend, I have," answered Levy. "I would like to be called Martin Luther."

"Well," beamed the minister, "you certainly have chosen an illustrious Christian name. May I ask the reason?"

"It's like this, sir," explained ex-Morris Levy, "I don't want to change the initials on my laundry."

✓ ✓ ✓

An atheist came to a rabbi with a peculiar request. "Rabbi," he said, "I have made up my mind to violate every precept in the Torah. I have already broken every one I can think of, but I am afraid I missed one or two."

"*Nu*, what do you want of me?" asked the rabbi.

"This. I'll enumerate all the commandments I have transgressed, and if you find that I forgot any, tell me so I can break them too."

The rabbi listened stonily as the sinner recited a long list of the most shocking misdeeds he had perpetrated.

"There is just one more sin you will have to commit to make your record complete," said the rabbi when the libertine had finished.

"Fine! Tell me what it is and I'll do it!"

"You forgot the injunction against suicide," snapped the rabbi. "Drop dead!"

✓ ✓ ✓

Jacob Goldfarb visited the Bureau of Motor Vehicles for a driver's license. Across the desk, an interviewer asked a few perfunctory questions:

"Name?"

"Jacob Goldfarb."

"Born?"

"Russia."

"Line of work?"

"A tailor."

"Religion?"

"Catholic, what else?"

✓   ✓   ✓

An agnostic and a rabbi were arguing about the existence of God, the soul, and man's spiritual relationship with the world.

"For your information," the agnostic said sarcastically, "the great philosopher, Spinoza, wrote that man in no way stands higher than an animal and that he has the same nature."

The rabbi nodded. "I remember the passage well. But tell me, why is it that the animals have never produced a Spinoza?"

✓   ✓   ✓

A lifelong backslider suddenly "saw the light" and approached the local rabbi.

"Rabbi, from now on I will attend synagogue services regularly," he promised.

"I'm glad to hear that," smiled the wise old rabbi, "but remember— going to synagogue doesn't make you a Jew any more than going to a poultry farm makes you a chicken!"

✓   ✓   ✓

Rabbi Izel Harif, the noted sage of Slonim, was visited by a worldly young man who fancied himself a firm atheist.

"Before one can accept or reject a philosophy, be it theocratic or not, and before one can believe or disbelieve in any given subject matter, he must first be familiar with the main thesis," the rabbi said. "Do you agree?"

"Of course," the young cynic agreed readily.

"Then let me ask you, have you mastered the Torah?"

"Well, I wouldn't go so far as to say I have mastered it. I read a little of the Bible when I was preparing for *Bar Mitzvah*, but that was years ago."

"And the Talmud?"

"Oh, come now, Rabbi! Nobody reads the Talmud any more!"

"Then how about our great philosophers?" Rabbi Harif persisted, his eyes glinting. "Have you studied, for example, Maimonides, Ibn Gabirol or Moses Mendelssohn?"

"I never heard of them."

"My dear fellow," sighed the rabbi, "you are not familiar with the Torah, you know nothing of the Talmud, and you never heard of our Jewish philosophers. Yet you have the temerity to call yourself a disbeliever. Young man, you are not an atheist—you are an ignoramus!"

✓ ✓ ✓

Jake Rubin fell in love with a *shikseh* and, after changing his name to James Robinson at her insistence, they were married. In due course they had a son whom they named Patrick.

One day, young Pat came home from school and announced that he was taking two days off from school because of the Jewish New Year.

"You'll do nothing of the kind!" rasped the father. "You're only half-Jewish, so be satisfied with just one day off!"

✓ ✓ ✓

Sammy had just joined the Catholic Church on the condition that he would henceforth obey all the laws governing Catholicism.

"Remember," warned the priest, "you are now forbidden to eat meat on Fridays."

"OK, I'll remember," Sammy promised.

But the priest had reservations about the new convert, so on the following Friday he paid an unannounced visit to the man's house. As he had somehow guessed, the former Jew was consuming a huge steak.

"This is disgraceful!" cried the indignant priest. "Didn't you promise to abstain from eating meat on Fridays?"

"Meat? Who's eating meat?" answered the other blandly. "This is *gefilteh fish.*"

"You must take me for a fool!" snapped the outraged priest. "How can anyone make fish out of meat?"

"The same way you made a Catholic out of a Jew," answered the convert smoothly. "I sprinkled water on it!"

✓ ✓ ✓

"Benny, I know this will surprise you, but I was just converted to Christianity," said Meyer.

"Well, of all the . . ."

"Look, I want you to do me a favor," Meyer interrupted.

"What kind of a favor?"

"I want you to get baptized also."

"You're *meshuggeh!*" exclaimed Benny. "Why should I do such a thing?"

"Because," answered Benny wistfully, "I'd like to have at least one Christian friend!"

✓ ✓ ✓

Shpetner was a woebegone figure as he stood before the minister, hat in hand.

"I want to be baptised," he said resignedly, all hope gone from his voice.

"Fine!" agreed the minister. "Be here at the church tomorrow evening at six and I'll teach you the creed and the fundamentals of Christianity."

"It has to be done today—now!" protested Shpetner sadly. "Tomorrow will be too late."

"Why?"

"Because tomorrow is Passover," sighed Shpetner, "and there isn't a piece of *matzoh* or a drop of wine in the house."

✔ ✔ ✔

Feitel and Feivel went together to the baptismal font, and the first to be called to accept Christianity was Feitel. When he came out of the inner sanctum, Feivel greeted him eagerly.

"*Nu*, Feitel, how did it go?"

Feitel ignored his friend and brushed by without a word.

"Hey!" called Feivel, "What's the matter with you?"

"Nothing is the matter with me," said the other with some asperity. "In the first place, my name is not Feitel, it's Phillip. In the second place, I don't have anything to say to you Jews. You crucified our Lord!"

✔ ✔ ✔

Two elderly Israelites were waiting in the church vestry for the minister. This was the day they were to be converted, but they had already been waiting for more than an hour and they were quite restive.

"He certainly takes his time," commented one.

"Yes, he does," agreed the other. "It's already late afternoon. Do you know what I'm thinking?"

"What?"

"I'm thinking it's time for *mincha*."

"You are absolutely right!"

And so, while they waited for the minister, both men stood up and recited the afternoon prayer.

✔ ✔ ✔

It was two days before Chanukah and Mr. Feldman, quite downcast, was trudging home. "Where will I get the money to buy presents for the holiday?" he asked himself sadly, thinking of his wife and children. On the way he passed a church, in front of which was a sign:

One Hundred Dollars Cash To Anyone
Who Joins This Church Today!

Here was the solution to Feldman's problem! He went in, joined, and was given the hundred dollars as the sign promised. That evening, at supper, he told his family how he had come by his sudden wealth. "And here's the hundred," he announced grandly, waving the money before them.

"Darling," said his wife, "you remember that cloth coat you promised me three years ago? Well it's on sale at Macy's."

"How much is it?"

"Only fifty dollars, and it's worth eighty-five at least."

Feldman peeled off five tens and handed them to her.

The son spoke up. "Pop, for a long time I've been saving up to buy one of those English bikes with three gear shifts. I already have most of the money but I need a little more."

"How much more?"

"Twenty-five dollars."

Feldman handed over the money.

"Daddy," said his teen-age daughter, "next week our school is having the most important dance of the whole year. If I don't have a new dress I'll simply die—I just know it!"

"Don't die, Sweetheart. How much is the dress?"

"Only twenty-five dollars, Daddy dear."

Feldman handed over the remaining $25, leaned back and grinned. "It never fails," he announced. "The minute we gentiles have a little money, you Jews take it away from us!"

✓ ✓ ✓

An elderly man who had been a confirmed atheist since his early youth, turned to spiritual matters as his life span drew to a close. At the age of seventy he decided to return to the faith of his forefathers.

One evening, for the first time since his *Bar Mitzvah*, he attended services at the local synagogue and heard the rabbi announce that his sermon for the following week would deal with the Great Flood.

After the services the man approached the rabbi.

"Rabbi," said the penitent, "I will be out of town next week, but I don't want you to think I am shirking my duty as a Jew. Please put me down for ten dollars for the flood victims."

✓ ✓ ✓

Whenever Reb Eliah Chaim Lodzer came to Marienbad, many people visited him to discuss both general and Jewish problems. During the course of conversation one man spoke highly of Chwolson, who had taken on the Christian faith, but nevertheless had made many sacrifices for the Jews. The listeners, anxious to hear Reb Eliah's opinion, regarded him curiously, though silently, waiting for him to speak.

"The problem, as I see it," Reb Eliah finally said, "is whether an apostate can still be regarded with the same honor that was accorded him before his conversion, considering his continued good works." Reb Eliah paused, cleared his throat, and went on. "I have a parable for you. A Jew who lived in Lithuania came to a very small town in a distant part of Russia where no Jews resided. He was a very religious man and had no place to eat. Since he was familiar with the procedure of slaughtering and koshering meat, he decided to buy a chicken and prepare a meal. But when he was through he realized that he had cooked the chicken in a pot that was not kosher."

Reb Eliah gazed about him and sighed. "Alas, of what consequence is the entire work when the pot is not kosher?"

✓   ✓   ✓

Yankeleh, the shoemaker, had been a self-declared atheist ever since he could remember, and he rarely missed an opportunity to jeer at all religious observances.

One day, when he was in his seventy-sixth year, he entered a synagogue on the Day of Atonement and prayed so fervently that beads of sweat stippled his forehead.

"I thought you didn't believe in God!" said the surprised rabbi. "Why are you here praying?"

"I may be an atheist," replied Yankeleh, unperturbed, "but I'm also a pragmatist. At my age, just suppose I'm wrong?"

✓   ✓   ✓

Two brothers were arguing.

"You say you are an atheist and you believe in nothing?"

"Exactly. I can only believe in something I understand."

"Well, that certainly explains why you believe in nothing!"

✓   ✓   ✓

A non-believer who took a keen delight in flinging his verbal barbs and arrows at the local rabbi, thought of an unusual question which he was sure would stump the holy man.

At their next meeting the atheist lost no time in broaching the subject. "Rabbi," he began sarcastically, "tradition tells us that when one meets a mad dog the only remedy is to sit down quietly. But when one meets a rabbi it is customary to stand up."

"The rabbi nodded. "Yes, that is true."

"In that case, what happens when one meets both a rabbi and a mad dog together? Do we sit or stand?"

"Hmmm, that is indeed a difficult question," answered the rabbi thoughtfully. "It seems to me that the only way to find out is to make a test so that we can observe the reaction of the people. I'll tell you what; let us walk along the street together, and we'll see what happens!"

✓   ✓   ✓

A rabbi discovered at the services that he was short the tenth man to complete the *minyan*. Just then, through the open window, he saw Klein, the town atheist, drunkard and general ne'er-do-well.

"Call him in," the rabbi ordered the *shammes*.

"What! That atheist—that no-goodnik!" the sexton cried.

"Let me remind you," the rabbi said placidly, "in order to increase the number one to ten, all we need is a zero!"

✓ ✓ ✓

Mordecai, the *moser*, was the most hated man in his small Russian community. Let it be said here that all such *mosrim* were paid tattlers who supplied information about their fellow Jews to the Czarist authorities. Almost without exception, they despised their own Jewishness even more than they hated their co-religionists.

One day, when the Russian police felt that Mordecai's information was too sparse for the month, he was unmercifully flogged as a reminder that he should be more energetic with his tale-bearing.

After the bloody whipping, the rabbi noticed that Mordecai was chuckling to himself.

"What in Heaven's name can you find to laugh about?" asked the holy man who had witnessed the beating.

"It makes me feel good to know that a Jew has been flogged."

"If you derived so much satisfaction from it, then why were you screaming while you were being whipped?"

"Because," retorted Mordecai, "I hate to see a Jew having so much satisfaction!"

✓ ✓ ✓

The elderly, very orthodox Rabbi Twersky, before leaving Los Angeles to take up permanent residence in Israel, enjoyed telling of the time when he did *not* have the last word. Translated into English by his impish *rebbetzn*, the story goes like this:

Rabbi Twersky paid an unannounced call at the Beverly Hills home of one of his congregants. It was not only *Rosh Hashana* but *Shabbes* as well. To his disgust he found the man playing cards with four other Jews.

"What kind of Jews do you call yourselves, playing cards on such a day as this?" he bellowed in a voice that would have intimidated an army sergeant. "Gambling on *Rosh Hashana*, and on a Saturday at that! You are sinful men! A pack of atheists—all of you!"

One of the players looked up from his cards. "Rabbi," he said quietly, "with all due respect to your position, I assure you there are no atheists in a high-stake pinochle game!"

✓ ✓ ✓

No matter how high their station, Jewish fathers are concerned about the possible conversion of their children, as witness this appealing little anecdote.

A rabbi, whose son announced that he intended to convert to Christianity, locked himself in the synagogue and began a fast, hoping that the

Almighty would intercede. After eight days of fasting, when his head began to swim and visions danced before his eyes, an eerie light illuminated the synagogue and there in the center of the glow was an indescribable *Something*. There was no question about it. As far as the rabbi was concerned, he was in the presence of the Most High.

"O blessed God," wept the distraught rabbi, "shed your compassion upon me and help me in this moment of sorrow. My son is about to turn Christian."

And from the holy illumination, God's mournful voice answered, "*Your son!*"

✓   ✓   ✓

After years of enduring the lame jibes about his name, Joseph Kissinger went to court and changed it to Roosevelt, who happened to be his hero at the time. But the jokes were now more pointed than they ever were before, so he changed his name to Carter. The liver pill jeers got the better of him and he changed it once again. In fact, he was in and out of court so often that his friends began to ask, "I wonder who's Kissinger now?"

✓   ✓   ✓

The day that Goldsmith was converted to Christianity he shortened his name to Smith.

It figures," said his former rabbi. "The man keeps the useless second syllable but casts aside his gold."

✓   ✓   ✓

Four Jewish apostates met on a train in Russia and began to relate the reasons which had prompted them to accept the Christian faith.

The first apostate said that he had saved himself from a pogrom by changing his religion. "The *mujiks* and Cossacks killed almost every Jew in the village," he explained, "so I converted."

The second apostate stated that he had wanted desperately to attend the university, but since Jews were not admitted he had become a Christian so that he might continue his education.

The third apostate explained that he had fallen madly in love with a beautiful Gentile girl and that she would not have him unless he accepted her faith.

When the fourth apostate related his story he said, "My reason is entirely different. I became a Christian because I was convinced that Christianity is superior to . . ."

"Now wait a minute," interrupted one of the Christian converts, "tell that to your Gentile friends!"

✓   ✓   ✓

A Jew-turned-Christian went into missionary work and upon arriving in a distant city he placed an announcement in the newspapers stating that he would prove to the satisfaction of all that Christianity is the only true religion for the Jew.

The advertisement enticed a large number of people to the assembly hall, including several young students of the local *yeshiva*. After the lecture the talmudic students proceeded to bombard the speaker with questions, quoting verse after biblical verse to disprove his thesis.

The discussion, which was conducted in English, grew terribly heated. After nearly an hour the missionary was not only exhausted but infuriated as well.

"Rascals, get out!" he shouted in Yiddish. "Can't you give a poor Jew a chance to make a living?"

✓ ✓ ✓

During the early regime of Alexander III of Russia, when pogroms and discrimination had been threatening the peace and, in many instances, the very lives of Russian Jewry, a number of Jews in the larger cities embraced Christianity as a means of self-defense.

One day a Jew by the name of Yankel met his friend Chaim on the main thoroughfare of Moscow and informed him that he had become a Christian.

"Why, I don't believe you!" cried Chaim. "You were always such an orthodox, pious man!"

"Chaim, believe me," answered Yankel fervently. "I swear to you as a Jew that I am now a Christian!"

✓ ✓ ✓

A young Jewish man called on a Catholic priest and informed him that he wished to join the Church.

"My son," the priest said, beaming, "I am indeed happy that the light of the new day has finally dawned for you. I cannot see you until the day after tomorrow, but at that time I will be only too glad to instruct you in the true and holy faith."

"But that will be too late, Father," insisted the young man. "I want to change my religion at once."

"Why the hurry? A great faith like ours cannot be imparted in a few minutes."

"Well it's like this, Father," explained the young man. "I just had a terrible fight with my wife and, before I cool off, I want to do something immediately to disgrace her."

67

Chapter Seven

Fibbers

Harry and Joe, two old friends, were comparing their exploits, each, as usual, trying to outdo the other.

"Once I caught a herring," Harry said. "I'm telling you, Joe, it was the biggest herring ever seen by mortal eyes. It weighed 500 pounds— at least."

"That's nothing, Harry," answered Joe. "Once, when I was fishing, I pulled up my line and what did I find on my hook but a ship's lamp. And I should live so, it had a date engraved on the bottom—1392; a hundred years before Columbus yet. But that's not all: Inside the lamp was a light, and it was still burning!"

Harry studied his friend's face for some moments without a trace of expression. Then he grinned. "Listen, Joe, let's compromise," he said. "From the herring I'll knock off 495 pounds, and you blow out the light!"

*   *   *

A villager was boasting about the piety of the town's rabbi.

"Believe me," he said earnestly, "my rabbi is so saintly he fasts every day in the week except Saturdays and Sundays."

"Now just a minute!" cried the other, a stranger in town; "I saw your rabbi eating just this morning, and I've only been here a few days. Why don't you stop lying?"

"Lying? Who's lying? You don't really know my rabbi! What you observed was a demonstration of his modesty. The only reason he ever eats on weekdays is to hide the fact that he's fasting!"

*   *   *

Here is an "inside" joke; one that will send many readers to the glossary in the back of this book for the definitions.

The *rebbeh* was in an exceptionally good mood at the Purim *se'udah*, and he offered a bottle of his favorite wine to the *chassid* who could tell the cleverest lie.

Several of those present recounted their tallest tales, and the *rebbeh* was

68

in a quandary as to who was the winner—until one of the *chassidim* spoke up.

"One Shevuoth," he began, "when we sat at the *seder* in the *sukkah* and chanted the Book of Lamentations, the Purim Players surprised us. With their *shofars* they blew out the Chanukah lights!"

✓ ✓ ✓

A rich man was enjoying the company of the celebrated wit, Herschel Ostropolier.

"Herschel," he said, "if you can tell me a really spontaneous lie —without thinking—I'll give you a ruble."

Herschel's answer was instantaneous. "What do you mean, one ruble—you just said *two!*"

✓ ✓ ✓

A poor Jewish farmer called on his affluent neighbor to borrow his donkey.

"I'm sorry, neighbor, but my donkey is in the next pasture right now," said the rich farmer.

At that moment the hee-haw of a jackass was heard, braying in the nearby stable.

"Your alibi wasn't very clever," said the poor man bitterly.

The well-to-do farmer made a show of being offended. "Now look, neighbor," he asked with dignity, "whom are you going to believe? Me or a braying ass?"

✓ ✓ ✓

Schechter, who traveled for Gotham Fabrics, and Pechter, who was on the road for Feldman's Frilly Frocks, met at Pennsylvania Station.

"Where are you headed for?" asked Schechter.

"For Washington, D.C.," answered Pechter.

"Ahah!" snapped Schechter. "You tell me you're going to Washington, D.C., maybe to call on the Garfinkel account, because you figure I'll think you are going to Philadelphia. But you already sold the Philadelphia account, so you really must be going to Washington. Pechter, why are you such a damn liar?"

✓ ✓ ✓

The State of Israel was only a few weeks old, and the fledgling nation had just trounced the invading Arabs. Promotions in the hastily organized army were rapid, so former Lieutenant Halevi suddenly found himself elevated to Major. He had not been in his new office more than a few minutes when someone knocked on the door.

The new Major, wanting to impress the caller, whoever he was, called, "Come in!" and at the same time picked up the phone on his desk and pretended he was having an important, high-level discussion. "Yes, Mr.

Ben-Gurion, I quite agree, but perhaps you had better reserve your decision until I have had a chance to go over the matter. Thank you, Mr. Ben-Gurion, and I'll expect you and the missus at my house this evening for dinner."

The Major then hung up the receiver and turned to the visitor who had been waiting patiently on the other side of the desk. "All right, young man," he said pompously, although he could not have been much older than the other. "What can I do for you?"

"Nothing, sir," replied the stranger. "I was sent here to install your telephone."

✔ ✔ ✔

Mrs. Klein: "Can you tell if your husband is lying or not, just by looking at his face?"

Mrs. Gross: "No trouble at all, Mrs. Klein. If his lips are moving, he's lying!"

✔ ✔ ✔

"Grandpa, tell me again about The Three Bears," pleaded little Morton.

"Ah, you don't want to hear that old story again," protested Grandpa. "Better I'll tell you about the One Bear."

"Ooh, goodie!"

"Well, when I was a young fellow in Russia, I would sometimes go to Siberia to hunt grizzly bears. One day, I was walking through the frozen tundra when suddenly, right in front of my nose, a tremendous female bear rose up before me. I quickly aimed my gun and pulled the trigger. No bullets! I was just about to turn and run when all at once she threw her arms around me and began to squeeze and hug me."

Morton's eyes were wide with excitement. "What did you do, Grandpa?"

"What could I do?" demanded Grandpa. "I kissed her!"

✔ ✔ ✔

"Oh, Grandpa," cried Mortie, clapping his hands, "tell me another story."

"Well, there was the time I went out west and discovered the Gold Rush in California. While I was returning home with ten bags of gold, I saw smoke signals. Soon I heard the pounding of thousands of horses' hooves, and in a few minutes I was surrounded by Redskins; thousands of them, whooping and hollering like crazy. They formed a circle with me on the inside so it was impossible to escape."

"What did you do, Grandpa?" asked Mortie, on the edge of his seat.

"What could I do?" answered the old man. "I bought some beads and a blanket!"

✔ ✔ ✔

FIBBERS

Moe: "I didn't sleep a wink last night. It was awful."
Joe: Why? You got insomnia?"
Moe: "No, a fly kept buzzing around and landing on my nose."
Joe: "So why didn't you brush him off?"
Moe: "I didn't know he was dusty."

✓ ✓ ✓

"George, I saw you kissing the maid today," said the wife grimly. "I demand an explanation."

"Now don't jump to conclusions," said the fast-thinking husband. "All I did was to complain that she hadn't dusted the living room properly and she attacked me with a broom. I had to bite her in self defense."

✓ ✓ ✓

Little Marvin came into the house with a new harmonica. "Grandpa, do you mind if I play this in here?"

"Of course not, Marvie. I love music. In fact, when your grandma and I were young, music saved my life."

"What happened?"

"Well, it was during the famous Johnstown flood. The dam broke and when the water hit our house it knocked it right off the foundation. Grandma got on the dining room table and floated out safely."

"How about you?"

"Me? I accompanied her on the piano!"

✓ ✓ ✓

Two New Yorkers were discussing the latest marvels of science. "I like this age of technocracy," said one. "I established a little electronics business and it's making money."

"By me it's just the opposite," said the other. "It has already cost me a fortune."

"How so?"

"Last year I went to the auto show and saw an all-electric car—no gas tank, no carburetor, nothing like that. You just plug it in a socket in your house and attach the other end to the car. I liked the idea, so I bought it and then took a trip to California. I didn't spend a penny for gas, it's true, but it still cost me three thousand dollars before I got to Los Angeles."

"How's that?"

"Look at the long cord I had to buy!"

✓ ✓ ✓

"The nerve of her!" exclaimed Braine. "That neighbor of mine called me an old fool."

"You don't mean it!" clucked her sister Sprinze. "Well, at least we know she's a filthy liar. You're not even forty yet."

✓ ✓ ✓

The loyal *chassid* was defending his rabbi to the skeptical Litvak: "Do you realize how great the *rebbe* of Sadigora is? Why, every Saturday afternoon God Himself descends from on high, enters the *rebbe's* study, sits down on a chair, and keeps company with the holy man."

"How do you know this actually happens?" queried the Litvak.

"There's no doubt about it. The *rebbe* himself told us so."

"Yes, but how do you know he's telling the truth?"

"Blockhead!" cried the *chassid*. "Do you think for one moment that God Almighty would have anything to do with a liar?"

1   1   1

You heard about the Yid who went to the Black Sea so he could fill his fountain pen free? His brother went to the Red Sea for the same reason.

Chapter Eight

Dirty Crooks

So many horses had been stolen in the area that Berel the merchant decided to hire a driver who was clever enough to foil the horse thieves. He found an exceptionally clever man in Kovacs.

On the first day, Berel stopped at a tavern for lunch and a spot of *schnapps*, and cautioned Kovacs to be especially alert because they were in the midst of the region where the stealing was the worst. Now Berel was convinced that his new driver was a very clever fellow, but just to make sure, he would go outside every few minutes to check on his new employee.

The first time he went out, he asked Kovacs what he was doing.

"I am wondering what happens to the hole after you eat the bagel," replied the driver.

"Yes, you are indeed a clever man," grinned Berel, returning to the tavern. A few minutes later, he again thought it might be a good idea to check on Kovacs, and, of course, his horses.

"What are you doing now?" he asked.

"I am wondering what happens to a man's lap when he stands up."

Berel grinned once more, returned to his lunch, and again decided to go outside to check on Kovacs.

"What are you doing now?"

"I am wondering what happens to a man's fist when he unclenches his hand."

By this time, Berel was almost convinced that his driver was a brilliant man, and one to whom he could entrust with his valuable horses. But just to make certain, he went outside for the last time.

"Now what are you doing?" he asked.

"I am wondering," said Kovacs, "who stole the horses!"

✓   ✓   ✓

For the third time in a year, Solomon the *ganeff* was brought before the rabbi on charges.

"Look, Solomon, I am a patient man, but enough is enough," said

73

the rabbi sternly. "I'm not going to punish you this time, but the next time you are brought before me I will turn you over to the authorities."

"Oh, thank you, Rabbi," cried the thief.

"Don't thank me, please! Just promise me that you will not steal again, and that you'll stay away from bums and loafers."

"I promise! I promise!" agreed Solomon hoarsely. "You'll never see me again, Rabbi!"

✓ ✓ ✓

Max was caught redhanded by a police officer in the very act of burglarizing a store. He was quickly brought to trial.

"How do you plead?" asked the judge.

"Your honor," answered Max, "before I plead guilty or not guilty I ask that the court kindly appoint a lawyer to defend me."

"Max, you were caught in the actual commission of a crime. What could any lawyer possibly say in your defense?"

"That's exactly my point, Your Honor," said Max. "I'm curious also to hear what he could possibly say!"

✓ ✓ ✓

Shmendrik, the *ganeff*, was at home when the police burst in and arrested him just as he was about to eat supper with his wife. The evidence against him was clear: eyewitnesses were ready to testify that he had robbed the Pitkin Avenue Department Store and made off with twenty-nine dresses valued at $3.95 each. After a search of his apartment, the cheap apparel was found.

"Shmendrik," said the judge, "do you admit you stole these dresses?"

There was no refuting the evidence. Shmendrik hung his head and mumbled, "I admit."

"Before I sentence you," the judge continued, "I would like you to explain something that has aroused my curiosity."

"*Nu?*"

"Why did you take only the cheapest, $3.95 dresses, when in the very next rack were hundreds of very expensive gowns and furs?"

"Please, your honor, don't *you* start that!" begged Shmendrik. "My wife has been nagging me about it ever since I brought the *shmattehs* home!"

✓ ✓ ✓

"There is not a *yishuvnik* in our town who is not an overly cautious buyer," sighed the merchant. "Take for example such a simple thing as a scythe. The peasant first tries it out by throwing it on the ground to see if it has the right ring. Then he tries it by breathing on the blade to see if it has the right shine. Then he tries it out on one of his hairs to see if it has the right edge. Finally, if it passes all these tests, he tries to steal it!"

✓ ✓ ✓

DIRTY CROOKS

Sam Benson, the most notorious thief in the entire community, called on the town rabbi.

"Sir, I found a purse full of gold. I would like you to help me locate the owner."

"Why of course!" exclaimed the surprised rabbi. "I'll make an announcement in the synagogue. The owner will undoubtedly claim his property."

A few minutes after Benson left, the rabbi discovered that his watch was missing. He immediately sent his *shammes* to bring the man back, and sure enough, he had it in his pocket.

"I just can't figure you out," said the exasperated rabbi. "Here you return a purse full of gold, and then you steal a watch that costs less than five dollars. I don't understand you at all."

"What's to understand?" answered Benson. "When it comes to returning a lost article, that's a *mitzvah*. But when it comes to stealing, that's business!"

✓ ✓ ✓

"Jacob Rappaport," announced the judge, "for breaking into a house in the middle of the night, I sentence you to two years in prison."

"But, your honor," pleaded Rappaport, "last time I was in court you sentenced me to a year in jail for breaking into a house during the day! If not in the middle of the night, and not in the middle of the day, just when am I supposed to earn my living?"

✓ ✓ ✓

Goldberg and Greenberg were suspected of burglarizing the Second Avenue Dry Goods Emporium, but the police could find no actual evidence. They were questioned in detail at the local precinct.

"You say you did not break into the dry goods store?" demanded the police lieutenant.

"Who breaks into dry goods stores?" retorted Goldberg.

"Did you or did you not steal nine boxes of linens?"

"Who steals?"

"Well, what kind of work do you do?"

"Who works?"

"Then how about you?" rasped the police officer, glaring at Greenberg. "What do you do for a living?"

"What's the matter?" snapped Greenberg. "It's all of a sudden against the law I should help Goldberg?"

✓ ✓ ✓

Art Zweig, the plumbing contractor, was hailed into court for crooked practices—again!

"Zweig," growled the judge, "this makes the fifth time in a year you've been in this court. You should be ashamed of yourself!"

"Now your honor, is that a nice way to talk?" asked Zweig reproach-fully. "After all, I've seen you here, too, five times. But do I criticize you?"

✓ ✓ ✓

Berman owed Bronstein $100 and, at last, when the note was more than a year overdue, he managed to accumulate enough money to repay the loan. They met in a small tavern and each ordered a glass of wine to celebrate the occasion.

As they were sipping and reminiscing over old times, a masked man entered the establishment, brandished a gun, and hissed, "Hand over your money, if you value your life!"

Berman, in a frenzy, snatched his wallet from a coat pocket and quickly thrust it into Bronstein's hands.

"Bronstein," he yelped, "remember, I paid you. We're even!"

✓ ✓ ✓

There's a moral to this one, and it doesn't necessarily relate to grand-fathers.

Grandpa Skolnik, a very clever old man, always cautioned his teen-age grandson to guard his health, not his wealth. So the youth took his advice, and while he was guarding his health someone stole his wealth. But there were so many clues left behind that it was easy to see that grandpa was the culprit, and the young man confronted him with the accusation.

"Yes, I'm guilty," admitted grandpa at once. "And let this be a lesson to you. Never watch your wealth—watch your grandpa!"

✓ ✓ ✓

Miriam was awakened by a strange noise in the middle of the night. She nudged her snoring husband. "Sam, wake up! There's a crook in the house!"

"All right, so there's a crook in the house. Go back to sleep!"

"Sam, don't you understand? Somebody broke in!"

"Keep quiet!" Sam hissed. "You know very well we have nothing worthwhile stealing. What should I do, go downstairs and admit it to a total stranger? Have you no shame?"

✓ ✓ ✓

Two thieving *yishuvniks*, Boris and Ivan, saw a Jewish wagoner hitch his horse and cart outside a tavern and then go inside.

"That's a fine-looking horse," said Boris greedily. "Young and strong."

"Let's steal it," said Ivan promptly.

"It's a little risky. The Jew will be coming out in a minute or two. If we're caught it's a good ten years in prison for us."

"I have an idea," said Boris. "We'll unhitch the horse, and you ride him out of town to our hideout, as fast as you can. Meanwhile, I'll get into the harness myself, in place of the horse."

When the wagoner came out of the tavern and saw a human being hitched to his wagon he was dumbfounded.

"What happened to my horse?" he shrieked. "What are you doing here?"

"*Shah!* Don't carry on so!" soothed the stranger. "I *am* your horse. Many years ago, when I was a young man, I could not stay away from loose women, and so, for my transgressions, the Lord punished me by changing me into a horse for eighteen years. My term just expired a few minutes ago and now I am a human being again."

The Jewish driver was full of compassion. "Oh, my dear man," he sighed, "when I think of all the times I treated you harshly I could weep. I made you stand outside in the rain and snow. I loaded the wagon with more than you were able to pull. I didn't feed you as well as I should have. Tell me, my friend, how can I make it up to you?"

"Well, I'll need a little money to get started again as a human being."

"Here's fifty rubles. Go your way, old friend, and stay away from naughty ladies."

On the following Tuesday, the driver went to the marketplace to buy a new horse, and lo and behold! there, tethered to a post, was his good old horse, up for sale.

The wagoner rushed over to the animal and threw his arms around its neck. "You old rascal," he whispered affectionately. "You transgressed again! I *told* you to stay away from naughty women!"

✔   ✔   ✔

The *maggid* had a preaching engagement in the next town and he hired a driver to get him there on time. On the way they passed a field of ripening corn and the driver, sorely tempted, drew up his horse and jumped down from the wagon.

"Listen, do me a favor," he said, glancing around, furtively. "If you see anyone looking, just holler. I'm going to pick some of that corn while you act as my lookout."

The driver was just about to pluck the first ear of corn when the *maggid's* warning cry sounded: "Someone is looking! Someone is looking!"

In a panic, the driver leaped into the wagon and urged the horse to a gallop. But, when he looked back over his shoulder, he saw no one.

"What's the big idea?" he complained. "Who was looking?"

"God," the *maggid* replied simply.

✔   ✔   ✔

The little man bowed his head in reverent prayer. "Thank you, God, for all our alert police officers and for punishing and jailing so many dirty crooks, pickpockets and *fenaiglers*. If it weren't for your Divine intercession, Lord, my profession would be so overcrowded that a poor thief like me could never earn a decent living!"

✔   ✔   ✔

Simon, the coachman, came home tired but happy one night, and, over a glass of tea and lemon, he told his wife how he had bamboozled a notoriously crooked Gypsy out of a valuable horse earlier in the day.

"All I paid for the horse was twenty *zlotys*," he bragged. "It's worth fifty, at least."

"That's good!" said the wife.

"No, that's bad," countered the husband. "It's a very small horse."

"Then he won't be able to pull a heavy load," observed the wife. "Yes, that's bad!"

"No, that's good. The horse is exceptionally strong. The only trouble is that he limps."

"Oh, that's bad. A crippled horse can't work!"

"No, that's good! The foolish Gypsy didn't notice the small nail in its hoof. I pulled it out and the limp is gone."

"Then you have a perfect horse for only twenty *zlotys*," the wife smiled approvingly. "That's good!"

"No, that's bad! By mistake I gave him fifty *zlotys*."

"*Oy vay!*" wailed the wife, "That's bad!"

"No, that's good," grinned the husband. "The money was counterfeit!"

✦　　✦　　✦

Only a week earlier, the popular rabbi had been given a new fur hat as a Chanukah present. Now someone had stolen it.

There was only one way to find out who had perpetrated this crime, so the rabbi sent for Louie, the town's king of thieves.

"How about it, Louie; do you think you can get my fur hat back?" asked the rabbi.

"Well, that depends."

"Depends? Depends on what?"

"On who took it," answered Louie. "In the event that one of my followers stole it, you can be sure I'll get it back for you. But if it was stolen by one of your followers, then, Rabbi, you might as well forget you ever had a new fur hat!"

✦　　✦　　✦

The new Commissar was determined to learn as much about his job as possible, and in the shortest time. On the first day he visited the prison and asked each of the inmates why he was there.

"I was accused unjustly," said the first prisoner.

"A case of mistaken identity," said another.

"I was framed," alibied still another.

Every one, in turn, insisted that he was completely innocent of the charges for which he had been jailed, until he came to the last inmate.

"My name is Isidor Fein. I'm serving a sentence because I stole an expensive silver candelabra."

"What!" roared the Commissar. "Guards, release this man! Turn him out, I say! We can't have this crook contaminating all the good, innocent men in this prison!"

✓ ✓ ✓

"Avrum," said one talmudic student to another, "I'm afraid I have committed a terrible sin."

"Oh, it can't be as bad as all that," said the other airily. "What did you do that was so terrible?"

"I stole a box of candles."

"Hmmm, that *is* serious! You'll have to atone."

"Yes, but how?"

"I know one way. You can show repentance by bringing five bottles of sacramental wine to the synagogue as a gift."

"Five bottles of wine! Are you out of your mind? You know I haven't a penny to my name. How could I possibly get all that wine?"

"The same way you got the candles," suggested the other.

✓ ✓ ✓

Jake had been a successful counterfeiter in the old country, so when he came to America he decided to follow the same profession. He took a one dollar bill and, with the fine precision work that had always been his trademark, he raised the figure "1" to a "9."

Full of confidence in his artistry, he went into Dave's pool-room, bought a pack of cigarettes and presented his nine-dollar bill in payment.

Dave, a counterfeiter himself for the past thirty years, took one look at the phony bill, nodded silently, and gave Jake some phony silver and two four-dollar bills as change.

The newcomer to our fair shores walked out, congratulating himself on his first easy mark.

✓ ✓ ✓

Then there's the man who lost his wallet, and his brother found it. Now he's looking for his brother.

✓ ✓ ✓

Ralph was on his deathbed, the pallor of eternal rest already on his face. Charlie, his business partner, hovered over him.

"Charlie, I have a terrible confession to make," Ralph said weakly. "I repent for my sins—truly, I'm sorry."

"What could you have done that was so bad?"

"Remember when someone robbed our company of $75,000 while you were on vacation? It was I who took the money."

"That's all right," soothed Charlie. "This is no time to think of things like that."

"And when you created that new pattern that would have put us ahead of every other garment maker in the country, it was I who stole the

79

drawings and sold them to our competitor before our own company could get it on the market."

"*Shah! Shah!* Try to rest," crooned Charlie.

"And that time a private detective caught you in that hotel with our head model—it was I who tipped off your wife so she could get evidence for the divorce." Ralph was now sobbing with remorse. "Oh, Charlie, please forgive me before I die!"

"What's to forgive?" answered Charlie. "We're even. I'm the one who poisoned you!"

✓ ✓ ✓

A man went into a store and ordered a tie. The clerk wrapped it up and then handed it to him.

"I changed my mind," said the customer. "I believe I'll trade this for a pair of socks instead."

"All right."

The customer selected the socks and when the clerk had wrapped the purchase and handed it to him, the man started to leave.

"Hey, you didn't pay for those!" called the clerk.

"What are you talking about?" retorted the man. "I just traded the tie for them."

"Yes, but you didn't pay for the tie."

"Why should I? Did I keep it?"

✓ ✓ ✓

During the turmoil occasioned by the Israel-Arab War of 1967, a group of Syrians broke into the Bank of Tel Aviv. They escaped with over a million dollars in pledges.

Chapter Nine

Miracles

A certain *tzaddik* of Lithuania, a *chassidic* rabbi with a wide reputation as a wonder-worker, was in his study when the door burst open and the *shammes* rushed in, his eyes alight with holy fervor.

"Rabbi! Rabbi!" he shouted, wildly excited. "A terribly crippled man just came into the synagogue. The moment he approached the *bimah* and laid his hand on the Torah he threw his crutches away! I myself saw the whole thing!"

The rabbi jumped up from his chair and raised his arms heavenward. "It is indeed a miracle from Heaven!" he cried, his face aglow with spiritual rapture. "Tell me quickly, where is the man now?"

"He's lying in the aisle," answered the *shammes*. "The poor man fell on his *tuchus*!"

🗸 🗸 🗸

For Ben Alpert the day was a total loss. First his daughter announced she was engaged to a *goy*. As a result, Muriel, his wife, came down with nervous prostration. Then his creditors told him they could no longer wait for payment on his overdue loans.

As if all that were not enough, that evening, as he was bemoaning his fate, the cry of "Fire!" resounded outside his window. Rushing into the street, he saw that his store was blazing furiously, the flames thirty feet high.

"Oh, God!" he wailed. "Strike me dead so that my sufferings may come to an end."

At that moment, a brick from the burning building broke loose and landed with shattering impact at his feet, missing his head by the merest fraction of an inch.

"Lord," he muttered crossly, "don't I have enough *tsorres* without you taking me so literally?"

🗸 🗸 🗸

Here is another of Sigmund Freud's favorite anecdotes, reported in his *Wit and Its Relation to the Unconscious.*

The well-known Rabbi Nathan was in the synagogue of Cracow when he suddenly screamed.

"Why did you howl like that?" asked his startled pupils.

"I couldn't help it," declared Rabbi Nathan. "Just a few moments ago the great Rabbi Solomon of Lemburg died."

The entire congregation marveled at this demonstration of the rabbi's telepathic powers and immediately went into mourning.

A few days later, however, a group of Lemburg Jews arrived in the city and contradicted Rabbi Nathan.

"We just left Rabbi Solomon," they insisted. "He is in perfect health."

Finally it became clear that the telepathic communication was in error, and the Jews of Lemburg siezed on the mistake to ridicule the rabbi of Cracow.

"Your rabbi made a fool of himself when he said that he saw Rabbi Solomon die. Our rabbi is still alive."

"What does that matter?" retorted one of Rabbi Nathan's students. "Isn't it amazing enough that he was able to reach telepathically all the way from Cracow to Lemburg?"

✓ ✓ ✓

Dr. Theodor Reik, in his analytical volume, *Jewish Wit*, illustrates that Christian Science is not the only religion in which medical science competes with the belief in prayer. Pious eastern Jews, Dr. Reik correctly points out, recited the text of the Psalms in emergency situations. This ritual was called "saying *tefillim.*"

A distraught mother came to the *chassid* about her sick child.

"Rabbi," she lamented, "my *ingeleh* is suffering already a whole week from diarrhea. I tried every medicine, but nothing will stop it.!"

"Don't worry," the *chassidic* rabbi comforted her. "All you need do is say *tefillim*. I have no doubt that you will witness a miracle."

Three days later the worried mother appeared at the rabbi's house again.

"Rabbi, I did exactly as you suggested, but now my little boy is suffering from the opposite symptoms. He can't go at all!"

"Say again *tefillim*," recommended the *chassid*.

"But Rabbi," protested the woman, "*tefillim* are constipating!"

✓ ✓ ✓

A Jew was crossing the street while the traffic light was green when he was struck down by a car. Pretending to be seriously injured, he immediately sued the driver's insurance company, claiming that he was now totally paralyzed from the neck down. Because the automobile had entered the intersection against the lights, the victim was awarded $50,000.

"We won!" shouted the man when he was returned home in an ambulance. "We're rich!"

"But what good is it?" asked his wife mournfully. "The insurance adjuster testified in court that he didn't believe you were paralyzed, and that he was going to keep an eye on you. Even the judge said that if you ever take so much as a single step you will be prosecuted for perjury and fraud."

"Ruthie, don't worry so much," he assured his wife cheerfully. "I know exactly what to do. First, we're going to hire an ambulance to take me to the airport. Then we'll have the attendants carry me into the plane and we'll fly to Europe."

"Europe! What are you going to do in Europe?"

"I'm going to visit Lourdes," he explained jubilantly. "And then, *oy*, will you see a miracle!"

✓ ✓ ✓

A certain rabbi of Prague, reputedly able to work miracles, was in his study when the quiet afternoon was shattered by a frantic pounding on the door. The sexton admitted a distraught woman.

"My husband has left me," she sobbed, handing the *shammes* the deserter's farewell letter.

"Hmmm, I'd better show this note to the rabbi," said the sexton. "Just wait here—I'll be right back."

He returned in a few moments and consoled the woman. "Be at ease, Madam. The rabbi sends goods news. Seventy-six hours, eighteen minutes and thirty-four seconds from now, your husband will return."

When the relieved woman had departed the *shammes* went back into the study.

"Why do you look so glum?" asked the rabbi.

"It's that woman; I feel sorry for her."

"What's the matter? Don't you believe I can work miracles?"

"That's not the point," answered the sexton. "You only saw her note. I saw her face!"

✓ ✓ ✓

At the height of a season of extraordinary drought the rabbi designated a day for fasting and prayer, and ordered all the Jews of the town to assemble in the synagogue. Before the services commenced, however, the congregants were surprised to observe in their midst Herschel Schuster who was notorious for his persistent immorality. Herschel, who was seldom seen in the house of God, walked over to the *shammes*, and asked permission to lead in the services. He explained that on this day he would be observing the anniversary of his father's death. The *shammes* flatly refused Herschel's request, but the rabbi reversed this decision and permitted the disreputable character to act as cantor for that morning.

When the service was over the rabbi was asked to explain the reason for his strange conduct.

"The Torah tells us that sinners brought on the great flood," explained the rabbi. "Now if a multitude of sinners could bring on a deluge, it occurred to me that one miserable sinner might bring us at least a little shower."

Chapter Ten

Rabbis, Preachers and Cantors

The itinerant preachers who traveled throughout the Jewish communities of Russia and Poland depended for their subsistence on the generosity of the various congregations to whom they preached. Sometimes a *maggid* was driven to desperation in his quest for food, as this tale indicates.

A certain preacher who had delivered a long and fiery oration found himself facing the prospect of going to bed hungry. The congregation apparently had been so carried away by his eloquence that his material needs had simply slipped their minds.

After a few minutes of hard thinking, the *maggid* decided to visit the rabbi's house where, he was sure, he would get something to eat.

Upon entering the rabbi's home he found a huge roast turkey on the table, but the rabbi uttered not a word which might be construed as an invitation to the uninvited guest. Eventually, the visitor realized that he would have to take matters into his own hands.

"I want to tell you an intriguing parable," began the starving orator. "Once upon a time a *maggid* and a rabbi took a walk. On the road they met a turkey, so the three walked on together. A little later the trio met the devil, so the four walked together. After some time, they reached a wide river. Now only the devil and the *maggid* could swim; the rabbi and the turkey could not. The question is: Who took whom so they could all cross the river?"

The *maggid* paused and searched the rabbi's face, but the latter shook his head in puzzlement. "I don't know," he admitted. "Who took whom across the river?"

"First they held a conference," said the hungry orator as he bounded to the table and grabbed the turkey roast. He ran to the door with his prize and shouted over his shoulder:

"It was decided that the *maggid* should take the turkey and the devil take the rabbi!"

✓   ✓   ✓

RABBIS, PREACHERS AND CANTORS

The rabbinical post was vacant in a Bronx congregation, and a rabbi who had recently given up a pulpit in Brooklyn applied for the position. The president of the Bronx congregation did the usual thing: he wrote a letter of inquiry about the rabbi to the Brooklyn congregation. Shortly thereafter he received the following answer:

"Our former rabbi can easily be compared to Moses, to Shakespeare and to God the Father."

The Bronx congregation was impressed and delighted with this glowing praise and so they appointed the Brooklyn rabbi to their pulpit. But it did not take them long to discover that their new rabbi was no genius. So, in a huff, the president wrote a sizzling letter to the Brooklyn congregation, upbraiding them for the deception and demanding an explanation. Several days later they were in receipt of the following reply:

"Why do you call us names? Who has deceived you? We answered you as we did for good cause.

"Our former rabbi can be compared to Moses because, like him, he knows no English; to Shakespeare because, like him, he speaks as if he had pebbles rolling around in his mouth; and to God the Father because like Him, our former rabbi is positively not human!"

✓   ✓   ✓

It was a warm summer's day and inside the synagogue the rabbi droned on and on—endlessly—his voice a deadly monotone. The congregation fidgeted, squirmed in their seats and tried to stifle their yawns. At length a few stole quietly out of the temple. Others followed suit until, one by one, the entire audience had departed.

But the rabbi, oblivious to anything but his own voice, continued to preach, his phrases as uniform as the buzzing of a swarm of bees.

The sexton walked down the aisle between the rows of now empty seats and, sidling up to the rabbi, managed to catch his attention for a fleeting moment.

"Rabbi," said the *shammes*, "here's the key to the synagogue. Would you mind locking up when you get through?"

✓   ✓   ✓

The distinguished Rabbi Henri Spalier, of Alsace-Lorraine, was asked by an unlettered but fervent Jewish farmer to come to his distant village and discourse on the Torah. But the ignorant peasants were anything but polite when he graciously consented to talk to them. Indeed, they were downright rude. They joked, talked of other matters and paid scant attention to the learned scholar.

Upon his return to Alsace-Lorraine, Dr. Spalier wrote a polite letter to the farmer, thanking him for the invitation and addressing him as *"Gaon."*

The untutored farmer was astonished. He knew full well that the title *"Gaon"* was reserved for the Grand Rabbis and most prominent of

Jewish sages in Europe. During his next visit to the big city, he called on Rabbi Spalier.

"I know I am far from being a genius," said the farmer. "Why did you mock me by calling me 'Gaon'?"

"I meant no disrespect, believe me," said Dr. Spalier. "I addressed you by that title because you are exactly that—Grand Rabbi, Gaon—in comparison with the others in your village!"

✓ ✓ ✓

There is always at least one Jew in every congregation whose main purpose in life seems to be making the rabbi's existence miserable. Questions! Questions! It's enough to drive a rabbi crazy.

One such congregant, forever plaguing the rabbi with riddles he hoped would confound him, asked: "Tell me, Rabbi, why is it that four questions are asked on Passover, but no questions on Yom Kippur or Rosh Hashanah?"

"It's very simple," answered the rabbi wearily. "To see a Jew wail and moan is not unusual, and raises no questions, but to see a Jew happy—that demands an explanation!"

✓ ✓ ✓

Not every rebbetzn is the sweet, even-tempered darling that much of Jewish lore would have you believe. Some can be as shrewish as the proverbial fishwife.

Take Rabbi Ackerman's wife, for example. One evening, after a long harangue, she heard him sigh, "Oh, if only women could be as tolerant as men; what a wonderful world this would be!"

Spitefully, she prepared supper—a tough old rooster with meat like leather. The rabbi ate, uncomplainingly. Why start another argument?

On the following afternoon she boiled a plump, juicy, very tender young hen, and the surprised but pleased holy man relished every morsel.

"I did that for a reason," said the rebbetzn, when he had finished. "Now you can see for yourself that the female is better than the male."

"Yes, I suppose you are right," the rabbi agreed slowly, "but only after she's been boiled for a few hours!"

✓ ✓ ✓

A man who had lived a life of depravity finally repented and yearned to walk in the ways of Jehovah. He went to the rabbi to admit his unworthiness and to beg forgiveness of the Almighty. But, in his newly-acquired saintliness, he was ashamed to confess the full extent of his past sins, even to the rabbi. So he explained that he was pleading for a friend.

The rabbi, long experienced with this mild form of deception, placed his hand on the other's shoulder.

"How much simpler it would have been," the rabbi said, smiling gently, "if your friend had come here personally and told me that *his* friend sent him."

✓ ✓ ✓

Anna Klein, a pious woman, had an abiding faith in the goodness and wisdom of her rabbi, so it was only natural that she would visit him when she was confronted with a number of domestic problems. For two hours, Anna unburdened her heart, telling the cornered rabbi of all the mean things her relatives were saying about her. Finally she rose to leave.

"Rabbi, when I came in here I had a terrible headache," she smiled. "But now, thanks to you, it's gone."

"Mrs. Klein, your headache isn't gone at all," responded the weary rabbi. "I have it!"

✓ ✓ ✓

It had been a long, hard day, and now Rabbi Seligman took off his shoes, sat back in his overstuffed chair, lit his pipe and sipped a little *schnapps*. Leah, his wife, sat opposite him, sewing.

"Leah, there is an old Jewish saying," he began; "When a man is asked for whom he is working, he usually says that he has few personal needs but that he must consider the welfare of his children."

"It's a very nice saying," commented the *rebbetzn*. "After all, when the child grows up, he too carries on the tradition by working hard for *his* own children."

The rabbi nodded thoughtfully. "Without demeaning our hallowed traditions, my dear Leah, I would like to see just one thing before I die— that ideal child for whom all the generations are slaving."

✓ ✓ ✓

A *yeshivah* student was having a discussion with his rabbi.

"Someday, I too hope to become a rabbi," said the youth. "Aside from my studies is there any other all-important qualification I will need?"

"Yes, the stimulus of imagination," replied the rabbi. "You will have to imagine that somebody is paying attention to what you say."

✓ ✓ ✓

An Orthodox rabbi newly arrived in the United States sought a position in vain. Finally he was reduced to seeking a post in a Conservative congregation, but again he could not find an opening. In desperation he applied at a Reform temple and luckily found an opening in a small, impoverished section of the city.

He observed the services for a few days and especially noted how the departing rabbi conducted the proceedings until he understood the operation of this unfamiliar, *goyishe* (to him) branch of Judaism.

"Members of the Reform Congregation, I greet you," he announced, his first time in the pulpit. "You will want to know a little of the background of your new rabbi. First I was a rabbi in Yekaterinoslav. There were Jews but no money. Then I was a rabbi in Berlin. There was plenty of money but no Jews. Now in this congregation," he concluded with an almost imperceptible sob in his voice, "there is no money and no Jews!"

*   *   *

"Rabbi," complained an aggravated young wagoner, "I am at my wits' end about my horses. They won't eat anything but *latkes* and *haman-tashen*. Already they're so skinny I'm afraid they won't last much longer."

"Let me ask you something," said the rabbi. "Do you pray every day?"

"Why, er—uh—not usually," the driver stammered.

"Do you wash your hands before every meal?"

"Not always."

"And do you ask God's blessing before you eat?"

"No!" the driver answered tersely.

"Then all is perfectly clear," explained the rabbi. "It is irrevocably intertwined with the divine law of compensation. Since you eat like a horse, your horses eat like humans."

*   *   *

A youthful talmudic scholar asked Rabbi Laizer Kelmer to ordain him as a rabbi. Rabbi Kelmer spoke to the youth and found him to be quite intelligent, though somewhat conceited. He decided to test the lad.

"What would you do if you were confronted with a case where a man cut his hand on Saturday, and the blood flowed profusely?"

"Just a moment, please, Rabbi Kelmer. I will consult the Talmud for the proper answer," said the candidate.

"Never mind, young man," interrupted the rabbi. "I suggest you go home and study some more. By the time you looked it up in the Talmud the poor man would have bled to death."

*   *   *

The Grand Rabbi of Vilna had just returned to the synagogue when the sexton, the worst *Yenteh Tellabendeh* in the city, accosted him in the foyer.

"Rabbi," he said sternly, "I have heard disturbing rumors that you speak to women on the street—in broad daylight! I did not wish to repeat this idle gossip, but today I myself saw you talking to a woman."

"*Nu*, what about it?" asked the rabbi placidly.

"But you are a man of God!" the *shammes* protested. "It is not seemly that you should stop to talk to females in public."

"My dear *shammes*," the rabbi said patiently, "which is better—to talk to a woman and think of God, or to talk to God and think of a woman?"

*   *   *

The rabbi and the *shammes*, like many other clergymen and sextons, were not very friendly. Nevertheless, they made a pretense of getting along for the good of the synagogue.

One afternoon while the rabbi was delivering one of his interminably long sermons, a loud snore almost drowned out his words.

"*Shammes*," the rabbi ordered, "wake that man up at once!"

"Wake him up yourself!" retorted the sexton. "You're the one who put him to sleep!"

✓ ✓ ✓

An arrogant young rabbi, more interested in tax and syntax than in his congregational duties, was appointed to a new synagogue. At the very first service, the cantor began a prayer with the word "Lord," whereupon everyone rose to their feet.

"What is the meaning of this impertinence?" roared the rabbi. "I gave no one permission to rise."

"B-b-but the word 'Lord' . . .!" the cantor stuttered. "We're supposed to . . ."

"Don't but me any buts!" interrupted the rabbi. "Who's in charge here—me or the Lord?"

✓ ✓ ✓

A certain rabbi who was a compulsive stammerer was asked by two members of his congregation to act as arbiter for them in a commercial dispute. The loser, a butcher by trade, was a man of violent temper who respected neither scholarship nor piety, and as soon as the rabbi-magistrate pronounced his verdict, he opened fire on him.

"You are a thief and a robber!" thundered the disgruntled litigant.

The venerable sage listened calmly to the epithets, and when the torrent subsided he answered, "And y-you are a s-s-stut-stut-stutterer."

"What! *I'm* a stutterer?" cried the furious man. "What kind of a silly statement is that?"

"W-well," explained the rabbi, "s-since you a-a-ascribed t-to me your own sh-shortcomings, I th-thought it no m-more than right I-I should r-re-ciprocate."

✓ ✓ ✓

A poor teacher went to see his superior at the Talmud Torah.

"I know you are very busy," he said, "but I just want to ask you one question."

"Very well," said the other curtly. "What is it?"

"Passover is almost here and I haven't any money to buy food for the holidays. Tell me, Rabbi, what shall I do?"

"That's simple," replied the other. "All you need do is to pawn your silver candelabra. That will bring you enough money for your needs."

"But who has silver candelabra?" asked the poor teacher. "I don't even know where to get any."

"Aren't you being just a little unreasonable?" snapped the rabbi. "You came in here and said you had only one question, and I answered you. Now you ask me where you can get a silver candelabra. That's an entirely different question, so go ask somebody else!"

✓ ✓ ✓

A prosperous lawyer visited his brother, a rabbi in a small village, and was appalled at his emaciated appearance.

"How can you survive on those starvation wages they pay you?" he asked, shocked.

"It's like this, dear brother," the rabbi answered, smiling tolerantly. "I might have died of hunger long ago except that I make it a practice to fast on Mondays and Thursdays. That way, I have enough food to last the week!"

✓ ✓ ✓

The rabbi had spent the better part of the morning in fervent prayer. When he was finished, a member of the congregation approached him.

"I hope you prayed for something specific," he said, not without a slight touch of sarcasm.

"I did," the rabbi answered mildly. "I prayed that the rich should give more to the poor."

"Let's hope God heard your prayers."

"I'm sure He did—at least half of it. The poor have agreed to accept the increase!"

✓ ✓ ✓

For centuries the orthodox rabbis of eastern Europe have followed in the footsteps of their fathers and forefathers. In some families nearly all male ancestors followed the rabbinical calling.

So it was only natural when a group of distinguished rabbis met in Budapest one day, that they proceeded to boast of their rabbinical genealogy. All, that is, except one. When the others eyed him questioningly, he said quietly, "I am the first rabbi in my family."

The others, though somewhat surprised by this confession, were too polite to make any comment, so each, in turn, began to expound *Torah* as taught by his respective ancestor.

Finally it was the obscure young rabbi's turn to offer his learned dissertation based on the revelations of his forefathers. There was an embarrassed silence, for the others had no wish to humiliate their colleague. But he arose confidently and began:

"Fellow rabbis, my father was a simple baker but he taught me something I shall never forget: that only fresh bread is appetizing, and that

I should always avoid the stale. And that, gentlemen, also applies to learning."

And with that, he sat down.

✔   ✔   ✔

Rabbinical students, like other young men, often bubble over from the sheer exuberance of youth. So it was not too great a surprise when a group of them were caught redhanded as they played pinochle on the Sabbath.

"What have you to say for yourselves?" the rabbi demanded sternly.

The first student made a good show of regret. "I'm sorry, Rabbi, but I simply forgot it was the Sabbath."

"Well, I suppose that is possible. I'll give you the benefit of the doubt this time, but don't let it happen again."

The second student was equally as glib with his excuse: "I'm ashamed to admit it, but I simply forgot that gambling on the Sabbath is prohibited."

"That too is possible. You are forgiven, but sin no more."

Then the third miscreant, the owner of the apartment in which the students had gambled on the Sabbath, approached the rabbi.

"All right, what is your alibi?" the elder asked. "No doubt you forgot something too."

"Yes, Rabbi," replied the young man dejectedly. "I forgot to pull down the shades."

✔   ✔   ✔

"Rabbi! Rabbi!" shouted the cantor in anguished tones as he burst into the synagogue.

"What is it this time?" demanded the rabbi, well aware of the other's propensity for high drama.

"This is serious. Meat is being brought into the city from the outside!"

"*Nu*, what about it?"

"What do you mean, 'what about it?' What kind of question is that for a rabbi to ask? The meat may not be *kosher*. We don't even know the slaughterers."

"My dear *Shammes*," the rabbi sighed, "if we can eat the meat of our own slaughterers whom we know so well, we shouldn't have any qualms about eating the meat of slaughterers whom we don't know at all—thank Heaven!"

✔   ✔   ✔

What did the Jews laugh at circa 300 C.E.? Pretty much the same things that tickle their risibilities today—the joke that shakes the listener with laughter or the quietly humorous tale that evokes an appreciative smile. The following anecdote falls in the latter category. It appears that it was first translated from the Yiddish to English in 1926 by Jacob

Richman in his *Laughs from Jewish Lore*. Whether the principal character lived some 1800 years ago, as claimed by Richman, or 200 years later, as stated by such authorities on Jewish wit and humor as Nathan Ausubel and Rufus Learsi, this anecdote is pre-dated only by a handful of pre-Christian era Jewish witticisms:

Rabbi Judah ha-Nasi, the editor of the compilation of texts which expound on the Talmud, and who lived some 1800 years ago, was lecturing before his students one day when his nostrils were assailed by the strong odor of garlic. Apparently one of his pupils had just eaten more than common sense dictated.

Irritated, the great teacher offered a terse observation: "Dirt in the garden is a natural concomitant of plant life—including such delicacies as garlic. But that same earth, in the kitchen, is unwanted dirt, nothing more. Pursuing the same analogy, garlic in the kitchen enhances and enriches by its fragrance, but in the classroom it is noxious and offensive. Therefore, will the student who is responsible for the effluvium be good enough to absent himself with all haste and as unobtrusively as possible?"

There was a hum of *sotto voce* discussion among the students as they translated the illustrious scholar's purple prose into lay language, but not a soul stirred. Evidently the garlic-eater was ashamed to acknowledge publicly that he was the cause of the beloved master's annoyance.

At length, a student, one Rabbi Haya, rose from his seat and walked out.

Now it was well known to all that Rabbi Haya never touched garlic; that, in fact, he despised it. Clearly, he had taken it upon himself to assume the guilt so that the lecture might continue.

But the good rabbi had not reckoned with conscience. Presently another student arose, his face crimson with guilt, and left the room. Another pupil observed the departure, his eyes wide with surprise. Then he too arose and slunk from the classroom. Then another, and another, and still another. Soon a general exodus began.

In a few minutes, the great Rabbi Judah ha-Nasi was facing an empty lecture room.

✓ ✓ ✓

A new immigrant made his way to Brooklyn in search of a cousin he had not seen since childhood in the old country. He stopped a man who looked Jewish and, in Yiddish of course, asked: "Sir, I am looking for Cantor Rosenzweig, of the Pitkin Avenue Synagogue. Can you give me directions, please?"

"Sure, I know the man well," said the passerby. "You are speaking of Cantor Berel Rosenzweig, a *chazzen* who can't carry the simplest tune. You'll reach the synagogue six blocks ahead, two blocks to the left and a block-and-a-half to the right."

The newcomer thanked him but soon had to stop someone else. Again he asked directions to the Pitkin Avenue Synagogue, explaining his wish to see Cantor Rosenzweig.

"Oh, you mean Rosenzweig the crook—the one who has all those phony sales every year. Sure, just turn left at the subway and walk two blocks."

He finally reached the synagogue and, in the lobby, he spied a man who looked as though he might be the long lost cousin.

"Pardon me," he asked politely, "but are you Cantor Rosenzweig?"

"Who, Rosenzweig the miser, who lets his wife and children starve while he buys for himself only the best? No, thank God, I'm not. But that is he, standing over there."

The stranger approached Cantor Rosenzweig, introduced himself and exchanged the usual greetings. At length, the visitor asked curiously; "Tell me, Cantor, why do you devote so much time to the synagogue? Is it the money they pay you?"

"I don't get paid," Rosenzweig said. "Not a penny!"

"Then why do you do it?"

The Cantor inflated his chest proudly. "Why, for the honor, of course!"

¶ ¶ ¶

A very poor widow rushed to the house of the rabbi, tearfully demanding that she see him at once. The *rebbetzn* quickly ushered her husband into the living room.

"What can I do for you, my child?" asked the rabbi.

"*Oy*, did something terrible happen to me!" she wailed.

"What's so terrible?"

"Rabbi, with my last few pennies I bought for the *kinderlach* and for myself a piece of *kosher* meat, but when I got home—who can explain it?—inside my bag was a strange package with, you should pardon the expression—ham!"

The rabbi nodded gravely. "That is not good."

"We have nothing else in the house to eat," the poor woman sobbed. "And no money to buy anything else."

"But what makes you so sure it's ham?"

"It *looks* like ham!" Tears coursed down the woman's cheeks.

"Madam, you are permitted to eat it," decreed the compassionate rabbi. "Take my word for it—the *flanken* is *kosher!*"

¶ ¶ ¶

A rare combination of scholarship, coupled with humility and naive sweetness, characterized many of the nineteenth century Jewish sages. Jacob Richman, almost a half century ago, recorded this enduring illustration:

It was customary in former years, when writing to rabbis, to precede their names with a long string of flattering titles. "*Harav, Hagaon, Hamaor Hagadol*" (Rabbi, Genius, Great Luminary) were among the shortest forms

93

of salutations with which Jews of yore would address their spiritual leaders, or anyone else reputed to be a Hebrew scholar.

That, however, made little impression on the recipients of the reverential correspondence. In fact, they were noted not only for their profound erudition but for their humility and utter disregard of their own importance.

Take the case of Rabbi Joseph Ber Soloveitchik, of Brest-Litovsk, who once sent a letter to a farmer who could scarcely read Hebrew. He addressed the rustic as *"Harav, Hagaon, Hamaor Hagadol."*

The countryman felt deeply insulted. To address an ordinary farmer in that fashion could be nothing but sarcasm. On his next visit to the city he went to the rabbi's house, letter in hand, and reproached him for his derision.

"True enough, I am an unschooled man," said the farmer, "but that does not entitle anyone to ridicule me. Perhaps if I had had the opportunity I too would have been a *lamdan."*

The holy man gasped in astonishment. "I insulted you? Why should I insult an image of God?"

The farmer displayed the letter and pointed to the offending salutations which he believed were intended in a pejorative sense.

The great rabbi took one look at the words he had written, and entreated; "Believe me, I meant no offense. That is the way they address me, too!"

✓ ✓ ✓

A young rake was brought before the rabbi on charges of breaking his engagement to a nice girl without good reason. Aware of the profligate's unsavory reputation, the rabbi sternly ordered that he pay a fine to the girl's parents.

"But, Rabbi, I was only engaged to her for a few weeks!" protested the youth. "She can always marry someone else—after all I didn't harm her!"

"This is not the first time you have cast off and humiliated a respectable Jewish girl," the rabbi answered slowly. "But that is beside the point."

"Then what's the reason for the fine?"

"Consider two apples that have fallen from a tree. One is picked up, washed and eaten by the one who found it. But the other is picked up by a pig—he rolls it around in his mouth and then spits it out. True, the pig only possessed the apple for a few moments and apparently did not harm it, but all the same no one will touch that apple."

"Rabbi," the young man said indignantly, "are you calling me a pig?"

"Well," answered the holy man, "let us be kind and say I am calling the girl an apple. *Pay the fine!"*

✓ ✓ ✓

The story is told of a rabbi who was not only an eminent scholar and a deeply pious man, but also a prosperous merchant. And because of his many good works, his unending acts of charity and his lively sense of humor, he was much beloved among the common people.

One day, calamity struck. The rabbi, because of misjudgment in a business transaction, was wiped out—completely ruined financially.

His disciples, however, remained fiercely loyal. Thinking to cheer him up a delegation went to his house, believing they would find him broken in spirit and in need of a few friendly words. But to their amazement they found him serenely engrossed in his studies.

"*Rebbenyu,*" they exclaimed, "why are you so calm? You are a poor man now! Don't you ever worry?"

"Of course I do," the rabbi answered. "But I thank God for blessing me with a quick mind. You see, the worrying that others do in a month takes me only about a half hour."

✓   ✓   ✓

It was a week before Passover when Rabbi Elijah of Odessa responded to a knock on his door. The day was unseasonably cold and the visitor shivered in his light, threadbare coat. The rabbi escorted him inside, invited him to sit near the stove, and gave him a glass of hot tea. "Tell me," he asked at length, "why do you look so depressed?"

"I'm desperate," the stranger complained bitterly. "In just a few days *Pesach* will be here and I have no money for matzohs, sacramental wine or meat; not even the barest necessities. My wife, my children and I are even too ashamed to attend synagogue for the holiday services because we're in rags."

The rabbi nodded understandingly. "Believe me, my friend, God will help you. He never deserts His children."

The visitor, unconvinced, was on the verge of tears, and the compassionate rabbi, a poor man himself, endeavored to comfort him.

"Let's figure out your needs," he suggested, getting a pencil and paper. "First, how much will you require for the matzohs, meat and wine?"

"Fifteen rubles."

"And how much for clothes for your wife and children?"

"Twenty-five rubles."

"How about a new suit for yourself?"

"That should cost about twelve rubles."

"Let's see," the rabbi said, adding up the figures. "You need a total of fifty-two rubles. I think we've solved your problem."

"What do you mean?" asked the impoverished stranger.

"It's as clear as glass," replied the rabbi confidently. "Now you need not worry about matzohs, meat, sacramental wine, clothing for your family and yourself—no, nor even attending the holiday services. You now have only one worry—where to get the fifty-two rubles!"

✓   ✓   ✓

Mrs. Morganstein was particularly impressed with the sermon given by the rabbi.

95

"He is an inspired man," she told her husband.

"You like his work that much you should tell him," reasoned Mr. Morganstein. "I think he'd appreciate it."

On the next *Shabbes*, after the services were over and the congregation had dispersed, she went over and shook the rabbi's hand.

"I especially want you to know that all of your sermons are marvelous," she gushed. "In fact you should have them published in a book."

The rabbi smiled good-naturedly. "Mrs. Morganstein, I can't help but admit that I am flattered. But to be perfectly frank, there are rabbis whose sermons are much better than mine."

"Nonsense!"

"Well then, perhaps my sermons will be published posthumously," said the modest rabbi.

"Oh, that would be wonderful!" cried Mrs. Morganstein. "Let's hope it's real soon!"

✔   ✔   ✔

Members of the congregation had told the rabbi that Mrs. Ginsberg was sick, so he went to visit her. He was pleased to find her sitting up, smiling and cheerful. She assured him that she would be well enough to attend the weekend services.

"On what subject will you be speaking, if I may be so bold?" asked Mrs. Ginsberg.

"The necessity for relaxation," the rabbi answered.

The woman beamed. "By me medical subjects are always interesting. Tell me, Rabbi, on what laxatives are you talking—natural fruit juices or Ex-Lax?"

✔   ✔   ✔

Cantor Rosenblatt could not sing a note but his conceit was so ingrained that all the hints and snide remarks made about his croaking voice simply did not penetrate.

He had just finished singing the service one evening when he was approached by a stranger. "It is truly a burden, this profession of ours," he sighed.

"Oh, you're a cantor too?"

"Good Lord, no! I'm a butcher."

✔   ✔   ✔

The cantor and the treasurer of the synagogue had been carrying on a bitter feud for many months, but it reached a climax one day when the cantor publicly denounced the treasurer as a crook who had been appropriating the synagogue's funds for his own use.

Understandably enraged, the treasurer complained to the rabbi who immediately sent for the slanderer.

"You have made a very serious charge against an honest man," the

96

rabbi said coldly. "You know as well as I that the accusation is untrue. I must insist that you make a public apology in the synagogue this coming Saturday. Nor are you going to mince any words about it, either. You will say 'I made a false charge and I apologize.'"

"All right, so I'll say it," the cantor grumbled.

"Let me hear you say it right now."

"I made a false charge and I apologize," the cantor mumbled almost inaudibly.

"That's no good!" the rabbi stormed. "You are to enunciate your words clearly and loudly enough for all to hear."

"Now just a minute, Rabbi," the cantor said resentfully. "I don't tell you how to interpret the Torah, so don't you instruct a cantor in matters of tone and voice!"

✦ ✦ ✦

Rabbi Goldman surveyed his new Torah class with a keen eye. Each semester he made it a point to familiarize himself with the incoming students, so he began at once.

"For my first lecture of the season I will speak of liars. I now ask that those of you who have read the twenty-fifth chapter of our text book to please raise your hands."

All but two of the students raised their hands.

"Very good! I can see that my opening subject is well taken. There is no twenty-fifth chapter in our text book!"

✦ ✦ ✦

"The trouble with you Jews," said a priest to a rabbi, "is that your people are too old fashioned and set in your ways. What you should do is catch up with the modern world—go in for public relations and advertising."

"My dear friend, you don't know anything about ancient Jewish history or you wouldn't say that," replied the rabbi, his eyes twinkling. "Our mighty Samson had the right idea about advertising more than three thousand years ago: He took two columns and brought down the house!"

✦ ✦ ✦

It happened in the mid-1800's. A pious *chassid* was relating the wondrous miracles wrought by his rabbi. "For example," he said, "our great *rebbeh* and several of his followers were taking a walk on a fast day when they noticed a Jew leaning against a wall and devouring a piece of bread and herring.

"'Infidel!' cried one of the *chassidim*. 'May that wall crumble and crush your renegade bones!'

"But the *rebbeh* spoke in gentle tones. 'He has ignored this holy fast day but perhaps he has a good reason for committing the sin. Let us remember that even a sinner is a child of God. Rather than curse him I

97

shall bless him, and I shall pray to the Almighty that the wall does not crumble and crush him, but that it remain standing.'

"And what do you think happened?" concluded the *chassid* triumphantly. "No sooner had the *rebbeh* uttered his pronouncement that the wall remained standing and the sinner escaped unharmed!"

✓ ✓ ✓

Two boys, Abie and Patrick, were having an argument about the respective merits of their spiritual leaders. Abie contended that his rabbi was the smartest man in the community while Patrick insisted that his priest was among the cleverest men in the entire country.

Soon the boys began to compare notes, each explaining the intellectual and social qualifications of his favorite. The Jewish boy, having a far greater knowledge of his rabbi's achievements than the Catholic lad did of his priest's, quickly won the argument. "Now, do you believe my rabbi is smarter than your priest?" exulted the Jewish boy.

"No, I don't," snapped Patrick. "It's no wonder your rabbi knows so much—you tell him everything!"

✓ ✓ ✓

During the days of Sabbatai Kohen, the great rabbi of the 17th century, the Jewish community of Vilna was looking for a *Stadt-hazan*, and Rabbi Moses Rivkes was considered as a candidate for this post of honor. Some of the community leaders, however, objected to Rabbi Rivkes because his voice did not measure up to the standards of former cantors of Vilna. So the case was referred to Rabbi Sabbatai Kohen who said that although he was aware of Rabbi Rivkes' deficiency as a singer he was still in favor of electing him *Stadt-hazan*. He was asked the reason.

"When you read the Jewish Code of Laws," explained Rabbi Kohen, "you will notice that the following are the requirements of a good cantor: He must be married, learned in the Law, God-fearing, of good reputation, and the possessor of a good voice. Rabbi Rivkes has the first four qualities in a satisfactory degree. It is true that his voice is horrible—but I ask you—is any man perfect?"

✓ ✓ ✓

The exuberant lady pushed herself through the crowd after services and shook the hand of Dr. Stephen S. Wise. "Doctor," she said animatedly, "after hearing you talk so often and so enthusiastically about Palestine I made it my business to see the country for myself. I have just returned from Palestine and I tell you it's a wonderful place. I was particularly impressed with Lake Tiberias and the Sea of Galilee. They are simply gorgeous."

"Madam," answered Dr. Wise, suppressing a smile, "the two happen to be synonymous."

"That may be," stammered the lady, taken aback, "but to me it seemed that the Sea of Galilee is much more synonymous than Lake Tiberias!"

✓   ✓   ✓

A rabbi was invited to speak to the patients at St. Elizabeth Hospital, an institution in Washington, D.C. for the mentally disturbed. He came prepared for any reaction that might ensue, so he was scarcely surprised when the chief psychiatrist warned him to disregard any comments the inmates might offer during his address.

After the rabbi had talked for about half an hour a member of his audience stood up in the center aisle and, in a loud voice, declared, "My God, this is awful! I never heard such a lousy speech in my life!"

The rabbi carefully ignored the interruption. When he was through, the psychiatrist ran up to him and warmly shook his hand.

"Rabbi," enthused the doctor, "you have no idea how much you've helped that poor man. Why, that was the first rational statement he has uttered in three years!"

✓   ✓   ✓

Before the service was over the president of the congregation decided to take the worshippers to task for their indifference.

"You refuse to pay your membership dues to the congregation," he scolded, "but when it comes to our cemetery you all want the pleasure of being buried there."

✓   ✓   ✓

"Rabbi," said the president of the congregation, "I was sorry to hear that you are planning to resign for another pulpit."

"You need have no fears," said the rabbi. "I am going to recommend a successor who will probably be a better man than I."

"That's precisely what worries me," replied the president. "Your predecessor told us the same thing."

✓   ✓   ✓

The call to a larger pulpit that came to a middle-aged rabbi in poor circumstances upset him completely. The salary offered by the new congregation was unusually attractive, and the *rebbetzn*, understandably, was anxious that he accept at once. Yet, he could not decide whether or not it would be wise to give up his present post. After all, he had been with his congregation for many years and he disliked the idea of leaving his many friends and familiar surroundings. Despite his wife's entreaties he continued to weigh the advantages and disadvantages.

Finally a trustee of the new congregation visited the rabbi's house to learn his decision. He was met at the door by the holy man's son.

"Has the rabbi made up his mind?" he asked the teenage youth.

"I really don't know," replied the son. "Papa is upstairs praying, but Mama is downstairs packing."

*   *   *

A well-to-do American Jew who had spent many years in a small town, moved to the city and was made chairman of the ritual committee of a large synagogue. Before the High Holy Days it was his duty to engage a cantor. When the transaction was completed, the cantor inquired, "How about a *shofar*?"

"Look, mister, you may be a great cantor but don't put on any airs with me," snapped the new chairman. "If I, a rich man, can drive my own car, then so can you—and without a *chauffeur*!"

Chapter Eleven

Religion

Religious controversy is the sauce and spice that adds zest to Jewish spiritual life. Sometimes, where no difference of opinion exists, it is manufactured. The story of what befell Robinson Krotzmeir when he was cast up on a desert isle is a *poopik*-tickling example.

The story began during the Hitler regime. The minions of the Third Reich were just about to nab Krotzmeir for deportation to a terminal camp, when he managed to escape through a back door and make his way to Rotterdam. There he stole a rowboat from the local *gauleiter* and headed out to open sea, hoping somehow to reach England and eventual safety.

But Robinson Krotzmeir was a landlubber of the classic order. He had never even seen an ocean, let alone embark on a long and perilous voyage without the slightest knowledge of navigation. But when a Jew is being pursued by the Gestapo, such minor details are ignored.

On the very first day he lost his oars and on the second a storm arose and blew him off course; in the direction opposite to the one he desired. Two weeks later, when his water and food had long since been consumed, he was cast up on a tropic isle—a lush, green little jewel somewhere off the coast of equatorial Africa, and far removed from the customary shipping routes.

Now Krotzmeir was an ingenious fellow. First he built a sturdy house as shelter from the drenching tropical rains. From vines he made fishing nets. In the interior he found an abundance of fruit, herbs and vegetables. In the hills there were wild goats which he soon domesticated, and which provided him with meat, milk, cheese, butter and skins for clothing. He even found a variety of partridge, closely akin to the ordinary barnyard chicken. Before long, Krotzmeir was living a baronial, if lonely, existence.

Let it be said here that Robinson Krotzmeir always walked in the ways of the Lord. Now that he was settled, he built a house of worship. For many years he lived the good life, knowing nothing, of course, about the outcome of the war or the fate of his fellow Jews.

One day, as he was casting his fishing nets into the sea, what did he behold but a ship on the horizon. And to his utter astonishment, as it hove in closer, he could see that the vessel flew an unmistakably Jewish flag! Quickly he lit a huge bonfire as a signal. The ship's officers lowered a lifeboat and rowed towards Krotzmeir's island. In the boat were the captain and a few members of his crew.

"I am Captain Ben-Halevi of the Israel Navy," the officer introduced himself.

Krotzmeir was thunderstruck. Israel? A navy? Jewish officers? He knew nothing of the new Jewish homeland, and his joy knew no bounds.

Nor could the captain contain his own curiosity. "How have you managed to survive all these years on this island?" he asked.

"By following the precepts and traditions of our people—that and hard work. Let me show you around the island," he said pridefully.

The captain was then escorted to the castaway's trim house, the vegetable gardens, the fruit orchards, poultry yard and goat stables.

"Amazing!" breathed the overwhelmed captain.

"Ah, but that isn't all! Just follow me."

At the end of a tree-lined lane, there stood two synagogues, one on either side of the road. Krotzmeir pointed to the structure on the left, on which he had painted a *Mogen David*.

"Here is where I attend services every *Shabbes* and all the Jewish holidays. It is my solace, my comfort and my source of inspiration."

"Remarkable! Truly magnificent!" exclaimed the captain. "And that other synagogue across the road—how often do you go there?"

Krotzmeir's face darkened. He jerked a contemptuous thumb in the direction of the other structure.

"That's a Reform Temple," he spat. "I wouldn't be caught dead in there!"

✓ ✓ ✓

A barrel-maker of Kiev who had a wry sense of humor did not believe in imposing on the Lord.

"Dear God," he prayed, "all I'm asking from You is bread to eat and clothes to wear. Nothing more. The *schnapps* I'll buy myself!"

✓ ✓ ✓

"Why is it," asked a priest of a rabbi, "that your funerals are so gloomy, while there are flags, statues and flowers in ours?"

"I really don't know," admitted the rabbi. "You are quite correct when you say our funerals are mournful and yours are cheerful. Perhaps," he concluded reflectively, "that is why I prefer to witness one of your funerals instead of one of ours!"

✓ ✓ ✓

Yankel was in dire need of money. His creditors were pressing him, his wife constantly harangued him for household expenses, and the children pestered him every day for school needs. In desperation he went to the synagogue.

"Oh Lord," he prayed, "give me $10,000! I promise You with my hand on the Torah, if You'll just give me the money I'll give half to charity."

He waited for a moment or two, and when there was no response from above, he added, "Look, Lord, if You don't believe that I intend to give half to charity, then You divide it Yourself. Give me my $5,000 now and the other $5,000 You can give to the poor Yourself. I trust You!"

✦ ✦ ✦

Reb Nathan Buchsbaum married off the last of his seven daughters, and by way of celebrating the momentous occasion, he invited a few friends in for some brandy. Between drinks, he asked his guests to participate in chanting a verse from the New Year's liturgy which says, "Man comes from dust and returns unto dust."

"Look, Reb Nathan," protested one of visitors, "after all, this is a party. Can't you think of a happier verse than that?"

"No, I can't," answered the host. "Dust to dust is the happiest verse in the Bible. Now if we came from gold and returned to dust we would really have something to complain about!"

✦ ✦ ✦

A poverty-stricken Jew in a remote Russian village, decided that the only way he could survive would be to petition God for help. Naively, the innocent man sat down and wrote a short letter:

"Dear God:

Unless You send me a few rubles I shall starve to death. All my life I have observed the Law, and now I appeal to You for help."

The post office was at the other end of the village, but the pious man simply tossed the letter into the wind, confident that it would be blown to Heaven.

A passerby found the note, read the pathetic lines and turned it over to the postmaster. He, in turn, delivered it to the Governor who was equally touched by the writer's simple faith.

The Governor, in his compassion, sent fifty rubles to the postmaster, with instructions that he was to deliver the money to the poor man. The postmaster complied at once.

A few days later another letter was brought to the postmaster by a passerby who had found it blowing in a field. It read:

"Dear God:

I thank You for the fifty rubles, but You must never send money through the office of the postmaster or Governor. Those dirty crooks probably kept half of what You sent!"

✦ ✦ ✦

Columnist David Schwartz, a perceptive student of human nature, made the following observations in *The California Jewish Voice*:

The most widely used word among Jews is "peace," *shalom.*

Isaiah foresaw the time when the sword would be turned into a ploughshare, the lion lie down with the lamb.

There is the story of the Jew who was in Moscow and, visiting the zoo, saw a lion and a lamb in the same cage.

"Wonderful!" thought the Jew. "The dream of Isaiah is realized."

He approached the keeper and voiced his approval. "This is indeed a testimony to religion," he said. "Tell me, my friend, how is it that you can fly in the face of earthly convention by making the lion lie down with the lamb?"

"Nothing to it!" replied the keeper. "Every morning, we simply put another lamb in the lion's cage!"

✓ ✓ ✓

And still another from the pen of David Schwartz, who tells of the man who opened one of the Gideon Bibles in a hotel room.

On the front page he read this inscription:

"If sick, read Psalm 18. If troubled about your family, read Psalm 45. If you are lonely, read Psalm 92."

He was lonely, so he opened to Psalm 92 and read it. When through, he noticed on the bottom of the page, the handwritten words, "If you are still lonely, call Hollywood 5-0394, and ask for Ida."

✓ ✓ ✓

Barney Wasserman, owner of the Gotham Paper and Twine Company, was hurrying home after a hard day's work when it began to rain. In a few minutes the rain turned into a deluge. Soaked to the skin, Barney looked for a place to hide, but the only open door he could perceive was at an old-fashioned revivalist hall with a huge sign proclaiming: "Enter And Be Saved."

So Barney entered.

Inside, the evangelist exhorted the congregation to "Come To Jesus!" Barney listened respectfully, rather admiring the preacher's sincerity and eloquence. At the end of his sermon, the minister announced, "All those who wish to enter the Kingdom of Heaven, please stand!"

Everyone arose except Barney.

"You, the brother in the last row," shouted the evangelist, "don't you want to enter the gates of Paradise?"

"Yes," Barney shouted back, "but what's the hurry?"

✓ ✓ ✓

Father Flanagan, of St. Thomas Aquinas, and Rabbi Metzger, of Beth El Congregation, both of the Bronx, were engaged in a technical discussion.

Said the priest: "I have noticed, Rabbi, that the Jews consider the time after sundown as belonging to the next day, which makes your holidays begin at sunset on the previous evening."

"That is so," agreed Rabbi Metzger.

"Then why is it that Purim is different from all your other holidays? You celebrate Purim with a feast on the *following* evening!"

"You might call it a matter of overlapping religious institutions, my friend," the rabbi grinned. "You Christians regard your holidays as beginning in the evening of the same day—exactly the opposite of our own practice. But your question about Purim prompts me to ask this question: "Why do you gentiles celebrate Christmas on the eve of the approaching day as we do our own holidays?"

"Hmmm," the priest muttered. "That is a good question!"

"Let me answer it myself," said the rabbi, still smiling. "We Jews are thankful to a *goy* named Haman for the festival of Purim, so we celebrate it according to the gentile fashion. On the other hand, you gentiles owe your Christmas to a Jew, so you observe it in the Jewish manner."

✓   ✓   ✓

A wealthy landowner burst into his home one day and, in a voice filled with despair, cried to his startled wife, "Marushka, there is a terrible rumor in town—the Messiah is coming!"

"So what's terrible?" asked the wife. "I think it's wonderful! Why are you frightened?"

"I have good reason to be afraid," he whimpered. "We have a fine dairy herd, a barn full of grain, and our orchards are laden with fruit. Now we will have to give up everything and follow Him."

"Compose yourself," said the wife soothingly. "The Lord our God is good. He knows how much suffering we Jews have had to endure. We had a Pharaoh, a Haman—always somebody; but our dear Lord got rid of them all. Just have faith, my dear husband. He will get rid of the Messiah also!"

✓   ✓   ✓

Among the best known, most oft-told of "Anglo-Saxon" Jewish vignettes is the following dialogue between priest and rabbi. The earliest published version which this editor was able to unearth appeared in a poorly-printed anonymous booklet dated London, 1891.

A rabbi and a priest were discussing the material advantages of their respective ministries.

"The trouble with being a rabbi is that you are in a rut," the priest said. "From the day you are ordained to the day you die there is no hope for promotion."

"And a priest . . . ?" queried the rabbi.

"Come now, Rabbi; you know better than to say that! I can become a bishop."

"So you're a bishop. So what?"

"Why, an effective bishop could be promoted to cardinal. What do you think of that?"

"So you become a cardinal. So what?"

"My dear Rabbi, a cardinal, as you should know, could become a Pope."

"So you become a Pope. So what?"

"Good heavens," the priest cried out in exasperation, "what do you expect a man to become—God?"

"Why not?" answered the rabbi calmly. "One of our boys made it!"

↑   ↑   ↑

Synagogues do not take up collections—"passing the plate"—as do Christian churches. Among the various means of raising funds is the sale of seats for the High Holy Days.

On one such holiday, Kaplan the milliner rushed to the synagogue in Los Angeles but was refused admittance by the guard because he had no ticket.

"Look, Mister, my partner is inside and I must see him immediately. It's very urgent!"

"No tickee, no admishee," said the guard, grinning at his own little pun.

"But you don't seem to understand," Kaplan persisted, "It's strictly business. We'll lose the shop if I don't see him at once. Please, I'm begging you like a gentleman, let me in for just two minutes!"

"Well, if it's just business then go on inside," said the guard grudgingly. "But remember, don't let me catch you praying!"

↑   ↑   ↑

A Conservative and an Orthodox Jew were discussing the Bible.

"Did you ever stop to think of the inconsistency of Genesis?" asked the Conservative Jew.

"There are no inconsistencies anywhere in the Bible!" said his Orthodox friend flatly. "Give me an example."

"Look at it this way: If God is omnipotent he could have created Eve with a wave of His pinkie, yes?"

"I suppose so. What about it?"

"Then why did He go to all the trouble of robbing Adam of his rib?"

"That's not an inconsistency," replied the Orthodox Jew tartly. "God was merely demonstrating the very significant lesson that nothing good can ever come out of anything stolen!"

↑   ↑   ↑

Jascha Heifitz, the revered violinist, was about to appear on stage and the auditorium was packed to capacity. Suddenly a little man with unmistakably Jewish features rose from his seat.

"Is there a Christian Scientist in the house?" he yelled, shattering the hushed quiet.

RELIGION

Every neck in the theatre was craned to see who it was that was shouting. Angry murmurs and cries of "throw him out" were heard.

In a few moments, however, an elderly lady approached the little man. "Pardon me, sir, but are you the one who caused all the disturbance?"

"Yes, Madam."

"I am a Christian Scientist. What can I do for you?"

"Do you believe that there is no physical reason for sickness? That it is only a question of mind over matter?"

"Yes, of course!"

"Then would you mind changing seats with me?" asked the man. "I'm sitting in a draft!"

✓   ✓   ✓

"*Oy,* if God would only help me until He helps me!"

✓   ✓   ✓

An Israeli army pilot was returning from a sortie over enemy Arab territory. Both wings were in tatters from anti-aircraft bullets, one of his engines had been blown off and the other was on fire. The controls were barely working and now the sounds of explosions could be heard in the vicinity of his gas tanks. The pilot picked up the radio-phone, called the tower at Tel Aviv Air Base, and reported the condition of his plane. He ended with, "Await further orders."

There was a long silence at the other end, and then the voice from the airbase intoned, "Repeat after me . . . 'I believe with perfect faith in the coming of the Messiah' . . .!"*

✓   ✓   ✓

A rabbi and a minister were discussing what it must be like in heaven. "One thing is certain," commented the minister, "we will have a good rest up there. No buying or selling is conducted in heaven."

"Of course not!" agreed the rabbi. "That is not where business has gone."

✓   ✓   ✓

Student: "Rabbi, why did God make man before woman?"
Rabbi: "Because He didn't want any advice on how to make man!"

✓   ✓   ✓

Mrs. Baumgarten was having tea with the *rebbetzn.* "Did you notice Mrs. Vogel's hair at Friday evening's services?" she asked the rabbi's wife. "I could swear she had it dyed."

"I really didn't notice," said the *rebbetzn.*

---

* The Hebrew prayer for the dying.

107

"And the nerve of that Mrs. Silvers coming to temple with a strange man. Her poor husband hasn't even been dead a year!"

"Frankly, Mrs. Baumgarten, I didn't notice that either."

"Well, did you notice that Sarah Bender? I swear, just because a girl is in college, does that mean she should wear a dress to synagogue with the hem above her knees? What did you think of that?"

"I'm afraid I didn't see that either."

"Oh, for heaven's sake!" snapped Mrs. Baumgarten. "What good does it do you to be a rabbi's wife?"

✓ ✓ ✓

An atheist and a rabbi were having an argument. The atheist maintained that if one lived an ethical, upright life he had no need of God. The rabbi asserted that these qualities were fine, but without spiritual values the real beauty of life could not be comprehended.

"I don't see where the recognition of beauty has anything to do with belief in God," protested the atheist.

"Let me illustrate," explained the holy man. "A believer, when he arises on a lovely spring day, goes to the window, breathes deeply and says, 'Good morning, God.' But when the atheist arises and goes to the window, he says, 'My God, what a morning!' "

✓ ✓ ✓

Berel: "It is a well-known fact that no pious Jew is permitted to walk about with his head uncovered, and yet how is it that in our Torah there is no commandment to this effect?"

Shmerel: "You are greatly mistaken, my friend. There are numerous places in the Torah where the sin of going hatless is pointed out to us. Take, for example, the passage in Genesis which tells us that 'Jacob went out from Beersheba and went towards Haran.' Now I ask you, Berel, can you possibly imagine a Jew like the patriarch Jacob walking all that distance in the hot sun without a hat?"

✓ ✓ ✓

Haikel: "Why is Jethro, the father-in-law of Moses, known in the Pentateuch under seven different names?"

Michael: "Figure it out for yourself. Jethro had seven daughters, right? Well, whenever he married one of them off the affair was so expensive he would be thrown into bankruptcy. To start back in business, each time he had to assume a new name. So there's your answer: Seven daughters, seven marriages; seven marriages, seven bankruptcies; seven bankruptcies, seven new businesses; seven new businesses, seven new names. It figures, yes?"

✓ ✓ ✓

Bienstock and Gold, two immigrant Jews, were sitting in an Orthodox synagogue discussing Reform Judaism.

108

"I have never been in a Reform temple," said Bienstock, "but I have been told that their worship is entirely different from ours. They have abolished prayer completely."

"I don't see how they can worship without prayers," reflected Gold. "Yet I have heard that on a holiday such as Yom Kippur, for example, Reform Jews spend most of the day at their Temple. What can they possibly do there all that time?"

The thought was so intriguing that Bienstock undertook to find out for himself, and on Yom Kippur he visited a Reform Temple. Considering it a breach of spiritual values, if not an outright sin to remain long, he left after a few minutes, completely puzzled by the silent prayers.

"Bienstock," said Gold when they met later, "what do they do there?"

"These Reform Jews have the most peculiar services you ever imagined," explained Bienstock. "Their cantor never opens his mouth and the congregation listens attentively."

✓   ✓   ✓

An immigrant Jew and a prominent cantor were passing the time of day in idle conversation. "Isn't it strange," remarked the old Jew, "that there are so many cantors in this country, yet American Jews are far from being religious?"

"Not so strange when you go back to the Torah," replied the cantor. "When God asked Moses to go and address Pharaoh he declined, stating that he was 'slow of speech and of a slow tongue.' But when he crossed the Red Sea we are told 'Then sang Moses.' Our immigrant Jews are only repeating the experience of our great Lawgiver: After crossing the Atlantic Ocean every one of them suddenly becomes a regular Caruso!"

✓   ✓   ✓

A gentile landlord called on his Jewish tenant to collect the rent which had not been paid for two months. He was told that the tenant was sick in bed and that he had not worked for six weeks. The landlord, an ardent Christian Scientist, stalked into the tenant's bedroom and began to censure him.

"You're not sick, you're just lazy," the landlord scolded. "Sickness is only an error of mortal mind, existing only in the imagination. A man can talk himself into anything."

"If that is so," replied the Jew, "then talk yourself into having received my rent!"

✓   ✓   ✓

The missionary, preaching to a small audience on New York's lower East Side, found business poor indeed. He talked himself hoarse in his effort to win souls for Christ, but the results were nil. Over and over again he warned his listeners that unless they stepped forward and accepted Jesus as their personal Saviour they were doomed to spend eternity in the hot place. Even this threat frightened no one. Finally the missionary descended from his platform to exhort listeners individually.

The first customer he approached was Sam Lachman, an immigrant Jew who had not been long in this country.

"Tell me, brother," said the missionary, "do you mean to say that you want to go to hell?"

"Vy not?" answered Lachman.

Chapter Twelve

The Sages of Chelm

A group of citizens in the town of Chelm were busily engaged in digging a foundation for the new synagogue, when a disturbing thought occurred to one of the laborers.

"What are we going to do with all this earth we're digging up?" he asked. "We certainly can't just leave it here where our Temple will be built."

There was a hubbub of excitement as the men rested on their spades and pondered the question. Suggestions were made and just as quickly rejected.

Suddenly one of the Chelmites smiled and held his hand up for silence. "I have the solution," he proclaimed. "We will make a deep pit, and into it we'll shovel all this earth we're digging up for the synagogue!"

A round of applause greeted this proposal until another Chelmite raised his voice in protest. "That won't work at all! What will we do with the earth from the pit?"

There was a stunned silence as the men tried to cope with this new problem, but the first Chelmite soon provided the answer.

"It is all very simple," he said. "We'll dig another pit, and into that one we'll shovel all the earth we're digging now, and all the earth we take out of the first pit. The only thing we must be careful about is to make the second pit twice as large as the first one."

There was no arguing with this example of Chelmic wisdom, and the workers returned to their digging.

✓   ✓   ✓

Everyone in Chelm was scandalized—a thief had broken into the synagogue and made off with the poorbox. The Council of Seven immediately convened and after some deliberation they arrived at a unanimous decision: A new poorbox would be installed, but suspended close to the ceiling so that no thief would ever be able to reach it.

But the moment the *shammes* heard about the decision he raised a new problem. "It is true that the box will be safe from thieves," he declared, "but it will also be out of reach of the charitable."

The Council of Seven held another hurried meeting, and once again the wisdom of Chelm prevailed. It was decreed that a stairway be built to the poorbox so that the charitable might easily reach it.

✓   ✓   ✓

The *maggid* of Chelm was returning home from a neighboring village where he had just preached a sermon. On the way he was overtaken by a farmer whose wagon was piled high with hay.

"May I offer you a ride?" asked the peasant courteously.

"Thank you," replied the *maggid*, climbing aboard the wagon. It was a warm, sunny day and soon the preacher fell fast asleep. But when he arrived in Chelm he could not find his notebook in which he kept his themes and parables.

"I must have lost it in the hay!" cried the *maggid*, greatly distressed. "Now some cow or goat or ass will eat it and become familiar with all my best sermons!"

The next evening, at the synagogue, he strode to the *bimah* and glared at the congregation.

"Fellow citizens of Chelm," he proclaimed, "I have lost my notebook in a load of fodder. I want you to know that if some dumb ox or ass ever comes to this town to preach, the sermon will be mine, not his!"

✓   ✓   ✓

The rabbi of Chelm entered the courtyard of the synagogue where he was to officiate at a wedding, and he immediately noticed that the young couple under the canopy was facing west.

"Surely," he protested, "you know that it is the custom among our people for the bride and groom to stand under the canopy facing *east*!"

The *shammes*, embarrassed at this oversight, rushed forward and turned the canopy around. But all noticed that the couple was still facing west. The Seven Elders of the Council of Chelm deliberated among themselves and then changed the position of the poles. But the couple still faced west.

A Galitzianer happened to be passing through the town and he took in the situation at a glance. Without a word he brushed the rabbi aside, muttered a few words of contempt to the *shammes*, and then turned the bride and groom around so that they faced east.

"I must say, that was a very clever trick," said the rabbi admiringly, even though he had just been jostled by the stranger.

"In Galicia, where I come from, we are all clever!"

"I can well believe it," said the rabbi. "Now I suggest that the people of Galicia learn some manners!"

✓   ✓   ✓

112

The rabbi was deeply worried. For weeks no one had come to him to judge a case and, being a poor man, he was desperately in need of the fees usually paid for his services.

One day, as he was standing at his window, wondering when he would get his next case, he saw Itzig the butcher and Shloime the baker in what appeared to be a sharp dispute. As they passed by they were waving their arms in emphatic gestures, and talking loudly and excitedly.

"Aha! A couple of litigants!" He threw open the window and called to them, "Let me adjudicate your dispute."

"Dispute? Who's having a dispute?" answered Itzig.

"We were just having a friendly discussion," agreed Shloime.

"Fine!" replied the quick-thinking rabbi. "Just step right into the house and, for a very small charge, I'll make out a certificate that you have nothing against each other!"

*　　　*　　　*

The *melamed* and the rabbi of Chelm were in a coffee house where they were discussing the economy of the town and how to improve it.

"There is one thing that depresses me," sighed the *melamed*, "and that is the injustice accorded to the poor. The rich, who have more money than they need, can buy on credit. But the poor, who haven't two coins to knock together, have to pay cash for everything. Do you call that fair?"

"I don't see how it could be any other way," answered the rabbi.

"But it's only common sense that it should be the other way around," insisted the *melamed*. "The rich, who have money, should pay cash and the poor should be able to buy on credit."

"I admire your idealistic nature," said the rabbi, "but a merchant who extends credit to the poor instead of the rich will soon become a poor man himself."

"So what?" retorted the *melamed*. "Then he'd be able to buy on credit, too!"

*　　　*　　　*

A fire broke out one night in the city of Chelm and all the inhabitants rushed to the fiercely burning building to extinguish the blaze. When the conflagration had been put out, the rabbi mounted a table and addressed the citizens:

"My friends, this fire was a miracle sent from heaven above."

There were murmurs of surprise in the crowd, and the rabbi hastened to explain.

"Look at it this way," he said. "If it were not for the bright flames, how would we have been able to see how to put the fire out on such a dark night?"

*　　　*　　　*

Tanchum the water carrier was a contented man. He had a good wife and he enjoyed his work.

Once, as he was filling his pails at the river's edge, he spied his wife on the bank, some distance downstream. As he watched, she placed the week's wash beside her and then extracted his drawers from the basket. As was necessary in the primitive laundering technique common to Chelm, she soaked the drawers in the water, then put them on a flat stone, and after that beat them with a stick. The process was repeated several times until the drawers were quite clean.

A wave of gratitude to the Almighty swept over Tanchum. He raised his eyes to the heavens.

"Blessed art thou, O Lord," he murmured. "I thank Thee for giving me the wisdom to get out of my drawers this morning—just in time!"

✔ ✔ ✔

Tanchum, the water carrier, was returning home one evening when a stranger rushed up to him and slapped his face.

"Take that, Meyer!" yelled the attacker.

Tanchum picked himself up from the street and stared at the man in amazement. Suddenly a broad grin spread over his face and then he laughed uproariously.

"Meyer, what are you laughing at?" exclaimed the other. "I just knocked you down."

"The joke is on you," chortled Tanchum. "I'm not Meyer!"

✔ ✔ ✔

The Council of Elders pondered a dilemma in penology. Suppose they caught a thief; what in the world would they do with him? There was no jail in the city, and the crime of stealing was hardly serious enough to merit exile from Chelm.

The seven elders discussed the problem at length but were making no progress until the rabbi came up with the solution: they would bore two holes in the wall of the bath house. The prisoner would be made to pass his hands through the holes and keep them there for as long as the judge decided was right and proper.

"That won't work," protested one council member. "Suppose he should simply withdraw his hands and walk away before he had served his full sentence?"

"That's no problem," answered the rabbi. "Once his hands are passed through the holes he will be ordered to make a fist, so he can't withdraw his hands without unclenching them!"

✔ ✔ ✔

The unique powers of reasoning among the Chelmites were not confined to the males. The ladies, too, possessed a superior mentality, as witness this account.

A traveler entered the city and dined at the local inn. When he finished his dinner he asked for the bill.

The woman who owned the little hostelry added up the costs:
"The chopped egg, bread and soup comes to seven *kopeks*," she said, itemizing everything very carefully. "For the fish is another seven *kopeks*. Altogether, eleven *kopeks*."

"But, Madam," corrected the honest stranger, "two times seven are fourteen!"

The woman silently added up the sum again and then shook her head. "No," she repeated, "two times seven are eleven!"

"How did you arrive at that figure?"

"Like this: I was a widow with four children. I married a widower who also had four children. Then we had three children of our own. Now he has seven children and I have seven children, and altogether we have eleven. Two times seven are eleven!"

The stranger, unable to find a flaw in this typical Chelmic logic, paid the account.

1   1   1

One Friday afternoon the first heavy snowfall of the year occurred in Chelm and the inhabitants rejoiced to see the lovely white blanket covering the rutted streets of their city.

But a sad note was struck by the rabbi. "The *shammes* will soon be passing through the town to call on the people to prepare for the *Shabbes*. He will leave ugly tracks in the beautiful snow when he walks on it."

At once, the seven elders of the City Council were called into session to solve the dilemma. The snow, they agreed, must be kept trackless, no matter what. But how to prevent the good *shammes* from tracking it up?

As might have been expected, the wise old rabbi again rose to the occasion. "I have it!" he cried triumphantly. He explained his idea to the Council and they agreed to the plan with shouts of joy.

When the *shammes* finally started on his rounds, he was made to stand on a table so that he might not make tracks in the pretty snow. And, in accordance with the rabbi's scheme, the table was carried through the town by the seven Council members!

1   1   1

Shloime, the young apprentice cobbler of Chelm, took as his bride a girl of his own age—eighteen. Imagine his surprise when, three months later, his new wife gave birth. Naive as he was about such matters, he was nevertheless astounded at this phenomenon, so he rushed to the rabbi's house for an explanation.

"Rabbi," he exclaimed, "you will find this difficult to believe, but my wife just gave birth to a baby."

"Wives usually do," commented the sage wryly.

"But we have only been married three months. My own mother, she should rest in peace, told me it takes nine months to make a baby. Believe me, I am terribly worried."

115

The rabbi stroked his beard and reflected upon this strange occurrence. When he had meditated long and earnestly he spoke to the young man, his voice unusually kind. "We will solve this mystery with talmudic logic, through the asking of questions. First, my son, you say you have been married for three months?"

"Yes, Rabbi."

"Your wife has lived with you for three months?"

"Yes, she has."

"And you have lived with your wife for three months?"

"Yes."

"There you have it, young man. Add up the total: three months plus three months plus three months. How much is that?"

"Nine months, Rabbi."

"Correct," said the rabbi gently. "Peace be with you and yours. Now go home to your wife and nine-month baby."

✓ ✓ ✓

The renowned Rabbi Eliahu of Chelm had amassed such learning and wisdom that his fame spread to the farthermost reaches of Poland. Wherever he preached, in the large city temples or the smaller village synagogues, he was accorded the most respectful and admiring welcome.

Now Rabbi Eliahu had a driver who, although he loved the scholar devotedly, also envied him his great popularity. One day, as he was at the reins, he turned to the revered teacher and voiced his inner feelings.

"Rabbi, please don't think me too impertinent, but I have a favor to ask of you. I realize only too well that I am an uneducated man—a nobody—but I too would like to be welcomed as you always are. Just for once I would like to know how it feels to have everyone look up to me and marvel at my wisdom."

The rabbi nodded sympathetically. "I can understand your feelings, my friend. But what is this favor you mentioned?"

"Suppose—just suppose—we were to change clothes. Then you would be the driver and I would be the famous Rabbi Eliahu of Chelm. Please, Rabbi, just for one day! Tonight you are supposed to speak before a council of our most learned scholars. I will do so and they will honor me instead."

Now the rabbi, scholar though he was, had never lost the common, earthy touch. He also had a keen sense of humor and the idea appealed to him, but he immediately detected the one flaw in the scheme that could only bring humiliation to the driver.

"I must point out to you," he said, "that just as the covers do not make a book, so the rabbi's clothes do not make a rabbi. You are not a scholar—you can scarcely write your own name—and you will be questioned by some of the most astute sages in all of Poland. You can't substitute *chutzpah* for talmudic learning."

116

"I'll think of something, Rabbi," the driver assured him. "Don't worry!"

So they exchanged clothes and soon they entered the city, Rabbi Eliahu guiding the horses and the driver sitting proudly beside him in the rabbinical garments.

As expected, huge throngs turned out to greet the honored guest. The "rabbi" thrilled to all the honors bestowed upon him. It was even more than he had hoped for. Meanwhile, hovering unobtrusively in the background, the vastly amused real rabbi watched with twinkling eyes.

Inside the synagogue, the imposter was given the seat of honor, a bowl of fresh fruit and a vase of flowers were placed before him, and the wise men of the city grouped themselves around the "rabbi."

"Learned Rabbi," one of the scholars asked, "would you be kind enough to explain this passage in the Law? It is very complicated and we simply cannot understand it."

The real rabbi tensed. "Now he's in trouble!" he thought. He held his breath, waiting for the driver to reveal his ignorance, yet feeling a wave of sympathy for the unlucky fellow.

But the driver calmly studied the sacred book placed before him, although he could not read a single word of the text. Then he spoke, his voice bitingly sarcastic:

"So you call yourself scholars? Is this the only question you could save to ask me when you know I can only visit you once a year? Why this passage is so simple even my driver could explain it to you."

With that, he called to Rabbi Eliahu, "Step over here, please, and explain the Law to these so-called scholars."

When the rabbi and the driver left the city the people marvelled anew, for not only was Rabbi Eliahu the most learned of sages, but even the humblest of Chelmic servants knew more than they about the sacred Law.

✔ ✔ ✔

Lemach ben Lekish, the wisest of Chelm philosophers, was having an earnest discussion with the *balegoleh*.

"I do not wish to sound sacrilegious," said Lekish, "but I believe I have discovered a major flaw in the order of creation."

"What kind of flaw?" asked the wagoner.

"It seems to me that it would have been better if women gave birth in the same manner as chickens."

"What! They should lay eggs?"

"Certainly! At least it would be better for the husbands. Suppose a man wants another child. So he tells his wife, '*Liebeh, hatch the egg!*' But if he has all the sons and daughters he wants, all he need do is say, '*Liebeh,* make me an omelette!'"

✔ ✔ ✔

Lemach ben Lekish, the dean of Chelm philosophers, failed to appear at the synagogue for the *Shabbes* services, and the rabbi, deeply worried about his friend, called at his home to see what was the matter. The philosopher's wife greeted him with a lament. Lekish, she explained, was ill. He would not speak a word but lay silently in his bed, a peculiar expression on his face. The rabbi immediately entered the bedroom.

"Lekish, I implore you, speak to me," he said earnestly. "Whatever thoughts may be tormenting you, it is better that you let them out rather than permit them to fester inside."

"Yes, Rabbi, there is a thought that is tearing me apart," said Lekish after a prolonged silence.

"Tell it to me."

"Well, suppose that every living human being became one gigantic man. And further suppose that all the trees on earth became one tree, and all the axes in the world became one axe. Now suppose that man took that axe and chopped down that tree and it fell into the ocean . . ."

"Yes—yes! Go on! Don't stop!"

". . . Can you imagine," whispered Lekish hoarsely, "what a splash that would make?"

✓ ✓ ✓

Herschel the water carrier had a son who would soon be Bar Mitzvah, so he went to the eminent Rabbi Eliahu to ask an intimate question.

"Tell me, Rabbi, how shall I introduce my son to the mysteries of reproduction? He will soon reach the age of spiritual manhood and it is time he learned about the birds and the bees."

"First of all," replied Rabbi Eliahu, "you must forget about the birds and the bees. It is a myth that has no reality in fact."

"How can you say that?"

"Because I proved it to my own satisfaction. I put a bird and a bee together in a cage, and although I watched them constantly for three days, I assure you, dear Herschel, nothing happened!"

✓ ✓ ✓

The whole town was assembled in the synagogue one Purim, but although it was now quite late the rabbi had not yet appeared. After awhile the townspeople grew nervous and a delegation went to his home to see if perhaps he had suddenly taken ill. The *rebbetzn*, however, said that he had left the house hours earlier.

Deeply concerned, the good people of Chelm went out to look for him; in the woods, in caves, in ditches, in wells—but no rabbi! Finally a boy came running to the searchers with gruesome news. He had found a headless corpse.

Now the townspeople were confronted with a problem. "How can we be sure that the body is that of our beloved rabbi?" they asked.

The populace grew even more disturbed when the president of the

Council of Seven spoke his thoughts: "It may be his body after all. Who can be certain that the rabbi had a head in the first place?"

To find out, they called the *shammes.*

"Did the rabbi have a head?" they demanded.

"Well, I know the rabbi had a beard because I saw him combing it," observed the *shammes* after pondering the question for some time. "But as to whether or not he had a head, I am not sure."

The Chelmites then thought of the keeper of the bath-house. "He should know," they chorused. "We'll ask him."

But the bath-house keeper was anything but helpful. "I know he had ears because they protruded out over his *yarmulkeh,*" he said slowly. "But as to a head, this I canot definitely say."

"There is only one person in all the world who can answer this question," they cried, "and that is the rabbi's wife."

So a delegation went to see the *rebbetzn.*

"Did the rabbi have a head?" they asked.

The woman remained silent for a long time as she tried her best to remember.

"This much I know," she announced finally. "The rabbi had a nose because he often said he liked the smell of my cooking. But to be honest with you, I really don't know if he had a head or not."

Now all this happened over a hundred years ago, and we are sorry we brought it up in the first place because, to this very day, the people of Chelm are still arguing about it.

𝟷   𝟷   𝟷   𝟷   𝟷

There are countless wise rabbis in the world, but none was as wise as the rabbi of Chelm, as this incident proves:

A farmer purchased a horse from a dealer but on the very next day he came to the rabbi with a complaint.

"I was swindled," he charged. "I paid out good money for that horse, but when I put it in the stable and gave it some hay to eat, it bit the wooden manger instead and broke its teeth. The seller should have told me the animal was that stupid. Do you call that an honest sale?"

The rabbi summoned the horse dealer to hear his side of the story.

"Believe me, in all the time I have had that horse he never bit the manger—not even once! Am I to blame for the farmer's hard luck?" complained the dealer.

The rabbi stroked his beard reflectively. "This dispute is indeed complicated," he said. "Come back this evening when I will have given it the deep thought it requires. At that time I will render my decision."

They returned that evening and the rabbi spoke to the farmer.

"I am sorry, but after due and deliberate consideration I find that I must rule against you. The Law simply isn't on your side. After all, who

119

forced you to put the manger near the horse's mouth? If you had kept your wits about you, you would have put it near his tail!"

✓ ✓ ✓

For months the people of Chelm were beset by worries. They worried about finances; they worried about health; they worried about politics— worry, worry, worry! To alleviate this alarming situation, the Council of Seven called a meeting of all the townsfolk.

A motion was made and duly seconded that Saul, the town *shikker*, be retained to do all the worrying for Chelm. As recompense, he was to be paid one ruble per week.

A wave of rejoicing greeted this wise solution to the problem, when the patriarch of the Council asked a question that silenced the throng. "If the *shikker* is given a ruble every week," he demanded, "tell me, what will he have to worry about?"

✓ ✓ ✓

A butcher came to the synagogue with a ritual question about a cow he intended to slaughter. The *shammes* admitted him. "What can I do for you?" asked the sexton.

"I must see the rabbi about something important," explained the butcher. "Is he here?"

"The rabbi is studying right now."

"Studying!" cried the butcher. "Is Chelm so poor it can't afford a graduate rabbi instead of a mere student?"

✓ ✓ ✓

The *melamed* of Chelm was speaking with his wife.

"If I were Rothschild, I'd be richer than he."

"How can that be?" asked the wife. "You would both have the same amount of money."

"True," he agreed, "but I'd do a little teaching on the side."

✓ ✓ ✓

He was a poor barrel-maker from Chelm and knew nothing of opulence and grandeur. After a particularly vicious pogrom he set out for more favorable climes and finally, after many months of walking, he arrived in Germany. There, in the Jewish cemetery at Frankfort-am-Main, he saw the magnificent grave of Amshel Rothschild, founder of the international banking clan.

"Now that's what I call living!" he breathed ecstatically.

✓ ✓ ✓

Leo returned home from the County Fair and his friend asked him if he had enjoyed the visiting carnival.

"I didn't like it at all," he spat. "The Fair should never have been permitted to come to Chelm. One of the guards spoke rudely to me and said they did not particularly welcome Jews."

"Why, that's terrible!" said the other. "What did you do?"

"I got my revenge," said Leo, grinning spitefully. "I bought a ticket but I didn't go in!"

✓ ✓ ✓

Two Chelmites were in the local coffee house discussing higher mathematics.

Said one: "It takes four hours to drive to the city with one horse, right?"

"Right!" agreed the other.

"So if I drove with two horses, doesn't it follow that I would cut the time in half—that it would only take two hours?"

"Like night follows day. It's logical."

"All right. So with the same reasoning, if it takes four hours with one horse and two hours with two horses, doesn't it stand to reason that with four horses I'd make the trip in no time at all—instantaneously, you might say?"

The other man scratched his head. "I don't understand something," he said, bewildered. "If it takes no time at all, why not just harness the horses and stay right here instead of making such a long trip?"

✓ ✓ ✓

The people of Chelm are still talking about the dispute that raged between Zvi the driver and Avrum the merchant. It seems that Avrum hired Zvi to bring back a consignment of glassware from a warehouse on the other side of town. But, because the roads were icy, and snow covered the ruts and holes in the road, Zvi's wagon skidded, swayed and slipped, breaking several expensive items of glassware in the process. The merchant contended that the driver was to blame and should therefore pay for the damage, but the driver adamantly refused, on the grounds that he could not be held responsible for the weather.

So Avrum the merchant hauled Zvi the driver up before the rabbi for adjudication of the argument.

The rabbi listened attentively to both parties and then ruled in favor of the merchant.

"Rabbi," asked Zvi, "on what do you base your decision?"

"On the Torah, of course," the rabbi answered.

"And when would you say the Torah was written?"

"When the Jews were released from bondage to the Egyptians. Moses went up . . ."

"No, I don't mean that," interrupted the driver. "I mean what time of the year was it written?"

"Now let me see," pondered the rabbi, "That would be on *Shevuos*— in the summertime."

"Exactly!" cried Zvi triumphantly. "The Torah was written in the summer when there is no ice or snow and the roads are not slippery. And that is why the Torah stipulates that I must pay the damage. If it had been written in the winter, Avrum the merchant would be required to pay."

The rabbi turned this new argument over in his mind. At last his face lit up. "The word of the Torah cannot be changed," he ruled. "You will have to pay. But hereafter, as a Jew who meets his responsibilities, you are ordered to break Zvi's glassware only in the summertime!"

✓ ✓ ✓

"Which is more important, the sun or the moon?" a citizen of Chelm asked the rabbi.

"What a silly question!" snapped the cleric. "The moon, of course! It shines at night when we really need it. But who needs the sun to shine when it is already broad daylight?"*

✓ ✓ ✓

There are many kinds of status symbols in the world. In America it may be a fancy new car, a pastel mink stole, or maybe a swimming pool. In India it is a white elephant or a sacred cow. In England it is a whole side of beef in the freezer. Not so in Chelm.

Two Chelmites were taking a walk, one carrying with him his status symbol—an umbrella. Suddenly it started to rain.

"Quick, open your umbrella!" cried the man who had none.

"It's no use," answered the other. "My umbrella is full of holes."

"Then what in the world did you take it for in the first place?"

The answer was perfectly logical—for a Chelmite: "I didn't think it would rain!"

✓ ✓ ✓

A Chelmite was drowning and set up a desperate hullabaloo: "Help! Help! I'm going under!"

A passerby on the shore heard the drowning man's shouts.

"Why are you making such a to-do?" he yelled back. "If you can't swim, can't you at least get out and learn how?"

✓ ✓ ✓

---

*Like many other witticisms in Jewish folklore, this joke was attributed to Chelm in the course of generations of story-telling. This editor's father, a serious researcher into ancient Hebraic tales, traced it back to the second or third centuries, C.E. Genesis tells us that the sun was created on the fourth day, but on the first day God separated light from darkness. This gave rise to the belief, especially among Christians, that the "light of day" had no relationship to the sun, which merely illuminated natural daylight.

In the fourth century, St. Ambrose wrote, "The light of day is one thing, but the light of the sun is another, adding luster to the daylight." The Jews could be condemned to torture or death on the Inquisitorial racks for disputing this silly assertion, hence a body of jokes on the subject. The above anecdote, only one of several, is a very early mockery of the inchoate Christian dogma.

THE SAGES OF CHELM

The sage of Chelm came home from the public baths without his shirt. "Where is your shirt?" demanded his shrewish wife. "How many times must I tell you to watch your belongings?"

"Well, it was like this," explained the sage; "someone else at the baths mistook my shirt for his so he took mine by mistake."

"*Nu*, then where is the other man's shirt?"

"He must have forgotten to leave his."

✓ ✓ ✓

Reb Yankel returned to Chelm after a two-day visit to the big city where he purchased goods for his little store.

"Believe me, Rivka, it is good to be back among the poor people," he said to his wife. "Whenever I travel among the rich I cannot help but notice that they are all selfish, greedy and dishonest, while the poor are very decent."

"You are quite right," agreed Rivka. "But tell me, did something happen in the city to remind you?"

"Yes," answered Yankel. "After running all day long from one business house to another, I discovered that my walking stick was missing. I knew I had forgotten it at one of those rich places but I couldn't remember which one. So early the next day I set out to look for it. I entered the first place and the millionaire owner denied ever having seen my stick. The rich owner of the second place also denied that I had left it there. All day long I re-visited every one of the rich places I had been and every one of the owners denied it. Finally, at night, I went into a very poor little restaurant where I had eaten the evening before and without a word the man handed me my stick.

"And there, my dear Rivka, you have the difference between the rich and the poor!"

✓ ✓ ✓

Rabbi Greenspan was both revered by the people of Chelm and loved at home as well, for he was a gentle soul, full of understanding and compassion.

It was Rabbi Greenspan's custom to enjoy an onion roll with his Sabbath dinner, and throughout their marriage the *rebbetzn* never failed to have a supply of the rolls on hand for the weekend. One Friday evening, however, as he sat down to his dinner, the good rabbi noticed that his onion rolls were missing. He asked his wife for an explanation.

"Something awful happened on my way home from the bakery," she said tearfully. "Some drunken soldiers grabbed me and stole all the dozen rolls."

The rabbi, kind man that he was, told her that he understood and that she was not to feel badly about something that was not her fault. He began to eat, when a sudden thought occurred to him.

"Look, as long as those soldiers were so busy stealing the rolls," he gently admonished his wife, "couldn't you have stolen at least one for your own husband?"

✦ ✦ ✦

The *melamed* of Chelm secured a teaching post in a neighboring town, but although the place was only a few miles distant, he visited his family only on Passover.

During one visit the rabbi asked him why he returned home only once a year. "After all," he pointed out, "you are near enough to see your wife at least once a week."

The *melamed* stared at him as though he had taken leave of his senses. "Rabbi, I come back once a year and each time my wife has a baby," he said. "Now you want me to come home every week. *Cholileh!* Do you realize what you're asking?"

✦ ✦ ✦

It was more than a week since Reb Yudel, the cobbler, had disappeared. Throughout the city grave speculation arose as to whether he had met with foul play or had simply abandoned his wife and hearth.

Reba, the wife, was especially concerned because, according to Jewish law, she was forbidden to remarry until Reb Yudel's death could be definitely confirmed. So, when a fisherman dragged a corpse ashore, she was as vitally concerned as anyone in the community. It was assumed that the remains were those of the missing cobbler, but to make certain, the rabbi summoned her so that she might offer proof that the body was indeed that of her husband, and consequently obtain her release so that she might marry again.

"Do you know of any distinguishing signs that will help establish his identity?" asked the rabbi.

"Certainly," replied Rebba. "After living with him for fifteen years who should know better than I? He was a stammerer and loved to sing old songs."

The rabbi smiled tolerantly. "Madam, such indications can hardly be accepted as evidence," he explained. "After all, he wasn't the only man in the world who stammered and sang old songs!"

✦ ✦ ✦

Simon the winemaker was deeply disturbed about a strange event that had occurred that morning, so he went to the wisest member of the Council of Seven for an explanation.

"It is an established fact that whenever a poor man such as I drops a slice of bread it always falls butter-side down," began Simon.

"Yes, that is true," agreed the Chelmic dignitary.

"Well, today I dropped my bread and it fell butter-side up!"

"What! Why, that's impossible!" exclaimed the Elder. "I never heard of such a thing!"

"But it happened!"

The old man considered the unusual occurrence for some time. At last he smiled as the simple truth dawned on him.

"Simon, go home and be at ease," he counseled. "You buttered your bread on the wrong side!"

✓   ✓   ✓

Two of the Seven Elders of Chelm were discoursing on the wonders of creation. It was a pleasant summer's day and the birds twittered above them while the cows grazed lazily in the meadow.

"The ways of the Lord are mysterious," said one philosophically. "Consider the birds and the cows. The bird is small and his needs are modest. Nevertheless he has been given wings and has access to the sky as well as the earth. The cow is big and her needs are much greater. What I can't understand is why the Lord, in His infinite wisdom, does not permit the cow to fly."

Just then a bird flew overhead and responded to the call of nature.

The embarrassed elder hastily wiped his sleeve with a handkerchief and muttered, "Now I know!"

✓   ✓   ✓

For twenty long years the wisest of the thinkers of Chelm had been absorbed in a philosophical question which no one had been able to satisfactorily answer: From which end does a man grow; from his head up or from his feet down?

One day the dean of the Council of Seven called a hurried meeting. "I have solved the problem," he announced.

"When I was a boy my father bought me a pair of pants. Now I recall quite vividly that the first time I put them on they dragged on the floor. But a few years later they were above my ankles. This led me to believe that a man grows from his feet down.

"That early recollection provided me with an answer—but an incorrect one," the sage continued. "In fact it was not until yesterday that the truth was revealed to me. You will recall that a company of soldiers marched through Chelm yesterday morning. Well, I examined them carefully and I noticed that their feet were all on a level, but some heads were higher than others, some lower. So we finally have our answer," he concluded as the Council members cheered madly; "A man grows from the head up, and not from the feet down."

✓   ✓   ✓

Reb Hirsch, owner of the Chelm tavern, decided to install a pool table in the dining area to attract more business. In the middle of the night, while the *landsleit* were asleep, the pool table was brought inside in sections and re-assembled. On the following day the huge table caused a sensation. "How did Hirsch get that immense piece of furniture through the small door?" was the overriding question. But Hirsch only smiled and refused to tell.

So the Chelmites sent for the oldest and wisest man of that city. The sage regarded the table for a long time, occasionally glancing at the small door and the even smaller windows, again returning his gaze to the large object before him.

At length he gave of his wisdom. "It is obvious that this table could not have been brought through this door, and that is where you have all made your error in judgment—you have been studying the problem from a mistaken premise."

"What premise, O learned one?" they asked.

"You have assumed that the tavern was built first and the table brought in afterward. Since that is plainly impossible, pure logic tells us that the table was brought in first and the tavern was built around it."

"But we have been in the tavern many times and no one ever saw this table before," one Chelmite reminded him.

"Are you going to believe the evidence of your own eyes as you see it today?" retorted the Elder, "or will you continue to refer to those silly optical illusions of yesterday?"

✓   ✓   ✓

Of all the grim events that befell the people of Chelm, none was so harrowing as the experience suffered by Reb Buchsberg and his wife—a drama that still lives in the annals of Chelmic literary history.

It happened on a sunny morning in June. Buchsberg's wife was preparing to go to market and was giving her husband explicit instructions before leaving:

"Whenever the baby wakes up you are to rock the cradle," she told him. "And be sure to watch the milk on the stove so that it doesn't boil over." She was halfway through the door when she remembered her husband's fondness for preserved fruit. "And don't touch that jar on the shelf," she warned. "It's rat poison!"

Now Reb Buchsberg was not only a Chelmite but a great intellectual as well. As soon as his shrewish wife was gone he contrived a plan that would permit him to carry out his wife's instructions and to study the Talmud at the same time. He tied one end of a length of cord to the cradle and the other end around his ankle. Then, seating himself beside the stove, he was able to rock the cradle and watch the milk at the same time, meanwhile reading the treasured book.

Suddenly, a chicken flew in through the window and overturned the pan of milk. Frantically, Buchsberg snatched at the pot in an effort to save it, but in leaping forward he gave the cradle a violent tug. The cradle turned over and the baby was thrown to the floor where it howled to the high heavens.

Reb Buchsberg was aghast at the havoc he had wrought. In his mind's eye, which was 20-20, he could just see his wife's reaction, and the vision was anything but pleasant. He knew that he could not possibly face her after this horrible fiasco. All was lost!

When the wife returned a half hour later, she found Reb Buchsberg stretched out on the bed, his face deathly pale. The baby still howled on the floor beside the overturned cradle. The pan of milk had splashed all over the stove and was now congealed.

Hot fury overcame her, and she cursed him through her angry tears. "*Shlemiel!* It's not bad enough you had to bring all this sorrow on my head, but do you have to lie there in bed?"

"Please," he moaned. "Have a little respect for my final hours!"

"*Wh-a-a-t!*"

"Yes, I'm waiting for the end. I just ate the poison in the fruit jar!"

✓ ✓ ✓

Two of the brightest scholars in all Chelm, if not the whole world, were discussing the difficulties involved in learning to spell the modern as well as the biblical words that were part of their studies.

"Let me ask you a question," said one.

"Ask!" replied the other.

"Who needs a *gimmel* in 'Noah'?"

"But there is no *gimmel* in 'Noah'."

"Tell me, why shouldn't there be a *gimmel* in 'Noah'?"

"But who needs a *gimmel* in 'Noah'?"

"Now just a minute," protested the first student. "That's the same question I asked you to begin with: 'Who needs a *gimmel* in Noah?' "

✓ ✓ ✓

Reuben Zalman, *chazan* of Chelm, was rehearsing a difficult passage for the following Sabbath's services when, to his annoyance, a group of laughing, shouting children stopped to play outside his window. He paused for a few minutes, hoping they would go away, but they had settled down to a Chelmic version of follow-the-leader.

In desperation, Zalman poked his head through the window and called out: "Listen to me, children. Go at once to the warehouse by the river. A horrible dragon is there. It rose out of the water with smoke and flames spouting from its tongue. It has scales like a fish, a thousand teeth and one big red eye in the middle of its forehead. Run quickly, *kinderlach*, or it will go back into the river before you can see it!"

Screeching and yelling, the children scampered toward the river to see the fearsome dragon. Cantor Zalman settled down for some serious rehearsing, but he was disturbed again—this time by a mob running toward the river.

"Where are you running?" he called out.

"Haven't you heard?" someone shouted back. "There's a dragon loose at the river. He has scales like a fish, flames leap from his tongue and he has an enormous red eye in his forehead! Hurry, or you'll miss it!"

The *chazan* grinned to himself, marveling at the power of a rumor, and went back to his work. Still, he thought, it is rather peculiar for so many people to believe in a dragon.

A few minutes later another great tumult interrupted his rehearsing. This time it was all seven of the Council of Elders, followed by their families and neighbors.

"Why are you all shouting and running so?" he cried out.

"Come see the dragon," yelled the dean of the Council. "He has scales like a fish, breathes fire and smoke and has a big red eye in the middle of his forehead!"

"No, it can't be!" muttered the cantor, returning to his studies. "Didn't I concoct that story in the first place? Still and all, why is it that so many respected people are running to the river! Is it possible . . . ? No, of course not!

But he had no sooner begun his rehearsals when another commotion drew him to the window. Again he saw a large number of people rushing pell-mell toward the river, but this time they were being led by the rabbi himself.

That did it!

Chazan Zalman grabbed his hat and rushed out into the street where he joined the running throng. "You never can tell!" he gasped.

�'s ✐ ✐

There are very few accounts of murder in Jewish humor. This type of violence has found but a small degree of acceptance among those tales designed to bring laughter to the House of David. Here is one of those infrequent anecdotes. It is attributed to Chelm, as are so many Jewish stories whose true origins have been lost in antiquity.

The town of Chelm was in an uproar. The townspeople had learned that Selig, the wine maker, had murdered a fellow Chelmite in a sudden burst of passion. The Council of Seven immediately convened to pass sentence and, as there was no question of the man's guilt, the injunction, "An eye for an eye and a tooth for a tooth," prevailed. The culprit was sentenced to death.

A murmur of approval swept through the onlookers at the trial, but the *shammes*, who had listened closely to every word, now raised his hand for permission to speak.

"I have heard the sentence and I consider it just," he began. "However, there are practical considerations which the learned Elders have not taken into account. For example, if you execute Selig then where will we obtain our wine? There is not another wine maker within forty miles of Chelm."

The patriarch of the Council nodded gravely, consulted with the six other members, and then addressed the townsfolk.

"It is true that Selig the wine maker is too valuable to our community to dispense with his services. However, justice must be done. Since we have two candle makers in Chelm where we need only one, it is decreed that one of them shall be executed instead."

✓ ✓ ✓

The *chazzan* of Chelm was about to marry off one of his daughters. Inasmuch as he was a poor man the congregation advanced him two hundred and fifty rubles, to be deducted from his salary during the next five years. The *chazzan*, however, was an honorable soul, and though he sorely needed the money he decided to unburden his secret thoughts to the congregation.

"Gentlemen," he began, "please understand that I am accepting your kind help on the following two conditions: Should I live five more years, that is your good fortune. However, should I die before the five years are up, that is my good luck!"

✓ ✓ ✓

Reb Leizer was a meek, kind-hearted Jew, living at peace with the world. But his wife's character was precisely the opposite. She was hot-tempered, malicious and uncharitable. Day in and day out she scolded her husband, berating him in the vilest language. Reb Leizer accepted his fate resignedly and seldom uttered a word.

One day she was in a particularly disagreeable mood, even for her, and swore at him unsparingly for hours on end. Toward evening, the woman's soliloquy took on a new, self-pitying turn.

"Oh, what a miserable fool, what a wretched, unfortunate cow I was to have tied myself to a *shlemiel* husband like you!" she wailed. "How could I be so stupid!"

Silently, Reb Leizer rose from his chair, walked over to the ranting woman and gave her a resounding slap in the face.

"Y-you hit me!" howled the astonished shrew.

"Yes," he cried, "and I'll do it again if you don't change your ways. I didn't mind so much when you reviled me, but when you insulted my wife that was a different story. I refuse to tolerate such impudence."

Chapter Thirteen

Fur, Fish and Fowl

Of all the eminent philosophers of Chelm, the only one who had never been confounded by a difficult question was the extraordinary thinker, Lemach. A group of students came to him one day, seeking to best him with their most puzzling riddles.

"Tell us, O great Lemach," said the spokesman, "why does a dog wag its tail?"

"You really should not bring me such simple questions," Lemach answered. "The dog is stronger than its tail. Otherwise the tail would wag the dog."

Another student asked, "Why does the hair on a man's head turn gray sooner than his beard?"

"It is because the hair on his head is twenty years older than his beard."

Again he was questioned: "Why is the sea salty?"

"Because," replied Lemach without hesitation, "so many salty herrings live in it."

Finally the students asked the one question which they were sure he could not answer. "All our lives," explained the spokesman, "we have noticed that whenever a dog passes water he holds up one leg. Pray tell us, why is this?"

"Surely you know the answer to that!" exclaimed Lemach. "It started thousands of years ago when a dog stopped at a tree to relieve his bladder. Suddenly a storm arose and a bolt of lightning felled the tree. The crashing trunk struck the little dog and killed it. Ever since then," concluded Lemach, "whenever a dog relieves himself he holds up the tree with one leg so it won't fall on him."

✓　　✓　　✓

Herman returned from morning worship at the synagogue to find his wife in tears.

"*Liebling*, what's the matter?" he asked.

"Somebody stole the five pounds of goose fat I prepared for *Pesach*," she cried.

"But that's impossible! There hasn't been anyone here but you and the cat." Herman looked at the cat with dawning suspicion. "There is no question about it. She ate it."

"I thought so too," said the wife as she dried her eyes on her apron, "but to make sure I put her on the scales and when I weighed her she came to exactly five pounds."

"Now we have a *real* mystery on our hands," said Herman thoughtfully. "We have discovered the five pounds of goose fat, but where do you suppose the cat went?"

✓ ✓ ✓

It was a bitter cold winter's day, a very long time ago when knighthood was in flower, as the saying goes. Sir Galahad, the pride of King Arthur's round table, set forth on a mission of derring-do.

The weather turned worse and soon the light snow grew to blizzard proportions. Galahad's horse, stumbling and exhausted, might have collapsed in another minute, but fortunately toward nightfall they came upon Shapiro's tavern. Grateful for this unexpected sanctuary, Sir Galahad rushed inside and warmed himself by the fire. His horse, poor creature, was bedded in the stable, safe at last from the howling elements.

"Mr. Shapiro," said the knight, "if you will provide me with another horse I will be on my way."

"What's the big rush in such rotten weather?" Shapiro wanted to know.

"I'm thinking of slaying a dragon," answered Sir Galahad. "I'll save you some of the meat."

"*Feh!* Dragon *flaish* my people don't eat! But no matter, a horse I haven't got for you anyway."

"But I'm a bold knight," protested Sir Galahad. "If you haven't a horse for me, how about that big St. Bernard lying there by the fire? A dog that size should be able to carry me easily."

"Sir Galahad," thundered Shapiro indignantly, "I wouldn't even consider sending a knight out on a dog like this!"

✓ ✓ ✓

Once upon a time, when the world was very young and the animals and birds could talk to one another, a pig saw a sparrow perched on an upper branch.

"Sparrow, drop to the ground," said the pig. "You need not be afraid. The Messiah has come: we will all now live like brothers and no one will eat another."

Suddenly there was the sound of furious barking.

"What is that?" quavered the pig, frightened. "You are high up in the tree. Look around and tell me what you see."

"I see a pack of hounds racing to this spot," said the sparrow. "They look ferocious and starving."

The pig at once took to his heels, squealing in terror.

"Why are you running away?" cried the bird. "You just said the Messiah has come—no creature will now eat another."

"Dogs don't believe in the Messiah," shouted the pig as he disappeared in the underbrush.

"Neither do pigs!" called the sparrow.

✓   ✓   ✓

A young talmudic student was working his way through a *yeshivah* as a part-time magician. He was very good, too. His feats of magic astounded even the veteran magicians on the Borscht Circuit.

Contributing to the scholar's success was Yoshke, a wise old parrot said to be a hundred and twenty years old. There were some who claimed that if it were not for the parrot's clever participation in the act the young man might have been a dismal failure.

But Yoshke had one very bad failing. Every time his master tried out a new trick before an audience, the parrot would shout out the answer; he'd give away the "secret" at once. The scholar could not get rid of his "assistant"—Yoshke was too valuable. So he tried newer tricks, but within a day or two the parrot would catch on to the secret and blurt it out to the audience. The student was desperate. It was apparent that unless he found a way to silence the big-mouthed bird he would soon be out of bookings.

Then one day, as his depression was at its lowest, and Yoshke had figured out his last trick, the young magician suddenly remembered his grandfather, Shmuel Baror, who lived in Tel Aviv. The old man was renowned as an authority on the Cabala, and reputedly was familiar with mysticisms, magic phenomena and certain aspects of witchcraft unknown to anyone else on earth.

"Why, of course!" the young magician exulted. "Grandfather can teach me magical effects that this smart-aleck parrot will never unravel—not in a million years!"

So he made arrangements for an immediate passage on the next ocean liner bound for Israel, and a few days later he and Yoshke were on board the glistening ship.

The first two days on the high seas were lovely, but on the third morning a raging storm erupted. Thunder rent the air and deafened the passengers. Jagged shards of lightning split the leaden sky. The ship rolled perilously in the mountainous waves, and suddenly a huge bolt of lightning hit the vessel. Immediately it began to sink. Everywhere, frantic passengers rushed to the life-boats, crowding the student-magician aside until he was the last one on board. He grabbed a life-preserver, fastened it around his body, clutched Yoshke the parrot to his bosom, and jumped overboard.

For more than an hour they floated in the sea until they were a safe distance from the doomed vessel. With Yoshke perched on his shoulder, they watched the ship sink lower and lower into the water until, all at once, it disappeared beneath the waves.

Yoshke seemed to wilt. For two days they drifted, but the parrot spoke not a word. In vain did the scholar try to get the bedraggled bird to utter a single syllable.

On the third day, the parrot broke its silence.

"All right," said Yoshke wearily, "I give up! What did you do with the ship?"

♪   ♪   ♪

The colonel at the local Cossack barracks invited a circus to perform for his soldiers. As a gesture to the townspeople of the nearby little village, he also invited them to attend.

The daring aerialists, acrobats and strange animals attracted everyone of the local inhabitants, including Hyman and his wife, Minnie. They viewed the fearless performers with unabashed admiration, and inspected the lions and tigers, the elephants and giraffes, with wide-eyed amazement. But when they came to the camel, Hyman drew up with an angry start.

"Minnie," he fumed, "just look what those dirty Cossacks did to that poor horse!"

♪   ♪   ♪

An elderly widow of Russia came to this country to live with her grandson, Donald Krass, né Doovid Krasnopolsky. Grandma loved America but her one big disappointment was her inability to learn even the rudiments of the English language.

One day her grandson's cat jumped on the table and helped herself to a plate of chopped liver.

"*Upsheek! Upsheek!*" Grandma yelled at the cat. But the cat, understanding not a word of Slavic cat-talk, regarded her placidly and did not budge.

The grandson, hearing the old woman's cries, rushed into the dining room and took in the situation at a glance. "Get the hell off the table!" he snapped.

The cat jumped down at once.

Grandma shook her head. "Who would have ever thought," she said wistfully in her flawless Yiddish, "that a plain cat would know more English than I?"

♪   ♪   ♪

A Jewish denizen of New York's lower East Side visited his country cousin, a dairy farmer in Connecticut. The cousin proudly showed his relative the new barn.

"Say, what kind of a cow do you call that?" exclaimed the city *landsman*. "I never saw one like it before."

"That's a cross between a Guernsey and a Holstein. It's called a Goldstein."

The city cousin grinned. "Next you'll tell me it doesn't give milk, only sour cream."

"Not at all," answered the witty farmer. "Instead of saying 'mooo,' this Goldstein says '*nu-u-u?*' "

✓   ✓   ✓

Television star Danny Thomas, a Lebanese who tells a Jewish joke better than most Jews, claimed that he bought a parrot from an Israeli seaman.

"Every morning," swears Danny, "the parrot would shout, 'Polly wants a *matzoh!*' "

✓   ✓   ✓

A Jewish cockroach was perched on a piece of moldy salami, eating his dinner. Just then, his friend, a gentile cockroach, came to visit for awhile.

"You should live at my place," said the gentile cockroach. "Instead of an old piece of salami, I can usually find bits of pork, ham and, on Sundays, bacon."

The Jewish cockroach looked up and glowered, but the other went on blithely. "Not only that, but the lady at my house keeps the place spic and span—the cleanest home in the whole city."

The other could stand it no longer. "What's the matter with you?" he shouted angrily. "Have you no manners at all? When you talked of pork and ham and bacon I said nothing. But when you try to turn my stomach with stories about clean, spic and span houses I want to ask you something—do you have to talk like that while I'm eating?"

✓   ✓   ✓

He was a frail, timid little man who lived in a village in Russia. At the moment, he was being buffeted by a fierce wind on a bitter cold day. Suddenly he was startled to hear a voice: "A big blizzard is coming. Go home as quickly as possible!"

He looked around but there was not a soul in sight, except for a horse that stared at him out of its intelligent, brown eyes. Terrified, he turned around and rushed home, his legs working like pistons. "Feigeleh," he screamed to his wife, "get me a little *schnapps* or I'll faint!"

"What happened? Why are you shaking so?" she asked.

He told her. "And there was not a human being anywhere around."

"All right, so he said there would be a big blizzard," consoled the wife. "But you don't need to get so excited. After all, what does a horse know from the weather?"

✓   ✓   ✓

A gorilla walked into Goldman's delicatessen and ordered a pastrami sandwich on pumpernickel with a piece of pickle on the side—to go.

FUR, FISH AND FOWL

"That'll be two dollars," said Goldman, handing the ape the sandwich. "And I must say, I never expected to see a gorilla in my store!"

"At two dollars for a pastrami sandwich," snapped the gorilla, "you never will again!"

✓   ✓   ✓

Two caterpillars, Izzie and Natie, were sunning themselves in the garden. A small shadow fell across them and they glanced up to see a butterfly overhead. It fluttered, swooped and did a few fancy Immelman turns on the air currents.

"Izzie," remarked Natie, "there's one thing for sure—you'll never get me up in one of those contraptions!"

✓   ✓   ✓

The two lovers had been separated for many weeks. Now they were together, exchanging endearments as do lovers the world over.

"I'll tell you a secret, darling," she murmured. "Whenever I received a letter from you I always kissed the back of the envelope because I knew you had sealed it with your very own sweet lips."

"Well," he stammered, "that's not quite accurate. I always moistened the envelope on Rover's wet nose."

✓   ✓   ✓

Saul, the rooster, and Hilda, the turkey, were in the barnyard chatting about their low station in life. But after Saul had gone on interminably for an hour or more about the many abuses he was forced to suffer, Hilda grew impatient.

"Listen," she began, "you think you got *tsorres*? Consider the poor turkey. First somebody gives him such a hit in the neck, his head flies off the handle. Then they tear off the wings, break his legs, knock the stuffing out of him, cut him to pieces and, as if all that weren't enough, they pick on him for weeks after."

✓   ✓   ✓

A Jew invited a friend to his home for the Passover celebration. The friend, in appreciation of this courtesy, went to a pet shop and purchased a trained parrot for his host.

The head of the family in due time began the *Seder* service, the first part of which speaks of the glories that await the Israelites in the future. "Next year let us hope that the Jews all over the world will be free from bondage," intoned the host, paraphrasing the Hebrew into English.

But the mention of the word 'Jew' had a peculiar effect on the parrot. "Kill the Jews!" it shrieked. "Christ killers!"

The host was furious. "How dare you bring this vile creature into my

135

home?" he shouted at his friend. "Is this your idea of a joke? Surely you must have known it was trained by a Jew-hater!"

But the friend was equally horrified. "Believe me, I knew nothing about his background," he insisted. "In fact, I just bought that parrot a few minutes before I came here. How could I have guessed that a bird with such a nose would be anti-Semitic?"

Chapter Fourteen

Marriage Brokers

A *shadchan* called on a young man of poor circumstances to attempt a match.

"Frankly," the youth said, "the only girl I would consider must be young, beautiful, come from a good family, and own a delicatessen."

"What!" shouted the indignant marriage broker. "You, a poor man, expect all that? You're not even passably good-looking and you have no trade. A girl such as you describe would have to be crazy to marry the likes of you!"

The young man shrugged. "So, she's crazy! As long as she has all the other qualifications, who cares?"

✓ ✓ ✓

For a month the *shadchan* had been extolling the many virtues of a young lady, until finally the prospective bridegroom became deeply interested. So the marriage broker arranged for the youth to meet the girl at a party at her parents' home.

But when the young man laid eyes on the intended bride his heart sank—and he blazed inwardly at the perfidious, lying broker.

All through dinner he maintained his composure, but at the first opportunity he drew the *shadchan* aside and hissed fiercely in his ear: "You fraud! You swindler! What did I ever do to you that you should fool me like this? Do you need the fee so badly? Why, this woman is a good twenty years older than I am. And that face—she should charge admission to look at it. Better yet, she should nail a board over it. And she's so near-sighted she squints. She has no teeth, she . . ."

"You don't have to whisper," interrupted the *shadchan*. "She's deaf, too!"

✓ ✓ ✓

"*Shadchan*, you told me a deliberate lie," a prospective groom complained. "I'm surprised—a man of your age and background!"

"I lied? What are you talking? She isn't beautiful by you? She doesn't

137

have excellent manners and she isn't a high school graduate? She doesn't sing like a knight in a gale? So where did I lie?"

"You told me her father was dead—that's where you lied! The girl told me herself that he's been in prison for the past ten years."

"*Nu*, I ask you," countered the broker, "do you call that living?"

↗   ↗   ↗

An old marriage broker who found it increasingly difficult to get around because of his arthritis and other afflictions that accompanied his advanced years, hired a young assistant.

"Do you know anything at all about this business?" asked the aged *shadchan*.

"Not a thing," replied the young man truthfully.

"Then give a listen. The main point in the matchmaking business is that you should always flatter the merchandise. It never hurts to exaggerate a little. In other words, spread it on good!"

"I understand perfectly," the new assistant grinned.

The next evening the old broker took the young man on his first call. "We have a chance for a good match," said the elder. "And there will be a substantial fee involved. The father of this young man is very wealthy. Just remember my advice: exaggerate, be enthusiastic and spread it on good and thick."

Seated around the table in the rich man's home, the broker started his pitch:

"Have I got a girl for your son! She comes from a long line of famous rabbis and wealthy bankers. Such *yiches* you never saw!"

"Wealthy bankers?" interrupted the assistant. "She's a member of the Rothschild family!"

The old broker experienced an uneasy moment—membership in the Rothschild family was too easy to check. Perhaps he should have cautioned his new helper not to get carried away.

"Another thing," the old *shadchan* went on, "she's always perfectly groomed, and on each pinkie she wears a ten-carat diamond ring."

"Ten carats! What are you talking?" the assistant burst out. "Those diamonds are at least twenty carats. I saw them with my own eyes! But beautiful as they are, they can't compare to her gorgeous face!"

The broker gulped. He knew that the rich man was aware that no woman could be that perfect. So he decided to play it down a little.

"Well, to be perfectly honest with you," he told the prospective groom's father, "she does have a slight imperfection. On her back she has a tiny wart."

"A tiny wart?" cried the assistant rapturously. "Believe me, it's a regular hump!"

The old broker glared at the young man as though he could throttle him with his bare hands. Somehow, he had to save the day or this rich client would be lost.

"There is one more thing," he said to the groom's father, smiling knowingly, in a man-to-man manner. "Your son will be especially pleased because this girl has a figure like an angel—36-21-36."

"And that's an understatement!" cried the assistant, butting in once more. "Her bosom is a good 50. Her waist? Figure it at least 39. And the hip measurement? Believe me, that girl has a *tuchus* every bit of 60 inches!"

✓ ✓ ✓

A certain *shadchan* was anxious to make a match between a promising young dentist and the daughter of a wealthy wine merchant. But there was one drawback: the young dentist was quite homely.

"I like her," the intended groom admitted, somewhat sadly. "But when she sees my face she'll undoubtedly refuse me."

"You just leave everything to me," said the broker confidently.

That evening the *shadchan* called on the girl and showed her the young man's picture.

"Oh, I could never marry him!" cried the girl. "Look at that face!"

"I'm glad you brought that up," said the canny broker, "because what you see is only an illusion. When he was born he was the most beautiful baby in the whole country."

"He certainly isn't beautiful now."

"But that's just the point! It was his hard luck to be accidentally exchanged at the hospital for somebody else's baby! Still and all, it's the same person, no?"

✓ ✓ ✓

Shadchan: "Why is it, a nice-looking man like you, you're not married?"

Herschel: "Because every time I meet a girl who cooks like Mama, she looks like Papa!"

✓ ✓ ✓

The matchmaker was very anxious to conclude a *chasseneh* between the son of his longtime friend and his own niece. It wasn't just the fee involved, either. The old broker was certain they would make a happy and loving couple. But the young man would have none of the prospective bride, a recent widow.

"You call this a good match?" he rebuked the *shadchan*. "That woman is the mother of four children!"

"All right, so she's the mother of four. By you this is bad? Take the word of an experienced man—it's much better so!"

"What do you mean, better?"

"My boy, did you ever stop to think that if you married a maiden and decided to have four children, what kind of *tsorres* you'd go through?"

"I don't think that's so much trouble."

"Ha! The experienced man is talking! You never had to go through four pregnancies! And you live two flights up in the apartment house so you have to carry your wife up the stairs when you bring her back from the hospital. So what happens? I'll tell you exactly what happens—you sprain your back and now you're both convalescing. And if your wife doesn't recuperate from the childbirth, what do you do? You send her to the Catskills for a rest, that's what!

"Here you are, living in the city and she's in the country. And who'll look after the *kinder* while you are working or maybe laid up in a sickbed, and she's away? Will you do all the cooking and cleaning and washing of diapers? You call that a kind of life?

"On the other hand, I'm offering you a fine-looking widow with four ready-made children: no fuss, no bother, no expense—custom-tailored, just for you. My boy, anybody who doesn't grab this proposition is out of his mind!"

✦   ✦   ✦

A *shadchan* was declaiming on the attractions of a hopeful bride, but the young man remained unimpressed.

"You're making a mistake by refusing her," said the marriage broker. "She has a speech impediment."

"Speech impediment!" echoed the man. "What kind of an inducement do you call that?"

The *shadchan* grinned knowingly and explained, "She can't say 'no'!"

✦   ✦   ✦

There seemed to be no question that the matchmaker had arranged a marriage, but at the last minute the fiancé changed his mind.

"What's wrong with the girl that you should back out like this?" demanded the *shadchan*. "She's a regular angel and pretty like a doll."

"It hasn't anything to do with that at all," the young man said thoughtfully. "I just realized that I simply don't believe in marriage."

"What kind of nonsense is that from a nice Jewish boy," the broker retorted. "A man without a wife is like a pastrami sandwich without a pickle; the spice and tang of life is missing. But with a mate at your side, life *means* something!"

"What, for instance?"

"Just think of it—you awaken in the morning and your loving wife brings you coffee in bed. She draws the water for your bath—even washes your back. At night, when you return home from work, do you eat alone like some poor bachelor? Of course not! Together you sit down at the same table and enjoy her delicious home cooking."

"Well, I have to admit, that part isn't so bad."

"None of it is bad, my boy! On the Sabbath you come home and the place is spotless. The furniture has all been dusted, a nice clean cloth is on the table, and there's the shining new silverware you got for a wedding

140

present. Then she lights the candles like a good daughter of Israel and together you eat her fresh-made chicken soup—it melts in your mouth."

"The more I hear the better I like it."

"That's not all, my young friend. Just think, you are at the dinner table and your bride tells you of the little happenings of the day in her own innocent, sweet manner. You listen and smile lovingly as she tells you one little story after another. And so she goes on talking while you sit there and listen. And she talks—and she talks—and talks—and talks—and talks! *Oy vay,* can a wife talk! It drives a man crazy!"

✔   ✔   ✔

The modern hippie is no latter-day phenomenon. He had his counterpart in the "old country" as witness this tale:

A young man with a scraggly, unkempt beard, his clothes filthy, his hair disheveled and uncut, decided that he would continue his Bohemian way of life without working, by marrying a wealthy girl. So he went to a *shadchan.*

The marriage broker made no effort to conceal his distaste for the unwashed specimen before him, but he did have a rich girl on his list who was seeking a husband.

"Take me to her right away," cried the disreputable slob eagerly.

"Not in your condition," protested the *shadchan.* "She'd have nothing to do with you. First you must shave, comb your hair, take a bath and put on some clean clothes."

"But suppose she still doesn't like me?"

"In that case," said the broker, "you can always dirty yourself up again."

✔   ✔   ✔

Shmuel the *shadchan* struggled valiantly for more than six months in an effort to unite a certain young man with one of his lady clients. But just as the fellow was about to accept, he learned that the girl limped.

"I'm calling the whole thing off," he declared. "I wouldn't marry a lame wife if she had the wealth of Rothschild."

Shmuel, at his unctious best, reasoned quietly with the youth. "You may not realize it at your age, my young friend, but you are displaying your crass ignorance—an ignorance that can only be surmounted by actual experience. Just suppose you married a girl with two strong and sound legs. What guarantee do you have that she won't fall and break one of them—or both? Do you have any idea of the anguish you will suffer while she is convalescing? Who will take care of the children, cook and clean house while she is laid up? Has it occurred to you that you could spend your life's savings to cure her? And without money, you surely know your health will break down; you'll lose your job because you are too weak to perform your duties.

"Now take this girl! Here is a bride who has already broken a leg,

141

and not only that but she has been cured with other people's money. Limp, shmimp—you have nothing more to worry about. Take her before somebody else grabs this prize!"

✦   ✦   ✦

The wily old broker knew he was going to meet with heavy resistance from this obstinate young man so he mustered all the arguments he could think of in his initial assault.

"The first thing I want you to understand is that this girl is a beauty," he began.

"Not interested," said the fellow curtly.

"Very well, if a lovely face and figure are not so important to you, I have another one; a nice-looking girl but not exactly beautiful. However, she has twenty thousand rubles and a sizeable income from her various properties."

"I have money of my own."

"Then maybe it's *yiches* that interests you, eh? Listen, I know just the girl for you. Her *mishpocheh* will leave you breathless—rabbis, bankers, merchants; believe me, you can't find any better!"

"Look, I'm telling you once and for all, I'm not interested," snapped the young man with finality. "When I marry it won't be for beauty, it won't be for money, it won't be for family. It will be for love!"

"Say, that's a coincidence!" cried the *shadchan*. "I have one of those also!"

✦   ✦   ✦

Not all marriage brokers are confined to Europe. A few ultra-orthodox Jews in America still cling to this form of "union by arrangement." Reputable (and sometimes not so reputable) brokers were especially busy around the turn of the century throughout New York. The following tidbit is dated circa 1903.

A woman called on Himmelfarb, the *shadchan*, and stated that she desired an immediate marriage.

"For an immediate marriage there will have to be an inducement," explained the *shadchan*. "Do you have *efsher* a dowry?"

"Two thousand dollars—cold cash!"

"A nice amount—a nice amount! For two thousand dollars I can offer you a writer."

"Please, no writers! I have enough trouble supporting myself!"

"Well, how about a nice young interne? I can guarantee one."

"Student doctors I don't need."

"Hmmm, you are being difficult, you know? All right, I'll give you a young rabbi."

"Spiritual talk I can always hear in the synagogue."

"A cantor?"

"No!"

142

"A violin teacher?"

"*Feh!*"

"Madam, just what do you want?"

"A working man!"

"What! A working man?" the broker cried in astonishment. "For only two thousand dollars? Why, I never heard of such *chutzpah!*"

✓ ✓ ✓

Shadchan Eisenberg was walking along the Miami Beach seashore one morning when a gigantic creature with two heads, a long, slimy tail and completely covered with barnacles, crawled out of the ocean and onto the beach.

The *shadchan's* first impulse was to take to his heels, but he conquered his inchoate fright and ran over to the weird denizen of the deep.

"Say," he cried, "have I got a girl for you!"

✓ ✓ ✓

"Harry, I found a young lady that's just right for you. Take my word for it, you'll want to marry her the minute you see her," enthused the *shadchan.*

"Who is she?" asked Harry suspiciously, quite familiar with the broker's propensity for exaggeration.

"Ida Kalman, the baker's daughter."

"Now wait a minute, I know her! She's not only cross-eyed but she's as bald as an olive."

"So what? That doesn't detract from her beauty."

"Beauty? She has a nose like an ant-eater. Besides, she's too skinny, she's flat-chested, and her teeth are crooked."

"Well, you have to admit she has a good heart."

"Perhaps. But how can you ignore the fact that she's a hunchback?"

"For heaven's sake, Harry, be reasonable!" cried the marriage broker. "So she's a hunchback! Can't you even overlook one little flaw in the girl who's willing to share your whole life?"

✓ ✓ ✓

The great Al Jolson told of a young man who accepted a dinner invitation to the home of a girl's parents. Neither had ever seen the other before, the match having been made by a marriage broker.

On the day after the tête-à-tête, the *shadchan* called on the youth. "Well," said the broker proudly, "wasn't that a fine, high-class family? And rich, too. Did you notice the pure sterling silverware?"

"Y-e-s, it was very fancy," the lad agreed hesitantly. "But one thing troubled me."

"What could possibly disturb you with such a wonderful family?"

"Do you suppose it is possible that they just borrowed that expensive silverware to make an impression on me?"

143

"What kind of crazy talk is that?" retorted the broker impatiently. "Who'd lend expensive silver to those crooks?"

✓ ✓ ✓

The *shadchan* heaved a sigh of relief when the man finally broke down and agreed to see the girl he had suggested. It had been a long, tough fight.

"There is just one qualification before I accept," the man said, interrupting the broker's happy thoughts. "Before I give you my answer I must see her in the nude."

"How dare you!" shouted the outraged broker. "What kind of a suggestion is that to make to a nice Jewish girl?"

"I insist."

The *shadchan* threw up his hands in resignation, and, his reluctance very apparent, went to the girl's house and told her of the fellow's decision. After strenuous objections, indignant tears and refusals, she finally agreed to appear before her "intended" stark naked.

"*Nu,*" said the *shadchan* the next day, "did you find her satisfactory?"

"No," said the man. "I didn't like her nose!"

✓ ✓ ✓

A *shadchan* was asked by a young artist to find him a suitable mate.

"I know just the girl for a creative man like you!" cried the marriage broker.

The next day the *shadchan* brought the girl to the artist's house. The young man was shocked with her appearance and at the first opportunity he drew the broker aside.

"What kind of a monster do you call that?" he hissed. "One eye slanted up, the other down; the left ear way up here, the right ear way down there; the forehead sloped back like a . . ."

"Look, you're an artist," interrupted the *shadchan*. "You should know better than anyone else—you either like Picasso or you don't!"

✓ ✓ ✓

He was a wealthy widower in his mid-seventies and anxious to remarry. The trouble was that the old lecher would accept no girl older than eighteen so, naturally, his rate of refusals was 100%. At last he went to a *shadchan* who introduced him to a likely young maiden.

The oldster took one look at the lovely girl and breathed, "Where have you been all my life?"

"Well," she said reflectively, "for sixty years of it, I wasn't even born!"

✓ ✓ ✓

Berel, the matchmaker, waited impatiently to hear the outcome of the introduction he had just arranged. His client was a wealthy young man who could be expected to pay a substantial fee—the girl was a pretty young thing and a good cook. There was no reason why this should not culminate in a quick marriage.

But when the fellow showed up, the *shadchan* could see, at once, that something had gone awry. "What happened?" he cried.

"There'll be no wedding," sighed the other. "She's too near-sighted. The poor girl said she couldn't see me from a hole in the wall!"

✓ ✓ ✓

A *shadchan*, noted for his sense of humor, enjoyed livening up a dull day, especially when his victim was a *nudnik*. It was on just such an idle afternoon that he happened to run into Yoshke the barrel maker.

"Yoshke, how would you like to marry the Czar's daughter?" asked the *shadchan*, his eyes atwinkle.

Yoshke furrowed his brow in deep thought. "No, I don't think I'll marry her," he said at length.

"But she's a real princess! What's your objection?"

"The Czar is a Christian, no? Well, I just couldn't marry his daughter —she's a *shikseh*."

"But think of it! She's not only gorgeous but the richest girl in all the Russias!"

"All right, as long as you put it that way, I'll marry her."

"Fine," grinned the *shadchan*. "Now that you're satisfied with the match all I need is the Czar's consent."

✓ ✓ ✓

Shadchan: "Have I got a girl for you! She comes with a dowry of ten thousand rubles."

Young Man: "That sounds interesting. Let me see her picture."

Shadchan: "Sorry, but with a ten-thousand-ruble dowry we never show pictures!"

✓ ✓ ✓

The *yeshivah* student came over to discuss terms with the prospective father-in-law, following an introduction by the village *shadchan*.

"What the *shadchan* told you about me is perfectly true," said the rich man. "I can well afford to give a handsome dowry to the one who is going to marry my daughter. As to the exact sum, I must say that it all depends upon which daughter is chosen. The one who marries my youngest daughter, who is twenty-five, receives three hundred rubles. My second daughter, who is thirty, will bring six hundred rubles, and my third daughter, who is forty, will bring nine hundred rubles."

"Sir," exclaimed the *yeshiva* student eagerly, "you got maybe a daughter in her fifties?"

✓ ✓ ✓

Itzik married a girl from Yehupetz, but three months later he divorced her. His next wife came from Kopulye, but again within three months the marriage landed on the rocks. Following the advice of a *shadchan*, Itzik's new wife came from Zhitomir. To Itzik's surprise he got along beautifully with his latest wife and they lived happily for a whole year after their marriage.

One day he happened to meet the *shadchan* who inquired about his third wife.

"Everything is rosy and my married life is a complete success," enthused Itzik. "From now on I intend to marry only girls from Zhitomir."

Chapter Fifteen

Marriage and Divorce

For six months business was so hectic at Barney Klein's shop that he invariably came home late for dinner. Every night, Barney promised faithfully he would be home earlier, but something always arose to keep him at the shop after hours. Finally, Mrs. Klein could stand it no longer.

"Barney, for more than six months I've been slaving over a hot stove so you should have *eppes* to eat when you get home—a hot, nourishing meal. But are you ever here on time? I should live so long! For the last time, Barney, I'm telling you—either you are here at six o'clock sharp every night, and not a minute later, or no more cooking. You can eat in restaurants."

Barney Klein was worried. After all, he loved his wife and realized that her resentment was justified. "From tomorrow night on I'm turning over a new leaf," he promised her solemnly. "Six o'clock sharp!"

The following day he closed up shop earlier than usual and was on his way home when, walking against the traffic lights, he was struck down by a car. An ambulance whisked him away to Bellevue Hospital where, fortunately, his injuries were found to be minor. They dismissed him shortly thereafter, and he continued his interrupted journey home. It was after eight when he opened the door to his apartment.

"What kind of an hour is this to come home?" Mrs. Klein wept. "The dinner is ruined—and after all your big promises, too."

"But I have an explanation," he told her reasonably. "I know I'm two hours late but I was run over by a car."

"So what?" she replied. "It takes two hours to get run over?"

✔   ✔   ✔

Tanteh was explaining why she never married:

"I have a dog that growls, a fireplace that smokes, a parrot that curses and a cat that stays out all night. So tell me, what do I need with a husband?"

✔   ✔   ✔

Mrs. Cohen appeared before the judge in a divorce action.

"How old are you?" asked the judge.

"Thirty-five," answered Mrs. Cohen promptly.

The judge noted her graying hair and wrinkled cheeks. "May I see your birth certificate?"

Mrs. Cohen handed up the document and the judge examined it closely.

"Madam," he said severely, "according to this certificate you are not thirty-five, but fifty."

"Your honor," countered Mrs. Cohen, "the last fifteen years I spent with my husband I'm not including. You call that a life?"

✓　　✓　　✓

"Mama, stop saying my boy friend isn't serious. I'm sure he is."

"Better you should listen to your mother. If he really loved you he'd at least write a few compromising letters."

✓　　✓　　✓

Max Gittelman celebrated his eightieth birthday party with his wife, Reba, and a few old cronies. When the guests left, Max sank down on the davenport, his expression weary.

"Max, are you all right?" Reba asked anxiously. "I told you a man your age is too old for a party. Maybe now you'll listen!"

"My dear Reba," replied Max patiently, "a man is not too old until it takes him longer to rest up than it did to get tired!"

✓　　✓　　✓

A jeweler boarded a train to the city to purchase some new stones. Inside the coach he sat down opposite an exquisitely beautiful woman. But his reaction was quite strange. Every few moments he would look at her and mutter *"Feh!"*

Another passenger, sitting next to the jeweler, became irritated. "Mister," he protested, "that woman is perfectly gorgeous. Why do you keep looking at her and saying '*feh*'?"

"I'm not saying that to her," replied the grumpy jeweler. "It's just that every time I look at this attractive lady I can't help thinking of my wife. *Feh!*"

✓　　✓　　✓

"Rabbi, I hear that my ex-wife is now sorry she divorced me."

"It is ever thus," sighed the rabbi. "Wives are like fishermen; they complain about the one they caught, and brag about the one that got away."

✓　　✓　　✓

MARRIAGE AND DIVORCE

A Jewish teacher fell in love with a *shikseh* and they were married, but only after she had promised the rabbi she would study Jewish lore and traditions.

The dedicated (and very much in love) bridegroom began her instructions with that part of the Bible which deals with Joseph and how he was sold into slavery by his brothers. The bride listened to the tale of Joseph's many hardships and, being a compassionate girl, she wept bitterly.

A year later, the husband again explained the same sad story, once more emphasizing Joseph's misery. But this time his wife grinned broadly, as though enjoying a huge joke.

"What in the world are you smiling about?" asked the surprised husband. "Last year, when I told you this story, you cried. Now you act as though I had said something funny! What's the idea?"

"Well, really, it *is* funny," she giggled. "After what happened to him last year you'd think the idiot would have better sense than to go back!"

✓   ✓   ✓

"Have I got a sanitary wife! A real fanatic! She's the only woman in all New York who washes the garbage before taking it outside!"

✓   ✓   ✓

Selma and Nathan, who had constantly made the air blue with their swearing at each other for almost all of their twenty-five years of marriage, promised faithfully, in the presence of the rabbi, that one would never curse the other again.

"Rabbi, I give you my word of honor, from now on our behavior will be above reproach," vowed Nathan as they were leaving.

Selma turned to the rabbi. "You really believe what Nathan just told you?"

"Certainly. Why not?"

"I'll tell you why, Rabbi. I should have so many good years, the number of curses that *momzer* will scream at me before we even get home!"

✓   ✓   ✓

The story of Rivka and Yankel proves that one can not only get used to anything but even grow to enjoy it.

Rivka, a lonely but very respectable widow, fell hopelessly in love with Yankel, a beggar who earned his daily bread by going from house to house and pleading poverty.

She implored him to seek honest labor and renounce the degrading life he had been leading until, one day, his resistance was finally swept away.

"Rivka darling, I'll make you a promise," he declared. "If you will marry me I give you my word of honor that I will continue to beg for only one year. After that, I'll get a regular job. By that time we'll have enough saved to give our marriage a decent financial start. But there is one condition."

"What's the condition?"

"That you go begging with me. Not only will we be company for each other but we'll make twice as much."

"But that's impossible!" she cried. "Everybody in town knows me. If anyone saw me begging in the streets I'd die of shame."

Yankel softened to her entreaties. "All right, then we'll go to another town."

So Rivka and Yankel were married. For a whole year they begged together, setting aside as much as they could against the day when they would retire from the *shnorring* business.

Whatever else might be said about Yankel, none can dispute that he was a man of his word. At the stroke of noon, on the fifty-second week, to the very second, he stopped short in the middle of the street.

"The year is up, Rivka, my love. Just as I promised, we are through with begging forever."

Rivka paused and studied the neighborhood with a trained eye. "Let's finish this row of houses first," she said shyly.

✓   ✓   ✓

"Izzie, wake up!" called the man's wife.

"Wh-what's the matter?" mumbled Izzie.

"You're talking in your sleep again. Why don't you control yourself?"

"All right, we'll make a bargain. You let me talk when I'm awake and I'll try to control myself when I'm asleep!"

✓   ✓   ✓

"You say you want a divorce but you wont tell me why?" the rabbi asked.

"I have my reasons," said the man stubbornly.

"I cannot understand what your reasons might be. Your wife is soft and gentle and, if I may say so, she is also quite beautiful and nicely proportioned. I really don't see what you have to complain about."

To the rabbi's surprise the man removed his shoe. "Take a good look at this shoe," said the man. "The leather is soft and gentle. It is a beautiful piece of work and nicely proportioned."

"Ah, a parable."

"In a way, Rabbi. I'm the only one who knows—it pinches!"

✓   ✓   ✓

Then there's the domineering wife who snapped at her long-suffering husband: "Stop beating around the bush already! If you have anything to say—shut up!"

✓   ✓   ✓

MARRIAGE AND DIVORCE

Meyer Saperstein was highly displeased with the way his marriage was turning out. His wife, a born "joiner," was always away, attending club meetings. There was the Ladies' Civic Club at the night school, the Women's Auxiliary of the Socialist Party, the Y.W.H.A., Hadassah, WIZO and several other groups which she attended with maddening regularity.

In desperation, Meyer consulted his rabbi.

"I need your advice," he said angrily. "Tell me something, Rabbi, do you believe in clubs for women?"

"Why, of course not!" exclaimed the rabbi, shocked. "A little slap with the open hand once in a while, all right. But what kind of a monster uses clubs?"

✓ ✓ ✓

"Abe, for heaven's sake, can't you talk to me once in a while?" scolded Thelma. "Your head is forever buried in books. You don't even know I'm alive. Sometimes I wish I were a book. At least you would look at me."

"That isn't such a bad idea," mused Abe. "Then I could take you to the library every few days and change you for something more interesting."

✓ ✓ ✓

"Rabbi, I want you to arrange a divorce," said the sad-faced old man. "I simply can't stand my wife another day."

"What! After living with her for forty years you want to cast her out? How dare you!"

"I don't blame you for being so indignant about those forty years," the oldster sighed unhappily. "I know better than anyone else I should have come to you years ago."

✓ ✓ ✓

A solicitor for the Jewish Home for the Aged called upon a well-to-do young couple for a donation. Hearing a commotion inside he knocked extra-loudly on the door.

A somewhat disheveled man admitted him. "What can I do for you?" he growled, clearly upset about something.

"I would like to speak to the master of the house," said the solicitor politely.

"Then you're just in time," barked the young man. "My wife and I are settling that very question right now!"

✓ ✓ ✓

"Ah, do I have a wonderful wife!" the young man enthused. "She's so good she gets all my shirts sparkling white—even my blue ones!"

✓ ✓ ✓

Rabbi Katzenelson had long grown accustomed to the peculiar demands made by couples seeking divorce, but he was more than disconcerted by the request made by Ruth Yelman who called on him one Friday morning.

The rabbi listened to her gravely and then spoke. "I have already had a talk with your husband, Mrs. Yelman. I understand that you are both agreed there is no other remedy but divorce."

"Absolutely!" agreed the woman. "But only on my terms."

"Terms? What kind of terms?"

"He has to leave me in the same kind of condition that he found me."

Rabbi Katzenelson, understandably misinterpreting her meaning, could only stare at her in amazement. "Madam, pardon me if I do not understand you correctly, but are you referring to your original condition of—ah—er—well—virginity?"

Now it was Mrs. Yelman's turn to be surprised. "Hardly that," she giggled. "I was widowed twice before. In fact, that's my very point. I was a widow when he met me . . . if he wants to go his own way, then he'll have to leave me as he found me—a widow!"

✔   ✔   ✔

"Nobody introduced me to my wife. We just happened to meet. I'm not blaming anybody!"

✔   ✔   ✔

Mollie was entranced with an expensive mink coat she had seen in an exclusive shop, and for days she cudgeled her brain to think of a way to bring up the subject to her husband. Suddenly she had an inspired thought.

"Sollie, last night I had a lovely dream."

"What kind of a dream, Mollie?"

"I dreamed that we passed by Saks Fifth Avenue, and there in the window was this gorgeous mink coat—only $6,200. And do you know what you did? You went right in and bought it for me, Sollie dear!"

"Say, that really was a wonderful dream! Hereafter, in all your dreams, you should wear it in good health, Mollie dear!"

✔   ✔   ✔

Shrewish wives have been the scourge of Yiddish menfolk since the earliest days of recorded biblical history. Gentile wives can be, and often are, shrews too. But they have much to learn from their sisters. The difference lies in the assertiveness of the males, as per this bit of wit.

A man was married to a woman whose commands to her husband were as sharp as the bite of a barracuda. It wasn't so much that he was a coward, or too timid to talk back, but you know how it is . . . let's keep peace in the family.

One day the wife invited a group from the local women's club to her house for tea and discussions. To make sure that her husband did not interrupt the goings-on, she ordered him into the closet and sternly told him to stay there until the last lady had left.

During their bridge game, the ladies of the club spoke of the authority they wielded over their respective husbands. Not to be outdone, the hostess informed the others that not only had she ordered her husband into the closet, but she could order him to come out, at will. "I'll prove it," she boasted.

"*Shlemiel!*" she commanded, "come out of that closet!"

No response.

"*Shlemiel!*" she called in a louder voice, "come out of that closet this instant!"

Nothing.

"*Shlemiel!*" she screamed at the top of her lungs, "I order you to get out of that closet this instant!"

"No, I won't!" came her husband's muffled cry from inside the closet. "I'll show you who's boss in this house!"

ꞏ   ꞏ   ꞏ

It was a cold, wintry night and they had just gone to bed.

"Goldie, why do you keep pulling away from me like that?" he asked.

"Your feet are cold."

"That's no excuse," he said unhappily. "You didn't act like this before we were married."

ꞏ   ꞏ   ꞏ

"Joey, what's the matter you can't bring me home a box of candy once in a while at least?" sniffled the wife. "Before we were married you were always bringing me little presents."

"*Shayneh,* tell me," asked Joey, "does it make sense a man should give worms to a fish after he catches it?"

ꞏ   ꞏ   ꞏ

The *melamed* brought his problem to the rabbi. "I'm ashamed to say this, Rabbi, but I want to divorce my wife," he confessed.

"Now see here," the rabbi scolded, "that is no way for a Godly man to talk. You, of all people! Surely you know what the Talmud says: 'When a man divorceth his wife not only the angels but the very stones weepeth!'"

"Yes, I know the saying very well, but if the angels and the stones must weepeth, that is their business. I want to singeth a songeth of joyeth!"

ꞏ   ꞏ   ꞏ

Everybody agreed that when Milton and Becky married it was a perfect match. Indeed, Milton was so much in love with his bride that he regularly brought home his eighty-dollar a week salary without even opening the envelope.

During the second month of their marriage, however, Milton opened the envelope before coming home, and gave Becky $79.50 of his eighty-dollar wages. During the third month he turned over to her $79.00 even.

Becky held her counsel, a growing worry nibbling at the corners of her mind. But, during the fourth month, when her husband handed over only $78.75, she confronted him with blazing eyes.

"All right, Milton, now it's finally out in the open," she cried. "Who is the other woman you're supporting?"

✔   ✔   ✔

"My first wife divorced me for religious reasons. She worshipped money and I didn't have any!"

✔   ✔   ✔

"My second wife divorced me because of illness. She got sick of me!"

✔   ✔   ✔

Grandma and Grandpa Vogel were reminiscing about their courtship days, with their teen-age granddaughter, an avid listener.

"Was Grandpa an ardent sweetheart?" asked the teenager, herself in the throes of her first adolescent love.

"The best," Grandma agreed, smiling.

"Oh, how romantic," sighed the girl. She turned to her grandfather. "Tell me, how long did you go with Grandma before you married her?"

"Hmmm, that takes me back many years," said Grandpa, rubbing his chin reflectively. "Now let me see; I went with your grandma for . . . ! Hmm, er, well, I went with her for . . . ! Say, come to think of it, what *did* I go with her for?"

✔   ✔   ✔

For twelve years Manny and Miriam had endured a nightmarish married life of bickering, cruel taunts and occasional physical altercations. Finally, and at long last, they agreed to put a legal end to their unhappy relationship.

Divorce, however, presented some unfortunate complications. In spite of their mutual dislike, Manny and Miriam had produced nine children, and now each demanded custody of five, leaving the remaining four progeny to the other. The only recourse was to ask the rabbi to adjudicate the case and grant them the hoped-for divorce.

The rabbi listened attentively to their respective arguments, and after failing to induce a reconciliation, he arrived at the only solution possible to a sensible man of the cloth.

"I know of only one way to divide your children equally between you," stated the holy man. "You now have an uneven number of off-spring, so you must wait another year before you part. Perhaps, during this postponement, you will have another child. Then, each of you will have five."

The couple agreed to this wise suggestion and returned to their home. For nine months the rabbi heard nothing from Manny and Miriam, until one day he met them on the street. He shook their hands warmly.

"It looks like you have given up the idea of a divorce," he said happily.

"No, we haven't," sighed Manny. "Complications arose about the division of the children."

"What's the matter?" asked the rabbi, turning to Miriam, "didn't you give birth?"

"Yes," she muttered glumly. "We had twins!"

✓ ✓ ✓

Mr. Rosen had just come home, tired and irritable. His wife intuitively felt that this was the wrong time to ask him for money but she needed it.

"Max," she asked hesitantly, "let me have five dollars."

"What, again?" he demanded. "What did you do with the five dollars I just gave you this morning?"

"What do you expect—an accounting?"

"Why not?"

"Well, a dollar here, a dollar there, you know how it is. That's two dollars, right?"

"Right!"

"And before you turn around, it's another two dollars, right?"

"Right! But that's only four dollars."

"Now just a minute!" she cried indignantly. "What do you want from my life—blood? I gave you a detailed accounting of the first four dollars. Do I have to account for the last miserable penny, too?"

✓ ✓ ✓

Ralph was lying on the living room couch, contentedly reading the evening paper.

"Ralph, close the window," complained Edith, his wife. "It's cold outside."

He moved not a muscle.

"Ralph, are you deaf? Would you please to close the window! I already told you—it's cold outside!"

No response.

"Ralph!" shouted Edith, "this is the third time I'm asking. Would you please be so kind to close the window? It's cold outside!"

With a grunt and a sigh, Ralph got up, went to the window, and slammed it shut.

"*Nu,*" he grumbled as he sank down on the couch, "so now it's *warm* outside?"

✓ ✓ ✓

"Rabbi, I need your advice; I'm desperate," cried the worried-looking little man. "I earn a very small salary—hardly enough to support my wife and eleven children. What's more, each year brings us another baby. Tell me, Rabbi, what shall I do?"

"You really want to know?" was the rabbi's terse reply. "Do nothing for a change!"

✓   ✓   ✓

Sybil and Marty lived in a comfortable apartment in Brooklyn, but Sybil was dissatisfied. Day in and day out she nagged her husband, urging him to move to a better neighborhood and a more expensive apartment.

"You can afford it," she scolded. "After all these years of skimping and saving we're entitled to a little luxury."

"But I like it here," Marty insisted, "Why move to a more expensive place? It just doesn't make sense!"

For months Sybil hammered and yammered at her husband but he could not be budged. Finally one evening, after dinner, Marty astounded his wife with a simple declaration:

"Sybil, at last you're getting your wish. Starting next month we'll we living in a more expensive apartment."

"Oh, that's wonderful!" exclaimed Sybil joyfully. "Did you find an elegant new house? On Park Avenue maybe?"

"No," said Marty. "The landlord just raised our rent!"

✓   ✓   ✓

Every summer, ever since their marriage twenty years before, she had nagged her husband to take a trip to the Thousand Islands. Finally he hit on a masterful compromise. He took her 1,000 times to Coney Island.

✓   ✓   ✓

The long wed couple had been watching a tender love story on television, and the wife was in a romantic mood.

"Tell me, darling," she said to her hubby, "if you had to do it all over again, would you still marry me?"

"I suppose so," he said laconically. "If I *had* to!"

✓   ✓   ✓

Mrs. Gold had been warned that her new neighbor was overly inquisitive, but she soon learned that the woman was probably the nosiest person she had ever seen in her life. Mrs. Gold, in self-defense, vowed that she would squelch the prying lady at the first opportunity.

One day the neighbor heard that this was Mrs. Gold's second marriage. She hurried over to the other's house to find out all the details.

"You're divorced?" asked the neighbor.

"No, my first husband passed away."

"Oh, is that so? Tell me all about it."

"Nothing much to tell," answered Mrs. Gold placidly. "He was bedridden and felt that he was dying by inches, so he went around to the back of the house and died by the yard!"

✓   ✓   ✓

Just a moment of silence for the husband whose breakfast consists of a three-minute boiled egg and a five-minute argument.

✓   ✓   ✓

. . . and another moment of silence for the fellow whose wife treats him like a god. Every morning, for breakfast, she gives him a burnt offering —his toast!

✓   ✓   ✓

Jack: "Are you married?"
Joe: "No, I look this way because somebody just stole my car."

✓   ✓   ✓

Sid and Suzie had spent the evening arguing over some trifle, and Suzie decided to make up.
"Wouldn't it be nice to have a few friends in tonight?" she suggested.
"Yeah," he grunted. "In fact even a few enemies would be a pleasure."

✓   ✓   ✓

Two buddies were having a beer and discussing whatever passes for wedded bliss.
"Is it true," asked one, "that marriage changes the personality?"
"In a way," answered the other, nodding. "Take my marriage, for instance. While we were engaged I did all the talking and she did all the listening. After we were married a few weeks she did all the talking and I did all the listening. Now we both do the talking and the neighbors do all the listening."

✓   ✓   ✓

"Since my wife started attending Adult Cooking School we're both much happier," boasted the young man. "Now we really appreciate simple, nourishing restaurant food."

✓   ✓   ✓

"Harry, why do you always stand outside on the porch whenever I sing?" asked the wife. "You know it hurts my feelings."
"What do you expect me to do?" demanded Harry. "Stay inside and have the neighbors think I'm beating you?"

✓   ✓   ✓

"Say, Honey," exclaimed the husband as soon as he returned home from work, "I really heard some gossip today."

"What kind of gossip?"

"I heard that the mailman has kissed every woman in this apartment building except one."

"I don't doubt it," replied the wife. "It must be that snooty Mrs. Karp on the ground floor."

✓   ✓   ✓

Joshua was an aesthetic youth with a great love for music, as well as the other arts. A rather shy fellow, he had never proposed to a girl, and his father decided to find him a suitable wife. After much discussion with two of his best friends, each of whom had a daughter, he gave his son a choice: He might marry a beautiful girl with no talent for music and little education, but with a fine cooking ability, or he might marry the daughter of his other friend. This one had a face that could curdle milk; her eyes were set too close together, she had no neck, her head seemed to be fastened to her shoulders with concrete, her nose could hold two dollars in nickels. But she had one virtue—a gorgeous voice. In fact, she adored all forms of music. The father showed his son a poster announcing the ugly girl's coming appearance at the Metropolitan Opera.

The youth's artistic sense overcame his attraction toward the beautiful girl, so he married the homely opera singer.

On the first morning after the wedding, he awoke, took one look at that face sharing his pillow and shook her. "For heaven's sake," he cried, "*sing* a little something!"

✓   ✓   ✓

"Just because we've been married for five years doesn't mean you can take me for granted," sniffed the neglected wife. "Why, I'll have you know that when I was young I could have married a real caveman." ·

"Naturally," said the husband. "When you were young that's all there were!"

✓   ✓   ✓

"All right, so I like to spend money," cried the resentful wife to her nagging husband, "but name one other extravagance!"

✓   ✓   ✓

"While we're on the subject of extravagant wives, let us consider the lady who was being very quiet while her grumpy husband toiled over his income tax returns. The doorbell sounded and a delivery boy was admitted with a stack of boxes from an exclusive milliner.

"What in the world is in all those boxes?" cried the husband.

"Hats—seven of them," explained the wife.

"Good God!" he exploded. "What do you need with seven hats?"

"Seven matching dresses," she told him.

✔   ✔   ✔

Mrs. Horowitz was talking to Mrs. Pomerantz, her neighbor. "I just can't stand that woman across the street . . . you know, the one who just moved in."

"Oh yes, the one who's always complaining about her husband."

"Believe me, it's worse than only complaining. She's terrible, the way she talks about him. Now take my husband; he drinks too much, he gambles, he stays out late—a worse husband you never saw in your life—he should drop dead! But do I ever say anything to anybody?"

Chapter Sixteen

Circumcisions and Bar Mitzvahs

Ben Landsberg, a staunch member of the Communist Party of America, was in a quandary.

"*Oy*, do I have big *tsorres!*" he complained to his brother-in-law.

"What kind of *tsorres?*" asked the relative.

"Any minute now my wife is expecting a baby. The doctor says it will be a boy. After all, she's your sister; you should understand my worry."

"Since when is having a baby boy something to worry about?"

"Look at it from my viewpoint. As a Communist I can't follow the religious practice of having the baby circumcised. On the other hand, I don't want him to look like a *goy* either. Believe me I got worries!"

A little later the brother-in-law accompanied Ben to the hospital. Ben went directly to the maternity ward while his relative waited in the lobby. A half hour elapsed before Ben returned, smiling cheerfully.

"*Nu?*" asked the brother-in-law.

"It's a girl, thank God!" exulted Ben.

"What do you mean, 'thank God!'" cried the other indignantly. "You Commies are supposed to be atheists."

"Of course! But in this case you got to admit that if there *is* a God He not only doesn't believe in circumcision but He's also on the side of the Communist Party!"

✦   ✦   ✦

A devout young Jew left his little village in Russia to seek his fortune in America. Many years later, having amassed his share of earthly goods, he decided to visit his aged parents in the land of his birth, and to relive a few nostalgic moments of his boyhood.

His eighty-year-old mother scarcely recognized him, so much had he changed.

"Your clothes are so strange!" she murmured.

"That's the way people dress in America," he assured her.

"But why aren't you wearing a beard like a good Jew?"

"But Mama, all men shave in the U. S."

"And the food? You at least keep a *kosher* kitchen in your house?"

"Well, to tell the truth, Mama, it is almost impossible to observe our dietary laws."

The old lady wiped a tear from her eye with a corner of her apron. Then a sudden, fearful thought struck her.

"Son," she asked anxiously, "are you still circumcised?"

✓ ✓ ✓

It has been said of Orthodox rabbis that they are quite stiff-necked, dour fellows. Actually they are flexible and, like their Reform and Conservative colleagues, possessed of a lively sense of humor. As the saying goes, read a little something:

Rabbi Friedman, whose wife was expecting a baby, was discussing the subject with a friend.

Asked the friend: "What are you hoping for—a boy or a girl?"

"I don't care which," said the rabbi, his eyes twinkling, "just so long as there's a *bris!*"

✓ ✓ ✓

A variation on the above bit of whimsy is the account of the friend who asks the rabbi, an expectant father, "Are you hoping for a boy or a girl?"

The rabbi answers, "Naturally!"

✓ ✓ ✓

"The Jews in America are so fancy," said the sage of a small Ukrainian village, "that when the *mohel* circumcises an infant he uses pinking shears!"

✓ ✓ ✓

Joel Goodrich, né Joseph Goodowitz, a third-generation American, had strayed long and far from the precepts and traditions of his people. So when his wife gave birth to their first child the young husband was at a loss as to the correct procedure to follow in naming the baby. But now that the time had arrived for the baby's circumcision he could postpone it no longer, so he decided to consult a patriarchal member of the local Orthodox synagogue.

"My son," the revered elder began, "you may not name a baby after its father or mother. It is traditional among our people to name an infant after some other member of the family who has passed away. In that manner the memory of the departed is kept alive."

"Which members of the family do you mean, sir?"

"Well, you can name the baby after your parents or others such as brothers, sisters, grandparents and so forth."

"But all of them are still alive," said the new father.

"Oh," the patriarch sighed apologetically, "I'm so sorry!"

✓ ✓ ✓

Twelve-year-old Sammy, an untutored denizen of New York's lower East Side, attended the *Bar Mitzvah* of his sophisticated cousin on the Grand Concourse.

After the ceremony, their grandmother served each a glass of milk and, in the middle of the table she set a platter containing two pieces of home-made cake. One piece, however, was slightly larger than the other.

Sammy, whose background was such that he knew no better, grabbed the bigger portion and stuffed it into his mouth. The well-brought-up cousin looked on, aghast. "What's the matter with you?" he cried. "Haven't you any table manners at all?"

"Why?" asked Sammy, genuinely surprised. "I did something wrong?"

"You took the biggest piece, that's what you did! Don't you know you're supposed to take the smaller one?"

"Well, what would you have done if you reached out first?"

"I'd have taken the smaller piece, of course."

"Then what are you making such a commotion about?" retorted Sammy. "That's what you got!"

✓   ✓   ✓

"Congratulate me!" enthused Hymie to his friend the butcher, as the latter was wrapping the *hock flaish*. "My Gertrude just gave birth to a fine, ten-pound boy!"

The butcher nodded absently, his mind on his work. "Really? With or without bones?"

✓   ✓   ✓

The wealthy and socially-conscious Mr. Archibald Schuyler threw a lavish party in honor of his son's Bar Mitzvah. During the festivities he was approached by one of the guests.

"Mr. Archibald Schuyler?"

"Yes."

"I have a message for you from my brother-in-law. He says he remembers you when you were Abe Schneider."

"What is your brother-in-law's name?"

"Donald Jackson."

"Oh yes, I remember him quite well. Good ol' David Jacobson!"

✓   ✓   ✓

Zimmerman, the big cloak-and-suiter, wanted to have the biggest *Bar Mitzvah* of all time for his son. So he mapped out a safari to Africa and chartered six DC-8's for his guests, and another six planes for the hunting and camping equipment, food and drink.

Everyone piled aboard and all the planes flew in formation to equatorial Africa. There, Zimmerman hired five hundred native pack-bearers and a dozen guides, cooks and a master chef. Then the huge procession started to wind through the dense jungle.

Suddenly the entire company came to a halt. Zimmerman, who was playing pinochle with a few of the guests on top of an elephant in the rear of the long line, called out, "What's holding us up?"

And the word was relayed back: "There's another *Bar Mitzvah* ahead of us!"

1   1   1

Around the turn of the century, when the Jews of New York were fighting for the right to organize their labor unions and the ensuing strife created much ferment and antagonisms, the police often used their clubs to crack the skulls of the striking garment workers. The epithet, "Cossack!" was frequently applied to the officers, many of whom were anti-Semitic. The following dialogue was a popular joke in the late 1890's and the first decade of this century.

A police officer passed by a home in which a circumcision had just been performed. As he watched, the *mohel*, whom the policeman knew, came out of the house.

"Hey, butcher, tell me something," said the officer jeeringly. "What do you do with all the pieces you cut off?"

"I'll be glad to tell you," answered the *mohel* courteously. "I send them downtown where they make cops out of them!"

1   1   1

Jewish wit and humor possesses a facility for the non-sequitur that is rarely equalled among other peoples. Author Alexander King, in his *Mine Enemies Grow Older*, reminds us of this perfect example:

One day a rich American Jew who was touring Russia, was compelled to lay over for a few hours in a small, remote village, because his car had broken down.

Deeply annoyed and irritated by the delay, he happened to consult his watch and noticed that the minute hand had become detached. So he decided to look around the main street of the town for a watchmaker who might make the necessary repair for him. He walked nearly the whole length of the street before he finally landed in front of a shop window where half a dozen assorted clocks and watches were displayed.

The door was a few steps below street level, and when he entered he found an old and venerable-looking Jew sitting at a lectern and quietly reading what was obviously the Talmud.

"I have to stay in this town for a few hours," said the visitor, "and this minute hand has somehow gotten loose. I am wondering if you could repair it for me?"

The old Jew looked up, slowly shook his head, and without a word returned to his reading of the Scriptures.

The visitor, thinking the old man might be a little deaf, now said in a much louder voice, "My minute hand has fallen off and I'd like you to fix it for me. Will it take very long?"

163

The old man again looked up, once more shook his venerable head, and again proceeded to immerse himself in the sacred tome.

Now the visitor was really getting irritated. He put his hand on the old man's arm and shouted, at the top of his voice, "Why don't you answer? Are you going to repair this minute hand for me or not?"

The old man looked up benignly and said, "I can't possibly do it for you."

"Why not? Are you afraid I'm unable to pay?"

"Not at all. I can't do it because I'm not a watchmaker."

"You're not a watchmaker? Then what in heaven's name are you?"

"I'm a *mohel*," explained the ancient one. "I circumcise the village children."

The visitor was stupefied. "Then what in the name of God are all those clocks and watches doing in your window?"

The old man regarded the intruder speculatively for a moment, and when he finally spoke there was an indefinable ripple of humor in his voice:

"Tell me, if you earned your living by circumcising babies, what would *you* put in the window?"

Chapter Seventeen

The Army—That's All I Need!

The Vietnamese war was raging on all sides of the small group of American soldiers. The sergeant drew up his isolated squad and barked, "This is it, men! The time has come to charge the Viet Cong. Get your bayonets ready—it's now man against man in hand-to-hand combat!"

Private Albert Silverstein raised his hand.

"Yeah, Silverstein," snapped the non-com. "What is it?"

"Sarge," quavered the private. "It's man against man?"

"You heard me!"

"Look," said Silverstein desperately, "how about showing me my man? Maybe he and I can work this thing out by ourselves!"

✓   ✓   ✓

During the invasion of Europe, in World War II, a Jewish private saved the life of General Dwight D. Eisenhower.

"You are a brave young man," exclaimed Eisenhower gratefully. "If I can do anything for you in return, just ask and I'll do it."

"Oh, thank you, Sir. I would sure appreciate it if you would transfer me to another company."

"But why?"

"My corporal doesn't like Jews."

"For heaven's sake!" cried the exasperated general. "Why didn't you ask me to promote you to a corporal instead?"

"Well, it's like this, sir," explained the youth. "The sergeant doesn't like Jewish corporals. The Lieutenant doesn't like Jewish sergeants. The Captain doesn't like Jewish lieutenants. The Major doesn't like Jewish captains. The General doesn't like Jewish maj . . . Please, General Eisenhower, why don't you do like I ask, and just transfer me to another company?"

✓   ✓   ✓

The ineffable distinction between sarcasm and biting satire is illustrated in this story—an exposition of the ultimate in "black humor."

During 1964 and 1965, the official reports from Washington were unanimous that the war situation in Vietnam was improving. So when Benny was drafted into the army, his father did not worry too much. After all, the newspapers, radio and TV all reported the improvements in the Vietnamese hostilities. Under these circumstances, the father was sure that his son would return home safely.

A few months later, to his utter shock, he was notified that his beloved Benny had been killed in combat—even as a television announcer was declaiming America's improved position.

The father called the family to his side and broke the stunning news. "Benny is dead," he said simply.

"But what did he die of?" moaned the sister.

And from the agony of his soul, the father cried out, "Improvements!"

✓ ✓ ✓

In 1966, when the United States embarked on a policy of bombing the oil depots in North Vietnam, thus "escalating" the war (to use the jargon of the day), many liberals and intellectuals raised their voices in opposition to the administration's military policy. A few, however, supported the government's stand, parroting the notion that unless we stopped Red China in Vietnam, hordes of Communist Orientals would soon invade Cleveland—and how would you like it if your sister was forced to marry one of them?

Among those who agreed with President Johnson was Dr. John Roche, professor of political science at Brandeis University, a keen scholar and provocative, liberal thinker on all matters except the unpopular war.

One day, Dr. Roche was lecturing on the necessity for our participation in the hostilities when a student interrupted his talk.

"Would Christ have carried a draft card?" shouted the heckler.

And Dr. Roche countered, "Would Christ have carried a Social Security card?"

✓ ✓ ✓

"What do I think of the Second World War?" asked Mama. "To tell you the truth, I saw it in the movies and I didn't like it!"

✓ ✓ ✓

There is a story of the First World War that does credit to both Jewish patriotism and ingenuity.

It seems that a Jewish boy of the American Expeditionary Forces would steal out of his trench every night, during the hours of ominous gloom and silence when the batteries ceased to scatter death and destruction, and return each time with ten or fifteen captives from the enemy camp.

This feat, repeated every night by the young hero, so impressed his superior officers that he was finally summoned to headquarters where he was commended for his heroism.

THE ARMY—THAT'S ALL I NEED!

"You have never told anyone how you have been able to capture so many prisoners," remarked one of the army dignitaries. "Just how did you manage it?"

"My method is very simple," replied the soldier with a beatific smile. "I sneak up to the enemy lines and call out, *'Yidden, ich darf a minyan auf kaddish,'** and instantly ten or fifteen Jews pop out to accommodate me!"

✓   ✓   ✓

The author's aunt, Bella Monoson, of Brooklyn, New York, is credited with this one.

An Israeli soldier, on vacation in the United States, ran into an American soldier. They struck up a conversation and soon were chummy enough to complain about conditions which soldiers of every army, in every century, gripe about.

"You can thank God you don't have to eat K-Rations," said the American GI. "As far as food is concerned, that's the biggest nothing since the invention of the zero."

"You're right!" agreed the Israeli soldier.

"Why, how do you know?"

"We have it too in our army. Believe me, my friend, Jewish K-Rations are just as bad as yours."

"What's Jewish K-Rations?"

The Israeli fighting man took a deep breath. "Jewish K-Rations include *katchkeh, knishes, kreplach, knaidlach, kishkeh, kasha* and *kugel.*"

The American GI laughed delightedly. "It's a good thing you guys don't have dessert."

"Sure we do," grinned the Israeli, *"kichel!"*

✓   ✓   ✓

The Russian equivalent of a drill instructor in the Czarist army had just taken command of a squad of raw recruits, nearly all of whom were rather doltish *yishuvniks*. The officer took one look at the vapid faces of his new men and realized that he would have to start with the most basic of instruction, using the simplest of terms.

"Now I want all of you to stand in a straight line," the officer began, "and when I count one-two-three, start to march—left foot first. At the count of three! Is that clear?"

"Tak totchmo!" roared the green troopers.

"Now, one . . ."

But no sooner had the officer uttered the count of 'one' when a Jewish recruit—the only one in the squad—marched off.

"Hey, *Zhid!*" bellowed the officer. "Stop where you are! What the hell's the matter with you? Didn't you hear me just say you were to march at the count of three?"

---

* "Fellow Jews, I need ten men to say the memorial prayer."

167

"Sir, I meant no disrespect," said the young Jew humbly. "If you will excuse me for saying so, we both can see that the rest of these recruits are a bunch of morons: they *must* wait until you count three. But I'm very quick, sir. I knew what you wanted the moment you said 'one'!"

✓ ✓ ✓

The Allied casualties that resulted from the D-Day invasion of Europe were frightful. In the American army, a Jewish soldier fell, critically wounded. A Catholic chaplain rushed to his side and showed him a cross with a crucified Christ on it.

"Do you know the meaning of this?" asked the priest.

"*Oy, gevald!*" moaned the soldier. "Here I'm dying with a bullet in my *poopik* and he wants to play guessing games!"

✓ ✓ ✓

A couple of talmudic scholars were standing on the platform of a railroad station in the heart of Russia, when two military trains, approaching from opposite directions, pulled in. The soldiers of one train all wore gray trousers and the soldiers of the other train all wore red trousers.

"The gray-trousered soldiers," explained one of the scholars, "are being transferred from Warsaw to Moscow, and the red-trousered soldiers are being transported from Moscow to Warsaw."

"I can't understand why the Czar is going to all this trouble and expense," said the other student. "Instead of transporting the soldiers, wouldn't it be much cheaper to transport just the trousers, and the soldiers could put them on right where they are? Then Warsaw would have red-trousered soldiers and Moscow would have gray-trousered soldiers."

"Don't be such a *shlemiel!*" cried the other impatiently. "What would they wear while the pants were being shipped?"

✓ ✓ ✓

Just prior to the Russian Revolution, a young Jewish soldier deserted his regiment. He was quickly captured and brought before the regimental commander.

"You are a gutless coward, a traitor to your country!" snarled the general. "Only a filthy deserter would run off as you did!"

"Sir," said the young soldier, "I had no intention of betraying the Fatherland. I ran away only because I hate the enemy so much I can't stand the sight of them!"

✓ ✓ ✓

Doctor: "Young man, is there any medical reason why you should not be inducted into the army?"

Draftee: "Believe me, Doctor, half of my insides are missing!"

Doctor: "What's your internal problem?"

Draftee: "No guts!"

✓ ✓ ✓

THE ARMY—THAT'S ALL I NEED!

Headlines throughout the world proclaimed that Egypt had attacked Israel and that both nations were now at war. The Israeli army was ready, but the Chief of Staff had no one to take over the command of the country's one and only submarine. An urgent call went out for an experienced captain. Answering the appeal was 'Albert Rothschild, scion of the immensely wealthy banking family, and a submarine officer in his own right.

On their third day at sea, an Egyptian destroyer was sighted in the heavy fog, only two hundred yards off the starboard side.

"Dive!" ordered Captain Rothschild.

Deep below the surface of the sea, they maneuvered into position to sink the enemy ship.

"Just bear in mind that torpedoes don't grow on trees!" Rothschild warned the chief gunner. "They cost $25,000 each, so take careful aim and don't fire until I give the order!"

"Yes *sir!*" answered the gunner with a snappy salute, gulping at the cost of the missiles.

"Enemy destroyer 150 yards off starboard!" called the first mate.

"Fire!" ordered Rothschild.

The gunner made no move to comply.

"Enemy destroyer now only 100 yards away," reported the first mate anxiously.

"*Nu*, what are you waiting for?" hollered Captain Rothschild. "Fire!"

The gunner stood as though frozen, not a nerve or muscle twitching.

"Enemy only fifty yards away and getting closer!" screamed the first mate hoarsely.

No move from the gunner.

"Allright already! FIRE!" bellowed Rothschild. "*I'll* pay for the torpedoes!"

✓   ✓   ✓

It is a scientific fact that continual drops of water will eventually erode a rock, but this story demonstrates how a pail of water can defeat an army.

It happened during the Franco-Russian War, at the time when Napoleon Bonaparte and his victorious armies had swept through Russian territory and had reached the Jewish Pale of Settlement.

One bright morning, a *melamed,* carrying a pail of water, was startled to see a full company of French soldiers approaching on the road ahead. Now it is well known among Eastern Jews that whoever meets a person carrying a pail of water will enjoy good luck. Conversely, should anyone meet a person carrying an empty pail, it will result in ill fortune.

The Almighty knows that the Jews of Czarist Russia had little reason to love their motherland; nevertheless they maintained a fierce loyalty to the land of their birth. So it was natural that the patriotic *melamed* should be thrown into near panic at the sight of the alien troops.

169

"Why should I bring good luck to the invaders?" he asked himself. "Napoleon's only purpose is to destroy Mother Russia." Suddenly he had an inspired idea. He quickly emptied the pail of its water and grinned as the French soldiers trudged past. "I fixed them good!" he thought triumphantly.

The moment he set foot inside his house, however, his wife, a shrewish woman, exclaimed, "Why do you bring home an empty pail? What happened to the water?"

"I dumped the water out as a military tactic," he explained, reminding her of the necessity of bringing bad luck to the French armies.

She listened in stony silence until her husband had finished, and then burst out wrathfully:

"*Shlemiel!* If two of the most powerful nations on earth are having an argument, who needs you to interfere?"

1 1 1

A Russian general, making a surprise visit to an isolated military post, was shocked to find the entire division in a disreputable state—their clothes filthy.

"Captain," he roared to one of the officers, "I want every man in this outfit to change his underwear at once!"

"But sir," the captain explained, trembling, "the men have no extra underwear."

"That's no excuse!" screeched the general. "Let them change with each other!"

1 1 1

Peter the Great once inspected a battalion of soldiers. Anxious to test the loyalty of his troops, he approached a big, overgrown *mujik* in uniform and said, "Listen, *zemlyak*, if I should tell you to shoot me, would you obey?"

"Yes, Your Majesty," returned the sturdy trooper. "I must do whatever my superiors tell me."

Putting the question to several other soldiers, the sovereign received the same reply.

At last the Czar approached a Jewish soldier. "And you, *Zhid*, would you shoot me if I ordered you to do so?"

"No, Your Majesty!" was the emphatic answer.

The great ruler was deeply moved. Here, at least, was one soldier whose love for his king outweighed his sense of duty. And an obvious Jew, at that!

"I'm sorry I called you a *Zhid*," crooned the monarch, full of emotion. "Tell me, my son, why wouldn't you shoot me?"

"Because I'm a *barabanschik*,"* answered the loyal soldier, "and I'm not supposed to do any shooting!"

1 1 1

_____
* A drummer in the army.

THE ARMY—THAT'S ALL I NEED!

The rabbi had just been given a chaplain's commission in the U.S. Army, and for his first tour of duty he was assigned to minister to the spiritual needs of the veterans in a mental hospital. The men, suffering from shell-shock, or combat fatigue as it is now called, listened politely as the rabbi developed his point that there is a divine reason for all that happens.

"Ask yourselves this question," he thundered like a prophet of old, "Why are we here?"

And a voice piped up from the rear: "Because we ain't all there!"

✓ ✓ ✓

A general was talking to the late Albert Einstein.

"Our losses in the last military campaign were relatively mild," the army officer commented with deep pride.

"Relative to *what?*" snapped the inventor of the theory.

✓ ✓ ✓

The Columbia Broadcasting System received this postcard complaint from a feminine viewer:

"I hate war. It's all we ever see on television!"

✓ ✓ ✓

Milton Berle, "Mr. Television" himself, was speaking at a Zionist banquet.

"While I was in Israel," he told the assembled guests, "they asked me if I would like to visit the tomb of Israel's unknown soldier. I said I would, and an escort picked me up in a limousine.

"When I arrived at the tomb I couldn't believe my eyes. There, in big letters, was inscribed, 'Here lies Israel's unknown soldier, Hyman Goldfarb, Furrier.'

" 'But I thought this was the tomb of an unknown soldier! How can he possibly have a name?' "

" 'As a soldier,' they assured me, 'he was certainly unknown, but as a furrier he was famous!' "

✓ ✓ ✓

TV and nightclub personality Mort Sahl was discussing his two years in the Korean "police action."

"I never saw any Koreans in Korea," he said, "except on Sundays when some of them used to come and watch us fight!"

✓ ✓ ✓

At the height of the Battle of the Marne, in the first World War, General "Blackjack" Pershing decided to visit the front line trenches for a personal appraisal of the military situation. A young Jewish corporal was assigned as his guide. "Please follow me, General," whispered the soldier.

171

"All right, lead the way," whispered General Pershing in return.

Silently they walked and sometimes crawled forward through the narrow trenches. "Are we very far from the front-line trenches?" asked Pershing after about an hour.

"Not too far," whispered the corporal.

Rather shamefacedly, the great general realized that he had raised his voice. "Sorry," he whispered.

They continued to move forward cautiously for two more hours.

"Aren't we there yet?" asked the impatient general, his voice scarcely audible.

"Almost," whispered the corporal.

But when they had not arrived at their destination after the next hour, the General's patience was at an end.

"Young man," hissed Pershing, "exactly how far are we from the front line?"

"About twenty-five miles, sir."

"Twenty-five miles!" roared the General at the top of his lungs. "Then why the hell have you been whispering all this time?"

"I'm not whispering, sir," replied the corporal, pointing to his throat. "I have laryngitis!"

✓ ✓ ✓

Private Cohen was rushing into the Army PX one night when he ran into a general and knocked him down. It was quite dark outside the Post Exchange, and Cohen snapped, "Why'ncha watch where ya goin'?"

The officer, his face a black mask of fury, struggled to his feet and roared, "Private, do you know who I am?"

"General Eisenhower, no doubt," sneered the impudent private.

"Exactly!" was the cold-as-ice reply.

The recruit swallowed hard, his mind a kaleidoscope of excuses, schemes and prayers. "Do you know who I happen to be?" he asked boldly.

"No, who?" asked the startled general.

"Thank God!" cried Private Cohen as he fled into the darkness.

✓ ✓ ✓

Sailor Jack Berger had only been in the Navy for three months and now he was taking his first ocean voyage. The ship was in the middle of the Atlantic when suddenly a storm burst upon them—a howling gale that soon had the ship sliding down the incline of tremendous waves, riding the crest for agonizing moments, and then pitching down again in a stomach-churning descent.

Berger, hanging on to the rail for dear life, gasped, "How far are we from land?"

"Only four or five miles," said the cheerful mate.

Berger felt a few seconds of relief, but quickly remembered that they

172

were three days out at sea. "Four or five miles!" he cried in disbelief. "What direction?"

"Straight down," grinned the mate.

✓ ✓ ✓

After a few years in the Navy, Berger became an expert seaman. In fact, his officers thought so well of him that they transferred him to the mighty Nautilus, America's first atomic-powered submarine. The pay was excellent, the prestige glorifying, and the young sailor quite contented.

After a great many months he was granted leave and visited his parents in Bensonhurst. As might be expected, he was asked how he liked being on the great submarine.

"It's wonderful," he enthused. "A nuclear powered submarine stays under water for two years without surfacing. The only time it comes up is when the crew has to re-enlist."

✓ ✓ ✓

Comic Joey Adams: "I was the only guy in the Army who was awarded the yellow heart."

✓ ✓ ✓

The war in Vietnam was being "escalated," and an instructor at the Saigon Military Police school was lecturing a class in practical defense and offense exercises. After presenting various problems to the recruits, and then explaining the solution, he pointed to Private Kaplan.

"Now then, Private, suppose you were all alone in the jungles when suddenly a Viet Cong guerrilla jumped out of the foliage and came at you with a two-foot knife. What steps would you take?"

"Big ones," said Private Kaplan.

✓ ✓ ✓

Sam and Leon were discussing the war in Vietnam which threatened to engulf all of American youth, including the college students. Sam was terribly pessimistic about the future, worried that he would never be able to complete his higher education, but Leon was an optimist.

"You'll graduate," Leon consoled. "You really have nothing to worry about. This affair may blow over, but even if the war escalates you still have two possibilities: You will either be drafted or you will not be drafted. If you are not drafted you have nothing to worry about, but even if you are you still have two possibilities: You may be sent to Vietnam or you might not be sent to Vietnam. If you are not sent to Vietnam you have nothing to worry about, but even if you should be sent to Vietnam you still have two possibilities: You will either be wounded or you will not be wounded. If you are not wounded you have nothing to worry about, but even if you are wounded you still have two possibilities: You may be wounded slightly or you may be wounded seriously. If you

173

are wounded slightly you have nothing to worry about, but even if you are wounded seriously you still have two possibilities: You may go either to the good place or to the bad place. If you go to the good place you have nothing to worry about, but even if you go to the bad place, you still have one possibility: War may not be declared because President Johnson said this is only a disagreement over conflicting ideologies, so you still have nothing to worry about!"

The Israeli-Arab War of 1967

"Where there are two Jews there are three opinions," goes an old Jewish saying. But a steadfast unanimity of viewpoint pervaded the entire House of Judah when, in June, 1967, Israel launched its "blintzkrieg" against the enemy which sought to exterminate her. The hostilities evoked an outpouring of jokes and witticisms that illustrated the smashing triumph as graphically as might any sober-sided historian.

But there was a vast difference between the drolleries occasioned by the war and those of the past. Historically, Jews have reserved their adulation and respect for the intellectual, the scholar and teacher, the rabbi and humanitarian. Military heroes—the warrior syndrome—are relatively few in number: Samson, David, Joshua, the Maccabees and the heroic defender against the Roman Legions, Simon Bar Kochba. But unlike the Quakers and a few other Protestant fundamentalists, the Jews are not now, and never have been, pacifists. Perhaps the answer lies in the sad fact that they have not had a national homeland to fight for since pre-Christian times. A quick perusal of the Torah, a reminder of the valiant Battle of the Warsaw Ghetto, a thought to the International Jewish Brigade under General Allenby, and the subsequent victories over the militant Arabs—all these should have recalled to the Jews their glorious past and capabilities.

Now, in the last third of the 20th Century, the accused became the accuser, the rabbit the hound, the intended victim the conqueror, and the object of post-Hitlerian genocide the magistrate of stern justice.

Withal, the Jewish penchant for humor continued unabated. Egypt's Gamal Nasser was dubbed Public Enema No. 1. Remarked the irrepressible Walter Winchell, "It couldn't happen to a Nasser guy—he's just an Arrable rouser."

The wry observations even invaded the sports arena. It was said that the former heavyweight boxing champion, Cassius Clay, who preferred to be called Muhammad Ali, changed his name to Al Malamud. In the baseball world there was this pithy evaluation of the Arab armies: The Mets, with guns.* And a popular question of the day was "What's the fastest

---

* As this was written (1967) the New York Mets were the perennial occupants of the last place in the National League.

thing on wheels?" The proper answer: "An Arab bicycling past the *Forverts* Building."

Moshe Dayan, the brilliant Israeli Minister of Defense, was much in the news and an object of admiring humor. "Mighty Moe," according to one quip, taught the big-talking Arabs the first rule of street fighting—the fist is quicker than the mouth! Dayan himself made the humorous statement that American GI's are not the only ones who gripe about army rations. "The only revenge I would take on the captured Egyptian soldiers," he grinned, "would be to make them eat the same food our boys eat."

On the eve of overwhelming victory, a spokesman for the U.S. Department of State advised the press that America would be "neutral in thought, word and deed." A prominent Jewish Democrat who invariably contributed substantial sums to his party's campaigns, sent this telegram to President Lyndon B. Johnson: "WHEN YOU AGAIN RUN FOR OFFICE I SHALL BE NEUTRAL IN THOUGHT, WORD AND DEED."

There was some apprehension among Jews in the Diaspora that Israel might suffer as a result of Arab refusal to provide oil in the future. But boycotts operate on a two-way street; the Israelis were anything but concerned. "The Arabs may have the oil," said General Dayan jauntily, "but we have all the credit cards."

Needless to point out, the lightning speed with which the Israeli army and air force clobbered its several opposing armies surprised the Egyptians. But they are a practical people. On the very first day of the war, when the trend had already been established, the Cairo-Hilton reportedly began taking reservations for *Bar Mitzvahs.*

Even the Soviet Union was taken aback by the swift advance. Russia airlifted 200 tanks to Syria, each equipped with back-up lights.

Nasser, caught with his pantaloons out of adjustment, complained to the United Nations that the war was unfair. "Israel has over two million Jews," he protested, "and we don't have any!"

In New York, the *Forverts,* disgusted with the UN's dallying at the height of the crisis, did a little transposing in its columns. Reading from right to left, as in Hebrew, the UN was changed to "NU?"

One cigarette company altered its television commercial to "Call for Philip Moishe."

Inevitably, Hollywood got into the act. At a Friar's Club banquet, a few days after the Six Day War, Frank Sinatra acknowledged the *fait accompli* of Israel's expanded frontiers. Joked the entertainer: "I'm going to Israel to see the pyramids."

Show business pundits quickly figured out the reason why Israel's performance was so decisive. George Jessel promised David Ben-Gurion he would send Darryl Zanuck over if the audition turned out okay.

Columnist David Schwartz, a very funny and quite perceptive observer, writing in the *California Jewish Voice,* informed his readers that Moshe Dayan's real name is Genghis Cohen.

Schwartz then went on to explain why Egypt lost the war. Nasser called his army chiefs of staff together and told them to copy the secret of Russian military success from Marshal Kutusov (who beat Napoleon). And that is exactly what the Arab officers did. They drew the enemy deep into their own territory and then waited for snow.

In a "truth is stranger than fiction" account, Schwartz also demonstrated that it is also often funnier. Discussing the miracles wrought by the Israel air force, the columnist described a conversation with Meyer Weisgal of the Weizmann Institute, who visited Los Angeles shortly after the war. Explained Weisgal: "Algeria came to the aid of Egypt after Egypt suffered its great loss of planes. Algeria dispatched two dozen air planes, but thinking to expedite things, sent them to El Arish, unaware that the Israelis had seized it. The Israel army has many young soldiers who are fluent in Arabic, and they signalled the Algerian pilots to land. When they did, they gave the pilots another signal—'HANDS UP!'"

But how can you top the one about the Israeli soldier who came upon a battered, burned-out Egyptian tank somewhere in the Gaza Strip? He posted this sign on the charred hulk: OIL AND CHICKEN SOUP DON'T MIX.

Chapter Eighteen

Anti-Semites

Eastern Europe

The Soviet Union requires its citizens who move from one part of the country to another, even though it may be the next town, to have a passport. Jewish citizens are the only group in that nation whose ethnic or religious origin must be identified; thus their passports are stamped "Jew." This practice stems from the bitter Czarist persecution of the Jewish people of old Russia where only a few privileged members of the House of Israel were allowed to reside in the larger cities. Those who did remain were often stopped by the police and asked to produce their *pravozhitelstvo*, the resident permit, or passport that allowed them access to the city. Those who trespassed in "Holy Russia" were subject to imprisonment, beatings and heavy fines—sometimes all three. The repressive regulations are embodied in much of the Jewish folk-humor of Eastern Europe.

✦   ✦   ✦

Two Jews were walking furtively on Nevsky Prospect, the chief thoroughfare of the former Russian capital, but only one of them had a residence permit. The other had entered the city clandestinely, in order to visit his mother who was ill. Suddenly an officer turned the corner, approaching them.

"Listen to me," said the passport holder to his frightened co-religionist, "run as fast as you can, and I'll follow you. I will be nearer to the policeman so he'll apprehend me first."

"B-but what will happen to you?"

"Never mind that! I can take care of myself. Now start running!"

The fugitive took to his heels like a frightened deer, the one with the permit following behind his friend. As expected, the officer pursued them, convinced that he had inadvertantly stumbled upon not one, but two of the despised *Zhids*. A much younger and faster man than the middle-aged victims, he soon caught his quarry—the Jew with the passport.

"Now I got you!" the cop thundered. "Where is your *pravozhitelstvo?*"

"Right here," said the panting Jew, producing the document.

177

The police officer examined it carefully, a bewildered expression on his face. Then his voice grew hard as suspicion dawned that he had somehow been duped.

"Why were you running if you have a permit?" he snarled.

"Doctor's orders, officer. He told me to run a mile every day for my health."

"How about that other *Zhid* who was with you? What was he running for?"

"The doctor ordered him to run a mile every day, too."

"Then why the hell didn't you stop when you saw me running after you?" cried the enraged officer.

"Because," replied the other sweetly, "I thought your doctor also ordered you to run a mile every day!"

✓   ✓   ✓

The Jews of Czarist Russia were not only required to obey the punitive laws but they were also forced to do homage to the police who vigorously enforced the purely anti-Semitic regulations. For example, a Jew who spoke with a government official, however minor his position might be, was expected to remove his hat or suffer outrageous punishment for the "affront."

A *gorodovoy*, or police officer, was patrolling his beat in Petrograd, when he observed a Jew who seemed to be acting in a peculiar fashion. From his furtive side-glances and timid manner, the policeman surmised that he had no residence permit in the city, and, like a bird of prey he swooped down on the intended victim.

"Stand where you are!" he commanded, collaring the quaking little Jew. "Where do you come from?"

The "prisoner" reached into his pocket and displayed his *pravozhitelstvo*. "I come from right here," he answered meekly, forgetting, in his confusion, to remove his hat.

The disappointed officer glared at the trembling "criminal."

"What about your hat?" he barked.

"My hat?" the Jew echoed, trembling in his shoes. "That comes from here too!"

✓   ✓   ✓

It happened during the reign of the viciously anti-Semitic Czar Nicholas. A mild-mannered, inoffensive Jew was strolling along one of the principal streets of St. Petersburg when he was nabbed by a police officer.

At the police barracks the Jew indignantly demanded that he be set free on the grounds that he was engaged in an essential industry and therefore had a perfect right to be in the city.

"What is this work of yours that's so essential?" asked the Captain of the Watch.

"I make buttonholes."

"Buttonholes! I don't see anything essential about that. My wife can even make buttonholes."

"Congratulations!" cried the Jew cheerfully. "Now your wife has a perfect right to live in St. Petersburg too!"

✓ ✓ ✓

Russia was not the only country in Eastern Europe where Jews were oppressed. Poland and Hungary were almost as bad, and often much worse.

In Budapest, the police broke into a Jewish home one night and dragged the father off to prison on the flimsiest of pretexts. Early the next morning the man's daughter went to the police station to plead for her father's release.

"Go to the priest," grinned the malicious police officer. "If he says I am to release your father, I'll set him free."

The girl knew that the priest was notorious for his zeal in attempting to convert Jews to Christianity, but she went anyway.

The priest listened to her anguished pleas for a few minutes and then pointed to a small statue of Christ.

"First kiss the groom," he commanded.

"Very well," answered the girl promptly, "but it is customary among the Jewish people that the groom first kiss the bride!"

✓ ✓ ✓

The following story may well elicit a sigh rather than a chuckle for those Jews who still remember Czarist oppression and the pathos of a people without a home.

Three weary Jews were caught as they attempted to sneak across the Russian boundary.

"Where were you three going?" asked the magistrate sternly.

"I was hoping to get to Palestine," said the first.

"My destination was Rome," said the second.

"My plan was to go to Australia," said the third.

"Australia!" exclaimed the surprised judge. "Why so far?"

"Far?" whispered the Jew with a catch in his voice. "Far from where?"

✓ ✓ ✓

In the days of Czar Nicholas, a friendly Jew boarded a train for Minsk. Opposite him, in the same compartment, sat a lieutenant of the Czarist army with a small dog on his lap.

The amiable Jew attempted to strike up a conversation but the Russian officer gave him such a withering look that he hastily retreated into silence.

But the lieutenant, not satisfied with silencing the hated Jew, kept stroking his dog and all the while maliciously calling the animal "Isaac."

Finally the Jewish traveler had enough. "It's too bad about your dog," he remarked innocently.

"What's too bad about him?" snapped the lieutenant.

"That he has a Jewish name."

"I still don't know what you are talking about."

"Well, if it weren't for his Jewish name," the little man explained politely, "he might someday be a lieutenant like his master."

✔   ✔   ✔

A prominent Jewish statesman was invited to attend a meeting of the Warsaw City Council. On the appointed day he arrived and seated himself in the left aisle.

A committee official approached him.

"Sir, Jew or not, you are an invited member and therefore entitled to sit on the right side."

"I'll sit on the left," the statesman replied calmly. "In Poland we Jews have no rights!"

✔   ✔   ✔

Just before the Russian Revolution, when that country was among the Allies at war with Kaiser Wilhelm's Germany, a Jew walked into a neighborhood store in Moscow to make a purchase. The proprietor looked at him contemptuously. "You are no longer welcome here!" he spat. "Get out of my store and stay out!"

"Why, what have I done?" asked the amazed Jew.

"I'll tell you what you and the rest of you Jews have done! While my son is in the army, fighting for honor and dignity, your son is still at home. And what is your son fighting for? Profit, that's what!"

"I'm sorry you feel that way," said the Jew, truly saddened. "My son may be called to defend Mother Russia at any moment. Meanwhile, let us bear in mind that your son and mine are both fighting for what each needs most!"

✔   ✔   ✔

Of all the Jews who suffered humiliations at the hands of anti-Semites in Russia, the Balkans and other areas of Eastern Europe, the least self-conscious of all was Meyer Kopetz.

Kopetz, the aged *chassid* of Stanislaw, decided to visit Cracow on a matter of business. In order to look presentable for this momentous journey, the saintly man donned his favorite silk gabardine and most impressive *streimel*, adorned himself with the newest prayer-scarf which had the longest fringes, and after combing his gray, patriarchal beard, went to the train, looking for all the world like a prophet who had miraculously stepped forth from the pages of the Torah.

Upon returning home, Meyer Kopetz appeared to be downcast and morose.

180

"What's the trouble, Meyer?" asked his wife. "Were you unable to complete your business transaction?"

"It was well taken care of, thank God," said the holy man, "but on the train several Poles constantly ridiculed Jews and Judaism. They said it loudly enough for me to hear, and it saddened me."

"Oh, Meyer, I hope you didn't argue with those anti-Semites they should beat you," cried the anxious wife.

"No, I didn't say a word," replied Kopetz, the venerable *chassid*. "I just acted as though I weren't Jewish!"

✦   ✦   ✦

Mendel Klotz and Moshe Zimmerman, two close friends, were walking along the main street in Odessa, engaged in an animated discussion. So absorbed were they in their conversation that they did not notice the two Russian Army officers approaching them, and consequently they did not get off the sidewalk and into the gutter as Jews were expected to do, so that their "betters" might pass without the contamination of a possible brush of shoulders.

Immediately the two were arrested and brought before the magistrate. Mendel was brought into the judge's chambers first, while Moshe waited in an anteroom.

"What have you got to say for yourself?" barked the Czar's defender of law, order and the rights of man.

"Your Grace, I was so involved in an argument with my friend that I did not notice the officers," explained the terrified Mendel. "I apologize. It will never happen again!"

"That's no excuse!" yelled the typical Russian judge. "Thirty days at hard labor!"

Mendel was escorted into the anteroom where Moshe was waiting.

"How d-d-did it g-go?" asked Moshe anxiously.

"We haven't a chance," groaned Mendel. "I received a thirty day sentence."

Now Moshe stood before the judge.

"All right, what's your excuse?" rasped the judge.

Moshe, numb with fright, could scarcely speak. "Y-y-your honor," he began, stuttering helplessly, "I-I-I tr-tried t-t-t- . . . !" Words failed him.

"Get this imbecile out of here!" the judge shouted to the bailiff. "I have no time for half-wits!"

Moshe walked into the anteroom, his face wreathed in smiles.

"How much of a sentence did he throw at you?" asked Mendel.

"None! I'm as free as a b-bird."

"What do you mean, you're free! How is that possible? We were both arrested on the same charges, yet I get thirty days and you go free?"

"The t-t-trouble with you, M-mendel," said his friend, "is that y-you don't know h-how t-t-to t-talk!"

✦   ✦   ✦

During the latter part of the 19th century a Russian Grand Duke, a member of the Czar's family, visited London and the Lord Mayor gave a dinner in his honor. Among the invited guests was the late Sir Moses Montefiore, famous millionaire and philanthropist. The Grand Duke did not relish the idea of dining with a Jew and in the course of the meal he remarked that upon his recent visit to Japan he found it to be truly unique in that it had neither Jews nor pigs.

The assembled guests pretended not to notice the slur, but old Montefiore responded coolly: "Sir, suppose you and I go to Japan. That country will then have a sample of each."

✔   ✔   ✔

A collector for a Jewish institution in Russia while passing through a forest was held up by an armed Cossack who robbed him of all his money.

"Let me ask a favor of you," said the collector to the Cossack. "The money you have taken from me belongs to an institution in the next city. When I get there and tell the people I have been robbed they will refuse to listen to me."

"There is nothing I can do about that," growled the Cossack.

"You can do me a small favor," replied the Jewish collector. "I will hang my hat on a branch of this tree and you will kindly shoot a hole through it so that they may believe I was actually held up."

The Cossack consented and shot two holes through the hat. The collector took off his coat and begged the robber to shoot two holes through each of his sleeves. Again the robber did as he was requested. Finally the Jew took off his vest and asked the robber to make another hole, but the robber said, "No more holes for you, *Zhid*. All my bullets are gone."

"That's all I wanted to know," retorted the collector. He leaped upon the Cossack, knocked him down, bloodied his nose, recovered his money and then tied him hand and foot.

The Cossack watched his intended victim depart and, as he struggled with his bonds, snarled to himself, "Well, this proves it: You simply can't trust a damned Jew!"

✔   ✔   ✔

A Jew and a Polish university professor were in the same coach on a train. The Jew, feeling sociable, greeted his traveling companion with a genial "Good morning, sir." The professor, an avowed anti-Semite, ignored him. The Jew repeated his greeting but the university man would not lift his eyes from the magazine he was reading. After being addressed the third time, the professor looked squarely at the Jew.

"Why do you persist in talking to me? Can't you see I have no desire to talk with an ignorant Jew?"

The Jew carefully hid his anger, and when he finally spoke his words were even and low. "An ignorant Jew is often more than a match for an educated bigot. I will make you a little wager to prove my point. First,

I will ask you a simple question. If you cannot answer correctly you will pay me twenty-five zlotys. Then you may ask me any question you like. But as I am only an ignorant Jew, according to your own statement, if I am unable to answer I will pay you only five zlotys. Is that agreed?"

"Agreed," said the university professor confidently. "Go ahead and ask."

"What is it that has three eyes, eats feathers and builds houses of solid gold?"

The professor wracked his brain for the right answer and made a number of wild guesses, but finally surrendered. "All right, I give up," he said. "Here is your twenty-five zlotys. Now tell me, what has three eyes, eats feathers and builds houses of solid gold?"

"I don't know either," replied the Jew. "Here are your five zlotys!"

✓ ✓ ✓

Ignace J. Paderewski, post-World War I premier of Poland, was discussing his country's affairs with the then President Woodrow Wilson.

"If all of Poland's demands are not granted at the peace conference," warned Paderewski, "I can foresee serious trouble in my country. Why, my people will be so angry that many of them will go out and massacre the Jews."

"And what will happen if we meet your demands?" asked Wilson.

"Why, my people will be so happy," replied the premier, "that many of them will get drunk and go out and massacre the Jews."

✓ ✓ ✓

During the Great War a lonely Jew happened to be in the same coach with a number of Russian soldiers. They began to molest the little fellow. One pulled his ear, another his hair. A third threw his lunch out of the window. The Jew was incensed, but wisely said nothing. But after having been annoyed and ridiculed for some time he rose from his seat and angrily shouted, *"Yekum purkan min shemaya hina vehisda verahemei vehayei ariha . . ."*

One of the soldiers who prided himself on his intellectual capacity, and unaware that the stranger had quoted an Aramic passage from the Sabbath morning ritual, exclaimed:

"Hey, hold on, boys! Leave him alone. This fellow isn't a Jew—he's a Frenchman!"

✓ ✓ ✓

Rasputin: "Your Majesty, the Jews are saying you are anti-Semitic. Why not kill them all as a lesson?"

Czar Nicholas: "Whoever said I was anti-Semitic is a liar. And to prove it, I certainly will not kill them all as you suggest. You should be ashamed of yourself for even thinking such terrible things. Kill half!"

✓ ✓ ✓

A young rabbi was traveling in a train from Minsk to Pinsk. His fellow passengers were three students from the University of Petrograd. Noticing his rabbinical garb and Semitic features the youths began to annoy him. Their taunts proved futile, however, for the holy man paid no attention to their jibes and jeers.

The students then devised a little game, each of them addressing the rabbi in turn:

"Good morning, father Abraham!"

"Good morning, father Isaac!"

"Good morning, father Jacob!"

It was more than the rabbi could endure. "You are mistaken, boys," he replied. "I am not any of the patriarchs. I happen to be Saul, the son of Kish, whose father sent him out in search of the lost asses. I am glad to see I have found them much sooner than I had anticipated!"

The Third Reich

A widely heralded circus was scheduled to appear in Berlin during the Third Reich. The featured attraction which everyone awaited with keen interest was to be a wrestling contest between a man dressed in a lion's skin and a wild, man-eating tiger.

But the man who was to do battle with the tiger became ill and so the promoters, unwilling to lose their main attraction, advertised for a substitute. For three days they advertised, with not a single applicant for the job, but on the fourth they were more successful: A sad-faced little man wearing the yellow Star of David patch on his arm, applied for work.

"We hadn't thought of giving employment to a Jew," the promoters said.

"But what else is there for a man of my religion?" the applicant replied bitterly. "All other employment is closed to me."

"You realize you may be killed," the circus entrepreneurs told him. "Even though you are only a Jew, you should know that the tiger is dangerous."

"My wife and children haven't eaten in three days," the Jew said wearily. "I have no alternative."

So, on opening day, before a capacity crowd, the Jew donned the lion's skin and, his teeth chattering with fear, he entered the tiger's cage.

"I have only one chance for survival," he said to himself. "If I can only frighten the tiger, or at least make him a little cautious, I might leave this cage alive."

Desperately, he dropped to his hands and knees, and, crawling on all fours, he roared like the king of beasts he was supposed to be. The tiger crouched, as though to leap, his cruel green eyes blazing.

"I'm going to die," the poor man thought dully. "This is the end." And in his last moment of anguish he cried out the Jewish creed that is recited when death is imminent:

"*Shema Yisroel!* Hear O Israel. . . . !"

And to his utter astonishment . . .

"*Adonoy Elohenu adonoy echod!* The Lord Our God, the Lord is One," recited the tiger fervently, completing the phrase.

"Wh-wh-why, you're not a real tiger at all!" gasped the pseudo-lion. "You nearly scared me to death!"

"*Landsman*," the tiger admonished irritably, "what makes you think you are the only Jew in Germany who's working?"

✓   ✓   ✓

Hitler had just become Chancellor of Germany, and in that accursed nation the Jews were beginning to experience a few of the evil omens of what was soon to happen to them.

A party of Germans, celebrating Hitler's political triumphs, were swaggering down a street in Berlin when they saw an aged, bearded Jew. They surrounded him, spat upon him, and hit him several crashing blows that knocked him to the sidewalk.

"Tell us, you Jew bastard, who caused the war?" their leader snarled.

The ancient one, wisely placing discretion before valor, replied, "The Jews."

The Germans roared derisively.

". . . and the pretzel bakers," the old Jew added, his eyes hot little points of anger.

The Germans were puzzled. "Pretzel bakers! Why pretzel bakers?"

"Why Jews?" shrugged the brave old-timer.

✓   ✓   ✓

A Jew, carrying a chicken under his arm, was walking along the street in Frankfort-am-Main when he was stopped by a storm trooper. "Where are you going, Jew?" demanded the Nazi.

"To the store, to buy my chicken some feed."

"What sort of feed will you buy for this chicken?"

"Corn."

"Corn, eh? Good Germans are going hungry while you Jews feed your chickens on the same corn we need for Aryan babies!" The Nazi advanced on the hapless Jew and knocked him to the pavement.

A few minutes later, another German, this time a civilian, stopped the Jew. "Where are you going, Dog?"

The Jew was well aware of what would happen to him if he again mentioned corn, so he answered, "Some wheat, I guess."

"Wheat, eh? Good Germans are going without bread because they haven't enough wheat, but you can give it to your chicken!" He slammed his fist into the little Jew's face. "For the glory of *Deutschland!*" he cried as the victim collapsed under the blow.

The poor, battered Jew eventually regained his senses and was challenged by still another German. "Where are you going?"

"To the store, to buy my chicken something to eat."

"What sort of feed will you buy for your chicken?"

"*Mein Herr!*" said the lacerated, still-bleeding Jew desperately, "I don't know what to buy him. I'll give him a couple of *pfennigs* and he'll buy whatever he likes!"

✦ ✦ ✦

Mahler, conductor of the Berlin Symphony Orchestra, was for years the target of the anti-Semitic press which ridiculed his Jewish physiognomy. And to tell the truth, the man did have a nose of majestic proportions. Had he been a Roman he would have been revered for it, but it was a convenient "handle" for the Germans.

One day, however, the conductor's patience snapped, and he accepted a similar position with the Vienna Symphony. Back in Berlin, the true music lovers at once noticed a decline in the quality of their symphonic concerts. Hastily they formed a committee and sent Mahler a letter in which they implored him to return.

"Conditions in the past few months have changed and the problems are much smaller," they assured him.

Mahler read the letter carefully and then answered, "Conditions may have changed, but my face hasn't. Problems may be smaller, but I assure you, I cannot say the same for my nose!"

✦ ✦ ✦

Hitler, in addition to his psychoses and delusions of omnipotence, was especially addicted to astrology, palmistry and other clairvoyant absurdities. So it was that, at the close of the war when defeat seemed certain, he sent for his favorite astrologer.

"Lloyds of London has refused to insure my life!" stormed Hitler. "I want you to tell me the truth—am I going to die?"

The astrologer went through the motions of making a forecast but was too frightened to voice his results. "My *Fuehrer*," he answered, trembling, "there is only one man in all of Europe who can tell you about your life or death with any certainty."

"Who is he?"

"Zelig Altman."

"A Jew, eh? Well, get him over here!"

"But, my *Fuehrer*, he is interned at Auschwitz."

"Very well," said Hitler, dismissing the astrologer, "I'll have him brought here."

"When am I going to die, Jew?" rasped Hitler, as soon as the concentration camp inmate was dragged in.

Zelig Altman scrutinized the lines in Hitler's palm and, for good measure, looked out of the window and gave the stars a quick once-over.

"The lines are indistinct, and the stars are not very bright tonight," the Jew began slowly. "But one fact is clear and prominent."

"What fact?"

"Not only the stars, but your life-line shows that no matter when you die it will be on a Jewish holiday!"

✓   ✓   ✓

Mama: "What do you think of Germans?"

Papa: "They should all put their shoes on backwards and get a bloody nose when they walk into themselves!"

✓   ✓   ✓

Loewenstein, who had escaped from Germany just minutes before Hitler's SS troopers raided his house, was in a Paris restaurant, sipping a cup of coffee, and minding his own business.

Two Germans entered the place and sat down at an adjacent table where, in loud tones, they discussed *Der Fuehrer*.

"Hitler is not as bad as his enemies say he is," remarked one.

"You're right," said the other. "The trouble with Hitler is that he is his own worst enemy."

"Not while I'm alive!" shouted Loewenstein.

✓   ✓   ✓

Some years before he became Chancellor, Hitler was making a speech in a Berlin beer hall, and as usual, his voice dripped with anti-Jewish vitriol. To his annoyance, he observed a man in the front row who smiled and chuckled throughout the talk.

When the address was over, Hitler sent word to the stranger that he wished to see him in a nearby coffee house. The man appeared a few minutes later.

"Tell me," said Hitler, noting the stranger's heroic nose, his patriarchal beard and his mannerisms, "aren't you a Jew?"

"Yes, I am."

"Then what were you so pleased about during my lecture? Have you any doubts about my intention to carry out my program against you and your kind?"

"I have no doubts about that at all," answered the old man. "That's why I laughed."

"I don't understand."

"Look at it from my point of view. We Jews have known enemies like you before. Pharaoh thought he could enslave us, and, in honor of our flight to freedom, we celebrate the beautiful festival of Passover.

187

Haman tried to exterminate us and, in commemoration of our survival, we celebrate the joyous occasion of Purim. The destruction of every such despot has brought us another glad holiday. Now you, Hitler, hate us more than did Pharaoh and Haman put together, so I smile and laugh in anticipation of the supremely happy holiday we will observe after we get rid of you, too!"

✓ ✓ ✓

Hjalmar Schacht, finance minister of the Third Reich, was ushered into Hitler's office where *Der Fuehrer*, more stone-faced than usual, awaited him.

"I hear that you have expressed some disapproval about the final solution to the Jewish problem," said Hitler coldly.

"Not at all, my *Fuehrer*," said Schacht. "I only meant that a few of the Jewish businessmen should be spared. The Reich still needs them. As a whole, they are more clever than their Aryan counterparts."

"Nonsense! No Jew ever lived who could outsmart a pure Aryan."

"Allow me to prove it, my *Fuehrer*. Come with me on a shopping tour of Berlin tomorrow."

On the following day, Hitler and Schacht stopped first at an Aryan store. "We would like to buy a left-handed teacup," said the finance minister.

"Sorry, I don't have any," replied the proprietor.

They stopped at another Aryan store and again asked for a left-handed teacup. As before, the store-owner answered, "Sorry, gentlemen, I don't have any."

Hitler and Schacht then entered a Jewish-owned shop. "We would like to buy a left-handed teacup," they said.

"What color?" asked the Jew instantly.

"Any color. It makes no difference."

The merchant withdrew one of the dozens of cups on the shelf and placed it on the counter with the handle facing the left side. "This is the only left-handed teacup in all of Germany," he announced. "I'll have to charge you fifty percent more because of its value."

"We'll consider it," said Schacht as he followed the outraged *Fuehrer* into the street.

"I told you those Jews were good businessmen," said the finance minister, smiling. "Who else but a Jew would have thought of such a clever way to sell goods?"

"Clever!" screamed Hitler. "What was so clever about it? That damned Jew was just lucky enough to have a left-handed teacup, that's all!"

✓ ✓ ✓

Hitler was vaguely dissatisfied with the glowing public opinion reports about him which he received almost daily from his propaganda minister,

Josef Goebbels. So he decided to go among the people incognito to find out for himself. He shaved his moustache, donned dark glasses and walked the streets of Berlin, listening to the comments of the citizenry.

Eventually, he landed in a theatre where the newsreel showed him making a speech. The moment he appeared on the screen, everyone in the audience rose, gave the Hitler salute and shouted, *"Sieg Heil!"* In all that audience, Hitler alone remained seated.

A Jew, standing next to him, grasped the *Fuehrer's* sleeve. "For heaven's sake, brother, get up on your feet," he whispered anxiously. "We all feel the same as you do, but why ask for trouble?"

✔ ✔ ✔

Soon after Adolf Hitler ascended to power, Germany was deluged with anti-Nazi jokes. Purple with rage, *Der Fuehrer* demanded that whoever was responsible for the non-Aryan humor be brought before him personally. Within a few days the Gestapo captured an outstanding Jewish writer known for his biting satire, and brought him to Hitler's bunker.

"What's your name, Jew?" snapped Hitler.

"Karl Mittelmann," replied the Jew.

Hitler repeated a joke about himself and asked, "Did you start that story?"

"Yes," confessed Mittelmann.

Hitler then recounted several other jokes and each time Mittelmann acknowledged his authorship.

Der Fuehrer, eyes glaring and canines bared, stalked about the room, his voice rising in a frenzy. "How dare you? How dare *any* Jew be so impudent? Don't you know that I am the leader of Germany's millions— the *Fuehrer* whose Third Reich is destined to last a thousand years?"

"Now hold on," interjected Mittelmann. "Don't blame me for that one. I never even heard the joke before!"

✔ ✔ ✔

Hitler had always secretly admired General von Hindenburg's military bearing—especially his typically short, Prussian haircut.

"How can I get my hair to stand like yours," Hitler once asked.

Answered the general, with scarcely concealed contempt, "There isn't a barber in the world who can do that for you. My advice is that you go to the Jewish quarter and listen to what the inhabitants there think of you. Your hair will stand on end within a minute!"

✔ ✔ ✔

Hans Pfeiffer, a staunch Nazi, went to the barn one morning, only to find that his prize ox was sick and unable to rise from its bed of straw. He called the only Aryan veterinarian in the community but the ox grew even more ill. Hans, a farmer for many years, recognized the death symptoms and knew that the animal must have immediate and proper treatment if it were to be saved, so, in desperation, he secretly called in Fleishman, the Jewish veterinarian.

Fleishman took one look at the supine ox, forced some medicine down its throat and then whispered in its ear. Immediately, the stricken beast leaped to its feet.

The Nazi farmer was astounded. "What did you say to the ox that made it jump up like that?" he gasped.

"I just used a little animal psychology, Herr Pfeiffer," said Fleishman. "I whispered the name 'Hitler' in its ear, knowing that there wasn't an ox in all Germany that wouldn't leap to its feet at its mere mention."

✓ ✓ ✓

A Jewish peddler of sea food was shouting his wares from a stall in Berlin. "Fish for sale! Fresh fish! Nice fat fish—as fat as Goering!"

A Gestapo officer heard the raucous chant and dragged the peddler off to the People's Court where the judge sentenced him to a year in a concentration camp.

After serving his term, the Jew returned to his business and again loudly announced his merchandise in the same sing-song voice: "Fish for sale! Fresh fish! Nice fat fish as fat as . . ."

"As fat as what?" snarled the voice of the same Gestapo officer who had sneaked up behind him.

". . . as fat as last year!" finished the peddler.

✓ ✓ ✓

Goebbels had written a propaganda speech for Hitler but they became involved in an argument over the proper use of the words "catastrophe" and "misfortune." Goebbels maintained that there was a difference in degree between the two, while Hitler insisted that it was purely a matter of semantics—that the words were synonymous.

To settle the difference of opinion they agreed to ask the first intelligent-looking person they met in the street, and that his decision would be final. They stepped outside the Reichstag and stopped a Jew, undoubtedly an intellectual judging by his appearance.

"Well," said the Jew, after they had explained the problem, "as one who appreciates the subtleties and nuances of language I must say that there definitely is a difference between the two words. For example, if the Reichstag should suddenly collapse and fall on you, that would be a catastrophe, but not necessarily a misfortune!"

✓ ✓ ✓

An Aryan entered a Berlin bus and noticed that the only vacant seat was next to a Jew, and on the seat beside him was a large package.

"Get that package off this seat!" ordered the Aryan.

"Why should I?" retorted the nervy Jew.

"You take that package off the seat or I'll call the conductor."

"*Nu*, so call him!"

The conductor, a burly, fierce-looking Nazi, descended on the little Jew and bellowed, "Take that package off the seat this instant or I'll throw it out the window."

The Jew shrugged. In a moment the hulking conductor seized the package and hurled it through the open window and into the street.

"Maybe that will teach you to respect the rights of your betters," snarled the conductor.

"Why should it teach me anything?" asked the Jew. "The package isn't mine!"

✓ ✓ ✓

A German entered a streetcar and, because there were no other seats available, had no alternative but to sit beside a Jew.

"I can see by your nose that you are a filthy Jew," said the venomous German. "Every thought in your head is concentrated on defiling blond Aryan girls."

The Jew ignored him, studiously fixing his gaze in another direction.

After a few minutes, the German broke the silence. "What time is it, Jew?"

The Jew did not answer.

"I asked you a question—what time is it?"

No reply.

"Listen, Jew, I'm asking you for the last time—what time is it? What's the matter with you, are you deaf?"

"No, I am not deaf," the Jew answered at last. "But if you can tell my sexual preferences by looking at my nose, you certainly should be able to tell the time by looking at the watch in my pocket!"

✓ ✓ ✓

A ferocious tiger broke loose from its cage in the Berlin zoo and ran amok through the city streets. The fierce beast frightened the citizenry out of their Aryan wits, and it might have killed several people had not a young Jew lassoed the animal and held it until the zoo officials came to the scene and returned the tiger to its cage.

A reporter brought the news to his publisher, the infamous Julius Streicher, who promptly wrote this headline:

FIERCE JEW ATTACKS HELPLESS KITTEN

✓ ✓ ✓

Nearly all of Germany's Jewish doctors and dentists had long since been sent to the death camps, so when Max Cohen suffered an impacted tooth, he had no choice but to visit an Aryan dentist. The Jew was seated, and the dentist asked the patient to open his mouth.

Max trembled, but did not comply.

"I said open your mouth!" the dentist repeated.

Max sat as though frozen in the chair.

"What's the matter with you?" exclaimed the dentist impatiently. "Can't you open your mouth when I tell you to?"

"I don't dare," whispered the terrified Jew. "I hardly know you!"

✓ ✓ ✓

Maximilian, the Aryan, and Joseph, the Jew, had been good friends before Hitler's advent to power. But now Maximilian, like most other Germans, considered himself a superman.

They met on the street one day and Maximilian deliberately looked the other way, but Joseph stopped him.

"We have come upon hard times," sighed Joseph.

"What are you complaining about?" spat Maximilian. *"Der Fuehrer* never promised you Jews anything!"

✓ ✓ ✓

A judge in Nazi Germany visited his club one evening and seemed to be unusually depressed.

"Why so dejected?" asked a colleague.

"I had a very difficult case today," sighed the judge. "A Nazi Party member stole a thousand marks from a Jew and I was forced to sentence him to a whole day in jail."

"That's not so bad," said the other soothingly. "After all, you had to keep up appearances."

"It wasn't that part of the case that really bothered me," explained Germany's upholder of the law, "but I was forced to sentence the Jew to no more than five years in a concentration camp for putting temptation in the Aryan's way."

✓ ✓ ✓

A badly frightened Jew stood before the bar of "justice" in a German court.

"The charge against you is very serious," intoned the judge. "You are accused of maligning the Nazi Party—the government itself."

"B-b-but Your Honor," stammered the Jew, "I was referring to the Communists, not the Nazis."

"Don't lie to me!" spat the magistrate. "The indictment accuses you of using the words 'murderers, gangsters and thieves.' This court knows exactly whom you meant!"

✓ ✓ ✓

Adolf Cohen went to the Berlin Municipal Court to change his name legally. When his case came up, the judge took one look at the application, another at the petitioner, and flew into a rage.

"What is this, another of your Jewish tricks?" he ranted. "Do you think that the Third Reich will permit you to hide your Jewish blood behind an Aryan name? Get out of this court. Your name is Cohen, and Cohen it will remain!"

"But Your Honor," protested the Jew, "I am perfectly satisfied with that part of my name. I only want to change Adolf to Abraham!"

✦ ✦ ✦

The German authorities knew that some Jews, desperate for survival, were attempting to escape deportation and death by posing as Christians. To put a stop to this practice, squads of SS troopers converged on churches throughout that sick nation. One such group entered a Berlin Evangelical Church while the services were in progress.

"I want to make an announcement to your congregation," said the squad leader.

The minister could only shrug helplessly.

"Fellow Germans," began the Nazi, "I am here in the interests of racial purity. We have tolerated the inferior race for far too long, and now the time has come when we must spew them out from our midst."

The Nazi glared at the congregation. "All those whose mothers and fathers were both Jews are ordered to line up outside this church—at once!"

A pitiful few rose from their seats and were hustled outside.

"And now, all those whose fathers were Jews are to get outside!"

A few more white-faced people rose and left.

"Finally, all those whose mothers were Jewish, get out!"

The minister took a figurine of Jesus Christ from its niche near the pulpit. "Allow me the honor, dear Lord, of escorting you to the door!"

✦ ✦ ✦

Two Jews sat dejectedly in one of the few restaurants still open to them in Germany.

"I just can't help but feel annoyed with our leader," said one.

"Shh! Quiet, idiot!" admonished the other, putting a finger to his lips. "Do you want to be sent to a camp for criticizing Hitler?"

"I was referring to Moses, not Hitler."

"Moses! What in the world are you talking about?"

"Did it ever occur to you that if Moses had not led our people out of Egypt," sighed the first Jew, "we would all have British passports today?"*

✦ ✦ ✦

* Egypt was a British protectorate until 1936, with complete independence granted in 1949.

Sol and Morty were walking along the *Kurfuerstendamm* when they came upon a sign on one of the buildings reading:

GESTAPO HEADQUARTERS
— Positively No Admittance —

"Look at that sign," whispered Sol to Morty. "So if admittance *were* permitted, do they really think we would go in?"

✐ ✐ ✐

Dr. Samuel Fishman, a once-famous physician in Berlin, was released from a concentration camp because the authorities felt he was about to die very soon anyway.

An old friend met him as the prematurely aged doctor was seeking a place to live.

"My God!" exclaimed the friend, thoroughly shocked. "Look at you! Your teeth are missing, your arm is twisted, you walk with a limp, your face looks as though it had gone through a meat grinder, and you weigh less than seventy pounds! What happened?"

"Nothing at all," said Doctor Fishman, smiling wryly. "I am just another atrocity lie."

✐ ✐ ✐

A German Jew was in a public park, sitting on a yellow-painted bench reserved for the "inferior race." He was absorbed in his newspaper, the Zionist weekly, *Juedische Rundschau,* and it was some moments before he realized that a Jewish acquaintance had also sat down on the bench and was reading Julius Streicher's *Stuermer.*

"I'm surprised at you," said the first Jew indignantly. "How can a Jew bring himself to read such anti-Semitic garbage?"

"To tell you the truth, it gives me a small measure of comfort," replied the other.

"Comfort? How can you derive any comfort from such a rag?"

"Let me explain. When I read *Rundschau* I am told of pogroms in Poland, of persecution here in Germany, of terrorism in Palestine, and other such happenings which depress me. But when I read Streicher's *Stuermer* I am told that the Jews are international bankers, that they control the press, that they dominate business—all this gives my morale a tremendous lift!"

✐ ✐ ✐

A couple of Jews were exchanging uncomplimentary remarks about Schickelgruber.

"What would please me most," said one, "is that Hitler should be changed into a lamp."

"Why so?"

"Because I would see him hang during the day, burn at night, and be extinguished in the morning."

✓   ✓   ✓

A teacher in a German private school was berating her only Jewish pupil.

"You are just like the rest of your race—selfish, greedy, and inconsiderate of others. Here your father pays tuition for only one student, but are you satisfied, Jew? No, you have to learn enough for three!"

✓   ✓   ✓

Propaganda Minister Josef Goebbels was touring the schools of Germany, helping to inculcate the Nazi philosophy in the minds of the very young. At one school he called on the boys to recite patriotic slogans.

"Heil Hitler!" shouted one pupil.

"Very good," said Goebbels.

"*Deutschland uber alles!*" another called out.

Goebbels beamed. "Excellent! And now, how about a still stronger slogan?"

A hand shot up and waved eagerly. Goebbels nodded and the little boy declared, "Our people shall live forever!"

"Now that's what I call a wonderful slogan!" exclaimed Goebbels. "What's your name, young man?"

"My name, sir, said the boy modestly, "is Israel Goldberg."

✓   ✓   ✓

It was Hitler's birthday and a time for celebration throughout Germany. In her classroom a teacher was addressing her pupils:

"Our beloved *Fuehrer* is more than just a leader; he is like our father. Now just suppose that he was really your father and you could have anything you wished, what would you want most?"

"I would ask him to make me a general!" shouted one boy.

"A *gauleiter!*" called another.

"A storm trooper!" yelled a third.

"An orphan!" shouted little Moishe.

✓   ✓   ✓

An aging, venerable Jew was drafted into a slave gang and forced to clean the latrines at the local army barracks. He was paid the equivalent of about 25 cents a day, in addition to the cuffs, kicks and curses he endured, but still it was better than being herded into Auschwitz. At least he could go home nights.

Each day, upon leaving the compound, he would push a wheel-barrow, filled with the filthiest straw, past the guardhouse. And just as regularly the guards examined the foul straw minutely, strand by strand, for they were certain he was stealing something. But what?

As the months dragged on, the old Jew waxed fat and sleek. The sentries were now convinced that he was taking something out of the army base and selling it on the black market. He surely could not be eating that well on 25 cents a day. So they reported him to the commandant.

He too watched as the old Jew trundled out his wheelbarrow of disgustingly dirty straw every evening, and like the others, he also was frustrated. The officer even went so far as to have the straw examined by chemists, but to no avail.

In 1945 the Allied armies rescued the Jewish people, among them the elderly patriarch. The old man, now free, asked a young American officer where he could find the former commandant of the German barracks. He was told that he had been imprisoned and would soon stand trial for his crimes. A few days later the old man secured permission to visit the German in his cell.

"Do you remember me?" the old Jew asked through the bars.

"Yes," snarled the German.

"You know, you were quite right when you accused me of stealing something from the army base every evening."

The German tried to ignore the visitor but he could no longer contain his curiosity. "I watched you wheeling out that damned straw every day for almost a year," he finally muttered. "We even used magnifying glasses. Tell me, just what were you stealing?"

"Wheelbarrows," the old man grinned.

✓   ✓   ✓

Author and radio-TV commentator Gloria Gundelfinger, of Los Angeles, a native of Great Britain, contributes this morsel as an illustration that the Germans were not the only ones who believed in the superiority of blood lines.

During the *blitzkreig* of England, a Nazi plane was shot down and the critically injured pilot was brought to London Hospital in the area of the city that was euphemistically called "bomb alley," the East End of London.

The German airman spoke excellent English, and while his battered face, broken ribs and internal organs were being patched up he poured forth a continuous diatribe against the British, the Americans, the democracies and especially against the Jews.

When Dr. Sidney Sontag, the chief resident physician, examined the obstreperous patient he ordered an immediate transfusion. Within a few minutes the German flier not only quieted down but was courteous and considerate of everyone with whom he came in contact.

"Isn't this change of attitude amazing?" a nurse asked Dr. Sontag. "An hour ago he was a raving madman, a dedicated Nazi with nothing but hate in his heart. Now he's a model human being."

"What's to be surprised?" asked Dr. Sontag. "He now has in him two pints of good Jewish blood!"

✓   ✓   ✓

During his brief stay in Paris after the fall of France, Hitler visited a French elementary school and interrogated the children about their political convictions.

Der Fuehrer pointed to a seven-year-old. "Now that France is on the side of the superior race, tell me, what would you like to be when you grow up?"

"A German officer," quavered the frightened child.

"And you," he said, pointing to another pupil, "What would you like to be?"

"An A-Aryan," sputtered the little boy.

"How about you?" he asked, nodding to another boy who happened to be Jewish.

"A Republican!"

"What!" stormed Hitler. "How can you even think of such a thing?"

"Because my father, mother, grandparents and great-grandparents were all Republicans."

"And if they were all murderers, would you be a murderer too?" boomed Hitler.

"Oh no," replied the boy. "Then I would be a Nazi!"

✓   ✓   ✓

Two judges in the land of the supermen were discussing the reasons why their courts were nearly always empty.

"I haven't had a case in over a month," sighed one. "I can't understand it."

"Well, I can," grumbled the other. "We haven't any work because a Jew will not sue another Jew, and he is afraid to sue an Aryan. An Aryan will certainly not sue a Jew because it would advertise the fact that he had business dealings with a Jew."

"What you say is true," acknowledged the first judge, "but still, one Aryan can sue another Aryan."

"No, they won't do that either," explained the other. "Where would they get Jewish lawyers to defend them?"

✓   ✓   ✓

Adolf Hitler, in his new Mercedes-Benz, was careening along a remote section of the *autobahn* when he lost control of the car and plunged off the highway and into a ditch. Flame and smoke leaped from the underside of the vehicle and the occupant could be seen vainly struggling to open the door from the inside. It was clear that the trapped *Fuehrer* would soon perish.

But at that moment an alert passerby came upon the scene, rushed forward and extricated the trapped man.

"You have saved my life," said Hitler, "and I am not ungrateful. Do you know who I am? I am your *Fuehrer*. Who are you?"

The rescuer blanched. "I—I am Israel Solomon, a Jew."

Hitler was taken aback for a moment, but then shrugged and said, "Well, Jew, you deserve a reward anyway. Ask any favor you wish and it shall be done."

"*Fuehrer*," replied Israel Solomon dejectedly, "the only favor I can ask is that you never breathe a word about this to a living soul!"

✓　　✓　　✓

Not long before Germany precipitated World War II by her attack on Poland, a group of supermen, headed by finance minister Hjalmar Schacht went to London. There they sought out Lord Rothschild and requested a huge loan for the Third Reich.

Schacht knew that Rothschild was Jewish, of course, but what the Germans could not blatantly steal from their victims they tried to get by stealth.

"Your Lordship can rest assured that we will be able to return this loan with interest," vowed the finance minister. "Our assets are enormous. Underground we have the largest coal and iron mines in all Europe. And I might add, above ground we have our great and incomparable Hitler."

Rothschild looked him straight in the eye. "I would consider such a loan favorably," he said, "if you would reverse those guarantees."

✓　　✓　　✓

Germany's military resistance was broken when the Allies swept into that country, but the spirit of Nazism lingered on. At a university in Hanover the history professor asked his students to recite the primary causes of the German defeat.

"It was the fault of the Jews," responded one student.

The professor beamed. "Very good, but can you tell the class what the Jews did to bring about this catastrophe?"

The student remained silent but another spoke up. "There were too many Jewish generals," he declared.

The professor was shocked. "That simply is not true!" he snapped. "There wasn't a single Jewish general in our whole army."

"Yes, sir, I know," answered the student. "I was referring to the American and British armies."

✓　　✓　　✓

Hitler had not yet been elected Chancellor of Germany, although he was already a power to be reckoned with in that country. Meanwhile, the Jews were still confident enough of the ultimate sanctity of decent government to talk back to their oppressors. It was under these circunmstances that a policeman, a staunch Nazi, swaggered down the street with a gigantic St. Bernard on a leash.

"That's a fine dog you have there," said a Jewish passerby. "What breed is it?"

"He's a cross between a mongrel and a Jew," spat the policeman.

"Aha!" retorted the nimble-witted Jew. "Then the dog is related to both of us!"

1   1   1

A Jew was walking on a street in Berlin when he accidentally brushed against a black-shirted storm trooper.

"Swine!" roared the Nazi.

"Epstein," said the Jew, bowing.

1   1   1

During the early part of the Hitler regime, prior to the infamous "final solution," German Jews taught their children to conform, outwardly, to Nazi customs, for the sake of survival.

One such Jew was teaching his young son how to conduct himself when eating in a restaurant where he might be observed by others. "When saying the blessing," he reminded the youngster, "the correct form of grace is 'Thank God and the *Fuehrer.*'"

"But suppose the *Fuehrer* dies?" queried the boy.

"In that case, my son," the father explained, "you just thank God."

1   1   1

A Jewish peddler, selling his wares from house to house, came to the home of a Nazi. The latter reached into the Jew's basket and picked up a pair of sun-glasses. "These are quite remarkable glasses," he said when he had tried them on. "As I look through them all I can see is a filthy pig."

"Is that so?" answered the Jew. "Let me try them on." He placed the glasses securely on his nose and peered at the German. "Say, you're right!" he exclaimed. "I see the same thing!"

1   1   1

Yoshke was the only Jewish boy in the class, and his German teacher delighted in humiliating him. On this day he felt particularly malicious. "Yoshke," he barked, "stand up and tell the class to which race the Jews belong."

"Semitic," replied the boy.

"And the Germans?"

"Anti-Semitic, teacher."

1   1   1

Two Germans noticed Ludwig Blau, a middle-aged man with Semitic features, board the train at Dresden. Grinning at this opportunity to annoy a Jew, they sat down beside him, one to his left, the other to his right.

"Tell us," said one, "are you an ignorant ass or a clever crook?"

The Jew thought for a moment and then answered calmly, "To tell the truth, I find myself somewhere between the two."

✓   ✓   ✓

A German army officer came to see one of the Rothschilds on business. The wealthy man happened to be occupied so he told the visitor to take a chair for a few minutes. The officer grew furious.

"How dare you ask me to take a chair?" he shouted. "Do you know that you are speaking to a prominent official of the German army?"

"Well, in that case," answered Rothschild unruffled, "help yourself to two chairs!"

✓   ✓   ✓

Israel Zangwill was clinging to a strap in a crowded street car in Berlin. He had finished a wearisome task at his office and, being without sleep for two nights, he could not suppress a wide, satisfying yawn.

A plump matron, standing beside him, snapped, "What are you trying to do—swallow me?"

"No, madam," replied Zangwill. "My religion prohibits a certain type of meat."

✓   ✓   ✓

The story is told of the time Israel Zangwill left London for Berlin to conduct some Zionist business. While in the German city he went into a restaurant and, because the place was crowded, he sat at a table occupied by two anti-Semitic *hausfraus*.

They glared at him as he opened a Yiddish newspaper and one of them remarked to the other, "Isn't there any place at all where a German can go without meeting a Jew?"

The unsolicited reply came from Mr. Zangwill: "Madam, you might try to go to hell!"

✓   ✓   ✓

Moses Greenspahn read an advertisement that a certain publishing house in Berlin needed a proofreader, and he applied for the job.

"We don't employ Jews here," said the foreman. "However, if you'll agree to be baptized I might make an exception in your case."

"Oh, no," replied Greenspahn, "I could never do that."

"Then get out," snapped the foreman. "As long as I am alive no Jew will ever be employed by this firm."

"I'll wait," said Greenspahn.

The United States

During the Second World War, a Mississippi dowager, product of an old Southern family still living in the ante-bellum age, decided to invite three soldiers at the nearby training camp to celebrate Thanksgiving at her colonial mansion.

She telephoned the camp and was referred to the lieutenant in charge of personnel.

"Lieutenant," she crooned, "send me three nice, lonely boys. It doesn't make any difference whether they are Northerners or Southerners, just as long as they aren't Jewish. No Jews, if you please!"

"Thank you, Ma'am," said the lieutenant. "You are a generous woman, and on behalf of the Army, I want to thank you."

On Thanksgiving Day a knock sounded on the door and when the lady went to admit the boys, there on the threshold stood three of the blackest Negro youths she had ever seen.

"B-b-but . . . there m-must be some m-mistake," she gasped, completely flustered.

"Oh no, ma'am," one of the young men assured her. "Lieutenant Goldstein *never* makes mistakes!"

✓ ✓ ✓

That some Jews have an almost paranoiac awareness of anti-Semitism, even in their own bailiwick, and often when there is no reason for their fears, is reflected in this psychologically revealing anecdote . . . an "inside" story told by Jews to other Jews.

The Bronx Park Express was running at top speed, carrying the weary toilers home. Above the deafening clatter of the wheels rose the stentorian voice of a stalwart, red-haired, ferocious-looking individual who appeared at the rear entrance of the car.

"Any Jews in here?" bellowed the giant.

The question was ridiculous. In that section of the East Bronx it would have been more sensible to ask if any gentiles were in the car.

There was no response. The gigantic proportions of the stranger, his hard face and belligerent manner made every Jew in the car exceedingly reluctant to acknowledge his religion. It was more than evident that this bellicose brute was just hankering to kill a few Jews.

"I said—any Jews here?" he boomed again, his voice louder and more terrifying than before.

A sepulchral silence was his only reply.

"Don't be such cowards," he shouted. "If there is a Jew in here let him stand up like a man and admit it!"

One young Jewish fellow was particularly stung by this insolent challenge. To be sure, he was no match for the towering monster, but his pride asserted itself and he decided to risk his life for the honor of his people. Besides, his girl was sitting next to him and he wanted to show her that he was a brave man and a proud Jew.

"I am a Jew!" he blurted out, rising from his seat. Pale as a ghost, glaring defiantly at the Goliath, he repeated, "I am a Jew! So what of it?"

There was a moment of tense silence in the car; the very air seemed electric with drama. A desperate battle seemed invitable—a battle which would probably end with the murder of the frail Jewish youth.

"Well, if you are a Jew," the giant said finally, "step into the next car."

"What for?"

"You see, today is the anniversary of my father's death and I want to say *kaddish*. But there are only nine Jews in the other car and I need one more to make a *minyan*. I'm afraid the synagogues will all be closed by the time we get home."

✦ ✦ ✦

Barney, a longtime alcoholic, was in a tavern, drinking. At the other end of the room sat an old friend. Gradually it dawned on him that every time Barney tossed down a jigger of whiskey he crossed himself. Unable to contain his curiosity, the friend approached the drinker's table.

"Barney," he said, his voice full of reproach, "have you forsaken the faith of your fathers?"

"Who me? Of course not!"

"Then why do you cross yourself every time you take a drink?"

"It's a matter of principle with me," said Barney. "Why should I give some anti-Semite a chance to say he saw a Jew drink like a fish?"

✦ ✦ ✦

The governor of the state held a banquet to which he invited civic and religious leaders, including the chief rabbi and the cardinal. The chef, though a gentile, was a considerate man, and went to great lengths to provide *kosher* food for the rabbi. But the cardinal was inclined to amuse himself at his Jewish colleague's expense.

"Have a piece of pork, Rabbi," said the cardinal. "And try some of this ham, too."

"Your Eminence," replied the rabbi, "surely you know that our people may not eat non-*kosher* food."

"What a pity," grinned the prelate. "It's delicious!"

When the meal was over and the speakers had finished their orations, the rabbi turned to the cardinal.

"Your Eminence," he said evenly, "please be kind enough to convey my greetings to your wife."

The cardinal drew himself up. "Don't you know that a priest is forbidden to have a wife?"

"What a pity," smiled the rabbi. "It's delicious!"

✦ ✦ ✦

ANTI-SEMITES

In the summer of 1912, long before the Germans had applied a race rationale to anti-Semitism, the following exchange evoked ribald laughter among the inhabitants of the East Side of New York, from Pelham Parkway to the Battery—and on into Brooklyn.

"The trouble with your people," said a Jew-hating merchant to a salesman, "is that you have become too proud."

"Look, mister, I only came here for an order," the salesman retorted, "but as long as you brought it up, what do you mean we've become too proud?"

"The Bible itself will bear me out. The biblical Jews only rode on donkeys. Even Moses, his wife and children rode donkeys, and what's more, your Messiah is supposed to appear on the back of an ass."

The Jewish salesman was honestly bewildered. "So how do you figure that makes us proud?"

"Simple. Today's Jew is too high and mighty to ride an ass. Nothing but an expensive horse will do for him."

"You have it all wrong, mister," said the salesman. "Our people started riding on horses because the asses were as stupid as some anti-Semitic merchants I could name. But we quickly found out that even a few horses are guilty of stupidity too. That is why, sir, there are so many more horses' asses than there are horses!"

✔   ✔   ✔

A bearded Jew, attired in old-fashioned garb, had some personal business which required that he leave his ghetto neighborhood. That afternoon he found himself in an exclusive area of New York's "silk stocking" district.

Feeling hungry, he entered a posh restaurant, but as soon as he was seated he was approached by a haughty waiter.

"I'm sorry, but we don't serve Jews here."

"Don't let that trouble you," said the old man placidly, "I don't *eat* Jews!"

✔   ✔   ✔

The two female pillars of the church were returning home from Sunday morning services when they spied ten-year-old Morty playing ball on the sidewalk.

"Who's that?" asked the first woman. "I don't seem to recognize him."

"Oh, he's the new boy in the neighborhood," explained the other.

"There's something different about him. What nationality do you suppose he is?"

"Why, American, of course."

"Well, you know what I mean—isn't he—er—ah . . ."

"Jewish?" the other woman finished for her. "Yes, I think he is. Why?"

"What a shame," responded the first. "Already a Jew—and so young!"

✔   ✔   ✔

A famous Negro boxing champion, an anti-Semite who shall charitably remain anonymous here, received his draft notice for army duty. After passing the physical examination he was passed on to the psychiatrist for the usual mental test.

"What is the meaning of rabies, and what would you do for it?" asked the medic.

"Rabies are Jewish priests," spat the fighter, "and I ain't gonna do nothin' for 'em!"

✓ ✓ ✓

Two school teachers, Sarah Goldberg and Patricia Johnson, met in Chicago during a National Board of Education convention.

After they had exchanged the usual introductory amenities, Sarah confided that she was Jewish and that she lived in Fresno, California.

"Well, that certainly is a surprise!" declared Miss Johnson stiffly. "I thought all Jews lived in New York."

"Why, we live everywhere, I'm proud to say. There is scarcely a city in the United States where you will find no Jews."

"Is that so? I'll have you know there isn't a single Jew in the village I come from."

Sarah smiled gently and murmured, "That's why it's still a village!"

✓ ✓ ✓

Mrs. Merriweather Randolph Jefferson Davis, the dowager of Charlottesville, Virginia, agreed to escort the younger members of the Southern aristocracy on a tour of Independence Hall in Philadelphia. In the teen-age contingent was the dowager's granddaughter, Susan, a modern and knowledgeable young lady.

During their visit they came upon the inscription engraved on the Liberty Bell: "Proclaim liberty throughout the land unto all the inhabitants thereof."

"Oh, I know where that comes from!" exclaimed Susan ecstatically. "That beautiful verse is from the Old Testament. It is one of the sacred writings of the Jewish people!"

"Well, I declare!" sniffed the dowager Merriweather. "First they take credit for the Ten Commandments, then the Psalms, and now this! What will those Jews be claiming next?"

✓ ✓ ✓

Ralphie Bortnik, a student at Benjamin Franklin University in Washinghton, D.C., was having a discussion with a foreign exchange student from Germany.

"Why is it that you Jews have never had a really great military hero in all your thousands of years of existence," sneered the German.

"What are you talking about!" retorted the offended Jewish boy. "We have had scores of outstanding heroes. For example there's Simon

Bar Kochba. For three years he stood off the might of the Roman Empire, defeating their legions with only a handful of defenders."

"You had to reach back almost two thousand years for that one," said the German, his voice oozing sarcasm. "Even here in America they can talk about more recent heroes—Paul Revere for instance."

"Paul Revere?" echoed the student innocently. "Oh yes, that's the fellow who had to run for help!"

✓ ✓ ✓

Avrum Rabinovitch had only been in this country for a few weeks when he discovered the Automat. For a man who spoke almost no English this was a God-send. All one had to do was insert a coin or two in the proper slot and the small window automatically opened, making the food inside the cubicle available to the customer. Small wonder then that Avrum was pleased with his discovery.

The new immigrant approached the baked goods section and decided to try the rolls. The price inscribed above the machine was ten cents.

"Where does the Torah say that you must put into a machine ten cents for five cents worth of rolls?" he soliloquized. "Why not five cents for five cents' value?" So he inserted a nickel and turned the knob but the machine did not respond.

"Aha! I see you are going to be stubborn about this," he said to the machine. "All right, to quarrel with you for a nickel it's a waste of time. You want ten cents I'll give you ten cents. Here are five pennies extra."

The machine, not geared to receive pennies, again did not respond.

"What do you want from my life?" cried the now angry Avrum. "You already got ten cents. Aha! Now I see! You want another five cents as a penalty. All right, I'll pay the fine."

He inserted another nickel but to his chagrin the machine still refused to work.

Just then a gentile went up to the machine, deposited a dime in the slot and promptly received his rolls.

Avrum Rabinovitch, his face contorted with rage, kicked the machine. "Anti-Semitic bastard!" he hissed.

✓ ✓ ✓

Little Hannah came home from school weeping. "The girls in my class called me names," she sobbed.

"*Shah, shah!*" crooned Papa. "What could they call you that was so bad?"

"They called me a dirty kike."

"So what did you do?"

"I ran away."

"Hannah baby," said Papa, "I hate to say this but a person must stick up for his rights. He must strike back, and never run away. Look at Cain

205

and how he slew Abel. If Abel had defended himself, who knows, he might be alive today!"

✓ ✓ ✓

Two pinochle players, between hands, were bemoaning the fate of their people.

"What have we really got to look forward to, Max?" said one. "Persecution, discrimination—even diseases like diabetes strike more Jews than gentiles. Now there's an American Nazi Party, the Ku Klux Klan is back, the States Righters are anti-Semitic, the John Birch Society doesn't like us—I tell you, Max, I sometimes think it would have been best if we'd never been born."

"Of course it would be best," sighed Max, "but who has that much luck? Not one in a thousand!"

✓ ✓ ✓

Anti-Semite: "One of the reasons we don't like you Jews is because you never contribute to charity unless it is run by a Jewish organization."

Mr. Shapiro: "You don't know what you are talking about. We Jews donate all kinds of money to interfaith charities. Take me, for example. I support Mental Health Week like crazy!"

✓ ✓ ✓

The paradox behind the trial and sentence of Adolf Eichmann was that there was no punishment commensurate to the magnitude of his crime. "After all," observed prosecutor Gideon Hausner, "you can't hang a man six million times."

During the Eichmann trial the subject of suitable punishment was debated in many Jewish publications, but the most appealing suggestion of all was written by a young soldier to the editor of the California *Jewish Voice*:

"Eichmann should not be hanged or imprisoned. Instead, he should be sentenced to live with my in-laws in the Bronx!"

Chapter Nineteen

These Wandering Jews

An elderly Jewish gentleman was standing in front of the ticket office in Grand Central Station. A picture of utter helplessness, it was clear that something dreadful was wrong with him. His elbows were closely pressed to his sides, his forearms were rigidly extended before him, and his hands, with palms turned toward each other some ten inches apart, were as stiff as boards. Apparently the poor man's arms and hands were paralyzed.

Another Jew approached the window and the helpless man faced him in a mute appeal for assistance.

"Can I do anything for you?" asked the compassionate stranger.

"Mister, please, put your hand in my pocket, take out the money, and get me a ticket."

Filled with pity, the man complied. He then helped him to board the train and assisted him into a seat.

When the train started its journey the sympathetic stranger remarked conversationally, "I suppose you are going to visit an out-of-town specialist?"

"A specialist!" echoed the elderly gentleman. "Why should I go to a specialist?"

"Don't you have some kind of trouble with your hands?"

"Who has trouble with hands?"

"If there's no trouble, then why do you hold them out in front of you like that? You couldn't even reach into your pocket to buy a ticket."

"My dear man," explained the oldster patiently, "my wife asked me to buy her a pair of shoes and this is her size!"

✦   ✦   ✦

There are a great many stories about the sinking of the *Lusitania*. Here is an eyewitness account that few gentiles have heard.

Hyman Baumgarten, emigrating to the United States, was a steerage passenger aboard the illustrious vessel on its ill-fated voyage across the Atlantic. He was sipping a glass of tea and thinking of nothing more important than the evening menu, when suddenly the ship crashed into a huge iceberg. History tells the rest. Almost at once the *Lusitania* began to list heavily. A few lifeboats were lowered over the side, but not nearly enough to accommodate the large number of passengers. Pandemonium raged throughout the ship. Everywhere people fought for life-preservers. Women screamed hysterically. Entire families, with their terrified children, leaped into the sea. Hundreds of others milled about on deck, yelling, crying and cursing, as the ship settled lower and lower in the water.

Of all the passengers, only Hyman Baumgarten was calm.

"What's the matter with you?" snapped the captain. "Don't you realize the ship is sinking? Aren't you at all concerned?"

"Why should I get excited?" countered Hyman. "Do I own this ship?"

*   *   *

Two men, emigrating to America, were assigned the same cubby-hole in the ship's steerage. They were only a mile or two out of the European port when one of them suddenly realized that his roll of bills was missing. He searched frantically in all his pockets and in every crevice of the tiny compartment, all the while eying his bunkmate suspiciously. But to his great relief he found his money inside a suitcase where he had forgotten it. He turned to the other man.

"I want to apologize, sir. I wrongfully suspected you of stealing my money."

"No apologies are necessary," replied the other. "I too made a mistake. I wrongfully suspected you of being a gentleman!"

*   *   *

Third class passengers on Russian railways often did not buy tickets; the conductors, who were an underpaid lot, gladly let them travel for a few *kopeks*. Occasionally, however, there appeared on the train a *malach-hamoves*, or controller, who searched the cars to apprehend any passengers without the required tickets.

The riders in one car of a train running from Vilna to Warsaw, learning that the *malach-hamoves* was about to enter, rushed to hide under the benches—their customary hiding place.

When the railroad officer entered the car and found it vacant his suspicions were instantly aroused. He looked around and noticed a pair of heavy boots protruding from beneath a bench. He kicked the man's feet. "Come on out of there!" he ordered.

To his surprise, it was not a Jew who arose but a husky *mujik*, definitely non-Jewish, and trembling with fear.

The *malach-hamoves* glared at him. "I suppose you lost your ticket," he said with heavy sarcasm.

"No, your excellency," said the peasant, trembling. "I have my ticket right here."

The railroad officer examined the ticket and then demanded to know why he had hidden himself.

"I thought everybody was supposed to hide when you came into a car," stammered the *mujik*. "I've been doing it all my life."

✓ ✓ ✓

A poor Jew, determined to go to America, had just enough money for his ship's passage, but not enough to get to Moscow where the local Jewish organization would help him with the extra costs involved. There remained only one way to get to the big city without paying the train fare, so he sneaked aboard without buying a ticket.

At the very next station the conductor grabbed him by the scruff of his neck and booted him off the train.

Picking himself up, the man limped back to the platform and sneaked aboard the next Moscow-bound train. Again he was discovered and, as before, the conductor kicked his behind and sent him sprawling from the train.

Twice more he stole aboard a train, and each time he was kicked in the rear and sent flying into the roadside.

Finally, when he had only nine more miles to go, he climbed aboard another train and sat down beside a paying passenger.

"How far are you going?" asked the stranger, making conversation.

"To Moscow," the poor traveler answered—"that is, if my *tuchus* holds out."

✓ ✓ ✓

Among the hundreds of immigrants aboard the *Mauretania,* bound for their new life in America, were two sojourners from Odessa. Soon they struck up a conversation with another Jew from Vilna, and to while away the hours at sea, they began praising their respective cities.

"In Odessa, nothing is too good or too expensive for us," boasted one. "Take the cantor of our synagogue, for example. Our cantor is indisputably the greatest in all the world. His voice is like an angel's. He costs us enough, you may be sure—twenty thousand rubles a year! His name is Marcus, by the way."

"Twenty thousand rubles a year!" exclaimed the man from Vilna. "Impossible!"

Now the second man from Odessa, the one who had remained silent, spoke up.

"Not impossible at all. There is much truth in what my friend says, except for a few minor details. First, the city is not Odessa, but Kiev. And the man's name is not Marcus, it's Brodsky. Further, Brodsky is not a cantor, he's a lumber merchant; and instead of making twenty thousand rubles a year he loses thirty. Everything else, you can take my word for it, is perfectly true."

✓ ✓ ✓

He was an old, insecure man who had lived on the lower East Side ever since emigrating from Czarist Russia. Now, for the first time, he was to ride on a train in America. His grandson was getting married in Boston.

Timidly he approached the information desk at Pennsylvania Station. "When do the trains leave for Boston?" he asked.

"Every day, Grandpa."

The old man digested the information, uncertainty still gnawing at him. "On Thursday also?" he finally inquired.

✦   ✦   ✦

A cantor of Minsk found himself stranded in a small village far from home. It was a wintry day and the heavy snowfall of the night before had stopped the one and only train that could have brought him home in time for the *Shabbes* services.

In desperation he hired a coachman to drive him to the city, fully aware that travel by horse and wagon over the icy roads might be dangerous. They started on their journey but before long they reached a hill.

"You will have to get out and help push," said the coachman. "My poor old mare isn't strong enough to pull the wagon up to the crest."

The cantor had no alternative but to get out and push. When they finally managed to get to the top, the cantor was about to return to the coach when the driver stopped him with a warning. "I'm sorry, but you will have to help me hold back the wagon on the downgrade. My poor old horse isn't strong enough to keep it from sliding down the icy road."

Again the cantor huffed and puffed as he held on to the wagon. Nor was this the only time. On several other occasions he was forced to leave the coach and help push it through mud, snow and slush, uphill and downhill, but at last they reached their destination.

"Do you mind if I ask you a question?" said the cantor as he paid the driver.

"Not at all. Ask me anything!"

"I had good reason to go to Minsk in this rotten weather because I have services tonight at the synagogue. You, of course, also had a good reason to go because you needed the money. But tell me something, what possible reason do you suppose the horse had?"

✦   ✦   ✦

They were two strangers in a first-class compartment of a railroad car and one of them lighted a cigar.

"Can't you see the sign?" said the other testily. "Smoking is not allowed here."

"Yes, I know," replied the offender calmly, as he continued to puff away.

"Look, mister, either you stop smoking or I'll call the conductor."

"Don't bother me," said the boorish man, blowing a cloud of smoke in his fellow passenger's face.

The enraged traveler immediately summoned the conductor. "He is violating the rules," he complained. "This compartment is reserved for non-smokers."

"And I say that he is the one who is violating the rules," argued the smoker. "He is traveling in a first-class compartment on a second-class ticket."

The accusing passenger turned pale and hastily left the compartment without another word.

When the train pulled into the station the two travelers met again on the platform. The curiosity of the non-smoker overcame his resentment.

"Are you a clairvoyant?" he asked. "How did you know I had a second-class ticket?"

"No, I'm not a clairvoyant," replied the other cheerily. "I saw a corner of your ticket showing from your pocket and it was the same color as mine!"

✓　　✓　　✓

Two Russian Jews were on board an ocean liner bound for their new home in America. One was a hunchback, the other sported a nose of majestic proportions.

For reasons known only to himself, the Jew with the oversized proboscis avoided the hunchback, but after a few days the need to talk with a fellow Jew overcame him and he finally engaged the other in conversation.

"My friend," he said, "I'm going to let you in on a secret. I am a Jew."

"Thank you for confiding in me," said the other, glancing at the man's tell-tale nose. "And secret-for-secret, I'll tell you one, too. Confidentially, I'm a hunchback!"

✓　　✓　　✓

The two emigrants, traveling alone from Poland to America, were seated on a bench on Ellis Island, waiting for customs clearance. Recognizing a co-religionist in each other, they wanted very much to talk, but hesitated. Each perceived in the other a certain aloofness and feared that the attempt might meet with a rebuff.

After an hour of sitting on the hard bench, one of the immigrants expressed himself. "*Oy!*"

"You're right!" exclaimed the other immediately. "That's just what I was thinking!"

✓　　✓　　✓

Bobeh Finkelstein, who could not speak a word of English, was placed on a train in New York, with her destination Washington, D.C. Carefully,

211

her son explained that she must transfer in Philadelphia, and the second train would take her all the way to Washington.

But in Philadelphia, *Bobeh* became confused and boarded the wrong train—one going back to New York. Before the conductor discovered the mistake, the amiable old lady noticed another woman sitting across the aisle with a Yiddish newspaper in her lap. Immediately they struck up a warm social chat.

"*Nu,* what are you going to do in Washington?" asked *Bobeh* Finkelstein.

"Washington? I just came from Washington. I'm going to New York to see my married daughter."

Bobeh sat bolt upright in her seat. "It's marvelous what these American railroads can do!" she exclaimed. "Here you sit on one side of the train and you're going to New York, and I sit on the opposite side of the same train and I'm going to Washington!"

✓   ✓   ✓

Reb Ellenbogen went to the railroad station to meet his wife who was expected on the next train. Just as he reached the building a man, running at full speed, raced past him, panting and glistening with perspiration from the unaccustomed exertion. He gazed wildly at the empty tracks and then collapsed on a bench, weeping.

"*Oy vay!*" the man groaned. "My train left without me! I was supposed to be in Prague tomorrow to get married. My fiancée will never believe me!"

Reb Ellenbogen's sympathies were aroused. "By how much did you miss your train?"

"Only by a minute—a trifling minute!" the man sobbed.

"Is that all?" cried Ellenbogen indignantly. "The way you are carrying on I thought you'd missed it by an hour!"

✓   ✓   ✓

Levy, Levinsky and Lubedoff, three traveling salesmen, met on a train going from New York to Los Angeles. They quickly formed a close friendship, and after talking about their respective lines of merchandise, they called the porter and requested a card table, a deck of cards and a bottle of vodka. They paid for all these services, of course, but they did not give George, the porter, a single dime as a tip. George, who had anticipated a substantial gratuity, was vastly annoyed.

"Man, them Jews are sho' stingy," he said to a fellow porter. "The mo' I see of 'em the mo' I believes they really crucified Christ!"

During the long ride to California the trio of salesmen did not alter their daily routine. They would order a table, cards, drinks, and each time they would pay for everything, but not once did they leave a tip. Meanwhile, George's irritation mounted with every hour.

But when the train finally pulled into Los Angeles, Levy, Levinsky and Lubedoff each handed him a crisp ten dollar bill and thanked him for his excellent service.

George sought out the other porter and proudly displayed the thirty dollar tip.

"I gotta admit I made a mistake," he said. "Them Jews didn't kill Christ. They jes' natch'ly worried him to death!"

✦   ✦   ✦

Yosselov had just returned from a business trip to Budapest, and after a glass of hot tea and some home-made cakes, he settled back. Yosselov was now in an expansive mood and he began to talk.

"You know," he said to his wife, "on the way back from Budapest I had a few uneasy moments. The conductor passed by and looked at me very strangely."

"What do you mean?" asked his wife.

"Well, he looked at me as if I had no ticket."

"So what did you do?"

"What could I do, *Leibeh*? I looked right back at him as if I did!"

✦   ✦   ✦

In a hot, dusty train unequipped with the luxury of water, and long before the advent of air-conditioning, an old Jew sat opposite a stranger in the cramped seats.

"*Oy!*" moaned the old man for about the ninetieth time, "am I thirsty!"

The younger traveler twitched with irritation. After all, he was thirsty too, as were most of the other passengers.

A few minutes later the old man's hoarse voice was heard again: "*Oy, am I thirsty!*"

The other traveler's nerves were now as taut as a violin string.

Three minutes later: "*Oy, am I thirsty!*"

Just then the train stopped at a station. The younger man hastened into the terminal building, bought three bottles of pop, and returned to the train, just as it was pulling out. He thrust all three bottles at the old man and cried, "Here, in Heaven's name, drink!"

"Thank you," said the old man, and poured the soda pop down his throat.

As the train started up again the young stranger settled back to enjoy the unaccustomed peace. But in a moment the tranquil quiet was shattered by a mighty sigh:

"*Oy, was I thirsty!*"

✦   ✦   ✦

A young rabbi was flying from New York to Los Angeles. They were 20,000 feet over the Rocky Mountains when, without warning, one of the engines fell off. The pilot, struggling with the controls, managed to bring the plane back to an even keel, and then asked the stewardess if the passengers were overly nervous.

"They're near the point of panic," she told him.

The pilot turned the controls over to the co-pilot and went back to where the rabbi was sitting. "The rest of the passengers are alarmed," he said, his voice urgent. "Do something religious."

So the rabbi took up a collection.

✔   ✔   ✔

El Al Airlines had just established trans-Atlantic service and was making its inaugural flight from Tel Aviv to New York. Once aloft, the pretty stewardess picked up the microphone and talked to the passengers:

"This is the first trans-ocean, non-stop flight from Israel to America. Just relax and enjoy the trip. You will know immediately if anything goes wrong. Our pilot will become hysterical!"

✔   ✔   ✔

The El Al plane from Israel to America was over the middle of the Atlantic ocean when suddenly an engine failed. The pilot at once informed the passengers that, unless a few of them bailed out, all the rest of the passengers would die. The plane load simply had to be lightened.

A Frenchman arose and yelled *"Vive la France!"* and leaped out of the open door. Then an Englishman arose and yelled, "Long live the Queen!" and jumped out.

Finally a Jew rose from his seat, yelled, *"Deutschland uber alles!"* and pushed a German out the door.

✔   ✔   ✔

Also aboard the El Al plane from Israel to America was Grandma, taking her very first flight. They had only been aloft for a few minutes when the old lady complained to the stewardess that her ears were popping. The girl smiled and gave the older woman some chewing gum, assuring her that many people experienced the same discomfort.

When they landed in New York, Grandma thanked the stewardess. "The chewing gum worked fine," she said, "but tell me, how do I get it out of my ears?"

✔   ✔   ✔

Moishe Margolies, who weighed all of 105 pounds and stood an even five feet in his socks, was taking his first airplane trip. He took a seat next to a hulking bruiser of a man who happened to be the heavyweight boxing champion of the world.

Little Moishe was uneasy enough before he even entered the plane, but now the roar of the engines and the great height absolutely terrified him. So frightened did he become that his stomach turned over and he threw up all over the muscular giant sitting beside him. Fortunately, at least for Moishe, the man was sound asleep.

But now the little man had another problem. How in the world would he ever explain the situation to the burly brute when he awakened? The sudden voice of the stewardess on the plane's intercom, finally woke the bruiser, and Moishe, his heart in his mouth, rose to the occasion.

"Feeling better now?" he asked solicitously.

✓　　　✓　　　✓

"But Papa, I don't want to go to America!"
"Shut up, Herscheleh, and keep swimming!"

✓　　　✓　　　✓

For years the Goldmans had wanted to emigrate to America but Mr. Goldman kept postponing the trip because of the cost. In fact, the man was so tight he squeaked when he walked. At last his wife persuaded him to buy the passage tickets, and all during the voyage he complained about the expense. The ship finally docked in New York, and Goldman and his wife were descending the gangplank when suddenly a deep-sea diver emerged from the water.

Goldman clutched his wife's sleeve. "Now why didn't we think of that?" he exclaimed. "With a suit like that we could have walked across too!"

✓　　　✓　　　✓

For lo these many years, Sol Bainkup had worked hard to build a paying clientele. Now he was acknowledged as one of the best salesmen of ladies' wear in all New York, and he had the bank account to prove it. But all during the long years of labor he had also nurtured a secret ambition. He wanted to devote the remainder of his life to the study of insects. Indeed, as an amateur entomologist, he was quite an authority. Came the happy day when he visited his last customer, closed his sample case for good, and retired. At last he could indulge his ambition: to hunt rare bugs in darkest Africa.

A few weeks later found him in the trackless jungle of the deepest Congo. Cutting his way through a tangled mass of vegetation he suddenly came upon a clearing, and there in the center was a grass-thatched hut. And to Sol's utter astonishment, who should be standing there but his old friend, Nathan, whom he hadn't seen in years.

"Nate, what are you doing here?" he gasped.

"I'm chief of the local Vayizmir tribe," Nathan explained. "How about you?"

"I'm an entomologist now. I came here looking for rare insects."

"Let me help you," cried Nathan, delighted to be of aid. He turned over a log and snatched up a crawly little bug with red feet. "How about this one?"

"Sorry, Nate. I got lots of those."

Nathan stooped over a large rock, turned it over, and picked up a hairy spider with wings. "Bet you ain't got one like this."

Sol shook his head. "I have five of them," he said.

Nathan climbed to the top of a coconut tree and captured a centipede with two heads. "Here's a specimen for your collection!" he announced excitedly.

Sol heaved a regretful sigh, "Too bad, Nate, but I have one of those with three heads."

Nathan shrugged and smiled wanly. "Well, I guess that's it," he said. "But, as one salesman to another, I certainly appreciate the opportunity for showing you my line."

Chapter Twenty

Death and Taxes

For years the men in the village had taunted Isaac the cigarette maker with the accusation that he mixed his tobacco with fifty per cent horse manure. They were only joking, of course, but the cigarettes had an abominable taste and they used the expression just to get even.

But now old Isaac lay on his death bed and the men of the village repented for having made his life miserable with their callous accusation. So a delegation went to see the dying man.

"Isaac," said a spokesman, "we are here on behalf of the whole village. We want you to know that we apologize and are sorry for saying that your cigarettes were fifty percent horse manure."

"Yes, that was a wrong thing to say," agreed the old man, even as the death rattle sounded in his throat. "I want all of you to know, before I pass on to my Maker, that they were a *hundred* per cent horse manure."

✦   ✦   ✦

A fabulously wealthy cloak-and-suiter went to that Great Garment Center in the Sky. Back on earth, as might be expected, his *ganseh mishpocheh* assembled in the attorney's office to hear the reading of his last will and testament.

The silence was charged with drama as the lawyer cleared his throat and read the deceased's last words:

"Being of sound mind and body, I spent every penny on young girls before I died!"

✦   ✦   ✦

Arnold Constable, who started out in life as Abraham Cohen, and who amassed millions on the stock market, fell gravely ill.

"Anna," he said to his beloved granddaughter, "I'm afraid my time has come. I'm dying."

"*Shah, shah!*" Anna crooned consolingly. "With your constitution you'll live to a hundred and twenty."

"What sort of silly remark is that?" retorted the cantankerous old stock broker. "Why should God wait until I go all the way up to a hundred and twenty when he can get me at only seventy nine?"

✓ ✓ ✓

Lena lay dying in her bed. "Morris, I heard what the doctor told you," she managed to gasp. "My hours are numbered."

Morris wept. "Tell me, Lena darling, is there anything I can do for you? Anything at all! Just name it!"

"Yes, Morris dear. I want you should promise me one thing before I go. When I die it is my dearest wish that you should marry my sister, Yetta."

Morris wept bitter tears, his sorrow almost approaching hers. "Lena, you haven't a thing to worry about," he assured her. "I've been thinking of nothing else for years!"

✓ ✓ ✓

Pomerantz the plumber was talking to the undertaker about the final disposition of his mother-in-law's remains.

"Shall I cremate, embalm, or just bury her as she is?" asked the mortician.

"Why take chances?" said Pomerantz quickly. "All three!"

✓ ✓ ✓

Yossele, a small boy who had been killed in a tragic automobile accident, lay in state at the mortuary. A quarrelsome couple—actually they couldn't stand each other—went to the funeral home to pay their last respects.

"Yossele, little angel, now that you have ascended to Heaven, pray for us whom you have left behind," the woman sobbed.

"On such an important mission you send a little child?" demanded her husband. "Why don't you go yourself?"

✓ ✓ ✓

A *Galitzianer* came to visit a distant relative in a small Russian town inhabited by only ten Jews. That night the stranger became acquainted with the tiny Jewish population when he attended services. Now this *Galitzianer* was a jovial, fun-loving fellow, so he thought he would amuse himself for awhile at their expense.

"There is something about this town that completely mystifies me," he began, his voice teasing. "Why do so few Jews need both a synagogue and a cemetery? As a practical Jew, it seems to me that you should have either one or the other."

"How so?" asked the rabbi.

"Well, if you all live, who needs a cemetery? But, on the other hand, if only one of you should die then you wouldn't have a *minyan*—and your synagogue would be useless. Right?"

DEATH AND TAXES

"Yes, that is correct," answered the rabbi after some soul-searching thought. "But we have another reason for our cemetery which seems to have escaped you."

"What kind of reason?"

"Suppose a *Galitzianer* should come here and die?"

✔   ✔   ✔

The venerable rabbi, known throughout the land as the holiest of the holies, lay in a coma, near death. Around him were grouped his worshipful disciples.

"What God-given virtue! What piety!" one of them exclaimed with deep feeling. "Nowhere can his equal be found."

"Yes, truly a man of God," agreed another. "None approach him in generosity."

"A wonderful family man; kind and loving to his wife, children—even his distant relatives."

"And a scholar! Who can compare with him in his understanding of Talmud, of Torah, and with such wise interpretations."

Now the grieving disciples lapsed into silent meditation. The absolute quiet continued for a minute or two when the rabbi opened one eye and watched them expectantly.

Finally, with an injured air, he asked, "What's the matter—about my modesty you can't think of anything to say?"

✔   ✔   ✔

A young couple went to the cemetery to pay their respects to a long-departed relation. A few feet away they saw a man bending over a grave and wailing bitterly.

"O woe is me! Dark is my lot! How sweet this poor life of mine might have been, how precious this world would have appeared, if only our Lord, may His name be sacred always, had spared your life." The stranger wept for a few moments and then moaned, "If only I could bring you back."

The young couple, a little embarrassed at witnessing the man's private torment, attempted to console him. "Are you weeping for your dear wife?"

"No," the man groaned from the depths of his heart. "I am grieving for my wife's first husband."

✔   ✔   ✔

David and Lisa, in the sunset of their lives, their children, grandchildren and great-grandchildren scattered to all parts of the country, were discussing what remained of their future.

"We have had a good life together," said Lisa contentedly.

"Yes, it has been good," agreed David. "And I'll tell you something, Lisa. If, God forbid, one of us should die first, I have made up my mind to spend the rest of my life in Israel."

✔   ✔   ✔

The critically ill woman called her husband to her bedside.

"Moishe," she said weakly, "I want you to know that I gave my burial garments to Yossele the tailor he should sew them for me."

"To Yossele!" he demanded sharply. "You should know better than that! He keeps a piece of work for weeks!"

✓   ✓   ✓

He was a poor man, and when his wife died he was somewhat apprehensive about the final expenses.

"How much will the eulogies cost?" he asked the local *maggid*.

"What kind of eulogy do you want? One with tears or without?"

"Why, what's the difference?"

"Five dollars," said the preacher.

✓   ✓   ✓

Had there been a Motion Picture Academy of Arts and Sciences a few centuries ago, Herschele Ostropolier would easily have been awarded an Oscar for his dramatic ability. Among the many legendary stories surrounding this real-life Jewish wit, the following is a good example.

Ostropolier once rushed into the office of the *Chevra Kaddisha* (burial society) and, his eyes brimming with tears, announced that his beloved wife had just passed away, and that he was without funds for a coffin and shroud.

A popular man in the community because of his unbounded humor and kindness, he was given the necessary money. An hour or two later, a committee from the society went to his house to take care of the deceased spouse. When they entered, however, they were astounded to see the "corpse" in the unghostly occupation of peeling potatoes.

"Herschele, how dare you make such fools of us!" they demanded. "You cheated the society out of much money. Just look at your wife—she's as alive and healthy as anyone here!"

Herschele Ostropolier drew himself up to his full height, his eyes blazing with righteous indignation. "Look, she's going to be yours sooner or later anyway. What kind of monsters are you, begrudging a man a few extra years of companionship with his own wife?"

✓   ✓   ✓

A much-loved holy man of Petrograd lay dying. In another room were members of his family and friends, none of whom the sage would allow to enter for a few last words.

Suddenly there was a knock on the door and who should be admitted but the notorious Bergdorf, a liar, cheat and scandal-monger. "I came to pay my final respects," he declared.

When the mortally ill holy man heard who had come to see him he immediately demanded that the visitor be permitted to approach his bedside.

"Sir," murmured Bergdorf in surprise, "I am at a loss to understand why you allowed me to enter your room when your family and close friends are kept outside."

"Dear Bergdorf," replied the sage weakly, "they have lived in accordance with the teachings of the Torah and I will soon meet them again in Paradise. But as for you," he concluded, extending a withered hand, "I want to say goodbye for the last time."

✦   ✦   ✦

Two brothers, a rabbi and a truck driver, who lived within a few blocks of each other, received a letter from the old country that their father had died. The missive reached the truckman, but as he was unable to read, he took the letter to his learned brother.

As soon as the rabbi glanced at the dire news he burst into tears and lamentations. "Poor papa! Poor papa!" he sobbed.

"What's the matter?" asked the illiterate brother apprehensively.

The rabbi told him, but instead of using the Yiddish word *geshtorben* (died), he employed the Hebrew term *niftar* (demised).

"*Unser fotor is niftar gevoren!*" the rabbi wept.

The untutored truck driver attempted to console his grief-stricken brother.

"*Niftar, piftar, shmiftar!*" he crooned tenderly. "What's the difference as long as he's healthy and making a living!"

✦   ✦   ✦

Rabbi Israel ben Asher, the beloved sage of Yekaterinoslav, lay dying. The local physician had done all within his medical power to fan the rabbi's spark of life but it grew dimmer by the hour.

There was only one remedy left—the most drastic alternative known to Jewry. All members of the community were called to a mass meeting and asked by the pillars of the town to contribute time from their own lives. The donated time would then be added to the rabbi's, in this manner postponing his death for several years.

When the populace was assembled, the *gabbai* mounted the platform, offered the prayer of *Mi Shebeirach,* and promptly donated one year of his life to the rabbi.

The congregants, all of whom loved the stricken holy man dearly, then formed a line and the *gabbai* wrote down the months or the full year (as some offered) of contributions.

Last in line was Leibush, the shoemaker, "I donate ten years," he said.

"What?" cried the *gabbai,* astounded by this lavish contribution. "Leibush, that isn't at all necessary. Ten years out of your life is too much!"

"Not out of *my* life," explained Leibush hopefully. "I'm donating the ten years out of my mother-in-law's."

✦   ✦   ✦

A man died suddenly in the market-place while doing business. So the rabbi sent the *shammes* to the dead man's wife.

"Be careful," he cautioned the sexton. "Break the news to her as gently as possible."

The *shammes* knocked. A woman came to the door.

"Does the widow Rachel live here?" he asked.

"I'm Rachel, and I live here," replied the woman. "But I am not a widow."

"You want to make a little bet?" asked the *shammes*.

✓ ✓ ✓

Mrs. Rubin had just read a newspaper article that the remains of Sir Winston Churchill would be interred in Westminster Abbey. She turned to her husband, her face puzzled. "Tell me, Max," she asked, "this Weinstein Churchill was a Jewish boy he should be buried in Westchester Abie?"

✓ ✓ ✓

The Jewish community, like any other group, has its share of agnostics and punsters who are indifferent to the tragedy of death, and who do not mind saying so on their tombstones. Here are two examples:

"I *Told* You I Was Sick!"
and
"You Wouldn't Believe Me When I Said My Feet Were Killing Me!"

✓ ✓ ✓

Mrs. Abrams' husband, Marvin, passed away and, in accordance with his last wishes, she had his body cremated. The ashes were put into an urn which she kept on the mantelpiece. For aesthetic reasons she never told a soul what was in the urn, but would say, instead, that it was merely an ash tray. As a result, whenever friends came to visit her they would often flick their cigar and cigarette ashes into it.

One day, as she was cleaning house, she picked up the urn in order to dust the shelf. "I don't know whether it's my imagination or not," Mrs. Abrams muttered to herself as she hefted the urn in her. hand, "but it seems to me that Marvin is putting on weight!"

✓ ✓ ✓

This old classic goes back to the 18th century, proving once again that a story need not necessarily be new to be witty.

Rabbi ben Asher, of Vilna, had known for some time that Marushka's father had died two years earlier in Yekaterinoslav. But, because Marushka was a frail, sensitive girl, the rabbi had not broken the sad news to her so that he might spare her the mental agony.

Now, he learned, Marushka had decided to visit her father in Yekaterinoslav to find out why he had not written in the past two years. Clearly, the time had come when Rabbi ben Asher must inform the young woman of her father's passing. But how to do so without seeming too abrupt was the problem. Determined to get it over with, he went to Marushka's house.

"I see you are preparing for a journey," he said, his face a portrait in innocence. "Where are you going?"

"To Yekaterinoslav, to see my father," she replied. "I haven't heard a word from him in two years."

"I wouldn't worry about that if I were you," said the rabbi, thinking quickly. "My father died more than *ten* years ago and I haven't heard a word from him—either!"

*   *   *

The man was a poor woodcutter, and with his advancing years his burden grew heavier and heavier.

He was carrying a heavy load of wood on his back one day, trudging wearily along the road, when he suddenly grew weak and dizzy. He let the bundle down and cried bitterly, "O Death, release me from this terrible existence!"

The words were no sooner spoken when the Angel of Death appeared. "You called me?" asked the sinister figure.

Astonished, and frightened beyond imagination, the woodcutter could only stammer.

"Yes, your excellency—your honor—your majesty—would you mind—er—ah—helping me get this bundle back on my shoulders?"

*   *   *

Stanley, who had been a waiter all of his adult life, suffered a heart attack and dropped dead while serving a table.

Fannie, his wife, was grief-stricken, but as an ardent believer in spiritualism she was certain that she would talk with her departed husband's spirit. For months she busied herself attending seances, talking with spiritualists and other cultists, but not once was she able to communicate with Stanley's ghost.

Then, one day, it struck her that a spirit would probably haunt that place where he had spent most of his mortal time. "To be sure!" she exulted. "Where else but at the restaurant?"

At once she telephoned the owner and after explaining her idea, she asked his permission to remain in the restaurant after closing time. Rather dubiously, he agreed, and that night she entered the darkened establishment and sat at a table.

"Stanley, can you hear me?" she called softly.

"Hello, Fannie! How's by you?" came the reply in Stanley's unmistakable voice.

"Stanley, darling, I can hardly hear you. Speak a little louder."

"I can't. It's bad for my heart."
"Then come a little closer."
"That too I can't."
"But why not?"
"That's not my table!"

✓   ✓   ✓

A millionaire died one day, after he had bequeathed half a million to the synagogue and another half million to his relatives.

At the cemetery, the rabbi noticed that among the well-dressed mourners was a shabby stranger who cried as though his heart were breaking.

"I noticed you weeping," said the rabbi. "Were you related to the deceased?"

"No, I wasn't related at all," replied the poor man, wiping his red-rimmed eyes.

"Then why do you weep?"

"I just told you—because I wasn't related!"

✓   ✓   ✓

Milton Rosen, a poor man all his life, was struck by a car and killed instantly. So his wife collected three thousand dollars from the insurance company.

But Mrs. Rosen was far from comforted. "*Oy*, what terrible luck!" she moaned. "Ever since we were married we lived in poverty, and now that we have a little something Milton has to go and die!"

✓   ✓   ✓

Mort Sahl, witty and urbane commentator on current events, made this observation on his Los Angeles television program:

"You haven't lived until you've died in California!"

✓   ✓   ✓

The authority formerly wielded by some Orthodox rabbis, especially upon the elderly, is illustrated in this story told many years ago by Muni Weissenfreund, otherwise known as Paul Muni, the stage and motion picture star.

Bobeh Margolies lay critically ill and breathing her last, when the rabbi was summoned to recite the confession with her. When the prayer was finished she turned to the rabbi and, in a very weak voice, she asked, "Rabbi, could I have please a little drink of water, or must I die right now?"

✓   ✓   ✓

Mannie and Murray had been lifelong partners in the *shmatteh* business, and both had prospered. So when Mannie died, Murray felt it only right that he give his old friend a fancy funeral.

DEATH AND TAXES

As the funeral cortege moved slowly through the streets toward Mt. Zion Cemetery, a huge coal truck accidentally pulled into the line of cars, directly behind the hearse, and in front of the car in which Murray was riding.

"If I hadn't seen this with my own eyes I'd never have believed it!" exclaimed Murray, his voice ringing with admiration. "Mannie not only knew where he was going, but he ordered his own fuel!"

✓   ✓   ✓

When Tsvi, the usurer, died, there were none to mourn his passing, except his immediate family. A grasping, greedy man, he had never contributed to charity, had charged criminally exorbitant rates of interest on the money he loaned, foreclosed on properties without a qualm and paid as little as possible to those who worked for him.

Apparently, Tsvi's sons and daughters inherited the same traits, for when they learned that the *Chevra Kaddisha* demanded 50,000 rubles for his interment, the sum to be charged against his estate, they reported the officers of the burial society to the rabbi for a *din Torah*, or judgment according to Jewish law.

"On what grounds do you charge 50,000 rubles, five times more than anyone else has ever paid for a grave?" asked the rabbi.

"Because of the Judgment Day," answered a spokesman for the society. "We stand on the principles of traditional Judaism. The Torah tells us that usurers will not be included in the miracle of resurrection when the Messiah comes."

"*Nu?*"

"Then it must be perfectly clear to you, Rabbi, that the body of the late Tsvi will not remain in the grave merely for the duration, but will stay there forever, throughout eternity."

"I still don't understand," said the rabbi.

"What's to understand?" demanded the representative. "If we had assigned the burial site on a lease basis until Judgment Day the price would not be so high. But we are not leasing it until the Messiah comes, we are selling the grave in perpetuity."

The rabbi nodded. "The way you explain it, it seems to me that 50,000 rubles is too cheap. Make it 60,000!"

✓   ✓   ✓

For years Ethel had tried to pursuade her unwilling husband to take out a life insurance policy, but to no avail. One day, when he had just recovered from a serious illness, she decided to have it out with him, once and for all.

First she tried tears. "You don't love me any more," she wept, secretly admiring her own acting ability. "If you did, you would provide for me in case something happened to you."

225

But he knew Ethel too well to be swayed by her crocodile tears. "Life insurance I need like I need three elbows," he insisted.

"Look," she said, trying another method, "my three sisters are all protected, so why not me? Are their husbands any better off than you?"

"So what have they got for their money? All they ever do is pay and pay and pay. There's no end to it."

"All right, so they pay," reasoned Ethel. "But you yourself always said I was luckier than my sisters. Who knows—this time I might strike it rich!"

✓ ✓ ✓

Chalk this one up to the irrepressible Harry Hershfield, veteran story teller for five decades:

An elderly Jewish man, a subway commuter all his life, was stricken with a heart attack while waiting for a train. A rabbi was summoned to the dying man's side.

"My friend, it is time to make your peace with God," the rabbi said. "Your prayers may determine whether you go to Heaven or to Hell."

"Rabbi, I don't really care which place I'm going," answered the dying man, "just so long as I don't have to change at Jamaica!"

✓ ✓ ✓

The old wine-maker of Bensonhurst was about to depart this mortal coil, so he called his only son to his bedside.

"My boy," he began, the death rattle already in his throat, "soon I shall be no more, but before I go I want you to know that I am leaving you my business."

"Thank you, Papa."

"There is one trade secret that you must know," the old man continued, his voice fading.

"What is that, Papa?"

"You have seen me pour water into the barrels, and you may have gotten the idea that wine is all water. Well, that is not so, my son."

The dying man's voice trailed off and the boy placed his ear an inch or two from his father's mouth. "Please, Papa," he implored, "don't leave with the secret locked in your heart! Just whisper it. I'll hear you."

The wine-maker stirred, and then in a scarcely audible voice he gave his counsel: "To each barrel of water you must always add two or three grapes!"

✓ ✓ ✓

Old Joseph had started out as a diamond cutter, and through hard work and good judgment he finally became the owner of a national chain of jewelry stores. He was wealthy indeed.

But now he lay dying, so he called his wife to his side.

"Goldie," he began, "I always meant to draw up a will but somehow I never got around to it. So pay close attention to my last wishes."

"Yes, Joseph, I'm listening," Goldie wept. "Whatever you want, it will be done."

"First of all, the business I leave to Harry."

"Oh, no, Joseph, not to Harry!" his wife protested. "With Harry it's girls-girls-girls! Leave the business better to Jerome. He's at least reliable, and he has a good head for figures."

"All right, let it be Jerome then," sighed the dying man. "To Harry I leave the stocks and bonds."

"Better you should leave *me* the stocks and bonds I should take care he doesn't squander it on women and cards."

"Very well, in your name I leave the securities. And the summer house I leave to our sweet Minnie."

"Minnie!" exclaimed his wife. "What for does Minnie need another summer house? Her husband didn't buy her one last year? Give it to Anna—her husband is a poor man. After all, she's our flesh and blood too."

"Fine! Anna gets the summer house," he sighed resignedly. "And to our youngest, Abe, I leave the car and the warehouses."

"But Abe has already two cars. What does he need with another one? And he wants to be a musician—what would he do with warehouses? Take my advice and give them to Louis."

That did it! Old Joseph had taken all he could of his wife's interference. Raising himself off the pillow, and summoning his last ounce of strength, he snapped, "Goldie, you are a good woman and you have been a fine wife and mother. But listen—who the hell is dying around here— you or me?"

✓ ✓ ✓

Two old friends met on the street and greeted each other effusively.

"There's something unhappy about you," said one. "Is business bad by you?"

"No, it isn't business," replied the other. "But only a few days ago I had the sorrow of burying my wife."

"What!" cried the first, amazed. "I distinctly remember going to your wife's funeral three years ago!"

"That was my first wife. This was my second who died."

"Oh, I hadn't heard that you were married again. *Mazel tov!*"

✓ ✓ ✓

Selig the *shnorrer* passed away and found himself before the Throne of Supreme Glory. He quickly noticed that the walls were of pure gold, the furnishings solid silver, and the floors and ceilings encrusted with precious stones. His lifelong habit got the better of him.

"O Lord," he began, "does all this wealth belong to you?"

"To Whom else?" replied the Lord.

"And is it true that time means nothing to you?"

"By Me a thousand years and a day they're all the same."

"Then," said the *shnorrer*, making his pitch, "how about lending me a million dollars?"

"Tomorrow," said the Almighty.

✓ ✓ ✓

The big cloak-and-suiter was breathing his last, but he still had enough presence of mind to dictate the terms of his will to his attorney.

"Abe," he said to his lawyer, "I want you to make a stipulation in my will that all employees who worked for me twenty years or more are to receive a bequest of $25,000 each."

"But you didn't start the business until ten years ago," protested the lawyer.

"I know," answered the dying man, "but think how nice it will look in the newspapers."

✓ ✓ ✓

A doctor at Mt. Sinai Hospital forever dispelled the mystery of life's end when he declared, "Death is simply nature's way of telling us to slow down."

✓ ✓ ✓

An efficiency expert died and was being carried to his grave by six pallbearers. As they approached their destination the lid of the coffin popped open and the efficiency expert sat up and shouted, "If you'd put this thing on wheels you could lay off four men!"

✓ ✓ ✓

A woman strode into the cemetery chapel and confronted the director. "I looked all over the cemetery and I can't find my husband's grave."

"What is the name, please?" asked the director.

"Myron Heffelfinger."

"Hmmm," grunted the director, after searching through the files, "there must be some mistake. All we have here is a Rebecca Heffelfinger."

"No mistake!" cried the woman. "It's my husband, all right. Everything is in my name."

✓ ✓ ✓

Old Mr. Koppelman's health was failing, so his family decided to send him to Palm Beach for two weeks. But as the little vacation drew to a close, the man died, and his body was shipped back to New York.

As the survivors gathered around the open casket to pay their last respects to the deceased, a nephew remarked, "Doesn't he look wonderful?"

"He sure does," said another family member. "Those two weeks in Palm Beach did him a lot of good."

✓ ✓ ✓

DEATH AND TAXES

Orthodox Jews do not believe in cremation, so it was with some misgivings that Rose said to her husband, "Honey, Mama telephoned me today. She made up her mind that she wants to be cremated."

"Fine!" answered hubby. "Tell her to get her things—I'll be right over."

✔   ✔   ✔

Rose's mother finally died, so the young woman informed her husband that just before the old lady passed away she had expressed a wish that he say the *kaddish* in her memory.

"Did you have to tell me that now?" he grumbled. "You just spoiled my whole day!"

✔   ✔   ✔

Let us not forget about the man who was looking so glum and despondent that a friend asked, "Morris, what's the matter with you? You look like last month's balance sheet."

"I'll tell you what's the matter," said Morris. "Remember two weeks ago, my *tanteh* Rozeleh died and left me $50,000?"

"I remember. What's so awful?"

"What's so awful? Remember just last week my uncle Chaim died and left me $75,000?"

"Yeah, I remember that too, but what's bad about that?"

"What's bad about it? This week . . . nothing!"

✔   ✔   ✔

She: "What's the difference between death and taxes?"
He: "Death doesn't get worse every time Congress meets."

✔   ✔   ✔

A Mohammedan emigrated to America sixty years ago and accumulated great wealth. Upon his death the rich man's will stipulated that his hundred-million-dollar bequest was to be divided equally among his three closest friends; a Catholic, a Protestant and a Jew. There was only one small provision: each of the heirs was required to deposit one hundred dollars in the coffin before it was lowered into the ground. This act, according to the deceased's statement, was to prove their good faith while the will was in probate.

As the coffin was about to be closed for the last time, the Catholic quickly deposited his hundred dollars inside the casket. The Protestant followed suit and placed his hundred dollars beside the Catholic's money. Then the Jew reached into the coffin, withdrew the two hundred dollars and replaced it with a check for three hundred.

✔   ✔   ✔

Chaim was in a romantic mood. He had been married for forty years and as he thought of his wife's loyalty and devotion his heart brimmed over with affection.

"Lena darling," he said, "I want you to know that I love you more than I can say. Rather than have anything bad happen to you, I would rather it happen to me instead. In fact, rather than have you become a widow someday, I hope God in His mercy first makes me a widower!"

✓   ✓   ✓

When Franklin D. Roosevelt died he went to heaven where he was welcomed by Moses. "Are you the Roosevelt that was just President of the United States?"

"The same."

"Ah, Franklin, you have my sympathy. I think it's a shame the way the world ignored your Four Freedoms," said Moses.

"Well, I suppose everything is relative," answered Roosevelt. "Your Ten Commandments aren't faring any better!"

✓   ✓   ✓

The superintendent of the cemetery was taking old Isaac Fox around and showing him the available family plots.

"The prices vary according to the location of the graves," explained the superintendent. "If you take my advice I suggest that you purchase this plot, close to the artificial lake. Look at the serene surface, the little ripples, the goldfish, the tinkling waterfall. After a hundred and twenty years, when you depart from this earth, what more ideal resting place could there be than next to this lovely lake?"

"What!" exclaimed Isaac. "Me and my rheumatism?"

✓   ✓   ✓

Walter Winchell relates the story of the ingrate son who could hardly wait to collect his dying father's inheritance. "Where do you want to be buried?" asked the son.

The father replied: "Why don't you surprise me?"

Chapter Twenty-one

Jewish Holidays

It was Yom Kippur, holiest of fast days, and Simon Dorman, of Dorman and Litvak, Furriers, was on his way to *shul*. He passed by a sea-food restaurant and, to his chagrin, spied his partner inside.

Bursting though the entrance, he ran to the man's table and bellowed, "Litvak, how can you sit here and eat oysters on this day of all days? It's a shame and a disgrace!"

"What's a shame and a disgrace?" demanded Litvak. "There's no 'r' in Yom Kippur?"

✓ ✓ ✓

Shabbes officially begins at sundown on Friday evenings. During this time, and on other Jewish holidays, the orthodox may not perform certain tasks—for example, lighting a fire for cooking, heating or illumination. In countless small communities throughout eastern Europe, these duties were traditionally handled by local gentiles who earned small gratuities for their services.

Berel, the butcher of a little town in the heart of the Pale of Settlement, and a scrupulous observer of religious injunctions, was busily engaged in his shop when a stranger entered and introduced himself as the new salesman.

"Where are you from?" asked Berel, noting the visitor's stylish suit.

"Born and raised in Kharkov," replied the salesman.

"Is that so?" exclaimed the butcher who had never been more than twenty-five miles from his village. "How many Jews are there in Kharkov?"

"Well, I'd say about fifty thousand."

"Hmmm, that is indeed a large number of Jews to be in one place. By the way, how many gentiles are there in your city?"

"Somewhere in the neighborhood of a million."

Berel's mouth fell open in amazement. "A million!" he finally gasped. "What possible use can only 50,000 Jews have for a million gentiles?"

✓ ✓ ✓

Rabbi Genzina Gribbn, of the Beth Yontif Temple in the Bronx, was an Orthodox cleric who observed the precepts of Judaism in the minutest detail. In the long, cold winter nights it was his custom to rise long before dawn and study the scriptures. A truly religious man, these were the most precious moments of his life.

Friday nights, when making a fire is prohibited, a lamp would be left burning all night for his habitual pre-dawn studies.

One Saturday morning when the venerable talmudist rose at the usual hour, he found, to his consternation, that the lamp had gone out during the night. To waste three or four precious hours was unthinkable.

The janitor, who lived downstairs, would gladly light the lamp, of course, but rabbinic injunction prohibits asking a *goy* to perform labor on the Sabbath (it must be arranged in advance), and Rabbi Gribbn was too devout a man to even entertain such a thought.

The good rabbi was in a quandary. Then a brilliant idea flashed through his mind. 'Why not induce the janitor to light the lamp through his own volition?'

When Rabbi Gribbn heard the janitor's footsteps outside, he opened the door and called out, "How's the weather?"

"Cold, Boss," came the answer.

"Why not step inside and have a nice glass of hot tea?" the rabbi suggested invitingly.

The janitor, delighted, entered the dark house.

"It's too dark in here to find the tea," said the rabbi, making a great to-do about fumbling in the shadows.

"Wait a minute, I'll light the lamp," volunteered the guest.

The lamp was lit and the janitor drained his glass to the last drop.

"Thank you, Rabbi Gribbn," he said gratefully as he strode out the door—first extinguishing the light.

❧   ❧   ❧

A well-to-do member of the American Council for Judaism hired an agnostic Jew to fast for him on Yom Kippur, while he himself gorged to his fill. But, came the Holy Day, he was taking a walk when he happened to glance through the window of a restaurant. There he saw the agnostic eating a hearty meal of *blintzes*, roast *flanken*, sundry vegetables, and *kichel*. In a rage, he dashed inside.

"Calm yourself and be reasonable," the agnostic said. "I have another customer who paid me more than you did. So today I fast for him and eat for you. Tomorrow, take my word for it, I'll fast for you and eat for him!"

❧   ❧   ❧

Max Greenberg openly admitted to the rabbi that he had failed to ask the Lord's blessing at dinner.

"Tell me, my son, why did you not say grace?" asked the rabbi.

"To tell the truth, I forgot to wash my hands before eating."

"*Oy vay!* A fine generation this is! How could a decent Jew sit down at the table without first washing his hands?"

"There was no point in washing my hands," explained Greenberg defensively. "The food wasn't *kosher.*"

"What! You miserable apostate! You ate *traif?*"

"But, *Rebbenyu,* you don't understand. They don't serve *kosher* foods in gentile restaurants."

"Why didn't a hole open in the earth and swallow me?" moaned the rabbi. "To think God let me live to see this day!" He buried his face in his hands for a moment, and then looked up as a thought occurred to him.

"Tell me, Greenberg, why didn't you eat in a *kosher* restaurant?"

"A *kosher* restaurant! What, on Yom Kippur?"

❧ ❧ ❧

Mama: "You know something, Ben? Those toys we gave the children for Chanukah are very educational."

Papa: "Yeah, they taught me how little I can get for a dollar!"

❧ ❧ ❧

Among the Orthodox, Zom Gedalia is a holiday set aside for fasting. It commemorates the assassination of the ancient leader, Gedalia, who attempted to reconstruct Jerusalem after the Babylonian exile.

One day a Jew was observed stuffing himself with food on this fast day.

"Doovid," his friend reproached him, "how can a good Jew bring himself to eat on Zom Gedalia?"

"Look, to butt in on my private affairs nobody needs," retorted Doovid. "As a matter of fact I never, never fast on Zom Gedalia!"

"Why not?"

"First of all, if Gedalia had not been killed he'd be dead by now anyway. Is this right or is this wrong?"

"Well, I . . ."

"Secondly, if I had been killed instead of Gedalia, he wouldn't be fasting for me. Is this right or this wrong?"

"Frankly, it . . ."

"And third and final, if I never even fast on Yom Kippur why should I fast on Zom Gedalia? Everybody knows that Yom Kippur is a holier fast day. Is this right or is this wrong?"

"This is right. But . . ."

"That's what I thought. So stop bothering me!"

❧ ❧ ❧

Some men are born with a natural facility that enables them to win any argument. Such a man was Winston Churchill; such a man was Disraeli; and such a man was a certain glib libertine in a small Lithuanian village

233

who was seen in a restaurant on Yom Kippur, openly feasting instead of fasting. He was hailed before the rabbi.

"Miscreant!" snapped the rabbi. "How dare you publicly defy this holy day by eating like a *chozzer* for all to see? You should hang your head in shame."

"Now let's not get too emotional about this," retorted the nervy culprit. "There's a reason for everything."

"You have a reason?"

"Look, suppose I was sick, would I be violating the Torah by eating on Yom Kippur?"

"Well," replied the rabbi, hoping there might be some extenuating circumstances, "it depends on the nature of your illness. If you were so critically ill that fasting might prove fatal, then I would say you were permitted to eat."

"Then in other words you do allow eating on Yom Kippur!" cried the offender with virtuous indignation. "But as a condition, you insist that I must practically be on my death bed. Shame on you! To think that a rabbi, of all people, would begrudge a fellow Jew his health!"

Chapter Twenty-two

Smoking, Drinking and Gambling

A bearded Jew, a venerable-looking patriarch, was arrested for imbibing too freely in public, and was hauled before a judge.

"Grandfather," the magistrate admonished, "how could a respectable old gentleman like you be found intoxicated in the street?"

"It's a lie, a conspiracy of the Police Department. I was not drunk then and I am not drunk now!"

"Look at you, you're weaving and staggering so you can scarcely stand. How did you ever happen to get in this condition?"

"Actually it is all quite simple," answered the ancient one. "I started out with the intention of taking only one drink. It was enough—I was satisfied! But that one drink made a new man of me, and the new man wanted a drink, too. After all, he was entitled, and when a man is entitled he's entitled and that's all there is to it. So he had his drink. Now there were two of us, yes? One and one is two. Now, your honor, everyone knows that when two Jews get together it is permissible that they share a little *schnapps*. Look it up in the Torah. Anyway, we made a few little toasts to each other and by this time we were both feeling joyous. And that's the whole point, Your Honor. On a joyous occasion a Jew is *supposed* to drink!"

✓   ✓   ✓

Meyer Meyerson, known to all as the worst *Yenteh Tellabendeh* in town, strolled into the lobby of the main hotel to buy a paper. While there he noticed a portly stranger smoking a huge cigar.

"My, such a fat cigar!" exclaimed Meyer, forgetting, as usual, to mind his own business. "It must have cost you a good fifteen cents!"

"Frankly, sir, it cost a quarter," said the stranger.

"What! Twenty-five cents for just one cigar in these hard times? How many do you smoke in a day?"

"Well, as a heavy smoker, I'd say ten."

"*Oy gevald!*" cried the *yenteh*. "Ten a day! That comes to seventeen-

235

fifty a week! And how long are you smoking this much, if I may be so bold?"

"Ever since I was eighteen years old," replied the matter-of-fact stranger. "I'll be sixty on my next birthday."

"Look, mister, I don't want you should think I'm sticking my nose into your affairs, but did you ever stop to consider that if you had saved all the money you spent for so many cigars you would have enough to own this hotel?"

The stranger blew a smoke ring and regarded Meyer coolly. "Do you smoke cigars?"

"Who, me?" Meyer snorted. "I should say not!"

"Do you own this hotel?"

"What a question! Of course not!"

"Well," said the stranger, blowing another cloud of smoke, "I do!"

1　　1　　1

A popular village teacher took to drink and before long the word spread among the children's parents and he lost most of his pupils.

The local rabbi pleaded with him to give up the habit. "There is no alternative," he said. "You simply must stop this nonsense."

"Give me one good reason," demanded the teacher.

"Give you a reason? You dolt! The reason is as obvious as that big nose on your face. You'll be able to teach again!"

"How do you like that!" declared the imbiber, talking to no one in particular. "Here I've been teaching for twenty years so I'd be able to drink, and you come along and tell me to stop drinking so I'll be able to teach!"

1　　1　　1

Eyes watering, his digestive system completely upset, and suffering from a wracking cough, Goldblatt finally submitted to a physical examination.

"Do you drink?" asked the doctor with studied casualness when he had completed a series of tests.

"Yes. About a quart of *schnapps* every evening."

"How about smoking?"

"Oh, three or four packs of cigarettes a day."

"Now see here, Mr. Goldblatt," said the doctor sternly, "if you want to live much longer you will have to quit drinking and smoking, and I mean starting right now. There is no other way!"

Without a word, Goldblatt got dressed and turned to leave.

"Just a moment," said the doctor, "this isn't a charity ward. You owe me ten dollars for my advice."

"Who's taking it?" snapped Goldblatt.

1　　1　　1

SMOKING, DRINKING AND GAMBLING

The renowned evangelist, Billy Graham, had come to town and the auditorium was packed. For the better part of an hour, Dr. Graham denounced the evil of drink, his impassioned denunciations taking in the distillers and sellers, as well as the imbibers.

The vast audience was enthralled with the fiery speech, but no one was as fascinated as Hymie Kaplan who had entered the hall only to get out of the rain, and who was hearing him for the first time.

Now the evangelist was winding up his lecture. "Who has the largest bank account?" he thundered. "I'll tell you who—the liquor store owner, that's who! And who lives in the finest house and in the most exclusive neighborhood? Again, the liquor store owner! Who buys his wife mink coats, Cadillacs and jewels? The liquor store owner! And who is keeping him in all this luxury? You, the working man who spends his hard-earned money for all that whiskey, wine and beer!"

At the close of the sermon, the audience rose as one and accorded him the most enthusiastic ovation he had ever received.

Hymie rushed up to the platform and grasped Rev. Graham's hand. "Thank you! Oh, thank you!" he cried. "You are indeed an inspiring man!"

"Then you are saved?" asked the good minister. "You've decided to give up drinking?"

"Well, no, not that," explained Hymie. "But I'm going right out and buy a liquor store!"

✓   ✓   ✓

It was Mendel's birthday so he treated himself to a fifteen-cent cigar at Sol Shimkin's. Outside the store he lighted it and took a few experimental puffs. The taste was abominable. He rushed back inside and confronted the tobacconist.

"Sol, how dare you sell me such a stinker?" he cried. "I pay you fifteen cents for a decent cigar and you sell me something that tastes like a rolled-up death certificate. What's the idea?"

"Mendel, take my word for it, you're a lucky man," said the store owner.

"Lucky? With such a cigar?"

"Yes," sighed Sol. "You only have one of those old stogies. I have a whole store full of them!"

✓   ✓   ✓

A renowned *chassidic* scholar had one minor vice—he enjoyed a nightly pipeful of fragrant tobacco. Even the ritual of lighting his pipe appealed to him.

One day the famous rabbi was visited by an obscure *chassid*. During a lull in their conversation the rabbi took out his favorite pipe and filled it with tobacco. The *chassid* immediately offered a lit match to his host as a token of respect. But the great man waved him away.

237

"I appreciate your match," the rabbi grinned, his eyes twinkling, "but I, too, enjoy catering to a respected scholar!"

✦ ✦ ✦

The rabbi was walking along Fordham Road, in the Bronx, when he met a rich fat man who was smoking.

"Why do you smoke? It is an awful vice!" the rabbi rebuked the man.

"I smoke to help me digest my dinner. To tell the truth, I over-ate," replied the other.

Further on, when the rabbi had reached the Concourse, he met a poor skinny man who was also smoking.

"Why do you smoke?" the rabbi said severely. "Don't you know it is a terrible vice?"

"I smoke to drive away the pangs of hunger," murmured the poor skinny man apologetically.

"Lord of the world!" cried the rabbi, lifting his eyes to the heavens. "Where is Your justice? If only the fat rich man would give the poor skinny man some of his dinner, both of them would be healthier and happier, and neither of them would ever have to smoke again!"

✦ ✦ ✦

A rabbi, looking through the window, saw a man and his son reeling in the gutter.

"I envy that father," said the wise old sage. "I do not yet know what my son will be, but that man has already succeeded in his ambition—he knows precisely what the future holds in store for his son."

✦ ✦ ✦

The last day of the Feast of Tabernacles, accompanied by the reading of the Pentateuch on Simchas Torah, is also celebrated by merriment. Sometimes the observant and faithful of the congregants participate a little too freely.

One such celebrant, having imbibed far more of sacramental wine than is condoned by Judaic tradition, was staggering home when he stopped on a bridge and looked down at the stream below. For a few minutes he could not believe his eyes. Reeling and swaying, he grasped the rail and peered down again. No mistake about it!

It was still down there when a policeman observed the swaying figure leaning over the rail, obviously in his cups.

"Hey there, get away from that rail!" yelled the cop as he ran to the elderly Jew.

The patriarch drew back at once.

"All right, Grandpop, go on home before I run you in," growled the policeman. "You ought to be ashamed of yourself—a man your age in this condition!"

"Very well, officer, I'll leave. But first, tell me, what is that shiny thing down there?"

The officer looked down and saw the reflection of the moon in the water below.

"That's the moon," he said.

"Exactly as I thought," the old man said, raising his eyes to heaven in an ecstasy. "Thank you, dear God. I really wasn't sure I'd ever get up here!"

ᕝ   ᕝ   ᕝ

"Rabbi, I know I am not permitted t'o smoke inside the synagogue, but tell me, may I smoke outside, on the temple grounds?"

"Yes, as long as no one sees you. Take my advice and smoke with the lighted end in your mouth!"

ᕝ   ᕝ   ᕝ

Dr. Mortimer Kaplan, professor emeritus of sociology at New York University, had a peculiar mannerism, as his thousands of students would attest: he was irascible and taciturn to those he liked—an approach intermingled with an intangible affection—but deceptively polite to those who incurred his disfavor. The only thing known about his private life was that he preferred—nay, insisted!—on being alone in the evenings when he would smoke and read from his hundreds of books.

Of late, however, another faculty member had made it a habit to visit the doctor every evening, much to the latter's deep annoyance.

One evening, the associate instructor arrived just as Dr. Kaplan had opened a book and filled his pipe.

"Do you mind if I smoke too?" the other asked genially.

"Not at all," said Dr. Kaplan, rather coldly."As long as you smoke as I do."

"How is that?"

"In our respective homes!" snapped the embattled professor.

ᕝ   ᕝ   ᕝ

It was a bitter cold day, typical of the harsh Russian winters, and the Jewish merchant was trudging along the icy road to his cousin's house, five miles away. He was bringing with him a gift bottle of vodka.

The merchant, of course, could afford to hire a coach for the long distance, but this was *Shabbes,* and the use of any transportation is expressly forbidden to the Orthodox Jew. As he walked along it began to snow, and the wind rose to a howling gale. He grew cold and miserable.

"Why not take a little drink of this vodka?" he said to himself. "It should at least help keep me warm."

He took a long drink, enjoying the warmth of the liquor as it exerted its authority on his insides.

A few minutes later, feeling a gentle glow diffusing his body, he decided that if one drink could have such a beneficial effect, two drinks would naturally make him feel twice as good. So he took another. Then another and still another.

He was prancing along the last half mile to his cousin's house, singing gaily, when his boisterous manner attracted the attention of a vile-tempered bull. The animal took one look at the raucous-voiced, reeling figure and decided to do battle. With nostrils flared, head lowered and horns at the ready, the behemoth charged. With a powerful sweep of his head the bull tossed him onto his back, while he raced toward the city at breakneck speed.

Soon the beast roared into town and shot down the main street, the merchant clinging desperately to a horn with one hand and clutching the near empty bottle with the other.

"*Oy gevald!*" cried the unwilling cowboy. "How will I ever explain this to my saintly cousin? Riding an animal on the Sabbath!"

✓ ✓ ✓

Milton Berle acknowledged that he was on the Drinking Man's Diet, an eating and drinking fad popular in 1965.

Said Miltie: "I get all my recipes out of Betty Cooker's Crock Book!"

✓ ✓ ✓

Here is an oldie but a goodie. A certain *shikker* of Brownsville was observed depositing pennies in a sewer. After each penny, he would gaze intently at the clock on the City Hall building.

A cop approached. "Go on home before I run you in for public intoxication," he warned.

"Who'sh drunk?" answered the swaying man belligerently.

"You are. Why else would you be putting pennies in the sewer and then staring at that big clock?"

"Clock?" cried the other, surprised. "I thought I was getting weighed."

✓ ✓ ✓

It was getting late and the traveling salesman had been driving all day. He was quite tired by this time, so when he saw the big neon sign, "Motel—TV," he pulled into the driveway, registered, and was assigned a "single" cabin. He undressed, ordered a beer and decided to relax while he watched television, but, for the first time, he noticed that there was no TV set in the room.

Indignantly he called the manager. "How can I watch television when there's no set in here?"

"Did I say anything about a TV set?"

"Of course! It says so right on your sign—TV!"

"Oh, that," replied the manager. "That stands for 'tourists velcome'!"

✓ ✓ ✓

A stranger weaved into a neighborhood tavern and, in a shaky voice, ordered a double whiskey.

"Tell me, how high does a penguin grow?" asked the agitated customer when the bartender brought his drink.

"Oh, about so high," answered the tavern keeper, placing his hand about two feet from the floor.

"You're sure? Positive?"

"Well, my kid—he's studying biology 'r something—he tells me they got penguins in the Antarctic about four feet tall. That's the biggest there is. Why?"

"*Oy gevald!*" moaned the stranger. "I guess I just ran over a nun!"

✐   ✐   ✐

Louie was driving along the highway at an excessive rate of speed when he hit a rock in the road, lost control of the car, and plunged down an embankment. Another motorist stopped and ran down the incline to offer his assistance. He pulled the shaken Louie from the wreck and noticed that he was weaving.

"Mister, have you been drinking?" he asked severely.

"What kind of a stupid question is that?" snarled Louie. "Of course I've been drinking. You think I drive like this sober?"

✐   ✐   ✐

The poor man was such a habitual drinker that even he was finally convinced that he was an alcoholic. At his family's urging he went to see a psychiatrist. After a lengthy consultation, the doctor sternly ordered that hereafter, every time the patient got drunk he was to report his transgression the very next day.

A few days later the patient staggered into the psychiatrist's office.

"I wanna report that I wash drunk lash night," he mumbled.

"For heaven's sake, man, you're drunk right now!" cried the doctor.

"Yeah, I know," said the patient, "but I'm gonna report this to-morrow."

✐   ✐   ✐

Mendel and Maxie were out on the town, and each had imbibed far more than was good for sobriety when, at the other end of the bar, they saw a familiar figure.

"Shay, isn't that the Gran' Rabbi of Chicago?" asked Mendel.

"It looksh a li'l like him," agreed Maxie. "Why'nt you go over an' ask him?"

So Mendel went over to the stranger. "Mishter, I don't shuppose you'd be drinking in a bar if it wash really you, but ain't you the Gran' Rabbi of Chicago?"

The stranger, a husky chap, glared at the innocent intruder and then swore horribly. Reaching back a huge fist he crashed it into Mendel's jaw

241

and sent him sprawling to the floor. For good measure he aimed a few kicks at the prostrate guy and then strode out of the tavern without saying a word.

Painfully, Mendel picked himself up, staggered back to his friend and lamented, "Darn it, Max, now we'll never know whether he was the Gran' Rabbi or not!"

✓   ✓   ✓

"I'm afraid," sighed Mama, "that our Herbie is a poor loser."

"What else?" retorted Papa. "You ever heard of a rich one?"

✓   ✓   ✓

"Did you win at the track today?" asked the wife.

"No," said the disgusted husband. "I think my horse just ran out of curiosity."

"Out of curiosity?"

"Yeah, he wanted to see if other horses also have fannies."

✓   ✓   ✓

The jockey was training his son so that he, too, might some day ride horses professionally. After the first day, the son informed his father that henceforth he intended to ride side-saddle.

"Why?" demanded Pop.

"So I can save a little place for the next time," explained Sonny.

✓   ✓   ✓

Junior: "Daddy, is it wrong to bet on the horses?"

Daddy: "Yes, the way I do it is."

✓   ✓   ✓

Yankel had had a trying day at the shop and he was tired. On the way home he stopped at a bar, thinking to relax a little. He ordered a vodka highball and the bartender mixed such a perfect blend that Yankel was sure the man could only have concocted it accidentally. To test him, Yankel ordered another. Once again, the bartender fixed a superb highball, the likes of which he had never tasted before.

"This is fantastic!" thought Yankel. "No one can consistently mix such a wonderful drink. I'll try him once more, just to make sure." So he called for another vodka highball, and sure enough the bartender brought him a superb drink.

"Mister," said Yankel, "I want you to know that never in my life have I ever had such a superior vodka highball. In fact, each one you mix is better than the one before. As a token of my appreciation I'm not only giving you a two-dollar tip, but I want you to have this also." So saying, he reached into one of his packages and brought forth a live lobster. He pushed it across the counter.

"Why, thank you, sir," the bartender beamed. "You mean to say I can take this lobster home for dinner?"

"Well, he's already eaten," said Yankel, "but I don't see why you can't take him to a nice movie."

✓   ✓   ✓

A Catholic, a Protestant and a Jew were enjoying a game of penny-a-point pinochle when the police burst into the room and arrested them for gambling.

When the case came up for trial each of them denied the accusation. The judge regarded them bleakly. "Were you or were you not playing pinochle for money?" he asked.

"I don't even know how to play the game," said the Catholic.

The judge turned to the next. "And you?"

"I wasn't even there," maintained the Protestant stoutly.

Now it was the Jew's turn. "And I suppose you too claim to be innocent?"

"Of course, your honor! Would I be playing pinochle for money by myself?"

Chapter Twenty-three

Eat a Little Something

Mrs. Goldsmith bought a two-pound carp but when she unwrapped it at home the stench was so abominable she was forced to open the windows. Wrinkling her nose in disgust, she re-wrapped the offending fish and hurried back to the store with it.

"Mr. Levine," she cried angrily, "without ice you keep a dead fish for a month? It stinks! I want my money back!"

"*Shrei nisht*, Mrs. Goldsmith," said Levine in a soothing tone. "I'll be glad to return your money. But you didn't have to bring back the proof. By me, your word is just as good as the fish!"

✓　　✓　　✓

Police Officer Mike O'Brien, whose beat was on the lower East Side of New York, struck up a conversation with Morty Zweig, proprietor of the Rivington Street Delicatessen.

"What makes you Jews so smart?" asked Officer O'Brien.

"I'll tell you a secret," answered Zweig, casting a furtive eye around him as though to prevent some unauthorized person from learning the mystery. "It's because we eat so much pickled herring."

The policeman was deeply impressed, and for the next six months he ordered pickled herring every evening at Zweig's delicatessen.

One afternoon he stalked into the little restaurant, his face flushed, his mouth drawn in a thin, hard line.

"See here, Mr. Zweig," he shouted, "for six months you have been charging me forty cents for a serving of pickled herring, and I just found out that I can get even a bigger portion around the corner for thirty cents."

"What did I tell you?" grinned Morty Zweig. "The herring is working already!"

✓　　✓　　✓

A youthful Reform Jew was twenty-five pounds overweight so he decided to go on a diet. But when the anniversary of his father's death occurred, instead of lighting a *yahrtzeit* candle he felt it would be more suitable to the occasion if he went to a *kosher* restaurant, diet or no diet. The very thought of eating his fill of anything that struck his fancy made his mouth water.

First he ordered a portion of *gribbn* swimming in *schmaltz*. Then he ordered roast potatoes, goose, vegetables, cheese cake and pudding. The young man devoured every morsel, and when he was finished, his diet all but forgotten, a wave of filial devotion overwhelmed him.

"Waiter!" he called. "Bring me another serving of cheese cake and pudding. My father deserves it!"

*   *   *

Rosen had always wanted to sample a piece of ham just to see what it would taste like, but being an observant Jew he never surrendered to the temptation.

One day, however, while he was in a strange neighborhood, he entered a restaurant and ordered a ham sandwich. But the moment he took a small, tentative bite, the sky opened above him. Lightning flashed and thunder crashed, and the rains came in a deluge. Frightened, Rosen cowered under the table.

"Lord," he moaned, "for a thirty-five-cent piece of ham, you have to make such a big tumult?"

*   *   *

A group of prosperous businessmen were dining at the Sam's Hotel in Oy Vegas.

"Seems to me you are getting a little slimmer," remarked one.

"I should be!" replied the other. "I went on one of those high protein diets. Nothing but expensive steaks and chops. And would you believe it?—in just two weeks I lost thirty dollars!"

*   *   *

In the first decade of this century, when bread was an inexpensive staple for the poorest immigrants, a newly-arrived *bobeh* purchased her first *chaleh* in America.

"*Nu,* how much?" she asked in Yiddish.

"Nine cents," said the baker.

"Nine cents for a bread? You're crazy! Seven cents, that's different."

"Look, Grandma, if I have to sell breads for seven cents I'll have to make them worse," pleaded the baker. "And as God is my witness, I couldn't make the bread any worse than it already is!"

*   *   *

The ladies of the Bronx chapter of Hadassah were about to hold their annual fish dinner. But this year all the banquet halls had been reserved and they had no place in which to hold the Zionist fund-raising affair.

The parish priest of St. Thomas Aquinas on 183rd and Clinton Avenue heard of their plight and graciously offered the use of his Sunday School auditorium, and even the services of the church chef. The ladies were very grateful, and that evening they sent the rabbi to the chef so that he might instruct the cook in the art of preparing *kosher* food.

When the main course was served, however, the women were horrified to see that the scales had not been removed from the baked fish. Immediately they sent for the priest who, in turn, demanded an explanation from the chef.

"But Father, I prepared it exactly as the rabbi instructed," he exclaimed. "He told me that Jews are absolutely forbidden to eat any fish that doesn't have scales!"

*   *   *

A Hebrew teacher was invited to the home of a gentile friend. He arrived just as the host was about to eat his dinner.

"Sit down and join me, my friend," said the Christian. He passed a plate of hors d'oeuvres across the table. "Try these delicious appetizers."

"I'm sorry, but we Jews are not permitted to eat non-*kosher* food," the guest said politely. "But thank you just the same."

A little later the maid brought in a huge roast with the juices still running down the sides, and with an aroma that made the Jew's senses reel. "Have some of this roast meat," the host offered hospitably. "And help yourself to some of this lobster tail, also."

"Again, I'm sorry," the other muttered reluctantly, stifling his desire with great difficulty, "but that too is forbidden."

"Oh, for heaven's sake!" cried the host, "your religion is far too strict. What would you do if you were cast up on a desert isle and the only food available was non-*kosher?* Would you just starve to death?"

"Well, no. If it is a matter of life and death our religion permits us to eat whatever is available."

The host pondered this explanation and then a fiendish gleam came into his eyes. He jumped up, drew a gun and, pointing it at his Jewish guest, he cried, "Start eating that meat or I'll blow your brains out!"

His face white, hands trembling, the Jew cut a slice of the roast and put it on his plate. As he began to eat his friend broke out in a wide grin.

"Look, my friend, I was only joking. I just wanted to see if you would actually touch non-*kosher* food if it meant your life or death. You're not angry with me, are you?"

"Not really," the Jew grumbled. "But the next time you pull a dirty trick like that, at least do it while the roast is still hot!"

*   *   *

A man with pronounced Jewish features stood before the display case and pointed to a tray.

"I'll have a pound of that salmon," he ordered.

"That isn't salmon, it's ham," corrected the clerk.

"Mister," snapped the customer, "in case nobody ever told you, you got a big mouth!"

✓   ✓   ✓

"A *nickeleh pickeleh*" is a hoary Jewish witticism popular around the turn of the century.

Mrs. Yontif, in the Delancey Street market, reached into the pickle barrel and withdrew a large, fat pickle.

"How much costs this pickle?" she asked.

"A nickel," replied the grocer.

"What! A nickel a pickle?" she cried with assumed outrage. "Too much!" She tossed the pickle back, plunged her hand deep into the brine and fished up a small pickle.

"*Nu*, how much costs this little *pickeleh*?" Mrs. Yontif crooned.

"That *pickeleh*," answered the grocer, also crooning, "costs only a *nickeleh*." *

✓   ✓   ✓

A very poor talmudic student was able to survive only because the villagers fed him every evening. But times were hard, the crops had failed and extreme poverty gripped the village. The only thing that had survived the drought was potatoes.

The poor student made the rounds of each home, hoping against hope that he would be served something other than potatoes which he had grown to detest.

Finally, at one cottage, when a platter of potatoes was placed before him, he asked his host, "Tell me, Reb, what benediction is said over potatoes?"

"What? You a talmudic scholar and you don't know the blessing for potatoes? Shame on you! Why, everyone knows you must say 'Blessed are the fruits of the earth.' In fact, you must say it over everything that comes out of the soil!"

"Yes, 'everything which comes out of the soil'—that I understand," sighed the scholar. "But what do I say when the potatoes are coming out of my ears?"

✓   ✓   ✓

It really happened.

The editor of this book was entertaining his friends, a Christian couple, Lindy Avakian and his wife Glynna. Chef for the evening was this editor's cousin, Yetta Koffman.

---

* The suffix, "eh," is a Yiddish idiom meaning "small" or "little," usually with a tender connotation. Thus, the play on words—the cost of a little pickle is a little nickel. Like the man said, it loses something in translation.

For the appetizer, Yetta served *gefilte fish*. It was the first time that either Lindy or Glynna had ever tasted (or even heard of) the Jewish delicacy, and they asked if it were possible to buy it "ready-made" in the stores.

"Sure!" Yetta agreed. "You can buy *gefilte fish* in jars. Go to Garfinkel's delicatessen on Sunset Boulevard. They'll have it."

"We must remember that, Glynna," said Lindy to his wife as they set out for the delicatessen.

All the way to the store they kept repeating the unfamiliar words, so that they would not forget: "*Gefilte fish*-Garfinkel's. Garfinkel's *gefilte fish. Gefilte fish*-Garfinkel's. Garfinkel's-*gefilte fish*."

Finally they entered the delicatessen, approached the display case and told the counter clerk, "We'd like to buy a jar of gilfinkels!"

✓   ✓   ✓

Isaac Ashkenasi, proprietor of the Orchard Street Hungarian Delicatessen, told the following story to Charles Spalding, this editor's father, early in the 1920's.

Mrs. Cronkheit, peering at the various meats in the showcase, pointed to a two-foot length of salami and said, "Cut me slices of that."

Ashkenasi withdrew the salami from the tray, placed it on the cutting board, and cut a few slices. "Enough?" he asked.

"Cut! Cut!" Mrs. Cronkheit ordered imperiously.

Ashkenasi shrugged and continued to cut additional slices, waiting for the lady to call a halt.

He was now a quarter of the way through the salami. "You're sure this isn't enough?" he asked, contemplating the large pile of slices he had accumulated.

"Cut! Cut!"

"She must be planning a party," thought Ashkenasi. So he continued slicing.

He was almost in the exact center of the salami, with Mrs. Cronkheit still urging him on. "Cut! Cut!"

"Okay, lady, it's your money," he muttered.

But just then, Mrs. Cronkheit threw up her hand in the manner of a traffic policeman.

"Now, from the middle!" she cried. "Cut me please five slices!"

✓   ✓   ✓

A very poor man burst into his house, breathless as though he had been running. "I've just been to see the richest man in town and I found him at dinner, eating *blintzes*. As I stood there and smelled their delicious fragrance the juices in me began to work. Those *blintzes* surely must taste wonderful. Believe me, when rich men eat something, it's *something!*"

Then the poor man sighed. "Oh, if I could only taste *blintzes* just once before I die!"

"I'd make them for you," said his wife, "but I have no eggs."

"So make them without eggs," he suggested.

"But what will I do for cream?"

"You'll have to do without the cream."

"Well, I'll try, but there isn't a grain of sugar in the house."

"Be inventive. Do without the sugar."

The wife, determined to please her husband, set about to make the *blintzes*, but without eggs, cream or sugar. A little later she placed them on the table before him. The husband started to eat, tentatively at first, and then judiciously. Gradually a look of bewilderment spread across his face.

"Believe me," he said, "if I live to a hundred and twenty, I will never understand what all those rich people see in *blintzes!*"

❦ ❦ ❦

What did the saltine say to the matzoh?

"You don't look it!"

❦ ❦ ❦

A recipe for an omelette in an old Gypsy cookbook begins: "Steal two eggs . . ."

❦ ❦ ❦

"A bagel," according to one wag, "is a doughnut with rigor mortis."

❦ ❦ ❦

Hy and Miriam had only been married for ten days and their wedded life was all sugar and spice and everything nice. So it was only natural that when Hy came home from work one evening and found his bride in tears he took her in his arms and caressed her tenderly.

"Miwiam, baby," he cooed, "tell oo big bwave Hymie aw about it, an' Hymie will tiss oo tearsies away."

"The dinner got scorched," Miriam sobbed.

"What!" gasped Hy, forgetting his honeymoon jargon. "You mean to say the delicatessen burned down?"

❦ ❦ ❦

"Lady," insisted the corner grocer, "these are the best eggs we've had for months."

"Then keep them," snapped the customer. "Who needs eggs you've had for that long?"

❦ ❦ ❦

Suzy was so much in love with Sol that she never noticed his deficient table manners. Now that they were man and wife, and married for lo these three days, she began to take cognizance of his comportment.

The very first time they left their honeymoon cottage to eat at a restaurant, she cried out in dismay when her loving Sol began to eat with his fingers.

Sol listened to her scolding for a minute or so and then answered her calmly:

"Honey, I'm sorry to disagree with my new bride, but I've always felt that if food wasn't clean enough to pick up with your fingers, it wasn't clean enough to eat!"

✔   ✔   ✔

Let us meditate quietly for a few sacred moments on the plight of Ruthie the new bride. She was getting along wonderfully well in cooking school until she finally burned something—the cooking school!

✔   ✔   ✔

Hubby: "Is this all you fixed tonight—salami sandwiches? I thought you were going to cook a big pot-roast."

Bride: "That's what I started to fix. But the pot-roast caught fire and it spread to the vegetables, so I had to put the blaze out with the chicken soup."

✔   ✔   ✔

When the hallucinatory drug LSD was a frequent subject of newspaper headlines, comic Dave Barry commented, "My wife is hooked on LSD: Lox, Salami and Danish!"

✔   ✔   ✔

The stylishly-dressed lady stopped at Tobatchnik's fish stand and examined his stock. After handling the fish for some time the lady started to walk away.

"Why don't you buy my fish?" asked Tobatchnik. "Don't you like them?"

"I certainly don't; they smell."

"You can't talk like that about my merchandise," retorted Tobatchnik. "It's not the fish you're smelling—it's me!"

✔   ✔   ✔

Mrs. Stein entered a *kosher* poultry store and asked the price of stewing chickens. "Forty cents a pound," said the butcher.

"Forty cents!" cried Mrs. Stein. "Why, just around the corner Ellenberger sells for thirty-six cents a pound."

"If Ellenberger sells stewing chickens for thirty-six cents a pound, why don't you buy there?" asked the butcher impatiently.

"Because he happens to be out of them today."

"Look, lady," said the butcher, "as soon as I run out of stewers I'll sell them to you for only twelve cents a pound—and you can't beat that price anywhere!"

Chapter Twenty-four

Waiters, Restaurants and Patrons

A small Jewish restaurant, seeking to expand its business, put in a line of Chinese food. A few evenings later a customer ordered egg foo yong.

"Tonight you're out of luck," said the waiter. "We used up the last egg an hour ago, and we don't have any yong left either."

"In that case," said the customer, "just bring me a bowl of the foo."

✓   ✓   ✓

To celebrate their fifteenth wedding anniversary, Sam and Thelma went to a fancy nightclub where they ordered exotic French dishes they couldn't even pronounce, drank imported wines, and enjoyed the floor show.

When they were ready to leave the waiter brought the check. But the moment Sam noticed the last item on the bill he hit the ceiling.

"Waiter!" he yelled, "what's with this cover charge business? We came here to eat, not to sleep!"

✓   ✓   ✓

At the turn of the century, two merry gentlemen, Gallegher and Shean, were evoking chuckles everywhere, especially among Jewish audiences. In their restaurant skits, Gallegher was usually (though not always), the long-suffering, frustrated patron, and Shean the bellicose waiter. Here are a few samples of their dialogue, now some seventy years old:

Gallegher: "Waiter, come over here!"

Shean: "On who are you hollering, on who?"

Gallegher: "I have a complaint. There's a black barley in my soup."

Shean: "So what? In this restaurant we don't draw the color line."

Gallegher: "That's not the point. This little black barley has feet. It's swimming around in the plate."

Shean: "What do you expect he should do? Lay there and drown?"

Gallegher: "Look, waiter, if you want me to pay for this soup, either help him climb out or stop him from making waves."

(And another):

Gallegher: "Waiter, what kind of a chicken did you bring me? One leg is shorter than the other."

251

Shean: "Mister, did you come here to eat the chicken or to dance with it?"

(And still another):

Gallegher: "Waiter, bring me a menu."

Shean: "Mister this is a restaurant, not a library. Did you come here to eat or to read?"

Some more . . .

Gallegher: "Waiter, my plate is damp."

Shean: "Eat—that's your soup!"

Gallegher: "But my other plate has a crack in it."

Shean: "Eat that too—that's your steak!"

✓ ✓ ✓

A Negro wandered into a small *kosher* restaurant and seated himself at a table.

A waiter approached. "Tonight we got *gefilte fish, borscht,* stuffed sweet-and-sour cabbage, *kishkeh* and *helzel.*"

The Negro, his face a complete blank, decided to order something more familiar. "You got any chitlins?" he demanded.

"Do I got *what?*"

"Never mind. Bring me a bowl of hominy grits."

"Whatever it is, we ain't got that either."

"Then bring me some hog jowls."

"Hog? In *here?*"

"F'r chrissake!" the Negro muttered in disgust as he rose to leave, "it'll be another hunnerd years before *this* place is ready for integration!"

✓ ✓ ✓

Morris had only been in this country for a few days and could not speak a word of English. Fortunately for him, however, he moved in with his brother who had left Europe years before. The brother found him a job in a garment factory and taught him to say "apple pie and coffee," so that he would not have to fix his own lunch every morning before going to work.

All was well for the first week or two, but one evening Morris complained of his noonday lunches. "I'm sick and tired of pie and coffee," he said in Yiddish. "How about teaching me something else?"

"Hmm," thought the brother. After a few moments, his face brightened. "I have it! Try this: chicken sandwich."

"Sheek'n senvidge."

"Again."

"Sheek'n senvidge."

"Okay, that'll do."

All through the morning, on the following day, Morris practiced the new words, and when the noon bell rang he went into the lunchroom and sat down at the counter. The short-order man approached, "What'll it be, buddy?"

"Sheek'n senvidge."

"On what?"

"Sheek'n senvidge," Morris repeated helplessly.

"Yeah, I hoidja. Ya wannit on rye 'r white—toast 'r plain?"

"Sheek'n senvidge," repeated Morris, almost sobbing.

"Say, you a wise guy 'r somethin'? Make up ya mind; rye 'r white—toast 'r plain?"

With a despairing moan, Morris gave his order: "Epple pie mit cawfee!"

✓　✓　✓

A man happened to find himself in a strange neighborhood, and as it was dinner time, he entered a small restaurant and ordered a plate of cabbage soup.

"I'm sorry but we're all out of cabbage soup—or any other kind of soup."

"Then bring me some roast chicken."

"Chicken we ain't got either."

"How about fish?"

"All out of that, too."

"Look, waiter, just bring me a glass of tea and a roll!"

"Good God!" the waiter exclaimed. "A man with an appetite like yours I never saw in my whole life!"

✓　✓　✓

A Texan came to New York for the first time and decided to sample that dish he had heard so much about—lox and bagels.

From the very first bite he loved it—so much, in fact, that he returned to the restaurant every day for two weeks and gorged on the delicacy.

On his last day in town, he called the proprietor to his table. "I want you-all to know how much I enjoyed that wonderful dish," he said earnestly. "But before I return to my oil wells in Texas I want to ask you a question."

"Sure! Go ahead and ask."

"Tell me, which is the bagel and which is the lox?"

✓　✓　✓

Mr. and Mrs. Jaffe were about to order supper in a Second Avenue restaurant where Al, the waiter, ruled his domain with the heavy hand of a tyrant. If the customer was properly respectful and displayed the right shade of humility, Al served with paternalistic benevolence. But woe betide the patron who did not know his place in the social order.

Mrs. Jaffe ordered veal cutlets and her husband requested the fish dinner. A few minutes later Al returned with Mrs. Jaffe's cutlets, but instead of the fish dinner he brought Mr. Jaffe chop-meat.

"You don't need fish tonight," said the waiter. "The chopmeat is better for you. Eat!"

The wife tasted her food first and beamed. "My, these cutlets are delicious," she told her husband. She cut a piece for him. "Here, have a taste," she offered.

Mr. Jaffe tried it and immediately his face lit up. "Say, that really is good!" he agreed. He turned to Al who was still hovering over the table. "Waiter, why didn't you bring *me* veal cutlets instead of this chopmeat?"

Al stared down at the customer as though he were a strange specimen under a wet rock. "Because you ordered fish," he snapped. "If you had ordered *borscht* you'd have gotten the cutlets."

"But my wife ordered veal cutlets and that's what you brought."

The waiter shrugged. "We were all out of *borscht*."

✓ ✓ ✓

A Jewish couple were dining out one evening at the neighborhood *kosher* delicatessen, when they were amazed to have a Chinese waiter approach to take their order. To their added astonishment, the suave Oriental addressed them in perfect Yiddish.

As soon as he had disappeared into the kitchen they motioned to the proprietor. "A Chinese waiter in a Jewish delicatessen!" exclaimed the man. "And not only that, but he talks Yiddish. How come?"

The proprietor looked around and put his finger to his lips.

"Shhhh!" he whispered. "He thinks I'm teaching him English!"

✓ ✓ ✓

Marty Singer had just opened his new tavern when a stranger walked in and ordered a glass of beer.

Without a word, the customer drank it in a series of long gulps, set the empty glass down, tossed a dollar bill on the counter and strode out.

"The nerve of that guy!" stormed Marty. "He comes in here, drinks my beer, leaves me a dollar tip, and then runs out without paying!"

✓ ✓ ✓

A gentile who fancied himself as something of a comedian was invited by a Jewish friend to dine at a *kosher* restaurant.

Thinking to have some fun at the waiter's expense, he ordered his meal and then said, "I'll have a yard of coffee."

Wordlessly, the waiter brought the food and then, without a change of expression, he dipped his finger into the coffee cup and drew a wet line on the table, thirty six inches long.

The so-called comic was up to the occasion. "Wrap it up," he said. "I'll take it with me."

The silent waiter contemplated this turn of events. Then he nodded, extracted a paper napkin from the holder, blotted the "yard" of coffee, and handed it to the insolent customer.

On the dinner check was added this item:

"Coffee to go—25¢. Container—$1.00."

✓ ✓ ✓

WAITERS, RESTAURANTS AND PATRONS

A late diner entered the Frailiche Fresser delicatessen on Hester Street and ordered roast duck.

"Sorry, no roast duck today. How about some nice roast chicken?"

"No, I don't want chicken. Roast duck or nothing!"

"Hey, Max," he said to the cook, "cut me a portion of roast duck from the roast chicken."

✓ ✓ ✓

For twenty years the same customer visited a certain Jewish restaurant and, without fail, always ordered the same dish—*borscht*! In all that time he never once complained about the food or service—the model customer.

One evening, when the waiter had served the customary plate, the customer called him back to the table.

"Waiter, taste this *borscht*!"

"Why, what's the matter with it?"

"Just taste it!"

"Listen, it's too cold, it doesn't taste right, whatever—I'll take it back and bring you another serving."

"Taste the *borscht*!"

"Why should I taste? You don't want it you don't want it. So I'll bring you a change. Why should I argue with a good customer?"

The customer, his face dark with fury, stood up. "For the last time, TASTE THE BORSCHT!"

Intimidated, the waiter sat down. "All right, if you insist." He looked around. "Where's the spoon?"

"Ah-HAH!" exploded the customer.

✓ ✓ ✓

A Jew and a German occupied the same table in a restaurant. The Jew ordered *gefilte fish* and the German ordered pork. Each recognized the origin of the other, and neither uttered a word throughout the meal.

When they had finished eating, the Jew decided he would have an after-dinner drink. "Waiter," he called, "the fish wants to swim."

The waiter, understanding perfectly, grinned and brought him a jigger of brandy.

But the German was not about to be outclassed by a Jew, although he did admire the other's cleverness.

"Waiter," he said loudly, "the pig wants to drink."

✓ ✓ ✓

It happened in a small restaurant in Flatbush. A regular customer sat down at his accustomed table and ordered baked flounder—the special for that day. He tasted it, quickly spat it out and pushed the plate away in disgust.

"Waiter!" he roared. "This fish not only tastes foul, it actually stinks!"

255

"That's impossible," the waiter protested. "You ate here a week ago, and you praised our fish to the skies."

"That was different. At least, then, it was fresh."

"Sir, I give you my word," said the waiter, "this is the very same fish!"

✓   ✓   ✓

It was their twentieth anniversary and Becky insisted that they celebrate at a swanky restaurant. They ordered the works—from pheasant under glass to champagne.

"Wasn't that a lovely meal?" cried Becky when they finished.

"To tell you the truth," said her husband as he studied the check, "I'm not sure whether we should have eaten it or had it appraised."

✓   ✓   ✓

"Waiter!" a diner barked angrily. "This *borscht* smells from kerosene!"

The waiter lifted the plate to his nose and sniffed deeply.

"What do you mean it smells from kerosene?" he demanded belligerently. "It smells like it's supposed to smell—from soap!"

✓   ✓   ✓

A well-dressed stranger entered Mama Eisenroth's restaurant on Avenue B and ordered the specialty of the house: home-made chopped chicken liver. It was perfectly delicious; far better than any he had ever tasted before. He called Mama Eisenroth to his table.

"Madam," said the stranger, "this chopped liver is the most flavorful, the tastiest I ever enjoyed in my life."

"Thank you," Mama beamed.

"Tell me," he asked, "is it cooked by electronics?"

"Why of course not!" replied Mama Eisenroth, shocked. "We're all Jewish here!"

✓   ✓   ✓

Yetta had not seen her New York relatives for several years, so she was understandably pleased when her Aunt Bella and Uncle Sam came to visit her in Los Angeles. To celebrate the reunion, she took them to Canter's restaurant on Fairfax Avenue.

"I'll have the *kreplach*," Yetta told the waiter.

"The *kreplach* is from last night," explained the waiter. "Better you should order something fresh-made—like stuffed peppers."

"All right, let it be stuffed peppers."

The waiter turned to Aunt Bella. "*Nu?*"

"Bring please the pot roast."

"Look, lady, the pot roast is strictly for the *goyim*. You want something special, try the *hock-flaish*."

"All right, so bring the *hock-flaish*."

Uncle Sam, who had been studying the menu carefully, now looked up. "Waiter, I can't make up my mind. What do you suggest?"

"*Suggest!*" cried the waiter indignantly. "On a busy night like this, who has time to make suggestions?"

✓   ✓   ✓

A suave beggar with the *chutzpah* of a lion, finished a hearty meal at Thaw's restaurant in New York and was contentedly sipping his coffee when the waiter brought the check.

"Sorry," said the diner nonchalantly, "but I don't have a dime."

The waiter called old man Thaw himself. "Mister, you'll pay for the meal or I'll call the police."

"That won't bring you any money," retorted the customer. "But I have an idea. I'll go out and beg until I reach the exact amount I owe you for my dinner. Then I'll come right back and pay up."

"How do I know you'll return?" asked the suspicious proprietor.

"Come along with me and watch, if you don't believe me."

"Who, me?" cried Thaw. "How dare you even suggest that a respectable businessman like me would be seen in the company of a disreputable beggar like you?"

"Well, if you refuse to be seen with me," the man said calmly, "I'll wait here in the restaurant. You go out and beg!"

✓   ✓   ✓

A vaguely familiar man walked into a restaurant on Second Avenue in New York, and demanded the best table in the house. Before he would even accept the menu he demanded that a tablecloth of the finest linen be spread before him and a vase with fresh flowers be placed on the table. Carefully he selected the vintage wines, but only after a long discussion with the waiter about the growing and bottling years. Then he chose the choicest cuts of meat, sending back explicit cooking instructions to the chef. He ordered caviar, as well as special sauces and gravies to go with the various exotic dishes he had chosen.

When he had finished the sumptuous repast, a full two hours later, and had sampled the imported champagnes, cognac and assorted Rhine and French wines, he lit a Corona-Corona cigar, summoned the waiter and asked for his check. He studied the $80.00 bill for a moment or two and then looked up at the solicitous waiter.

"Waiter," he asked, "do you recall ever seeing me before?"

"Why—why—you do look a little familiar."

"Well, I should be. One day last year I was out of work and dying of hunger. I ordered a meal, and then I told you I was unable to pay. Do you remember that, my good man?"

The waiter was growing increasingly uneasy, sensing that his tip would be small. "I have a hazy recollection," he admitted.

But the customer was relentless. "Let me refresh your memory. There

I was, cold, starving and broke. And because I could not pay for the meal you called the manager, and both of you threw me out into the street."

The waiter was truly embarrassed by now. "If there is anything I can do . . ." he began apologetically.

The customer nodded. "Yes, as a matter of fact, there is. Please be kind enough to call the manager again. I'm afraid I can't pay this time, either!"

✔ ✔ ✔

"Waiter, come here!" called a diner.

"You got troubles, Mister?"

"I ordered the special for today—chicken soup with *farfel*. But there's no chicken or *farfel* in it. You call this a special?"

"Sure—that's what makes the soup so special!"

✔ ✔ ✔

"Congratulations, I heard your restaurant burned down!"

"So what's to congratulate?"

"All your customers are bragging that it's the first time your place ever served hot food."

✔ ✔ ✔

"See here," complained a disgruntled patron, "I ordered vegetable soup. What's the idea of bringing me a bowl of chicken soup?"

The waiter peered closely at the soup. "But it *is* vegetable," he insisted. "Look, there's a piece of celery floating on top."

"Oh, excuse me," apologized the diner, "I thought it was a feather!"

✔ ✔ ✔

"Bob, did you have to disgrace me at the banquet tonight?" demanded the wife. "All through the meal you just ate soup and ignored the steak and everything else."

"I didn't have any choice, Selma," replied the husband. "There was a leak in the ceiling and I had to keep on eating the soup or drown!"

✔ ✔ ✔

"Hey, Louie, I heard that you saw the President's daughter at the restaurant last night."

"I sure did!"

"What happened?"

"I sent the waiter over to her table to ask her for a dance."

"Did she dance?"

"Yeah—with the waiter!"

✔ ✔ ✔

"Waiter, how come there's no coffee on the menu?"

"Because I wiped it off! You think we're a bunch of slobs around here?"

✓ ✓ ✓

Diner: "Do you serve wild rice here?"

Waiter: "No, we use tame rice and mish it around until it gets mad."

✓ ✓ ✓

Alan considered himself something of a wit, so when he noticed a sign saying "We prepare every type of sandwich," he called the waiter.

"Is that sign true?" he asked.

"Yes, it is," answered the waiter.

"Then bring me an elephant steak sandwich on toast."

The waiter stared at the wise guy for a moment and then replied, "I'm sorry, sir, but we can't start a whole elephant just for one sandwich."

✓ ✓ ✓

Harry returned home in a high fury. "That waiter at Epstein's Deli is the freshest guy I ever met in my life," he stormed.

"Why, what happened?" asked his wife.

"I told him I couldn't eat my salad unless I had some Russian dressing, so he brought me a picture of Khrushchev putting on his pants!"

✓ ✓ ✓

For years Shmendrik had been eating at the same restaurant without incident, but this evening the meal was abominable. The roast chicken was tough as an O'Sullivan heel, the peas were like B-B's, and the mashed potatoes reminded him of wallpaper paste.

"Waiter," he yelled, "I can't eat this meal. Call the manager!"

"It wouldn't do you a bit good," said the waiter. "He won't eat it either!"

✓ ✓ ✓

A Galician *chassid* was walking on a main thoroughfare in Vienna in search of a *kosher* restaurant. He finally located one of those Jewish restaurants that cater to the tourist trade. In the window was a large portrait of Moses. So the *chassid* went inside and seated himself at a table. A waiter approached and handed him a menu.

"What's this?" asked the startled Jew, pointing to a printed legend on the menu.

"It says '*kosher*-style food our specialty.'"

"I can read," snapped the *chassid*. "But what do you mean, *kosher-STYLE*? Food is either prepared in accordance with Jewish law or it isn't. There is no such thing as *kosher-STYLE*!" he concluded, quite correctly.

"Look, mister, you can't talk that way about this place. We're all Jews here. Can't you see that picture of Moses in the window?"

"Yes, I can see it," replied the Galician as he rose to quit the place. "But I'd feel a lot more certain about the food if you were hanging in the window and Moses were waiting on the tables."

Chapter Twenty-five

Show Biz

Hollywood—where the average actor has more lines in his face than in his script. The only town in America with wall-to-wall lawyers and psychiatrists. A city where the apartments are 80 by 15 by 30: If you don't pay eighty by the fifteenth—out by the thirtieth! Yet, Tinseltown, as it is sometimes called, has more to it than appears on the surface. Take away that outside tinsel and you'll find—more tinsel!

✓   ✓   ✓

Dorothy Rochmis, gifted motion picture reviewer for the *California Jewish Voice*, contributed this bit of whimsey:

A famous movie star was having difficulty pursuading a sweet young thing to go to his house and listen to his stereo set.

"Look," he implored, "how long have I known you?"

"About an hour," she estimated coyly.

"All right then," he stormed, "in all that time have I ever lied to you?"

✓   ✓   ✓

The late Joseph Schildkraut, idol of New York's Yiddish Theatre some five decades ago, was in his dressing room, preparing to go on stage.

It was Halloween, and the four-year-old son of Joseph Schildkraut was out "trick or treating."

There was a timid knock on the door and Schildkraut impatiently called through the door, "Come in! Come in!"

"Twick 'r tweat!" piped the little boy.

The actor, already late for his stage entrance, dashed out the door, crying, "Look, kid, go see my manager!"

✓   ✓   ✓

Joey Bishop tells about the entertainer, Frank Sinatra, who was dining out one night when a young high school lad came up to his table.

"Mr. Sinatra," said the teen-age boy, "my name is Bernie Rosenberg. Would you please do me a favor?"

"What kind of a favor?" Sinatra asked.

"Well, I'm here with my girl and I want to make a good impression on her. I certainly would appreciate it if you would drop by my table and say 'Hi, Bernie!'"

"OK, kid, I'll try," said the singer, smiling.

A little later he dropped by the boy's table and said, "Hi, Bernie!"

The boy looked up at him and snapped, "Don't bother me now, Frankie. Can't you see I'm busy?"

✓   ✓   ✓

Comic Lou Alexander was in the middle of his act at a Beverly Hills night club one evening, when one of his contact lenses popped out of his eye. It landed right in the drink of a man sitting at a ringside table.

"Sir," deadpanned Lou, "I'm afraid my eyeball is in your highball!"

✓   ✓   ✓

Al, Morris and Sidney, three brothers, purchased a run-down movie house. Two things were necessary, they decided, if the theatre was to make money. First they would have to remodel the place, and then they would have to book better quality motion pictures than had the former owner.

"Al," said Morris, "the seats are rickety and the material is torn. The stuffing even shows through. Now I suggest that we recover the seats with leather."

"Leather is too expensive," Al protested. "I think the seats should be covered with a strong material like mohair."

Al and Morris argued back and forth about the durability and expense of leather versus mohair but neither could agree. They turned to the third brother who had not uttered a word during the entire argument.

"Sidney," they asked, "what would you like to see the seats covered with?"

"Fannies!" replied Sidney tersely.

✓   ✓   ✓

"*In der beshreinking zeigt sich erst der Meister*," said Goethe. (The master knows how to limit his field. He does not spread himself too thinly.)

They tell a story of the great female star of the Yiddish stage of by-gone days. Despite her age—and she was sixty if she was a day!—she was always surrounded by a host of admiring, handsome young males. One night she came home after a performance and found five of them encamped on her doorstep.

"Listen," she said, "I'm very tired. I've had a hard day at the theatre. One of you will have to go!"

✓   ✓   ✓

There is an endearing and enduring quality to *Yiddishkeit*—the syndrome that encompasses all those things associated with Jewry. It is a quality that admonishes as it instructs, but with humor; sometimes gentle, sometimes devastating. The accented English used in this delightful story is not employed to mock those who have not mastered the language but to make a valid point: an expression of pleasure at the "return of the native."

Vaughn Platzer, well known Hollywood theatrical agent, was in her office one morning when the phone rang. The caller was an old friend who insisted, for old times' sake, that his daughter be given an audition. Vaughn shrugged. "Okay, send her over."

An hour passed when there was a knock on the door and in walked Rachel Goodowitz. She had a nose like an anteater's. Her hair, unbrushed and lusterless, hung like wet hay down her spine. Her dress was rumpled and three sizes too large. In short, she looked like something offered at a rummage sale by the Salvation Army. But the shocker came when she opened her mouth to sing: "Yenkeh Dreidel vent optahn he's riding on top a pony." The poor girl's accent was so thick it was scarcely understandable.

"Listen, Rachel," Vaughn began slowly, "I like your father and I'd like to help you start a career as a singer, but I'm going to give it to you straight—you have no chance in show business. It would be an act of cruelty to encourage you. Take my advice, Kid, and go home, find a nice husband and raise a family."

One day, several years later, Vaughn received an engraved invitation to the Governor's Annual Ball, a swanky affair attended by the elite of political and social society. Heading the entertainment, according to the invitation, would be the sensational new singing star, Raquel Goodrich.

Ensconced in the front row, Vaughn was tingling with anticipation as the curtain rose, for she had heard much of this new vocalist who had won national acclaim. But when the entertainer finally appeared in the spotlight, Vaughn gasped. There, poised and smiling confidently on stage was none other than Rachel Goodowitz. And what a transformation had taken place! Gone was the frumpy dress. Now she wore a gorgeous gown— a Dior, no less! Her hair was beautifully coiffeured, she had undergone a nose job, and—miracle of miracles!—when she began to sing her diction was absolutely impeccable:

> "Getting to know you,
> Getting to know you but nicely,
> You are precisely
> *Mein gless* of tea."

✓ ✓ ✓

Morrie Ryskind, syndicated columnist for the Hearst press, recounts a glorious moment in an old Fanny Brice show.

Fanny had bought what seemed to be an ideally located restaurant right off a heavily traveled road. She did some refurbishing, put up enticing signs—but, instead of stopping, the cars continued to whiz by. "At sixty miles an hour," noted Fanny with a sigh.

Desperate, she sought an attraction and, since at that time Negro jazz bands were beginning to come into their own, she signed with a booking agent for the services of the "Ethiopia Dixie Jazz Band." New posters heralded the advent and some customers actually showed up on the opening date. But the band was late in arriving, and Fanny used all her alibis to stall the patrons who were demanding their music as promised.

Finally, however, the band appeared. But, to her astonishment, their complexions and accents were clearly those of Manhattan's lower East Side, and were neither from Dixie nor Harlem, let alone Ethiopia.

"You swindlers!" shrieked Fanny in understandable dismay. "You got some nerve to call yourselves Ethiopians!"

"Now let's be reasonable about this," said the leader. "If you buy a suit from the Eagle Clothing Company, do you expect maybe to be fitted by an eagle?"

✓   ✓   ✓

Cantor Yehudi Rosenblatt had a magnificent voice, but for years he struggled in anonymity and poverty. One day Rosenblatt's old music teacher brought an impresario to the synagogue, and the cantor's very real talent made an immediate, favorable impression. From then on, the former cantor's rise was rapid.

From the recital stage, recordings and television, Rosenblatt went on to grand opera, scoring success after heady success. Now, at La Scala in Milan, he was making his Italian debut in *I Pagliacci*. Even his old music teacher, seated in the gallery, was on hand for this auspicious occasion. No one was disappointed. When Rosenblatt sang the famous *Vesti la giubba* aria, the applause was deafening—so tremendous, in fact, that the company could not go on with the opera and he had to sing an encore. And another. And again. Finally, after he sang eight full encores, he stepped to the footlights and waited until the audience was completely silent.

"My friends," announced Rosenblatt, "we have made history here tonight. I say 'we' because you, the audience, contributed as much as I. So far as I know, nobody in the history of La Scala, not Martinelli, not Schipa, not Gigli, not even Caruso himself ever sang *Vesti la giubba* more than six times. And you, my dear friends, have caused me to sing it eight. This is the greatest moment of my singing career—I shall never forget it. But there is still the rest of the opera to perform and my throat is becoming just a bit tired. So I ask you, dear friends, do not ask me to sing this aria again."

In the gallery, Rosenblatt's old singing teacher cupped his hands to his mouth and bellowed—

"You'll sing it 'til you get it right!"

✓   ✓   ✓

SHOW BIZ

During the first few years of the 1900's, when the Yiddish theatre flourished on New York's East Side, there was a talented actor named Barney Halpern. He earned top money, at least for those days, but because he spent all his money on women he was always without funds. Among his lady friends was a burlesque stripper who was his favorite.

"How is it, Barney," she once asked, "that I make only a fraction of what you earn, yet I have everything and you are always broke?"

Barney gazed about her apartment and noted the many gifts she had received from him and her other admirers. Then, as she slipped out of her dress and into a sheer negligee, he again studied her sinuous figure.

"It's very simple, dear," he said with a deep sigh. "The same thing that is making you so rich is making me poor!"

✓ ✓ ✓

Artie Feldman had always wanted to be an actor, even as a small boy. When he finished high school and refused to "waste his time" in college, his indulgent parents sent him to Actors Studio where he could learn his craft as a performer. The great day arrived, a year later, when Artie was given a role in a stage play about the war in Vietnam.

The Feldmans arrived at the theatre before curtain time; he in a new tuxedo purchased especially for this auspicious occasion, she in a new gown. Their hearts were bursting with pride as the theatre darkened and the first act began. But as act one neared its end, their son had not made an appearance.

"Maybe he got sick," whispered Mrs. Feldman worriedly.

They sat through act two. Still no Artie.

As the third act unfolded and the parents watched in silent despair, suddenly—lo and behold!—just as the play neared its end, there was Artie! Breathlessly they waited for him to speak, to portray an active character in the story, but, in his soldier's uniform he merely stood at attention, his rifle at his side—a faceless, anonymous GI on guard duty.

Mr. Feldman boiled inwardly at this humiliating role given to his talented son. Was this a part for such a fine actor? Now the curtain was about to come down and Mrs. Feldman brushed a sympathetic tear from her eye. At this, the father's resentment exploded.

"Artie," he yelled from the audience, "for God's sake, say a few words! If you can't, then at least shoot a little!"

✓ ✓ ✓

That inexhaustible fount of humor, Georgie Jessel, was fulfilling one of his functions as "Mr. Toastmaster, U.S.A.," at a Friar's Club banquet. He was discussing Frank Sinatra.

"All right, Sinatra likes girls," said Jessel without the trace of a smile. "So what else should he do—play with a knife and maybe cut himself?"

✓ ✓ ✓

265

An actor who was an expert in chemistry phraseology, finished a torrid love scene at Paramount Studios in Hollywood and was asked by producer George Sidney to describe his reaction to a kiss by the glamorous leading lady.

Said the actor: "The pituitary gland immediately manufactures a potent adreno-corticotrophic substance. At the same time the adrenal glands are stimulated, the blood pressure rises, there is a swift breakdown of white blood cells, the pulse quickens, the circulation jumps and the heart action speeds up."

Sighed George Sidney: "Let's hold back the scene and release the comment!"

✓   ✓   ✓

When convivial people are gathered together do they really *listen* as the others tell their favorite jokes or are they in a state of suspended animation until the moment they can tell their own? This mirthful vignette provides an answer:

A group of America's top comedians were invited to a party at the home of a movie star in Beverly Hills. As the cocktails took their cumulative effect, the comics began to relate their pet jokes. All during the telling, the others, their faces expressionless, would wait for the punch line and then leap into the momentary breach with a story of their own. If they were actually listening to the stories told by their colleagues, it certainly was not evident in their reactions.

When the party had been in progress for two hours, a late comer arrived, his face downcast, his voice depressed. A fellow comedian handed him a drink and asked, "What's the matter, Miltie? You look like death warmed over."

"I had an awful experience today," explained Miltie, close to tears. "My house burned down this morning. The wife and kids are in the hospital with second and third degree burns. The garage caught fire, too, and my new car was destroyed—and me without insurance. The cops suspect me of arson and right now I'm out on bail. To top it off, my neighbors almost died when some sparks set their house afire and they're suing. *Oy vay!* Have I got trouble!"

Replied the other fellow quickly: "You think *that's* funny? Listen to *this* one!"

✓   ✓   ✓

Here is one of those true incidents that prove the adage, somewhat paraphrased, "truth is funnier than fiction." It happened at Niagara Falls on June 28th, 1966, as this anthology was being written.

Producer Martin Manulis and director Clive Donner ran into communications problems at the Canadian Falls while scouting location sites for their motion picture titled "Luv."

266

SHOW BIZ

While checking accommodations at a local motel, the owner, Jake Levine, asked Manulis what they would be doing at Niagara Falls.

"We'll be making 'Luv.'"

"I see. Who'll be making love?"

"Jack Lemmon and Elaine May."

"They're married?" the motel man asked.

"Yes, but not to each other. You see . . ."

"Look, mister, we're a respectable place," Levine the motel man muttered through the slamming door. "Let them make love someplace else!"

✓   ✓   ✓

The renowned musicologist and conductor, Leonard Bernstein, was to appear at the Rockefeller Center Music Hall in New York to conduct one of the most widely heralded concerts of his career. Three days before, one of the trumpet players came down with the flu, and Bernstein was told by the musicians' union that the only trumpet player available as a replacement was a jazz musician.

"I don't want a jazz musician," complained conductor Bernstein. "They are a seedy-looking lot, they don't hit the notes right, and most of all, they're unreliable."

However, as no one else was available, he took the jazz man, who surprised the conductor (and everyone else in the symphony orchestra) by showing up in a brand new suit, hitting all the notes perfectly, and appearing early on each of the three days of rehearsals.

After the last rehearsal, just before the opening-night's grand performance, Bernstein took the jazz musician aside and said, "I am very happy you are playing for us, and we really needed you. You dress well, play beautifully, and I am especially pleased you were on time for rehearsals. Reliability—I like that in you."

"Well, man," the jazzist replied, "it's the least I can do for you, 'cause I won't be able to make the concert tonight!"

✓   ✓   ✓

It was back in the 1920's when Manhattan's show business fraternity began the exodus to Hollywood, seeking wider horizons on the silver screen. In 1926, Lena, the Yiddish Theatre's "Queen of Palesteena," suddenly packed her bags and moved from New York to Los Angeles.

"How come you made such a sudden decision?" she was asked.

"Two reasons," explained Lena. "Nobody lives in New York anymore, and it's too crowded."

✓   ✓   ✓

There are many apocryphal explanations of how Jewish entertainers acquired their Anglo-Saxon names. Bernie Schwartz, of the Bronx, for example, can regale his listeners with many differing accounts describing how he became Tony Curtis. But he has yet to match the following story.

During the era of silent movies it was not entirely necessary that an actor speak English with perfection. As long as his lip movements approximated the printed dialogue on the screen he was not too concerned with diction. So when Berel Bienstock, a leading actor of the Yiddish stage in Europe came to this country, he was confident that he would soon be working in the "flickers."

Sure enough, his famous name had preceded him, and when he landed on Ellis Island he was hustled aboard a train and sent to Hollywood. But before he left for the motion picture capital, his new manager cautioned him to change his name. "You'll never be accepted as a star with a name like Berel Bienstock," he said. "Take my advice and Americanize it."

The suggestion was a valid one to Bienstock, and all the way across the country he kept selecting likely names and then discarding them —selecting and discarding—for six days, until he finally picked one as the train pulled into Los Angeles.

After checking into a hotel he immediately went to see a movie producer, with a scrapbook loaded with newspaper articles and favorable reviews he had accumulated in the years he performed in Europe. A secretary ushered him into the producer's office.

"What is your name?" asked the movie maker abruptly.

Bienstock's mind went blank. To save his life he could not remember the American name he had chosen. There remained only one thing—to make an honest confession.

"*Schoen fergessen,*" he said.*

And a new star was born when the producer wrote down the man's name—

Sean Ferguson!

✔   ✔   ✔

For two years Harry Herzog had been trying to break into show business, but Broadway's "big time" eluded him. He joined a drama workshop, attended coaching classes and pestered the casting directors for a part, no matter how small, just so he could have a showcase for what he firmly believed was his monumental acting ability, but no one would give him that all-important "break."

Just when life seemed to be at its lowest ebb and he was wondering whether he could afford the gas to attempt suicide, he received a special delivery package. Inside the large envelope was a script and a note from a theatrical agent. "You are to report to the Shubert Theatre on June 8th, ready to work."

Harry was overjoyed. Here at last was the one chance he had been

---

* "I've forgotten !"

praying for. Yes, he would be ready on time if he had to stay up night after night, studying his part.

He opened the script and searched every page in the first act but could not find his name or his part. The second act was no different. With a sinking heart, hoping that he had not been sent the script through an error, he examined the third act. Page after page he turned, scrutinizing every line. Nothing! Suddenly, there on the very last page, he found his name. His part contained only one line of dialogue, but it was better than nothing. At least he was in a regular Broadway play. He read his line again.

The play was titled "The Battle of Gettysburg." At the sound of booming guns, he was to cry out, "Hark, I hear a cannon roar!" Thereafter, every hour on the hour, every half-hour, every minute of the day, he repeated his single line—"Hark, I hear a cannon roar!" Harry had no intention of forgetting his role. No *sir!*

Came the big night. Harry dressed carefully in the costume the director had sent, and was about to leave when he noticed that the clock on the dresser was an hour ahead of the time on his wrist-watch. The awful truth descended on him like a drumroll of disaster. *Daylight Saving Time!* He had forgotten to move his watch up one hour ahead.

But there was still a chance he might reach the theatre in time for the third act. The subway was now out of the question. Feverishly he called a taxi. All the way downtown, from Bronx Park South to the Shubert Theatre, with the cab careening through the streets, he kept repeating his one line—"Hark, I hear a cannon roar! — Hark, I hear a cannon roar! — Hark, I hear a cannon roar!"

He arrived just as he was due on stage. The director was wild. "No time for excuses now," he barked, waving Harry's explanation away. "You're on in ten seconds. You're sure you know your part?"

"Hark, I hear a cannon roar!" echoed Harry. "I know that line like I know my own name."

"OK—NOW!" snapped the director, giving him a push that sent him flying on stage.

The lights dimmed to red. Flashes of gunfire illuminated the theatre. And then the mighty cannon roared.

Harry jumped a foot in the air and yelled, *"Oy gevald!* What was that?"

✔   ✔   ✔

The young couple were in the fourth row at the concert of an internationally famous tenor.

"Oh, what a beautiful voice," exclaimed the girl.

"What's so wonderful about it?" asked the jealous youth resentfully. "If I had a voice like that I'd sing just as well!"

✔   ✔   ✔

269

The following story was popularized by Jewish comedians during vaudeville's heyday, and is paraphrased today by actors to express discontent with their agents.

The vaudeville monologist would tell of running into a relative who, he knew, had been reviling him behind his back as a tightwad.

"How can you, of all people, say that about me?" he asked reproachfully. "Didn't I pick up the tab for your son's orthodontics? Didn't I pay for his Bar Mitzvah, and foot the bill for your daughter's wedding party? And when your wife became ill last summer, didn't I pay for her operation?"

"Big deal!" the kinsman replied sarcastically. "But what have you done for me lately?"

✓   ✓   ✓

Excerpt from a lecture given by Dr. Ralph Rosenthal, professor of music theory at a large mid-Western university:

"Listening to a cool jazz vocalist may be an experience in aesthetics for some people who find it more rewarding than the caterwauling of modern folk singing. Today's folk singer is an anatomical wizard. He can strum one chord with one finger on one string, screw up his face, wiggle his behind, and all the while sing through his nose by ear."

✓   ✓   ✓

Excerpt from an after-dinner speech by Samuel Goldwyn, pioneer motion picture executive:

"The movie industry is essentially what the words suggest—an *industry!* Its primary function is to entertain, not to educate, although, however, occasionally a 'message' may be included when it does not detract from the entertainment value of the film. Many lengthy books have been written on the subject, but I can sum it up in six words: 'Messages we leave to Western Union!' "

✓   ✓   ✓

A self-styled impresario went to the entertainment manager of a swank Las Vegas casino. "Boy, have I got an act for you!" he enthused. "People will come from all over the country to see it. With an act like this you can't help but make money."

The manager agreed to audition the act, so the impresario brought in a suitcase. He whistled once, and out popped fifty mice, each dressed in a tuxedo and carrying a musical instrument. They jumped up onto the suitcase where they set up their tiny music stands and sheet music. They tuned up their violins, set up the percussion section, and blew tentative notes on their various trumpets, saxophones, clarinets, woodwinds, trombones and other instruments.

Then the impresario lifted his baton and the mice began the "Poet and Peasant Overture." They played gloriously, with the music sounding as though it was a performance by the London Symphony Orchestra. When the concert was finished, the impresario whistled once more and the mice bowed in unison, packed their instruments and sedately marched back into the suitcase.

"Well, what did I tell you?" smiled the impresario. "Isn't this a terrific act?"

"Well, yes, frankly; it is," admitted the manager. "But with my clientele, I'm afraid I can't use them."

"Why not?"

"It's that drummer. Sorry, but he looks too Jewish!"

✓ ✓ ✓

For weeks, Julius had badgered his elderly father to come to the circus with him to witness a phenomenal new act. "You'll be amazed," said the son. "Wait till you see the man shot out of a cannon 150 feet in the air—and all the while playing a violin solo."

Reluctantly, the old man accompanied his son to the circus and finally the featured act was announced. The son was on the edge of his seat with restrained excitement as the performer entered the mouth of a huge cannon, carrying a violin. The old man sat back, reserving judgment. Then there was a roar and the man was shot out and sailed through the air high above their heads, toward a net on the other side of the vast auditorium. And just as the advertisement proclaimed, he played a fiddle while hurtling through space.

When the act was over and the entertainer had taken his bows, Julius turned to his silent, unresponsive father. "Well, Pop, what did you think of it?"

"Believe me," said the old man, "a Heifetz he ain't!"

✓ ✓ ✓

Proud fathers sprout in every environment—the poor and the wealthy. So it might have been expected that conductor Leonard Bernstein's next-door neighbor insisted that he attend the local high-school concert where his fourteen-year-old son was leading the orchestra for the evening.

When the concert was at an end, the proud papa beamed, "You must admit, my son is rather young to be leading a concert band."

"Not the way he leads it," said Bernstein.

✓ ✓ ✓

Shall we simply ignore the fellow who wrote music only when he was in bed? He composed sheet music.

✓ ✓ ✓

Herschel Bernardi wittily illustrates the rise and fall of a movie star with a few choice phrases. Bernardi, famed for his Broadway portrayal of Tevya in "Fiddler on the Roof," among many other fine roles, explains

271

that when he was an "unknown," seeking a career in show business, the producers would ask, "Who's Bernardi?"

As his star began to brighten, the producers would ask, "Where's Bernardi?"

When he finally became a star, they would demand, "Get me Bernardi."

Later, they began to say, "Get me a Bernardi type."

Until—the inevitable—"Who's Bernardi?"

✓ ✓ ✓

Philosophy Department: No matter where you live, there are hidden blessings. Even Hollywood has its resident advantages. At least, out there, you can starve without an overcoat.

✓ ✓ ✓

A new arrival to this country had never in his life seen a stage play. On his first day of leisure, he walked up to the ticket window of a theatre and asked the price of admission.

"Downstairs, the tickets are $4.80," explained the ticket clerk. "Upstairs, the price is $2.20."

"Is that so?" said the surprised immigrant. "Tell me, what's playing upstairs?"

✓ ✓ ✓

Jacob Lefkowitz sat next to an arrogant looking Pole at a vaudeville show in Warsaw. The performer was a young violinist whom the Pole admired audibly.

"That violinist is Jewish," remarked Lefkowitz.

The next act was a folk dance given by a dark-eyed girl.

"She too is a Semite," commented the Jew.

The Pole glowered but made no reply. The third performer was a singer.

"Another Jewish boy," said Lefkowitz.

"O Jesus!" barked the exasperated Pole.

"Also a Jew," concluded Lefkowitz.

✓ ✓ ✓

Roger Wolfe Kahn Jr., the society bandleader, was the son of the multimillionaire financial wizard. When Kahn Jr. decided he wanted to lead a band, his father hired the greatest musicians available and they gathered for their first rehearsal.

Young Roger, who had never conducted before, raised his baton and the rehearsal began. In the middle of the first number the percussionist banged his cymbals.

The fledgling bandleader tapped his baton against the music stand and stopped the rehearsal.

"All right," he barked, his face livid, "who did that?"

✓ ✓ ✓

SHOW BIZ

Wherever musicians gather, the story about Yehudi Menuhin's encounter with an avid fan is told and re-told. It seems that Menuhin was scheduled to give a concert at Carnegie Hall on the night of one of New York's worst blizzards. At curtain time, the famed violinist walked out on the stage and there was only one man in the audience. So Menuhin announced that the concert would be postponed and the money refunded for the tickets.

"But I'm a great fan of yours," insisted the man in the audience. "You can't do this to me. I paid for my ticket and I want to hear you perform."

The violinist apologized and said he was sorry but there would be no concert that night.

"Now look here," argued the man, "I have followed your career for years. And since I came here in this terrible storm I think you should at least sing one little song!"

♪ ♪ ♪

Lefkowitz decided to encourage patronage in the dining section of his small delicatessen by adding music for his customers' listening pleasure. "It'll be like a little night club," he said to himself. So the first thing he did was to install an electric organ.

Now a problem arose. "Who was to play it?"

He called the musicians' union. "For my electric organ, send me please an organizer," he said, proud of his newly acquired musical knowledge. "Also, for the rest of the orchestra I'll need a saxist, a drummist, a fiddlist and a harper."

Chapter Twenty-six

The Tot-Rod Set

Mrs. Cohen was deeply concerned about a strange psychosis that had recently overwhelmed her little boy, Louie. He could no longer eat his once-favorite dish, *kreplach*. Indeed, the very sight of the delicacy made him physically ill. So she took him to a famous child-psychiatrist for consultation. The doctor listened carefully to her account of the boy's symptoms and reactions, and then nodded gravely.

"It is all very clear, Mrs. Cohen. Louie has developed a Freudian block which causes a combination anxiety-fear complex. My advice is that you show him, step by step, just how *kreplach* are made. Let him see all the harmless ingredients. In fact, let him help you prepare them. That should remove his fear and solve the problem once and for all."

That evening, with a prayer in her heart, Mrs. Cohen called Louie into the kitchen to help her make the *kreplach*.

"Look, Louie darling," she began, "here is the dough and here is the chop-meat. See, I roll out a little dough and make a square."

Louie smiled delightedly.

"Now you try it," she said, watching him closely as he rolled out a piece of dough into a reasonable square, smiling as though he enjoyed the process very much.

Mrs. Cohen was quite pleased with his progress. "I told you there's nothing to fear," she encouraged the boy. "Now we put a little chop-meat on the square of dough—*azoi*."

Louie loved the game. He put a measure of meat on his piece of dough as his mama had instructed.

"Now do as I do," continued Mrs. Cohen as her young son bobbed his head enthusiastically. The mother folded over one corner of the dough, and Louie did the same. Then she folded over another corner and Louie followed suit. Mrs. Cohen folded over the third corner, and Louie, grinning with pleasure at this new game, also folded over the third corner.

"And now," said the mother, "we fold over the last corner—like this!" The boy then folded over *his* fourth and last corner.

"You see?" Mrs. Cohen laughed triumphantly, "there's nothing at all to fear. Take a good look at what you made."

Louie took a good look, broke out in a sweat, and moaned—
"*Oy, kreplach!*"

✓   ✓   ✓

New Neighbor: "Hello, little boy. What's your name?"
Little Boy: "My name's Benjy. Are you the 'Awful People' who just moved next door?"

✓   ✓   ✓

Mrs. Greenbaum was at her wits' end about her nine-year-old Myron's conduct. He played hookey from school, used naughty words, was fresh to his own father and bullied children smaller than himself. In desperation, Mrs. Greenbaum took Myron to a psychiatrist, but after a few sessions the doctor threw up his hands in defeat.

"But what will I do?" wailed the mother. "He can't go on like this."

"That's true," agreed the psychiatrist. "I have only one suggestion— take him to your rabbi. Only God can help that boy."

So Mrs. Greenbaum took Myron to a stern old Orthodox rabbi, a no-nonsense type who could instill fear and awe in entire congregations. For a week he delved into Myron's psyche, talking to him, listening carefully, and evaluating all phases of the boy's personality. Finally he called the mother into his sanctum.

"Mrs. Greenbaum," the rabbi declared, "you will have to handle Myron with extreme tact. Remember, you are dealing with a sensitive, high-strung, intelligent little *momzer!*"

✓   ✓   ✓

Morris had been a very good boy all week, so Mama decided to reward him with a trip to the movies. The film was *Quo Vadis*, a picture about the early persecution of the Christians by the Romans.

During the arena scene in which a group of Christians are thrown to the lions and torn to pieces, Mama, unlike the wide-eyed little Morris, turned her head from the grisly spectacle. A few moments later she heard her son quietly weeping.

"Morris, honey, it's only a picture," she said soothingly, while regretting she had taken him to see the film. "Those people aren't really being killed."

"It's not that," answered Morris, his voice brimming with sympathy. "It's that poor lion in the corner. He didn't get a single *goy* to eat!"

✓   ✓   ✓

Hebrew Teacher: "That will be all for now, Rosie. I have a headache."
Little Rosie: "Oh, I know about that. Moses had a headache, too!"
Hebrew Teacher: "Moses had a headache? Where did you hear that?"
Little Rosie: "Grandpa told me. He said God gave Moses two tablets."

✓   ✓   ✓

Georgie's mother had sent her son off to school in plenty of time, but along the way he found it necessary to play with a stray dog, watch a house under construction and study the posters outside a movie theatre.

"You are fifteen minutes late," said the teacher when he finally reached his classroom. "What is your excuse."

"My farver made me work in the garage," replied Georgie promptly.

"Very well! Ask your father to give you a note to that effect and bring it with you tomorrow, otherwise I'll speak to him myself!"

"What?"

"A note—a written excuse. You know very well what I mean, young man!"

Georgie did indeed know what she meant, but he also knew that he would be punished; not only for being late without reason, but for fibbing. So he compounded the felony by writing the note himself:

> Deer Teechur,
>   Pleaz excuse Georgie for beeing late yestday becase he worked in the grage for me.
>
>   My Farver

✓   ✓   ✓

Little Jerome was playing on the sidewalk when an old man, quite taken by the boy's sweet innocence, stopped and patted him on the head. "What is your name, my child?" asked the elderly gentleman.

"Why, the same as my papa's," answered the surprised boy.

"I mean, what are you called when, say, it's time for supper?"

"Gee, mister, nobody ever called me in my whole life," said Jerome. "I'm always the first one at the table!"

✓   ✓   ✓

The Eisenbergs had struggled for years to better their circumstances and now they were able to move from the teeming East Side to Central Park West.

In their lovely apartment, replete with new furniture, drapes and carpets, Mama and Papa Eisenberg, together with their five-year-old daughter Becky, should have been supremely happy. But they were not. The parents noted, with pangs of sadness, that Becky, who attended the local kindergarten, had not been invited to any of the kiddie parties, either at school or by the swanky children in the neighborhood.

At long last, however, the great day arrived when little Becky received an engraved invitation to attend Sarah's sixth birthday party in one of the apartments in their building. The Eisenbergs were thrilled. They bought their daughter a new party dress, and coached her in the social graces in preparation for the big event.

"Don't accept second helpings of anything," Mama cautioned. "Remember to say 'please' and 'thank you' and above all, you must curtsy like Mama taught you."

When the fateful day arrived, they gave Becky an expensive gift for the other child, and Mama escorted her to the apartment where the party was to be held.

Their hearts were bursting with pride for the two hours that Becky was absent. "It looks like we've been accepted socially," said Papa.

"Unless Becky does something wrong," Mama said nervously.

By the time Becky returned they were on the verge of mental collapse. "Oh Becky, did they like the birthday present?" cried Mama excitedly.

"Yeth, Mama."

Papa gave her a loving pat on the head. "Then what did you do?"

"I ate thome cake and had a glath of chocolate milk—and I didn't athk for thecondth."

"Oh, I'm so proud of my darling," gushed Mama. "A real little lady!"

"So what did you do next?" queried Papa.

"Then we played ring-around-the-rothie. I liked it. All the kidth made a big ring and they put me in the middle and they all danthed and thang around me, and Tharah'th mama and papa were watching, too."

Papa Eisenberg was ecstatic. "Our own little Becky the center of attraction! Now I'm positive we're in the social swim!"

Mama took Becky in her arms. "And while you were in the middle of the circle, with all those children dancing and singing around you, and Sarah's mama and papa watching, tell us, darling, what did you do?"

And Becky answered—

"I thwew up!"

*   *   *

Joey was the only one at home when the telephone rang.

"Hullo, it's me," shrilled Joey.

"Is your father at home?" asked the caller, hearing the childish voice.

"Nobody here 'cept me. I'm Joey."

"Well, Joey, will you please tell your daddy that Mr. Schwartz called?"

There was an uncertain pause on the other end of the line and the caller added, "Perhaps you had better write that down."

"OK, wait'll I get a pencil and paper."

After some time, when the boy had found a pencil and paper, had a drink of water and stopped to look out the window at his neighbor's cat, he returned to the phone. Joey had forgotten the man's name so the caller repeated it.

"But I can't spell that name," Joey complained. "It's too hard."

"All right, I'll spell it for you," said the caller, wishing he had hung up long ago. "S-C-H-W-A-R-T-Z."

There was utter silence at the other end of the line while Mr. Schwartz fumed impatiently. It was certainly taking the boy long enough to write down the eight letters.

At long last Joey spoke, his voice sounding very small.
"Mister, how do you make an 'S'?"

✓　　✓　　✓

It was Saturday afternoon and Stanley's day for the movies. To find out what picture was playing, he called information as he had seen his parents do.

"What's the number for the Bijou Theatre?" he piped.

Information gave him the number, and suggested that perhaps the next time he could find the number in the directory.

"Yes, ma'am, I know," explained Stanley, "but I have to stand on the phone book to reach the telephone."

✓　　✓　　✓

It could only have happened in Beverly Hills.

Seven-year-old Irving Kornblum, son of a wealthy movie producer, was tardy for school. He handed the teacher a note from his mother:

> "Please excuse Irving for being late. Due to the heavy rains, our electronic gates would not open and he had to wait for the butler to arrive and boost him over the wall."

✓　　✓　　✓

The following Hebrew-school compositions appeared in the *California Jewish Voice,* under the by-line of Sholom Staiman, and titled "What I Like About Chanukah"—A View from the Third Grade.*

> Its a good thing teacher said to write what I like about Chanukah not what I like *most* about Chanukah. Because she said not to write presents because its mersenry. So I will say that I like lots of things about Chanukah in fact everything about Chanukah. Which includes presents I can't help it.
>
> DAVID GOLDFINGER

> My father doesn't understand Chanukah at all. He thinks if you light candles and dovin a lot that its a big deal. He hardly knows anything else, like presents. Of course thats not important. That's what I like about Chanukah.
>
> JON ROBIN BLOOM

> What I like about Chanukah is mirakuls. Thats some story about that little bit of oil lasting eight days. Boy. Our candles in half a hour are p-o-o-f-t. That was pretty good mirakuls for those days. Today of course we have better

---

* Quoted here with permission of the publisher.

ones. In fack we have a nite lite that lasts a hundred years. Expect when my father kicks them or bumps into them and brakes them. So far we had 3 and none of them has lasted the hole hundred years.

HUBERT HORATIO LEVY

Heres what I like about Chanukah besides presents.
1.
2.
3.
If I think of any more I will write them next year.

SANDRA STEIN

Once there were 2 baby hippipatomuseses. A boy and a girl. There names were Freddy and Flossy. When they were seven months old there mother found out they were twins. Hippipatomuseses like Chanukah a lot.

HEATHER HURWITZ

What I like about Chanukah is we get about eleven boxes of Chanukah candles in the male. We use to have to buy them in the store. Now we get them in the male for nothing. I don't know why Daddy says it costs ten times as much this way. I think it surtinly is nice of people to send us so many.

CLAUDIA COHEN

What I like about Chanukah is to go to Shul and pray a lot and fast and do everything like I should. I sure am not loking for presents but will not send any back if I get some for bein such a good boy.

RICHARD SILVERSTEIN

I like Chanukah but it should be a Jewish holiday too, like not going to school. Other kids don't have to go to school on their Chanukah which is approximetly December 25.

MAUREEN FINKLESTEIN

I like lotkiss the best but I have truble this year because my Mom is all exited about calrese. Skim milk is Okay but not having lotkiss on Chanukah is offul. P.S. Even if kids call me fatso I'd rather have lotkiss than be a skiny old thing any time.

CHARLES Z. LEVIN

279

I use to like Chanukah a lot better. We use to get lots of present from all the aunts and uncles and cuzins and even from other people I gess mothers friends. Now we get hardly any. I know why because mother talks on the phone and I understand Yiddish a little bit. They made a secret pack and us kids are getting robed. But I don't know what scratching each others backs has to do with Chanukah.

What I like about Chanukah is some people like my grandparents at least don't listen to my mother.

HERBIE SCHWARTZ

What I like about Chanukah is its dependable. It comes faithfully every year and you get presents wether you want them or not. So I am not mersernary in fact half the time it takes me by surprise I hardly know its coming.

ARTHUR EDWARD ANGEL

I like the spirit of Chanukah. Everybody is happy and cheerful. It seems like (peace on earth good will to men) thats crost off because my father said he didn't think it would go over very well. It seems like everybody is happy and cheerful.

GEORGIA GOLDBERG

What I like about Chanukah is you don't have to wurry about anybody jumping around on your roof or climin down your chimny. And that's a lode off my mind. Chimnys and roofs cost mony.

ANTOINETTE APPELMAN

I wish Chanukah was today. Then Judah Macabbee could of really slautrd those enemies. I would of been with him and we would of used atomic weppons. That's what I really like about Chanukah.

PAUL COHEN

P.S. Nickname is Judah Macabbee

✓   ✓   ✓

"Now, Herbert, aren't you ashamed for having forgotten your pen? What would you call a soldier who went to battle without a gun?"

Herbert knew the answer to that one. "A general," he piped.

✓   ✓   ✓

A knock sounded on the door, and Mortie opened it.

"I'm here to see your old tub," said the stranger, putting down his bag of plumber's tools.

"Mama," cried Mortie, "there's a man here to see Aunt Sophie!"

✓   ✓   ✓

Suzie brought a note to school which explained her absence the day before. The teacher smiled gently. "So you have a brand new little sister?"

"Uh-huh," nodded Suzie. "And we want you to come over after school and see the baby."

"Oh, I couldn't do that so soon after the stork came," laughed the teacher. "I'll wait until your mother is better."

"Oh, you needn't be afraid," said Suzie confidently. "Daddy told me it wasn't catching."

✓ ✓ ✓

It was a busy day for Suzie, what with a new little sister in the house and Daddy taking care of Mommy, so when someone knocked on the door Suzie answered it.

"I'm from the Humane Society," the dog catcher growled. "Does your dog have all his licenses?"

"Yes, sir," quavered Suzie. "He's just crawling with them."

✓ ✓ ✓

Mom and Pop had gone to the movies and Grandpa was telling seven-year-old Julie a story. But Julie, utterly fascinated, kept watching her heavily-bearded grandfather as he smoked a cigar down to the nub while he told the bedtime story.

Suddenly Julie interrupted the fairy tale. "Can you spit through your whiskers?" she asked quickly.

Grandpa smiled. "Why sure, Julie."

"Then you better start. Your whiskers are on fire!"

✓ ✓ ✓

It was the first day of school and the teacher asked all those who had been seriously ill to raise their hands. Little Willie waved his hand wildly for attention.

The teacher nodded to him. "Yes, Willie, what was your trouble?"

"I once swallowed my father's pen."

"My goodness!" cried the teacher in mock dismay. "What happened?"

"He had to use a pencil!"

✓ ✓ ✓

"Actually, I like all my new pupils except Webster," said the teacher.

"Webster? I don't know of any Webster in your class," said the principal.

"Well, his name's really Eisenberg, but I call him Webster because words can't describe him!"

✓ ✓ ✓

This anthology has set no definite age limits on the "tot-rod" set, so in all candor, we stretch the point with the following rib-tickler:

Two newborn babies were lying in their respective cribs in the hospital's maternity ward when one of them turned to the other and said, "I'm a little boy."

"I don't believe it," said the second baby.

"Oh, is that so!" said the first one. "Well, you just wait until the nurse leaves the room and I'll show you."

As soon as the nurse left the ward, he kicked off the blankets, lifted his foot in the air and said, "See? Blue booties!"

✓ ✓ ✓

Rabbi Twersky was taking his evening constitutional down the avenue when he came upon little Seymour standing on tiptoe, trying to reach a doorbell.

"Hello, Seymour," greeted the rabbi, recognizing the boy. "Let me help you."

The boy waited until Rabbi Twersky had pushed the buzzer, and then he shouted, "Thank you, Rabbi. Now let's run like hell!"

✓ ✓ ✓

A missionary from America went to Israel to "save the souls of the poor, uninformed children who had not learned of Christianity." He visited a *kibbutz* and there, to his horror, he observed a bunch of pre-schoolers frolicking in a lake—as naked as the day they were born.

"You children should be ashamed of yourselves," he scolded. "This is disgraceful. Shame! Shame!"

That night he sent a telegram to missionary headquarters in the United States, urgently requesting that swim suits be airmailed at once—and the garments soon arrived. He distributed them to the four-and five-year-olds, admonishing, "Now you can cover your shame." The children accepted the swim suits with whoops of delight.

That afternoon, one of the little boys' parents happened to visit the lake where the kids enjoyed their daily swim. The father called his four-year-old Avrum to his side. "Why are you wearing that suit?" he asked.

"So I won't be ashamed," replied the boy, "whatever that means!"

✓ ✓ ✓

Although Yetta was almost five years old she still retained the habit of sucking her thumb. Her mother, after many attempts to break her of the annoying practice, snapped, "If you don't stop sucking your thumb you'll swell up and bust!"

The frightening admonition penetrated deeply and little Yetta there-after restrained the impulse. On the following Saturday the mother invited her married sister and a few friends over for tea. The sister, it should be noted, was quite obviously pregnant, though no one in the group made any reference to her condition—at least, not until Yetta spoke.

With her mother's warning still ringing in her ears, she waggled an accusing finger at the lady's protruding stomach, closed one eye, grinned knowingly, and in the midst of the deathly silence, blurted out, "Oooh, *Tanteh*, I know what *you've* been doing!"

✓ ✓ ✓

It was the first day of school and the kindergarten teacher was calling the roll and, incidentally, obtaining the required family data. She pointed to the first little boy. "Your name, please?"

"Joey Kaplan."

"And what is your father's name, Joey?"

"Papa."

The teacher hid a smile. "I didn't mean quite that. What does your mother call him?"

"Nothin'," replied Joey promptly. "She likes him."

✓ ✓ ✓

"My, my, what a sweet little boy!" crooned the unsuspecting old lady to the fresh little kid. The boy glared at her and deliberately lit a cigarette.

"My dear," cried the nice old woman, "does your mother know you smoke?"

"No, lady!" retorted the brat. "Does your husband know you talk to strange men?"

✓ ✓ ✓

"What yould you like for Chanukah?" the mother asked her ten-year-old daughter.

"A mirror, Mommy."

"What a peculiar request! Why?"

"Because," sighed the girl, "I'm getting too big to make up in the door-knob."

✓ ✓ ✓

Aunt Sylvia gave her small niece a lovely birthday present and the child was ecstatic. "Oh, Aunt Sylvia," breathed the little girl, "thank you, from the top of my heart and my bottom!"

✓ ✓ ✓

"Bobby," scolded the small boy's mother, "your face is clean but how did you manage to get your hands so dirty?"

"Washing my face," replied Bobby.

✓ ✓ ✓

"Reuben, stop making so much noise!" cautioned the mother of a six-year-old as he slammed the door behind him.

"Why, whatsamatter?"

"Mrs. Schwartz, next door, is expecting a little visit from the stork."

"Gee, Ma, I hope it doesn't scare her," said Reuben. "She's pregnant!"

✔ ✔ ✔

It was a wintry day in New York and young Maxie slipped on the icy sidewalk. A kind old man helped the boy to his feet.

"How did you come to slip on the ice?" asked the oldster.

"I didn't come for that," explained Maxie. "I come to see my grandma."

✔ ✔ ✔

Fresh Little Kid: "What do they call frozen ink?"
Gullible Little Kid: "Iced ink."
Fresh Little Kid: "You can say that again!"

✔ ✔ ✔

Mr. Kalmanson took his young son to the zoo for the first time.

"You see that animal?" asked Mr. Kalmanson, pointing to a caged lion. "He is called the king of beasts."

"Why is that, Papa?"

"Because he's so ferocious. He has tremendous strength and a vicious temper. Why, with those big claws and sharp teeth, if he ever got out of that cage he could tear me to pieces."

"Papa," said the little boy, a worried look on his face, "if he should, what number bus do I take to get home?"

✔ ✔ ✔

Let us close this chapter on a less sanguinary note.

Rabbi Montague Isaacs, spiritual leader of Congregation Tifereth Jacob, in Los Angeles, illustrates the importance of prayer in the following supplication offered by a small child:

"Dear God, take care of Daddy, Mommy, brother and sister, uncles and aunts, grandpa and grandma; and please, God, do take care of Yourself, or else we are all sunk!"

Chapter Twenty-seven

Communication

A devout Catholic girl awoke one night with the uneasy feeling that she was not alone. Raising her head from the pillow she was aghast to see a looming figure inside her bedroom, his forbidding outline silhouetted against the window. As he approached her bed she could discern his wicked fangs in the shadowy darkness.

But the girl had been warned about vampires by her parish priest and she knew exactly what to do. Quickly she reached for the crucifix that she always wore around her neck, held it out at arm's length, and cried, "In the name of the Father, the Son and the Holy Ghost, begone!"

But the vampire, menacing as ever in his black cape, continued to move closer. Now she threw off the covers, scrambled out of bed, and thrust the cross right into his face. "In the name of our Lord and Saviour, begone!" she shrieked.

"Dollink," he grinned, "it vouldn't do you a bit good!"

ℐ   ℐ   ℐ

The creator of this hundred-year-old quatrain has long been lost to posterity:

> Roses are reddish,
> Violets are bluish,
> If it weren't for Christmas
> Everyone would be Jewish.

ℐ   ℐ   ℐ

It happened years ago in Atlantic City, so it is said. The boardwalk was jammed with Sunday visitors, thronging the promenade from one end to the other. In the milling crowd was an old woman who gazed about in a bewildered manner, a look of utter helplessness in her eyes. Suddenly she noticed a bearded man, and hobbled over to him.

"*Kenst reden Yiddish?*" she asked hopefully.

"Hah? Ya talkin' t'me, Lady?"

Disappointed, she turned away, but soon saw another prospect. She touched his arm.

285

"Kenst reden Yiddish?"

"Scoosa me, Senora, no spikka da English."

"Gevald!" she moaned, as he hurried on. Again she looked about for someone who might understand her. Finally, a well-dressed, portly gentleman walked by. She hurried to him.

"Kenst reden Yiddish?"

"Ya, tanteh," he replied, smiling genially. *"Ich jahrshtay Yiddish."*

"Oy, Gott sie dank!" she cried elatedly. *"Zogt mir,* vot time it is?"

✓ ✓ ✓

Papa: "New York, in the summer, is the hottest place in America."

Mama: "No it isn't! Last August when I went to Washington, D.C. for Thelma's wedding, it was so hot there I almost died of heat prostitution!"

✓ ✓ ✓

Mendel had not been in this country long before he moved from the crowded tenement area of New York's East Side to Schenectady, where he bought a small farm. He was returning from town where he had just picked up a load of manure, and was driving his quarter-ton truck briskly along the highway, when he was flagged down by a police officer.

The cop thrust his face into the cab and asked belligerently, "You got a governor on this truck?"

"A governor?" gasped the politically-minded Mendel. "Who am I to have a governor on my truck? That stuff you're smelling—it's fertilizer!"

✓ ✓ ✓

A vignette is told about the father of the late George Gershwin, the composer. The older man, who had a pronounced Jewish accent, escaped getting a traffic ticket one day when he told the officer he was George Gershwin's father.

The policeman thought he had said *"Judge* Gershwin!"

✓ ✓ ✓

A young cub reporter who had just been hired straight out of journalism school, asked Adolph S. Ochs for some instructions.

"Young fellow," said the famous publisher of the *New York Times,* "all I have to say is this: In promulgating your esoteric cogitations and articulating superficial sentimental and psychological observations, beware of platitudinous ponderosity. Let your extemporaneous decantations and unpremeditated expiations have intelligibility and veracious vivacity without rodomontade and thrasonical bombast. Sedulously avoid all polysyllabic profundity, pusillanimous vacuity, pestiferous profanity and similar transgressions.

"Or, to put it a bit differently," he concluded, "talk simply, naturally, and above all, don't use big words!"

✓ ✓ ✓

COMMUNICATION

Benny Bender was madly in love with Eva, and for her birthday he decided to buy her a recording of her favorite song, which was all he could afford. So he telephoned the local record shop, unaware that his dialing was rather careless.

"Yeah?" came a voice.

"Say, have you got 'A Boy Named Joey'?"

"No," was the gruff response, "but I got twelve children in Russia."

"That's a record?"

"I don't think so, mister," replied the voice, "but in Yekaterinoslav, believe me, it's above average."

✓　　✓　　✓

When Dr. Syngman Rhee, Korea's first president, arrived in the United States as a guest of *Life* magazine, a young cub reporter named Izzy Kaplan was assigned to show the foreign visitor the sights of the city.

Somehow they became separated and Izzy telephoned *Life*'s editor to ask for help in locating Dr. Rhee.

"What! You mean to say you lost the president of Korea?" screamed the editor, instantly visualizing an international incident should anything happen to the guest. "Listen to me, Kaplan, you have one hour to find him—or you're fired!"

Izzy called every embassy and legation in town. He telephoned the mayor, the chief of police, hospitals—everyone he could think of who might know of President Rhee's whereabouts. Just as his hour was up, who should come strolling toward him but the missing diplomat himself, smiling and unharmed. A wave of relief all but engulfed the young reporter. He rushed forward and grasped the president's hand, crying—

"Ah, sweet Mr. Rhee of *Life*, at last I found thee!"

✓　　✓　　✓

Jews the world over are noted for their eloquent and very expressive use of their hands when speaking. The gestures, of course, are not limited to the Jewish people; Latins and the French, for example, also gesticulate as an adjunct to speech. Anyway, it brings to mind this anecdote:

A Jew was taking a Sunday excursion on the Staten Island ferry when he fell overboard. Unable to swim, he set up a terrific din with his screeching and yelling for help. But, by the time the ferry stopped and reversed itself to where he was last seen floundering in the water, he had already reached the side of the boat.

He clambered aboard unaided, threw himself on the deck to catch his breath, and then gasped, "Believe me, if I hadn't hollered so, I would never have made it!"

✓　　✓　　✓

Although, broadly speaking, jokes which rely on Yiddish-accented English have no proper place in authentic Jewish wit, a few depend on that very accent to make their point. Here is an illustration:

A newly married couple decided to go on a cruise to Hawaii for their honeymoon. On the way they fell into a mild argument as to the proper way to pronounce it—Hawaii or Havaii.

"The real natives of the Island call it 'Havaii'—with a 'v'," insisted the bride.

"No, they say it with a 'w'," maintained the groom stoutly.

Finally they agreed to ask the residents themselves how they pronounced the name of their home.

When the ship docked at Honolulu, the young marrieds descended the gangplank and at once spied a true native of the Islands. He was bedecked in a gay, floral-pattern shirt, Bermuda shorts, and he was wearing a lei around his neck.

"There's a real oldtimer," said the groom. "Let's ask him."

They approached the man. "Sir, please settle a little argument for us. How do you pronounce the name of this place—Hawaii or Havaii?"

"Havaii," answered the stranger immediately.

"See? I told you so!" cried the delighted bride. "It's *really* Havaii!"

But the bridegroom was now studying the man's features closely. "Tell me," he finally asked, "how long have you lived here in the Islands?"

Smilingly, the man told him: "Two veeks!"

✓   ✓   ✓

Florence Zimmerman, who lived with her aged, Jewish-speaking mother on the East Side, fell in love with Al Mudrik, a wealthy piece-goods wholesaler. They were soon married and, changing their name to Murdock, moved to a fashionable town house on Fifth Avenue. Then they invited Florence's mother to come live with them.

"Mama," cautioned the daughter, "the first thing you must do is to learn to speak English. Al speaks no Yiddish, and neither do any of the guests we invite to our parties."

"All right, Feigeleh, I'll learn English," promised Mama.

The old lady was as good as her word. For over a year she studied, poring over books and attending night classes at the local public school. Now the daughter felt that her mother could safely attend their next party.

It was quite a banquet. Among the many notables at the table were statesmen, bankers, famous artists, industrial magnates and other outstanding personalities. Mama sat at Florence's right hand. On Mama's left was a well known television commentator whom the elderly woman recognized at once. During a lull in the conversation Mama turned to the commentator and began talking to him in Yiddish. A deathly silence fell over the guests as all eyes turned to the old lady who was speaking this strange tongue.

Horrified, Florence fought for self-control and then tapped her mother's arm. "Mumsie dear, remember what you promised? Nothing but English." She turned to another guest and murmured, "She's so quaint, isn't she?"— but boiled inwardly at her mother's breach of etiquette.

COMMUNICATION

Mama remained silent for a few moments and then turned once more to the TV commentator. With devastating clarity, she said, "You a no-good anti-Semite bestid!" Quickly she turned to her fainting daughter and beamed, *"Feigeleh, ist gut gesagt?"*

✓ ✓ ✓

Roth, the manufacturer, and Rochmis, the wholesaler, enjoyed a fine business relationship for many years, but they got into a dispute about a shipment of garments which Roth swore he had sent and Rochmis insisted he had never received. Thereafter, on the first of each month, Roth would send a bill, and just as regularly Rochmis ignored it.

But when a year had passed without payment Roth instructed his accountant to draft a telegram demanding his money. Dutifully, the accountant prepared this telegram:

DEBT NOW A YEAR OVERDUE. REMIT AT ONCE. CAN WAIT NO LONGER.

But Roth hit the ceiling. "Who needs so many words?" he said crossly, his sense of frugality outraged. "You couldn't make it shorter?"

"I don't see how," answered the accountant.

Roth grabbed a pencil and quickly reduced the telegram to one word: NU?

And the reply which came back from Rochmis the same day read: SUE!

✓ ✓ ✓

A very old woman, one of the few survivors of a concentration camp, was sent to America after her rescue by the Allies, to live with her widowed grandson. As virtual boss of her grandson's house her declining years were rich with peace and joy, but she had one problem: unable to speak a word of English, she had difficulty with her shopping. She would go to the store and point out the items she wanted.

One day she set out to buy a chicken, but unable to ask for it in English, she tried to communicate in sign language. First she flapped her arms wildly in the air, and then, to make doubly certain that the butcher understood her, she began to crow like a rooster, her shrill voice echoing throughout the store.

The butcher grinned. "Grandma," he said in Yiddish, his voice very kind, "just tell me what you want. You don't have to wave your arms around like that and make chicken noises."

"Blessed be the Lord! You speak perfect Yiddish!" cried the old lady, her face crinkled in pleased smiles. "Now I can stop talking to you in English!"

✓ ✓ ✓

Mama Kalmanson, holding the first check she had ever received in her life, went to the bank to cash it.

289

"You'll have to endorse it," said the teller.

"What means endorse?" asked Mama.

"Just sign it on the back, the same as you do in a letter," the teller explained.

Blushing fiercely, Mama took a pen and wrote on the back of the check:

"Lovingly yours, Miriam Kalmanson."

✓   ✓   ✓

Mrs. Berger had just finished reading a letter from her son in Los Angeles when a neighbor dropped in. "Ah, good morning, Mrs. Gold," she smiled. "A letter from my son, Solomon."

"*Nu*, how's by Solomon?" asked Mrs. Gold conversationally.

Mrs. Berger's face clouded. "Terrible news. Without a penny of insurance his house burned down. And at the store his partner stole all the money and ran away—the big *ganeff*! So what does my Solomon's wife do? I ask you. Does she stick by her only husband? No, she has to desert him for a rich real estate man. Even the children she took. Now my Solomon he has no home, no business, no wife, no children. *Ach!* It's terrible news for a mother!"

"But you were smiling when I came in!" cried Mrs. Gold.

"Well, yes," she acknowledged. "It's all a bitter nightmare, of course, but does my Solomon write a beautiful Yiddish! Just to read his letters, believe me, it's a pleasure!"

✓   ✓   ✓

Mama and Papa Jacobson were dubious about their brand new son-in-law, and worried as their daughter, Edith, set off on her honeymoon with her husband.

A few days later, Mama and Papa's sense of forboding grew when they received this telegram from Edith:

THE HONEYMOON IS FINE BUT THE MARRIAGE IS GETTING SHAKY.

✓   ✓   ✓

Grandpa Isaacs wanted to make certain that his grandson at Harvard did not forget the Day of Atonement, so he sent the young fellow a telegram:

YOM KIPPUR STARTS TOMORROW.

The grandson immediately wired back:

THANKS FOR TIP. BET FIFTY FOR ME—WIN, PLACE AND SHOW.

✓   ✓   ✓

The moral to the following very ancient story, is: "Most people will help one who has fallen, before they will help to keep him from falling."

COMMUNICATION

It was a wintry day. Ice and snow covered the streets of the Russian city, and the pious but desperately poor Jew trudged along, begging a crust of bread, a penny, anything to take home to his starving wife and children. There were many jobs he might have filled but the Czar had prohibited Jewish people from taking them.

He had suffered many cruel rebuffs, kicks and taunts when suddenly he slipped on the ice, fell, and broke his leg. Passers-by called an ambulance and he was taken to the hospital.

Word soon spread in that small town that a starving man, begging for a little food or a penny or two for his family, had broken his leg and was in the hospital. Donations quickly rolled in, together with much warm clothing, baskets of food and an offer of employment.

That night he sent his wife a letter:

"God in heaven has been good to me. Today, in His infinite kindness, He broke my leg!"

✶   ✶   ✶

Harry Karp, a proud and brand new father, sent his parents a telegram: WIFE BORE SON. HARRY.

A few days later, he received a stern letter from the elder Karp:

"For notifying me about the blessed event, I thank you. But a telegram should never contain a single unnecessary word.

"For example, why did you have to include your name, 'Harry'? Who else would give a son to your wife—the President of the United States?

"And why did you put in 'wife'? Were you afraid maybe I would think Queen Elizabeth made for you a baby?

"Then you included the word 'bore.' You think I might believe the child was hatched from an egg, like a chicken?

"Finally, why do you have to put in 'son'? Does anybody send a telegram to announce the birth of a daughter?"

✶   ✶   ✶

Mama was writing a letter to her daughter in San Francisco.

Dear Sadie,

You ask how is it I should get a busy signal when I telephoned you on Chanukah, so I'm explaining. I dialed the access number and then the area code and then the information number and then I got another number, so I dialed again the access number and then the area code and then the number information gave me and that, dear Sadie, is how I got the busy signal."

✶   ✶   ✶

Shortly after Justice Arthur Goldberg was appointed as Ambassador to the United Nations, President Lyndon Johnson, so the story goes, suggested that he first take a short vacation in order that he might be thoroughly rested before starting his new duties at the UN.

Ambassador Goldberg agreed, and flew to the Swiss Alps. There, on his first day, he was caught in a huge avalanche and was reported missing. For two days, searching parties of the Red Cross trudged through the snow seeking the missing official. Finally, on the third morning they spotted him on a snow bank.

"Mr. Goldberg! Mr. Goldberg!" the leader cried. "Thank God we found you! We're from the Red Cross."

Goldberg eyed them warily. "Sorry, gentlemen," he said, "but I already gave at the office!"

✓ ✓ ✓

"Dear Mama,
    Please forgive me for not writing sooner but I have been very busy. My career as a model got off to a good start. Next month my picture will be in Harper's Bizarre."

✓ ✓ ✓

In the City of Czarist Petrograd there lived a merchant who was planning to emigrate to America, "the land of milk and honey." He had already sent his wife and children to the United States and as soon as he had saved enough money for his passage he proposed to follow them.

One day he received a telegram from his wife, reading:
SAYS TO OPERATE OPERATE
Sorely troubled, the merchant immediately wired back:
SAYS TO OPERATE OPERATE
The very next morning he was summoned to police headquarters where he was confronted with copies of the two telegrams.

"There's no use in your denying it," rasped the police chief. "You are using a secret code with persons in another country. If you're smart you'll confess. We have ways of getting the truth out of you, as you must know." There was pure menace in his voice.

"Your excellency, this is no code," protested the merchant. "It is a simple exchange of messages. Let me read the telegrams to you."

"Are you implying that we can't read?"

"No, but—but . . ."

"Oh, stop stammering! Go ahead and read them."

"You see, your excellency, my wife in America is ill, and before she left we decided that she would go to a surgeon if her condition did not improve. She did so, and sent me this telegram: 'SAYS TO OPERATE. OPERATE?'

"And I replied: 'SAYS TO OPERATE? OPERATE!'"

✓ ✓ ✓

COMMUNICATION

Rabbi Mordecai Koppelman of Brooklyn arrived in San Francisco for a rabbinical conference, but when he checked into the Mark Hopkins hotel he found that he had forgotten his bedroom slippers. So he sat right down and wrote an air-mail letter to his wife:

> "Dear Leah:
> Send me at once your slippers. I wrote 'your slippers' because if I wrote 'my slippers' you would read it as my slippers and you would send me your slippers. And what do I need with your slippers? So I am saying plainly you should understand—'your slippers' and not 'my slippers,' so that you should read it your slippers and send me my slippers."

*   *   *

Two ancient Israelites were sipping tea in the kitchen of a small house in Warsaw. The news from Hitler's Third Reich had been very bad that morning. Without a word they brooded in silence for what seemed hours. Finally, one spoke:

"Oy, vay!"

Sighed the other: "You're telling me!"

*   *   *

Two university lads decided to compile a Yiddish-English dictionary, much as in the style of the glossary in the back of this book. They were both well versed in the grammar of the mother tongue and they proceeded rapidly in the task. However, when they reached the D's they ran into trouble. The word that stumped them was 'disappointed.' They cudgeled their minds for the Yiddish equivalent but neither could think of the answer.

"Say, I know what to do!" exclaimed one. "I'll ask my mother. Yiddish is the only language she understands. Believe me, she'll know the word for 'disappointed.' "

He soon had his mother on the phone. "Listen to me carefully, Mama," he said in Yiddish. "Every Friday night I come home so that you, Papa and I can have dinner together. Right? Okay! Now suppose, next Friday I telephoned you just as you were about to set the table and I told you I wouldn't be able to come. What would you be?"

"Oy, Ingeleh!" she cried, *"Azoi* disappointed!"

*   *   *

Before Harry Berman opened his own store on Second Avenue he was a traveling salesman for a silk house in New York. Once, when he returned from a trip to Chicago, the sales manager greeted him. "So what's new in Chicago?"

"Nothing new," was the laconic answer.

"What! In such a big city like Chicago there's nothing new?"

"Well, a dog barked."

"Why?"

"You see, a store was on fire and I guess he got excited by the big crowd and the policemen."

"Policemen were there too? What for?"

"They were arresting the guilty man for arson. To tell you the truth, the man who set fire to the store was your brother. I suppose he did it for the insurance."

"Hmmm," replied the sales manager reflectively. "All I can say about that rascal is that he's done it before. With that brother of mine, setting fires is nothing new."

"Just like I said," explained Harry. "In Chicago there's nothing new!"

✔ ✔ ✔

"There are no real Indians left in America!" declared Rabinowitz. "I can prove it! A few years ago I decided to find out for myself so the first place I visited was Coney Island. Of course, I expected to find a few phonies there, but I thought that one or two might be the genuine article. Finally I saw two Indians who really looked authentic. So I sneaked up behind them and heard one Indian say to the other: 'So how's by you the grandchildren?'

"And the other Indian answered, 'Oy, such little angels you never saw!'

"Well, nobody needs to tell me what kind of Indians *they* were, so I headed for the Chicago World Fair. There, I thought, I would find living, breathing Indians. At first I thought that the Indians who were performing for the crowds were real, but after listening closely to the war-whoops I asked myself, where have I heard those sounds before? Suddenly I remembered! They were imitations of the *shofar* on Rosh Hashanah! I heard them all: *tekiah, shevarim, truah!*

"In the end, I made my way to the far west, to a place called Dead Man's Gulch. This time there was no doubt about it. I had finally discovered a real Indian. His name, he told me, was Squatting Bull. I talked to him for over an hour and was convinced that he was no counterfeit for tourists. He spoke grandly of Indian history, displayed a sound knowledge of Indian lore and smoked a pipe of peace. He even had a bow and arrows.

"And then it happened! He stood up in all his primitive majesty and turned around. And there, sticking out of his back pocket—I should live so!—was a copy of the *Forverts!*"

✔ ✔ ✔

"Hello, Mr. Goldblatt. How's by you?"

"Eh-eh!"

"And the store—it's making money?"

"Hah!"

294

COMMUNICATION

"And Mrs. Goldblatt—she's in good health?"

"Mmm-mmm!"

"Well, goodbye, Mr. Goldblatt. It's a pleasure having a heart-to-heart talk with an old friend."

✓ ✓ ✓

During the height of German depredations against the Jews, a squad of Gestapo agents swooped down on a Jewish farmer on the outskirts of Berlin and hauled him away to a concentration camp. His wife, a gentile, was permitted to remain behind. As was the case in the earlier days of the holocaust, a few letters were somehow smuggled in and out of the camp.

In one such letter the wife complained bitterly that, although she had plenty of seed potatoes she would be unable to plant them because she could not plow the field by herself. The camp inmate pondered the problem for several days until he finally hit on an idea. He wrote her a brief note telling her that she was to forget about plowing the field. "Don't touch a single spot," he cautioned her. "That's where I buried the rifles and grenades." Then he mailed the letter quite openly.

A few days later several truckloads of Gestapo agents descended on the farm, each with a shovel. All week they dug in the field, turning over every shovelful of earth with great care. At last, finding no guns or bombs, they left. The bewildered wife immediately sent her husband another letter in which she explained the strange occurrence. "The field," she told him, "has been sifted from one end to the other."

And the husband wrote back, "Now plant the potatoes!"

✓ ✓ ✓

The clerk at the Post Office window recognized the next man in line as a newly arrived immigrant. "Let me see if you addressed the envelope properly," he said kindly.

The newcomer, grateful for his American friend's interest, handed over the letter and the clerk read

> Willi Eisenstadt,
> Berlin,
> U. S.

The clerk grinned. "Berlin is in Germany, not the U. S. You'll have to change it."

"But that U. S. doesn't stand for United States," protested the other.

"No? Then what does it mean?"

"It means," explained the immigrant, "upstairs!"

✓ ✓ ✓

Levy was on tenterhooks, waiting in the corridor outside the maternity ward for news of his wife. After an interminable wait the doctor emerged and shook his hand warmly. "Congratulations, Mr. Levy, you are the father of quadruplets."

"*Oy vay!*" moaned the shocked husband. "You mean one of those things that runs around on four legs?"

✦ ✦ ✦

Max was sitting in his office when the intercom buzzed. He flipped the switch and his partner, Sam, in the next room, said, "Listen carefully, I got an important telegram."

"So go ahead and read it," said Max.

"Wait a second. The secretary's here; she'll read it."

The secretary began: "Must have ten gross . . . stop . . . Ladies' gloves . . . stop . . . Assorted colors . . . stop . . . Pay top price . . . stop . . ."

"Sam!" roared Max into the set, "Leave the girl alone and let her read the telegram. This is business!"

✦ ✦ ✦

For years Sol had been using pay telephones, and like most other callers, there were numerous times when he failed to contact his party but nevertheless lost his dime. So it was with a pleasant feeling of revenge that he heard his dime fall back into the return box after he had successfully completed a call. He fished out the dime, put it in his pocket and was about to leave the booth when the phone rang. He picked up the receiver.

"Are you the person who just finished a call at this number?"

"Yes, I am," answered Sol.

"Your dime was returned to you by mistake," the girl explained. "Will you please redeposit it?"

"I'm sorry, ma'am, but it's against my policy to do that," replied Sol in a fairly good imitation of her voice. "But if you will give me your name and address I'll be glad to send you the ten cents—in stamps."

✦ ✦ ✦

Moses Mendelssohn was a poor boy when he arrived from the town of Dessau to study in Berlin. His first visit was to the rabbi who found him unusually well versed in Jewish law.

The rabbi was anxious to retain the boy in Berlin, but being unable to help him financially, he addressed a flowery letter to a prominent Jewish banker in the city. In this letter, the rabbi informed the rich man of Mendelssohn's knowledge and ability, and that the youth was worthy of support. Mendelssohn took the document to the banker who read it carefully and then chatted with the young man for a few minutes.

Completely satisfied, the banker added the following postscript to the rabbi's letter: "I fully endorse your sentiments!"

✦ ✦ ✦

COMMUNICATION

A cloak and suit manufacturer was so incensed with a delinquent customer that he sat down and wrote him a sharp note:

"Dear Sir:
Who promised to settle up for everything by the first of the month? You! Who failed to keep his promise? You! Who then is a damned liar?

Yours truly,
DAVID COHEN."

✔   ✔   ✔

Mrs. Levin was opening her mail and came upon a wedding invitation. "Meyer," she called to her husband, "Abe Epstein is marrying Sarah Solomon. The announcement just came."

Meyer scrutinized the invitation and handed it back. "We ain't going," he said tartly.

"Why not?" asked the surprised Mrs. Levin.

"Because they got a lot of nerve to send such an invitation. Just look at that R.S.V.P. You call that good manners?"

"What's wrong with those letters? What do they stand for?"

"Don't you know?" stormed Meyer. "They mean Remember Sending Vedding Presents!"

✔   ✔   ✔

Kaplan was seated comfortably in his living room one evening when a rock crashed through the window and landed at his feet amidst a shower of splintered glass. To the rock was attached a note: "Unless you pay us $10,000 according to instructions, we will kidnap your wife."

After some thought, Kaplan sat down at his desk and penned a reply:

"Gentlemen:
Your rock of this date received. I don't have $10,000 at this time. However, keep in touch, as your proposition interests me.

SOL KAPLAN."

Chapter Twenty-eight

Education

Of all the *yeshivahs*, *talmud torahs* and other non-secular schools in New York, none was so dear to the heart of Rabbi Emmanuel Goldman as the Freeman Street Elementary Day School in the Bronx.

One day the famous educator paid a visit to the school, popping in unexpectedly on a class of second graders. The flattered and flustered teacher introduced him to the pupils. "Children, this is Rabbi Emmanuel Goldman."

One little girl skipped to the front of the class and tugged at his sleeve. "Emmanuel . . ." she started to say.

The teacher, horrified, interrupted the six-year-old. "Rosie, you must never, never say 'Emmanuel!' You must say 'Rabbi Goldman'!"

Well, teachers are always right, so the little girl began again:

"Rabbi Goldman is my kid brother's name."

✓ ✓ ✓

Papa came home early one evening and confronted Mama with a stern demand. "I want a new Hebrew teacher for our Herbie. I went to the school today and the old teacher is no good."

"Impossible!" protested Mama. "All the parents say he's a fine teacher! In fact, he's been teaching for twenty years."

"That's exactly the trouble," replied Papa. "For a man who has been teaching for twenty years he's too healthy. Everybody knows that a good teacher, after two or three years, should have high blood pressure— or at least TB!"

✓ ✓ ✓

Rabbi Golden was lecturing his advanced class of biblical students when he spied a boy in the back row whose head was lowered, as though deeply engrossed in a book.

"Young man, I don't want to accuse you unjustly," said the patient rabbi, "but it seems to me you are reading a book. Are you trying to improve your mind?"

298

"Sir, I wasn't reading," replied the boy guiltily. "How can I be improving my mind when I was just listening to you?"

✓ ✓ ✓

The teacher at the *cheder*, after explaining the meaning of *Pesach*, asked the young pupils to use the word '*matzohs*' in a sentence.

"*Matzohs* are eaten at the *seder*," said Jerry.

"Very good," smiled the teacher. "How about you, David?"

"*Matzohs* are made without salt," responded David.

Izzy, who had been in this country for only a few months, raised his hand. "Time *matzohs* on!" he shouted triumphantly.

✓ ✓ ✓

The teacher at the YPSL (Young People's Socialist League) Sunday school on the East Side, was explaining the three fundamentals of socialism.

"Always remember, children, that socialism stands for Liberty, Equality and Fraternity," she instructed.

All the children remembered the slogan except Abie who could never recall more than two of the terms. Finally an idea occurred to the teacher. She handed Abie three buttons.

"Now take these buttons home with you and every time you look at them you will remember the three principles of socialism."

On the following Sunday the teacher asked Abie if the three buttons had helped refresh his memory.

"They sure did!" responded Abie. "They stand for Liberty and Equality!"

"What happened to Fraternity?" asked the dismayed teacher.

"Oh, that! Mama sewed it on Pop's old pants!"

✓ ✓ ✓

Rabbi Mordecai Kantor was a martinet and demanded the very best of his pupils. So it was to be expected that he would blow up when little Joseph handed in a poor paper.

"This is the worst Yiddish composition it has ever been my misfortune to read," stormed the rabbi. "It has so many errors I can't understand how one person could have made all these mistakes."

"One person didn't," muttered Joseph defensively. "My father helped me."

✓ ✓ ✓

Aaron, the scholar, although only fifteen years of age, had won fame and acclamation for his great learning. Day and night he studied. He studied while he ate, while he walked, while he bathed—some said he even dreamed of books. At home, in the university, everywhere, the boy studied.

His reputation ultimately reached the chief rabbi of Vienna. "The lad might be a valuable assistant," the eminent man thought, so he journeyed to the town in which the youth lived and approached the local rabbi.

"I have heard much of this boy's learning. Tell me, Rabbi, is it true that he knows so much?"

The wise old rabbi smiled. "You ask for the truth? Well, frankly, the boy studies so much he just hasn't the time to really *know!*"

✓ ✓ ✓

A Chicago couple decided that it was high time their little Velvel learned how to pray in Hebrew, so they employed a rabbi to teach him. But Velvel simply could not absorb the instructions. He knew all the latest rock 'n roll songs and could recite the baseball scores by rote in both Leagues for as far back as 1904. But no matter how the rabbi tried, the boy could not learn to pray correctly. Finally, in desperation, the rabbi seized on the idea of teaching the youngster the *kaddish*—the prayer for the dead.

But the moment Velvel's parents learned of this they rushed to the rabbi's house and confronted him angrily, and with some fear.

"What is the meaning of this?" they demanded. "We are still in our thirties—a long life is still ahead of us."

"Now don't get excited," admonished the rabbi calmly. "You can live to a hundred and twenty, but take my word for it, Velvel still won't know how to say the *kaddish!*"

✓ ✓ ✓

A class of talmudic students were having a discussion as to the origin of earthly objects and subjects. First they argued the age-old question as to which came first, the chicken or the egg. But Judaism has an answer for that, as one student promptly pointed out: the chicken came first otherwise the egg could not have been laid—and the original chicken had to be created by God.

"I have another question," interjected a student. "Which came first, the doctor or the lawyer?"

The students burrowed into their books but could find no answer that satisfied all of them, so they consulted the rabbi.

"The doctor came before the lawyer," said the rabbi, unhesitatingly.

"How so?" shouted the students.

"Because a doctor was essential as soon as man was created, when God cut out Adam's rib. The lawyer wasn't created until later, when Cain slew Abel."

✓ ✓ ✓

An aspiring young author whose ambition greatly exceeded his talent, visited his instructor after school hours.

"Sir, I have just finished my new masterpiece," he began proudly.

"It is called 'The Hands of Moses.' I would appreciate your honest opinion of the book."

The instructor flipped through a few pages of the manuscript—and that was enough! He was aghast at the poor sentence structure, the meandering plot, the hackneyed phrases and clichés.

"Young man," said the teacher at length, "I have one slight suggestion to make."

"What is that?" asked the would-be author eagerly.

"Change the title from 'The Hands of Moses' to 'The Face of God.' "

"But *why?*"

"Because it is something one can't look at!"

✓ ✓ ✓

We Jews, too, have our quota of absent-minded professors.

A *yeshivah* instructor, his mind on the next lecture, met his son in the school's corridor.

"Good morning, Morty," he said, "how's your father?"

✓ ✓ ✓

The son of an Orthodox Jew told his father that he was studying Darwin's theory of evolution.

"What's that?" asked the old man.

"According to Darwin," explained the son, "we are all descended from monkeys."

The old man turned purple with indignation. "What kind of nonsense is that?" he shouted. "Is that the way a decent Jew—my own son—talks?"

"But Papa . . . !"

"Please, don't but me no buts. I don't want to hear another word. *I* certainly don't come from monkeys. Maybe *you* do!"

✓ ✓ ✓

During the mid-1960's, elephant jokes were all the rage. But what the average gentile did not know is that we Jews have been laughing at the same witticisms for Lord knows how long. Here are just three examples:

At Adult Night School, in New York, in the summer of 1912, a teacher asked a newly-arrived immigrant, "Where are elephants found?"

The student, honestly perplexed, asked, "How can you lose an elephant?"

———

A professor of zoology at Harvard, some years ago, asked his graduate students, among whom were several foreigners, to write papers on the elephant.

A German student wrote: "An Introduction to the Bibliography for the Study of the Elephant."

A French student wrote: "The Love Life of the Elephant."

An English student wrote: "Elephant Hunting."
A Canadian student wrote: "Breeding Bigger and Better Elephants."
Izzy Kaplan, also a student in the class, wrote: "The Elephant and the Jewish Problem."

———

Before we leave the subject, we are reminded of the teacher who told her class: "An elephant never forgets."
And Moe Meisner, sitting in the back, muttered, "After all, what has an elephant got to remember?"

✓ ✓ ✓

A young stranger in New York was seeking Columbia University but the many directions he had received only confused him and he became lost. Luckily, he saw a scholarly old gentlemen approaching with a load of books under his arm. He stopped the professorial man.
"Tell me, sir, how do I get to Columbia University?"
The old man deliberated the question for a moment or two and then replied, "Study, young man. Constant study!"

✓ ✓ ✓

Theodor brought home his report card and his father was shocked at the low grades his son had received.
"There must be a reason for your poor marks," said the father. "Is it that you don't apply yourself? Don't you study?"
"But I do apply myself, and I do study," protested Theodor. "It's just that the teacher doesn't like me because I'm Jewish."
The father was disturbed at this evidence of anti-Semitism, having grown up with it himself in the old country. To spare his son such bigotry in the future he arranged with a minister to baptize the boy in the Christian faith. Thus it was that Theodor Cohen became Throckmorton Kane, a gentile.
At the end of the next semester, however, Throckmorton's report card was even worse than before.
"What's the excuse this time?" snapped the father. "Surely your teacher isn't prejudiced against you now."
"It isn't that, Papa," whined the boy. "All the other kids in my class are Jewish and it's just impossible for a Christian like me to compete!"

✓ ✓ ✓

Moses Rosenblatt, the *shochet*, was very proud of his grandson who was in his first year at Harvard. He was also intrigued with the courses the young fellow was taking.
"Tell me something," asked Rosenblatt, "what is this psychology business all about?"
"Well, it's a comparatively new subject," the grandson began. "They didn't know much about it when you went to school."

EDUCATION

"*Nu,* so enlighten me."

"Psychology," explained the youth in his best textbook manner, "is the science which deals with mental phenomena; the systematic study of consciousness and behavior; that is, the mind as displayed in traits, feelings, action and so forth."

"And what does that mean in plain language, if I may be so bold?"

"Simply put, it means how one acts, what he says, what he does . . ."

"Oh!" Grandpa Rosenblatt exclaimed. "So that's psychology! This is new by you? When I was a boy we called it ordinary *Yiddishe saichel!*"

✓ ✓ ✓

Sammy came home from school before lunch one day, and his surprised mother asked him why he had been let out so early.

"The teacher told me I need a bath," Sammy explained. "She said I have B.O."

Furious, the woman grabbed her coat and stalked to the school a block away. She confronted the teacher in the classroom.

"Listen," she fumed, "nobody claimed my Sammy is a rose. I'm sending him to school you should learn him, not smell him!"

✓ ✓ ✓

The modern, sophisticated Jewish mother bears little resemblance to her old-fashioned counterparts of past decades. Some of them have not only been assimilated into American society, they often out-assimilate their contemporary gentile sisters. Here is an illustrative example:

Mrs. Royteborscht was commanded to appear in school by an irate teacher who could no longer put up with little Montgomery Royteborscht's conduct. But what the teacher did not know was that Mama Royteborscht had not only majored in psychology, she had also married a psychologist. Naturally, she read all her husband's technical journals and considered herself an expert on the subject.

At school the next morning, the teacher at once launched into her complaint. "Your son's deportment is undermining the discipline of the whole class. I hate to say this, but Montgomery needs a spanking."

"I will permit no such thing," snapped Mrs. Royteborscht. "That sort of corporal punishment could very well result in a traumatic shock that would remain with him throughout his life. You see, Montgomery's problem is psychological—he is always suspecting others of plotting behind his back. True enough, he needs discipline, but a spanking—well, that would be behind his back. So if you *must* chastise him—whack him good while he's looking!"

✓ ✓ ✓

Child psychology is an art, not an exact science, as Mrs. Royteborscht had occasion to demonstrate. Once again her son Montgomery was making a pest of himself at school, and once again the teacher sent for the mother.

Mrs. Royteborscht listened patiently as the teacher itemized all of Montgomery's vicissitudes, leaving out nothing and adding a few of her own invention. But there was no question about it: the boy was disrupting the class. "Well, are you going to punish him or not?" asked the teacher, still glowering.

Mrs. Royteborscht nodded. "Yes, but we must consider his delicate, sensitive nature. Physical abuse could cause a Freudian complex, so what we must do is frighten rather than strike him."

"And just how do we do that?" asked the suspicious teacher.

"Simple—the next time my Montgomery misbehaves, grab the boy in front of him and give him a smack in the face."

✔ ✔ ✔

Leibush Himmelfarb was only a poor immigrant tailor, but ever since his son Yankel was born he had cherished one ambition: his son would receive a higher education in the best university in America. Yankel would have all the advantages that he had never enjoyed: prestige, social standing, a respectable profession and financial security.

The great day finally arrived when Yankel graduated from Roosevelt High School in the Bronx, and with joy in his heart, Leibush sent his son off to Harvard.

Vacation time soon rolled around and the pride of the family returned home for the summer. Old Leibush Himmelfarb listened avidly as Yankel told him of college life and the fraternity he had joined.

"About your education," Leibush interrupted. "What are you studying?"

"Many subjects. Languages, calculus, political science, philosophy and so on."

The word 'philosophy' was especially appealing to the uneducated, proud father. It sounded recondite and very, very learned. "Tell me, Yankel," he said, "what is this 'philosophy'?"

"Philosophy is—well—it's rather difficult to explain. I'll give you an example. You are now in New York, right?"

"Right!"

"Well, by using a series of deductions I can prove that you are not really in New York but in Philadelphia. That's philosophy. It never fails because, like logic, its laws are solid and certain!"

Old Leibush's face fell. Was this what he had sent his son to Harvard for? Was this the result of his many years of struggle?

"I am not an educated man, Yankel," said the tailor, "but I have learned one thing; nothing is certain to us humans except death."

"You just don't understand philosophy," said the young man, smiling loftily.

Suddenly the old man lashed out and struck his son on the jaw.

"What was that for?" cried the astonished Yankel.

"I want you to prove your theory," answered Leibush placidly. "Prove to me how I can be in Philadelphia instead of New York, and also tell me who just hit you while I was away!"

✓ ✓ ✓

"How is Goldie doing with her school work?" asked the proud papa.

"Well," his wife said reluctantly, "I hate to tell you, but her teacher kept her in after school—a whole hour!"

"Why? What did she do?"

"She couldn't remember where the Dardanelles are."

"*Aiee,* that child!" sighed papa. "Last week she couldn't locate the Straits of Gibraltar, this week she can't find the Dardenelles. Believe me, if I told her once I told her a hundred times, 'Goldie, please—try to remember where you put your things!'"

✓ ✓ ✓

"Marvin," said the teacher, "can you use the words 'effervescent' and 'fiddlestick' in one sentence?"

Marvin, who had only been in this country a few months, thought awhile and then smiled. "Yes, ma'am," he answered. "Effervescent for long blenkets the fiddlestick out!"

✓ ✓ ✓

The teacher had spent an exhausting half hour explaining the reasons for Lincoln's greatness. Now she called on Solly Weinberg to answer a question.

"Who wrote the Gettysburg Address?" she asked.

Solly, who fancied himself as somewhat of a comedian, replied, "Not me!"

The other pupils broke into raucous laughter and the teacher scowled. "Solly," she snapped, "I want you to bring your father here tomorrow morning."

The next day she told Mr. Weinberg how his son had disrupted the class with his wise-guy attitude. "And when I asked him who wrote the Gettysburg Address, he said 'Not me!'"

"Well, to be frank, Madam," replied the father, "I know that Solly is no angel, but he is not a liar either. If he says he didn't write it then he didn't write it!"

At home, he told his wife the whole story, but instead of agreeing with him her face clouded with annoyance.

"How could you be so silly!" she cried.

"Why, what did I do wrong?"

"I'll tell you what you did wrong! First you should have apologized for Solly, and then you should have told the teacher, like a gentleman, that although he wrote it this time, he would never do it again!"

✓ ✓ ✓

Barney and Sol, not long in America, enrolled in night school and because they were apt students, they quickly mastered the English language. Indeed, so proud were they of their new tongue that its correct usage became something of a contest between them.

Barney soon married a lovely girl, but within a few months she began to have an affair with Sol. One day, Barney returned home unexpectedly and found his wife in Sol's embrace.

"I am surprised!" shouted the outraged husband.

"No Barney, it is *I* who am surprised," corrected Sol. "You are astonished!"

✓   ✓   ✓

Bella was the only Jewess in her class at an exclusive school in Scarsdale. Quite rightly, she considered herself a lucky girl since, in those days, only gentiles were admitted.

Bella's closest friend was Cynthia, a Greek Catholic. When the girls took their final examinations Bella passed with straight A's but Cynthia failed miserably.

"I just can't understand it," complained Cynthia. "Just before the tests I lit candles to St. Peter, St. Barnabas and several other saints, and look what happened!"

"I lit a candle too," said Bella.

"What! You, a Jewess, lit a candle? To whom?"

"To nobody. I lit the candle and stayed up all night, studying!"

✓   ✓   ✓

Whether apocryphal or not, this campus favorite merits a niche in this anthology. It is the story of the eminent Morris Kaplan, of UCLA's English Department, who met in battle with no less a dragon than Amy Lowell, of the Massachusetts Lowells—reportedly on speaking terms with no one but the Cabots, the Lodges and God. The incident took place at a performance of a play by Shakespeare, presented by the University's drama class.

Miss Lowell was an ample lady and she more than filled her seat. Her seat was between the aisle and Professor Kaplan's seat, and once she was *in situ*, the professor had a hard squeeze to get by. He managed it with some stepping on toes, only to find that Miss Lowell chose to remain seated during the intermission. It took one more squeeze to get by her at the beginning of the first intermission, and yet another to get back at the close. Nor was Miss Lowell showing pleasure at being squeezed by. At the beginning of the second intermission, Professor Kaplan started out again, and Miss Lowell decided she had had enough.

"Young man," she announced in the voice that some Boston ladies still believe will check angels in their flight and send all mere mortals reeling, "I am Miss Lowell of Brookline."

But Kaplan was neither checked nor routed.

"Your address, Madam," he said, "is a matter of no importance to me."

✓ ✓ ✓

Mason Gross, president of Rutgers University, tells of an incident that occurred when he was a professor, and taught an introductory course in philosophy. He had barely begun the course when a student, arriving late for an afternoon conference, blurted out, "Look, I don't know nothin' about Aristotle and Pluto!"

"Sir," Professor Gross replied, "for millennia now, philosophers have been seeking what they call 'self-evident truths.' You," he added, "have just formulated one."

✓ ✓ ✓

Professor Morris Cohen, a legend at CCNY, also conducted an introduction-to-philosophy course. The semester was almost at an end when a coed arose in the role of intellectually ravished virtue, and declared, "Professor Cohen, you have knocked a hole in everything I have ever believed in and you have given me nothing to take its place!"

But Professor Cohen had a mind well poised against the slings and arrows of outraged virtue.

"Young lady," he replied, "you will recall that as one of the labors of Hercules, he was required to clean out the Augean stables. He was not, let me point out, required to refill them."

✓ ✓ ✓

An ignoramus managed to get himself invited to a party attended by world-renowned scientists. Among them was Albert Einstein. The illiterate guest immediately made a nuisance of himself by dogging the illustrious physicist's heels and offering what he thought were very profound observations.

"Tell me, Dr. Einstein," asked the pest. "What, in your opinion, is the difference between time and eternity?"

"Sir," answered Einstein, "if I took the time to explain the difference, it would take an eternity!"

✓ ✓ ✓

It was the first day of school and the teacher decided to get acquainted with her kindergarten pupils. She pointed to the first little boy in the nearest row and said, "Tell the class your name, like a good little boy."

"C'neelie," he answered promptly.

"Oh, no!" the teacher corrected. "In school you must give your proper name—Cornelius."

"Cornelius," said the little boy dutifully.

She nodded to the next youngster. "And what is your name?"

"Julie."

"Not 'Julie'!" reproved the teacher. "Your name is Julius. Now let me hear you say your name again."

"Julius!"

She then pointed to the third child in the row. "Tell us your name, young man."

"Bilious?" he asked uncertainly.

✔   ✔   ✔

Benny sauntered into the classroom a half-hour late.

"Why are you so tardy?" asked the teacher.

"My father needed me at home."

"Couldn't your father have used someone else instead of you?"

"No," answered Benny. "I had to get a spanking."

✔   ✔   ✔

Dr. Reuben Klein, professor of Jewish studies at Columbia University, was a brilliant instructor. However, because of his irascible disposition and stiff examinations, he was not too popular with his students.

One day his students sent him a small statue of a jackass made of sugar, as a Chanukah gift.

Not to be outdone, Professor Klein sent them a photograph of himself on which he had inscribed these words:

"Thank you for your picture. As a return courtesy I am sending you mine."

✔   ✔   ✔

"Rachel," roared the indignant father, "for the last time, I will not permit you to quit school and go to work. The trouble with you is that all you ever think about is boys—boys—boys!"

"That's not true, Daddy," the girl cried. "The only time I ever think of boys is when I think!"

✔   ✔   ✔

Herb Edelson, the shoemaker, was extraordinarily proud of the fact that, after years of heartache and struggle, he had been able to send his son, Harold, to college where the youth had earned his degree in the liberal arts.

But old Herb wanted his son to know that his father was no slouch either when it came to education, so, to impress the lad, he studied up on Shakespeare.

Harold," the old man began, "I can't understand why everybody makes such a to-do over Shakespeare. After all, except for the *Songs of Solomon*, what else did the man write?"

"Why, Pop," exclaimed the son, in surprise, "Shakespeare didn't write the *Songs of Solomon*!"

"He didn't! Well how about that? Now I have even less respect for him!"

✓ ✓ ✓

The young man had all the aptitudes to become a fine mechanic or a plumber. But he insisted, against his father's wise advice, that he go to college.

The rabbi came to call one evening, and said, "I hear your son is attending a university. What will he be when he graduates?"

"As near as I can figure," sighed the father, "about thirty-five or forty."

✓ ✓ ✓

Little Sidney had just transferred to a new school and been placed in a class that may have been a trifle too advanced for his seven years. The very first day, the teacher called on the boy to answer questions.

"Sidney, please tell the class why we raise sheep."

The boy maintained an embarrassed silence.

"But surely you know what we get from sheep!" the teacher said.

"Wool," Sidney finally answered.

"Correct! And what do we make from wool?"

"I—I really don't know."

"You don't know? Of course you do! Tell me, what is your jacket made of?"

"From my father's old pants," Sidney mumbled.

✓ ✓ ✓

"And now children," said the first grade teacher, "if anything important happened in your family over the weekend you may tell the class."

Jerry raised his hand. "My daddy went hunting and with only one bullet he shot a duck in the foot and in the head."

"What, at the same time? How could that happen?"

"I think," said Jerry, "the duck was scratching his head."

✓ ✓ ✓

Why is it that it takes some girls four years to get a sheepskin and only one day to get a mink?

✓ ✓ ✓

"My cousin is in medical school," said comic Joey Adams. "He isn't studying anything—they're studying him!"

✓ ✓ ✓

An exasperated father, who had been sending large checks to his son at college but without receiving any reports on the lad's progress, finally sent a terse note. Either the youth give him a report on his education or else—no more money!

Back came a telegram: "Getting along wonderfully in everything, Dad, except school!"

✓ ✓ ✓

A worried, Orthodox mother consulted a naive rabbi about her young son's enrollment in a strange school. "I don't like it there," she complained.

"Do they allow smoking among the pupils?" asked the rabbi.

"No!"

"Well, do they allow drinking?"

"Not that, either."

"Then what's to worry?"

"Well, I hate to say this, but I heard they allow dates."

"Oh for heaven's sake!" grumbled the rabbi. "Be reasonable. After all, how can they hurt him if he doesn't overeat?"

✓ ✓ ✓

Teacher: "Children, did you know that it is possible to play the piano by ear?"

Fresh Kid: "So what? My grandfather is always fiddling with his whiskers!"

✓ ✓ ✓

"You're sure you can teach my Walter to play the piano?" asked the doubtful mother.

"Listen, I can teach any child, including your boy," boasted the music teacher. "Why, in just a few months he'll be able to discuss such terms as *pizzicato, pianissimo, allegro* and *fortissimo*."

"What kind of language is that?"

"Italian, of course."

"Mister, for five dollars a lesson," snapped the mother, "you could at least teach him in English!"

✓ ✓ ✓

"Jacob, do you mean to say you don't know when Columbus discovered America?" demanded the teacher. "It's right on page one of your history book—1492."

"Oh," said the crestfallen Jacob, "I thought that was his telephone number."

✓ ✓ ✓

"Barbara," said the fourth grade teacher, "what are assets?"

"I think," answered Barbara, "they're baby donkeys."

✓ ✓ ✓

EDUCATION

Gentiles aren't the only ones who can laugh about their absent-minded professors. Dr. Mordecai Singer of CCNY, who was then teaching a class in introduction to philosophy, was in his study when his housekeeper came into the room and said, "The hospital just called. It's a boy, Dr. Singer."

The good professor, busily correcting term papers, looked up from his desk. "Well," he said, "ask him what he wants."

✓ ✓ ✓

A story that dates back to 1915 tells of the second grade teacher at P. S. 6, in The Bronx. She was adored by her little pupils because of her ability to tell interesting stories and yet hide the "educational value" of her parables.

One day, Jenny Goldstein asked the teacher why her stories were "so nice."

"Perhaps it is because I have no moral to tell," she answered.

That evening, little Jenny was discussing her school activities with her father. "Do you know why I like my teacher, Daddy?" she began. "It's because she has no morals."

✓ ✓ ✓

Dorothy was so excited she could barely wait for her father to return from work. Her parents had both been born in the Ukraine and she was anxious to tell her Daddy that she had been studying all about Russia. As soon as he relaxed in his favorite chair, Dorothy climbed into his lap and said, "Papa, we learned all about Russia today."

"Well now, I'm glad to hear it," smiled the father. "Did the teacher tell you who the former ruler was?"

"Uh-huh. The Czar."

"Good for you, Honey. And what was the Czar's wife called?"

Dorothy clapped her hands in pleasure. "I know that, too. The Czarina."

"That's right, dear. And what were the Czar's children called?"

"Hmmm." Dorothy puckered up her brow and concentrated. "I think," she said tentatively, "they were called Czardines."

✓ ✓ ✓

"Solly," asked the rabbi of his little student, "who was the father of Abraham?"

"Lincoln," answered Sollie.

✓ ✓ ✓

Teacher: "The New York Aquarium now boasts a man-eating shark."

Fresh Pupil: "That's nothing. Once, in the park, I saw a man eating herring."

✓ ✓ ✓

A public school teacher was explaining the wonders of the four seasons to her third grade pupils. She expounded at length on the bounty of summer, the glories of budding spring, the loveliness of autumn and the beauty of winter when a mantle of snow covers the bare trees and rocks.

The next day she quizzed the children on the lesson. The first boy she called on was Sidney Greenberg.

"Sidney," asked the teacher, "how many seasons are there?"

"Two."

"Why, Sidney, you know better than that. Which two seasons do you mean?"

The boy, whose father was in the cloak and suit business, answered promptly, "Busy and slack."

1 1 1

Teacher (in an East Side grammar school): "And now, children, tell me some names of objects that begin with the letter 'T.' "

Patrick: "Tigers and trains."

Elizabeth: "Tables and typewriters."

Izzy: *"Tallis* and *tefillin."*

Chapter Twenty-nine

Science

Benny's old grandfather, a gray-bearded patriarch from Poland, was very much puzzled by all the newspaper publicity given to Albert Einstein and his theory of relativity.

"Tell me, Benny," he asked his grandson when he returned from college for a weekend visit, "who is this Einstein and what is this relativity business all about?"

"Dr. Einstein is the greatest living scientist," enthused Benny, although a little uneasy about his own knowledge of the subject. "Relativity is—well—it's hard to explain. Let's put it this way: If a man's sweetheart sits on his knee, an hour feels like a minute. On the other hand, if the same man sits on a hot stove, a minute feels like an hour. That's the theory of relativity."

Grandpa, who had known his share of con men and *shnorrers* in his time, looked shocked. After an interval of stunned silence, he gasped:

"And from this your Einstein makes a living?"

✔   ✔   ✔

Papa had attended a few adult education classes in preparation for his citizenship papers and felt he was now an authority on national and international affairs.

One evening, as he and his wife were settling down for an hour or two of their favorite television programs, a bulletin announced that the Soviets had launched Sputnik, and that it was in orbit around the earth.

"What I can't understand," said Mama, "is why the Russians should be so far ahead of the U.S. in space."

"That's easy," replied Papa with a kind of wild logic. "They don't have to spend all their time fighting Communism!"

✔   ✔   ✔

It isn't generally known, and this is an important "first" for this anthology—but a Jewish scientist invented a time machine a few years ago, traveled to the future and returned with this story. At the risk of

313

scooping the *New York Times* and the *Jerusalem Post*, here is the exclusive account:

Our scientist was catapulted into the year 2081. Israel's space program had just paid off when Zvi Halevi, its first astronaut, was launched from a point in the Negev desert and zoomed spaceward, on target for Mars. All the time, he was in radio contact with the authorities in Tel Aviv.

Three months later he landed on the Red Planet and his radio messages were flashed back to Israel. On the fourth day of exploration, he astounded the world by telegraphing the existence of life there. "I have just found a beautiful feather," he flashed.

"What kind of feather?" the Israelis flashed back.

"How should I know?" radioed the astronaut. "What am I, a milliner?"

*   *   *

Manny and Moe were nobody's fools. After all, they had made a fortune in the auto supply business when no one else would touch it. So when they heard about the race to the planets between the Soviet Union and the United States, they figured there must be something valuable up there—else why the big rush?

They held a conference and decided, in the interests of rugged individualism and free private enterprise, to get there first; before the Soviet Union, and before the official U.S. Government astronauts. Together with their wives they collected wheels, wire, glue, electric bulbs, pliers, screw-drivers—the works! They were very handy with tools, and before long they had built a space ship. And so, as Manny's wife finished the *aleph-baiz* countdown, Moe's wife lit a match and touched off the fuse that sent their hubbies toward Mars, thus beating the Russian and United States goverments to the first landing on the alien planet.

Right away, Manny and Moe were made welcome by the Martian diplomats and they began a conducted tour of the strange world. They went to factories, parks, private homes and wherever else their little Jewish hearts desired. The Martians loved them.

On one of their tours, Manny and Moe were escorted through a huge industrial plant. "This is a baby factory," explained the two-headed, five-eyed Martian. "Our babies come off this assembly line."

The earthmen were naturally taken aback by this. When the Martian asked why they were so surprised, they told him, in all the intimate details, exactly how babies are conceived on Earth.

"Well, if that isn't the darndest thing I ever heard!" exclaimed the Martian. "That's exactly the way we make automobiles up here!"

*   *   *

A young science major was watching television one evening with his aged grandfather. Soon a newsflash appeared on the screen showing a space ship being launched for a trip to the moon.

SCIENCE

"Grandpa," said the youth, glad of the chance to display his scientific knowledge, "did you know that it costs three billion dollars to place a man on the moon?"

Grandpa was unimpressed. "Is that so?" he asked. "Including meals?"

✓ ✓ ✓

A rabbi and a priest were discussing the achievements of Judaism and Christianity.

"Rabbi, with all due respect to your men of science," said the priest, "we Catholics were the first of the modern scientists."

"How so?" asked the rabbi.

"Well, only a few years ago, while digging in the catacombs where the early Christians hid from the Romans, a group of archeologists uncovered a long wire."

"What does that signify?"

"It proves that we Catholics were the inventors of telegraphy, almost two thousand years ago."

"Frankly," said the rabbi, "I don't see anything so astounding about that. When the archeologists found the Dead Sea Scrolls, did you know that they dug a hole thirty feet deep and there, on the bottom, was no wire at all?"

"What in the world does that prove?"

"That proves that long before the Christian era we Jews had wireless!"

✓ ✓ ✓

Albert Einstein had just finished a detailed lecture about his quantum theory and his various speculations concerning relativity. When he completed his talk he was observed to retire glumly to his study.

"That was a brilliant discourse," commented another professor. "What possible reason could you have for looking so downcast?"

"Reason enough," replied Dr. Einstein. "My wife doesn't understand me."

✓ ✓ ✓

Two aged gentlemen were sunning themselves in Central Park—in those days when it was safe to do so.

"I tell you, Mr. Gold, it's a miracle to me the way modern science has changed everything. Take our grandfathers and great-grandfathers, for instance. How do you suppose they ever managed to live without television, radio, telephones, jet planes—all the modern wonders of science we have today?"

"That's just the point," replied Mr. Gold, nodding wisely. "They couldn't live without those inventions—that's why they're all dead now!"

✓ ✓ ✓

Harry Levine was a pragmatic, stolid sort of man. Nothing excited him. He had worked hard all his life, saved his money, and now owned a thriving, small hotel near Cape Kennedy.

One day, astronaut Gordon Cooper, who was stationed at the missile launching center, stopped at the hotel and engaged a room. A few minutes after he checked in, the house phone rang at the downstairs desk.

"This is Mr. Cooper in room 209," said the astronaut. "Where can I wash up?"

"At the end of the hall," answered Levine.

He turned to a maid who was sorting out the linen and remarked: "How do you like that? Here the government is sending Cooper out into space to look for Mars, and in a little hotel like this he can't even find the bathroom!"

✓ ✓ ✓

Alex, the Bar Mitzvah boy, told his rabbi he just couldn't understand how television works.

"How is it possible," he wondered, "to have a screen with pictures in houses throughout the country—and no wires?"

And the wise old rabbi answered, "So tell me, Alex—*with* wires you'd be able to understand?"

✓ ✓ ✓

The early telephones were primitive devices compared to the sophisticated electronic devices of today. Especially crude were the phones in a little town in Belgrade at the turn of the century.

It is told that Rabbi Gronsky was called to the house of a critically sick man who died within minutes of the good rabbi's arrival. It befell him to inform the deceased's relatives, but he was at a loss as to how to use the telephone. He asked one of those present how to operate it.

"First you crank the handle with one hand," he was told. "Then you hold the phone close to your ear with the other hand."

"What!" cried Rabbi Gronsky. "Then what will I talk with?"

✓ ✓ ✓

Georgie: "America's scientists are the greatest in the world."

Grandpa: "What's so great?"

Georgie: "Look at their achievements! Computers that can figure out problems that would take a human being a hundred years; space ships to the planets; mechanical hearts. There is absolutely nothing our scientists can't solve!"

Grandpa: "So why don't they invent something we shouldn't have to return to the bathroom to jiggle the hook?"

✓ ✓ ✓

A science major, proud of his vast knowledge, was bragging to his grandfather. "And furthermore," he went on, displaying his intimacy with

316

interstellar physics, "did you know that an astronaut's space suit costs over $60,000?"

"It's too much," said grandpa placidly, "considering that it only comes with one pair of pants."

✓   ✓   ✓

No one will take an oath that this anecdote is true, but the central character of the story, Albert Einstein, himself laughed when he heard it.

A group of nuclear physicists gathered in the gambling town of Las Vegas for a symposium. During their free time they congregated in one of the casinos, and it soon became apparent that Dr. Einstein was spending all his time at the dice and roulette tables.

"Einstein is gambling as if there were no tomorrow," remarked one of the scientists.

"What bothers me," said another worriedly, "is that he may know something."

✓   ✓   ✓

Some years ago Professor Albert Einstein and Dr. Chaim Weizmann sailed together to America on a Zionist mission. When they arrived in New York City, Dr. Weizmann was asked how he and the famous savant had spent their time on the boat.

"Throughout the voyage," Dr. Weizmann replied, "the learned professor kept on talking to me about his theory of relativity."

"And what is your opinion about it?"

"It seems to me," concluded Dr. Weizmann, "that Professor Einstein understands it very well."

✓   ✓   ✓

Professor Higgins: "Good morning, sir. How are you?"
Professor Einstein: "Relative to what?"

✓   ✓   ✓

Irving was deeply engrossed in a book on astronomy one evening when he came upon a startling passage. "Grandpa," he exclaimèd, looking up, "it says here the world will end in a billion years."

"What did you say?" cried Grandpa, his face ashen.

"The world will come to an end in a billion years."

"Oh," replied Grandpa breathing a sigh of relief. "I thought for a moment you said a million!"

Chapter Thirty

Culture

Alexander King, in his poignant and sometimes hilarious *Mine Enemies Grow Older*, observes that a joke is not necessarily a Jewish joke because the protagonists are called Abie and Jakie. In nine out of ten cases, says King, that is just a facile device for putting across a rabidly anti-Semitic point. An authentic "Jewish outlook" on life is nicely illustrated in the following story, one of the many which King tells so well.

One Sunday afternoon a couple of culture-bound young Jews, a brother and a sister, were determined to drag their poor old father to the Metropolitan Museum of Art. They nudged and maneuvered him from room to room until the poor old guy, who had spent most of his life standing over a pressing iron, nearly passed out from boredom and exhaustion.

But his daughter, determined to rally his flagging strength and attention, suddenly pointed to a large canvas of the Nativity, and said, "You see that painting over there, Papa? You know what the museum had to pay for it last year? Three quarters of a million dollars!"

The old man raised his eyeglasses higher on his nose and took a long, tired look at the canvas. "It's a family, eh?" he said.

"Yes," said his son.

"And this," he said, pointing at the Virgin, "this is the mama?"

"Yes," said the son.

"And this is the baby, eh? And why are they all sitting in this stable? And why are all those animals sniffing around them?"

"Because." said the daughter, "they were terribly poor people and they had no place to stay, except in the stable. You understand?"

The old man sadly shook his head from side to side and gave a great big sigh. "That's gentiles for you," he finally said. "Here they are, without a cent to their name, but they go and have expensive pictures taken."

✓   ✓   ✓

It was eight o'clock one morning when the telephone rang in Mrs. Offenberg's Whitechapel flat.

"This is the Third Secretary of the Order of the Garter," said the

318

unctuous voice on the other end of the line. "Her Majesty, the Queen, confirms that your daughter may make her presentation at the Court of St. James this Whitsunday."

"*Oy*, your Lordship," gasped Mrs. Offenberg, "have you got a wrong number!"

✓ ✓ ✓

No one is forcing you to believe it, but there's a matron in Beverly Hills who is so wealthy and eccentric that when she has a cold she first calls in a decorator before she lets the doctor paint her throat.

✓ ✓ ✓

When Manny Applebaum was promoted to foreman of the shop, his wife was overjoyed. Now she could have the things her artistic nature had always craved. As soon as the children were sent off to school, she went to Macy's and began selecting new wallpaper. But although she pored over dozens of patterns, nothing seemed to conform to her ideas of decorating.

"Perhaps," volunteered the weary sales clerk, "madam would like a border?"

"What kind of suggestion is that?" retorted Mrs. Applebaum. "My husband is now the shop foreman. Who needs a boarder?"

✓ ✓ ✓

Composer: "Well, hello there! If it isn't my old friend, the poet. How's your literary career progressing?"

Poet: "It couldn't be better! My poems are now read by twice as many people as when I first started."

Composer: "Well, *mazel tov*! I didn't know you'd gotten married!"

✓ ✓ ✓

Mrs. Weiss had recently come into a vast inheritance and, in keeping with her new position in society, had become a connoisseur of the arts. This, despite the fact that the only pictures she had ever seen were snapshots of her grandchildren and the reproductions on the calendars from the local mortuary.

Somehow she managed to wangle an invitation to the home of the great Picasso for a private showing of his latest works. Mrs. Weiss gushed over every painting, commenting with what she thought were knowledgeable critiques of each. Finally her attention became riveted on a display over the door. "*Oy*, Mr. Picasso," she exclaimed, "that is what I call a masterpiece—a regular dream! And the colors—beige on black; so artistical! The web effect, that I like. A sheer spider web? A futuristical waffle iron, maybe? What do you call it?"

"Mrs. Weiss," said Picasso coldly, "I call that an air conditioner!"

✓ ✓ ✓

Morris and Sol, two lifelong friends, finally retired from business, and they decided—more as a status symbol than for any other reason—to take a vacation in the modern, sophisticated manner, as befits men of circumstance and position. An African safari was the answer!

They arrived in the Congo, were outfitted by a supplier with tropical helmets, guns and all the accoutrements necessary for a successful hunt.

The next morning they set out for an area known to be inhabited by lions and tigers. As they were stalking through the jungle, about fifteen or twenty feet apart, Sol felt a heavy paw on his back. He stopped, rigid with fright, and too scared to turn around.

"Morris," he called, terror making his voice hoarse, "What's that pushing me from behind? A tiger? A lion?"

"How should I know?" Morris shouted back. "What am I, a furrier?"

✓   ✓   ✓

The age of Bar Mitzvah is supposed to bring with it the adult wisdom that a boy will need to meet the challenges of life. But a few do not attain such wisdom until they are much older.

Many friends and relatives had been invited to Jack's Bar Mitzvah party. A caterer had arranged everything beautifully, including an orchestra hired for those who wished to dance. But, of all the famous notables in attendance, the most important, by far, was Hyacinth DuPont, imperious matriarch of the DuPont clan of industrialists. She had condescended to accept the invitation only at the insistence of her husband who had some business dealings with the boy's father. After all, even to a multi-millionaire, a dollar is a dollar. There was still another reason why the dowager had been reluctant to come to the party. A formidable woman of extreme girth, with a bust measurement in the high fifties, she weighed three hundred pounds and waddled like a duck.

The festivities were at their height when Jack's mother noticed that no one had asked Mrs. DuPont to dance. She quickly drew her son aside.

"Jack, be a good boy and dance with Mrs. DuPont."

"Aw, Mom, have a heart!"

"Please!" she urged. "And be sure to say something nice to her. It'll be good for Daddy's business. Flatter her good!"

So the boy approached Mrs. DuPont. "May I have the honor of the next dance?" he asked in his most formal manner.

The matriarch thought this the cutest request she had heard in years and, smiling, she joined him on the dance floor. When the music stopped, Jack remembered his mother's admonition to say something complimentary.

"Mrs. DuPont," he said, "it was a pleasure to dance with you. You sweat less than any other fat lady I ever danced with in my whole life!"

✓   ✓   ✓

320

CULTURE

Lazar Brodsky, the lumber king of Kiev, was an immensely wealthy man, and like the Rothschilds of London and Paris, he was an almost legendary figure to his oppressed, impoverished co-religionists. It was the ambition of many Jews to meet him personally—or, at least, to catch a glimpse of the magnate through a window.

A certain Jew of a small Lithuanian community, through the influence of a prominent friend, was fortunate enough to enter the portals of the Brodsky mansion and have a peek into the living room. There he beheld two young ladies, the philanthropist's daughters, he was told. They were playing a duet on the piano.

When he returned home and his townfolk began to bombard him with questions about the millionaire's splendor, he stopped them with a disparaging shrug of his shoulders.

"Frankly, I wasn't at all impressed," he said. "I fail to see why people rave so much about Brodsky's wealth. Just imagine! Two girls forced to play on one piano! That's riches?"

✓ ✓ ✓

Mrs. Ginsberg: "Thank you for a lovely party, Mrs. Leibowitz. I want you to know your brownies were so tasty I ate four!"
Mrs. Leibowitz: "Five, but who counts?"

✓ ✓ ✓

Harold Solomon, the wealthy contractor from Bensonhurst, went to Florida and hit the big time in real estate. He built himself a palatial residence and then invited some friends over to see his new "town house." First he escorted them through the extensive kitchen and servants' quarters. Then he showed them the huge den and master bedrooms.

Then, with a flourish, he opened the floor-to-ceiling French doors and ushered them into the largest of the rooms. "This," he announced, "is the dining room. In here, twenty-five people can have dinner—God forbid!"

✓ ✓ ✓

Stanley and Clara, poor all their married lives, won first money in the Irish Sweepstakes.

"Let's go to Hawaii," cried the joyful wife. "I'd just love to visit the Islands!"

"A waste of good money," objected Stanley. "We already saw all the interesting ones."

"What are you talking about?" asked the surprised wife. "Which islands?"

Stanley, always the loyal New Yorker, took a deep breath, and then told her: "Manhattan, Staten, Ellis, Fire, Long and Coney!"

✓ ✓ ✓

Louis Pintner had been promising his wife and seven children that he would take them on a picnic one weekend, but time and again he was compelled to postpone the occasion because of business. One lovely June day, however, he cleaned out his truck, loaded his family aboard and, with happy shouts, they set out for a carefree day in the country.

They were about fifty miles from home, in an unfamiliar part of the state, when Mrs. Pintner cried out: "Oh, look at that beautiful park! Let's stop here!"

They turned off the road, parked, and seated themselves on the well-kept grass and proceeded to unwrap their picnic lunch—a huge variety of goodies including hardboiled eggs, pickles, olives, fried chicken, apples, oranges, soft drinks, potato chips, cookies and candy bars. After all, Mrs. Pintner had been planning the outing for months. They were all ravenous, and soon the area was littered with orange peels, egg shells, pop bottles and other debris.

Suddenly the pastoral quiet was shattered by an angry voice. A uniformed guard strode into the picnic circle and demanded, "What are you doing here?"

"What's the matter?" asked Pintner. "This is a public park, isn't it?"

"This is nothing of the kind!" barked the irate guard. "You happen to be on the property of the Burning Tree Golf Club—the most exclusive in the United States!"

"I never heard of it!" said Pintner defensively.

"I'll have you know that some of the most prominent men in America play on this course. Why, just to join this club you have to pay an initiation fee of $3,000. The annual dues alone come to $500. The club spends a fortune just to keep these grounds in good shape. Now look what you've done with your picnic garbage—ruined a $5,000 piece of property. I ought to knock your teeth out!"

"Just a minute," said Pintner with sweet reasonableness. "Is this a way to get new members?"

✓ ✓ ✓

Mrs. Pollack and Mrs. Golom both belonged to the group of *nouveaux riches* who, despite their lack of education, were eager to be seen in concert halls and the theatre.

One Saturday night, Mrs. Pollack telephoned Mrs. Golom. "This evening," she boasted, "we are going to the *Marriage of Figaro.*"

"What's the matter?" asked her friend. "You can't send a telegram?"

✓ ✓ ✓

Mollie Goodstein, budding young daughter of Mrs. Henrietta Goodstein, President of the Krasnopolsker Ladies' Progressive and Sick Benefit Association, rose to make her speech. She had been asked to report on what cultural work the organization could do.

CULTURE

In excellent English the young woman told the members that the best thing they could do was to help fellow immigrants to be naturalized. "I cannot think of anything finer for this club than naturalization work," concluded Miss Goodstein. Her remarks were applauded thunderously.

It was a great ordeal for the mother to follow her daughter. Mrs. Goodstein had not mastered English, but to talk Yiddish at this point would have been a terrible comedown. She therefore continued in broken English:

"Ladies, I rise to secon' my daughter's mawshun. I know a nice Jewish woman in my block who came a long time ago from ol' country, and yet she does not have her—ah—natur . . . natural . . . naturaliz . . ."

A member interrupted. "Madam President," she said, "why don't you say in plain Yiddish: 'tzidditzin papers'?"

✓ ✓ ✓

George Jessel, an art connoisseur, telephoned his mother and told her he had just purchased a Rubens.

"Rubin? Rubin the delicatessen man?"

"No, Mama, Rubens is a painter," he explained gently.

"Oh, this I didn't know," she said breathlessly. "Listen, Georgie, ask him how much he'll charge to paint the kitchen!"

✓ ✓ ✓

Aging Max Bloom was very proud of the fact that he had arrived in this country without a penny to his name, and through hard work and perseverance, had managed to send his son to college. Recently, his son had been promoted to the managership of Carnegie Hall, and tonight, old Max was to attend his first performance.

They arrived at the concert hall a half hour before curtain time and Max noticed on a large sign at the door:

TONIGHT ONLY!
"HAMLET—OR THE PRINCE OF DENMARK"

The old man turned to his son, his voice disapproving. "What kind of manager are you?" he scolded. "On opening night, you still don't know which program you're playing?"

✓ ✓ ✓

The Tremont Avenue auxiliary of Hadassah notified its members that, as a fund-raising device, the club would present a performance of Shakespeare's *King Lear*.

Among the spectators was Mrs. Kowalsky, attending the first stage play of her life. She was simply enthralled with the presentation and when the actors had taken their bows she called out, "Author! Author!" just as she had seen in the movies.

Mrs. Kowalsky's thoroughly assimilated son, seated next to her, whispered fiercely, "Mama, for God's sake, stop hollering so! Shakespeare is dead!"

"Oh, that's too bad," she replied sympathetically. "It's the same with all great artists—they don't live long enough to see their plays performed."

"It's not that, Mama," the son hissed, as other patrons nearby stared at them curiously. "He was taken long ago."

Mrs. Kowalsky, who had been born and reared under the oppressive reign of the Czar, clucked compassionately:

"*Oy*, poor Shakespeare! I didn't even know he'd been arrested!"

✓ ✓ ✓

This editor's uncle and aunt, Sam and Bella Monoson, collaborated on this delightful offering:

Sadie Hirschkowitz, a poor widow, awoke one morning to learn that a distant relative she had never seen had died and left her a sizable fortune. Nothing would do, of course, but that she immediately move from her East Side flat to a beautiful apartment on Riverside Drive. In her new home, the first thing Sadie did was to call in an interior decorator—a bleached blonde young man named Sylvia—you know the type.

"Mrs. Hirschkowitz," he lisped, "would you like the decor in Italian Rennaissance?"

"Eh-eh!"

"How about French Modern? That's perfectly adorable!" he said in his soprano voice.

"Mmmmm!!"

"Well, many discerning people today prefer German Provincial."

"German? *Feh*!"

"I have it! Perhaps you'd like Colonial English!"

"English-shminglish!" retorted Sadie. "Listen, just make it so that when my friends come to see me, they should take one look at my fancy furnishings and they should drop dead!"

✓ ✓ ✓

An elderly couple, recently emigrated from Europe, decided it would be nice to meet some of the people who sunned themselves in the nearby park every day. In order to show that they were "educated," they brought along a copy of the *New York Times*, although neither could read a word of English.

They found a bench near other Jewish gossipers of the afternoon, sat down, opened the newspaper, and pretended to read.

"Yankel," whispered the old lady to her husband, "turn your part of the paper around. You're holding it upside down!"

"How do you know?" her husband whispered back, just as fiercely. "You can't read English either."

"See the picture of that man?" she asked, pointing to an advertisement. "By you he's walking on the ceiling?"

✓ ✓ ✓

CULTURE

Madame Cornelia Broadbottom was planning the coming-out party for her debutante daughter and sought to hire the best entertainment available, so she sent for the famed concert violinist, Jascha Heifetz.

"My fee will be $5,000 for the evening," Heifetz told her.

"Very well, my good man," agreed Madam Broadbottom, "but there is one stipulation upon which I must insist. I do not permit Jewish entertainers to mingle with my guests."

"In that case," replied Heifetz, "my fee is only $500."

✓ ✓ ✓

It was Goldie's second week in America, and today her cousin Reuben was going to show her the cultural sights of New York. Reuben had been in this country for almost a year and was quite proud of his familiarity with the city's points of interest.

Goldie and Reuben visited the Museum of Art, the Bronx Zoo, the Statue of Liberty, and finally went over to Riverside Drive to view Grant's Tomb.

"This is where President Ulysses S. Grant is buried," explained Reuben, bursting with pride over his knowledge of Americana.

Goldie looked up at the imposing edifice and gasped in awe. "Tell me, why is the building so high?"

Reuben scratched his head for a moment and then his face lit up. "I think," he replied, "it's because he was buried standing up!"

✓ ✓ ✓

"Mama, I'll be a little late for dinner this evening," said the young man. "I'm going to the new art gallery."

"It doesn't sound like a decent place for a nice Jewish boy," said Mama dubiously, thinking of the nude paintings that might be on display.

"It's perfectly respectable," smiled the son. "And to prove it, I'm thinking of bringing Whistler's Mother home for the living room."

Mama gasped. "But there's no place for her in the living room. She'll just have to sleep with your sister!"

✓ ✓ ✓

Three somewhat overdressed, bejewelled ladies were dining in a posh hotel, each of them trying to outdo the other in the matter of wealth.

"When my diamonds get dirty I have them cleaned only at Tiffany's," said the first in her typical grand manner.

"Tiffany's! What's Tiffany's?" sniffed the second lady. "My husband won't allow me to have them cleaned anywhere but at Cartier's. Not only that, but Mr. Cartier's got to do it personally."

"Who knows about cleaning diamonds?" said the third airily. "When my diamonds get dirty I just throw them in the garbage can!"

✓ ✓ ✓

Grandma Himmelfarb had not been in this country long when her son made a success with a new line of blouses, and his small shop suddenly became a large manufacturing concern. In keeping with their new social status, the entire family moved to Tarrytown so that they might mingle with the commuting *hoi polloi*.

But Grandma soon learned that she was being ignored by the *hoi*, to say nothing of the *polloi*, because she was unable to discuss the subject of opera with some degree of familiarity. So, at her first opportunity, she attended a performance of *La Traviata* at the Metropolitan Opera House.

At the next meeting of the Tarrytown Ladies Guild, the president of that association asked Grandma Himmelfarb what she thought of the heroine.

"*Oy!*" gushed Grandma ecstatically. "Never in my whole life did I hear such a beautiful *matzoh*-soprano!"

✓ ✓ ✓

Seymour and Ruthie Kolnitz, prosperous citizens of Olympia, Washington, decided to celebrate their twentieth wedding anniversary with a trip to New York—the first time either had been to the city ever since they landed at Ellis Island many years before.

They checked into a hotel and, in order to save time, took a guided tour of the places of interest. The sight-seeing bus visited Chinatown, the East Side, the famous buildings, and then New York's exclusive "Silk Stocking" district on Fifth Avenue, adjoining Central Park.

"On our right," said the guide, "is the Vanderbilt mansion."

"Cornelius Vanderbilt?" asked Seymour, trying to impress his wife with his worldly knowledge.

"No, William," corrected the guide.

"And here is the magnificent Astor residence," the guide continued.

"John Jacob?" queried Seymour.

"No, Vincent," answered the guide.

"And here," announced the guide, "is the world famous Christ Church."

Ruthie tugged at her husband's sleeve and hissed: "Seymour, don't ask any more foolish questions. You'll only be wrong again!"

✓ ✓ ✓

Simon Halevi, a pleasant though vain sort of chap, suddenly acquired great wealth. To impress his relatives, friends and neighbors, he bought a Lincoln Continental and a Rembrandt.

At lunchtime, he telephoned his wife. "Harriette, I ordered a Lincoln Continental and a Rembrandt," he told her. "Have they been delivered yet?"

"One of them came," Harriette answered uncertainly, "but I don't know which."

✓ ✓ ✓

CULTURE

Society parvenu Tillie Golden went to a literary tea, just so she could boast to her old friends of her intimacy with *belles lettres*.

"Have you read the *Kinsey Report*?" she was asked.

"No," replied Tillie. "I'm waiting it should come out in the movies!"

✓   ✓   ✓

Mama: "What's the matter you're not seeing that nice young dentist anymore? You told me you both like the same things."

Daughter: "We do, Mama. He and I like the same books, the same plays, the same food. The only trouble is we don't like each other!"

✓   ✓   ✓

For twenty-five years Anna and Aaron had scrimped and saved, doing without all of the luxuries and many of the necessities of life. Every penny they could spare was invested in stocks and bonds. Suddenly, one morning, they awoke to find that a soaring market had made them rich beyond their wildest dreams.

Both were ambitious and insatiable social climbers. They bought a town house and hobnobbed with the elite of Long Island, Cape Cod, Penobscot Bay and—what else?—Miami. For their housewarming, they invited the *crème de la crème* of *Who's Who*.

After a princely banquet, Anna ordered the special society orchestra to play some appropriate music, and their first offering was a selection from Brahms.

"What kind of funeral music is that for such a happy occasion?" demanded Anna, breaking the enraptured silence like a bombshell.

"Shh—it's Brahms!" snarled Aaron, *sotto voce*, a cautioning finger to his lips.

"Oh, Brahms!" said Anna brightly. "I met him on the West Side the other day. He was walking on Fifth Avenue, and we bowed to each other."

All eyes turned toward Anna who was blissfully unaware that she had committed a monumental boo-boo. But the distinguished guests were too well-bred, of course, to correct her.

That night, when everyone had gone home, Aaron turned on her, absolutely furious. "Never in my whole life was I so disgraced!" he shouted. "You and your big mouth!"

"What are you talking? I said something wrong?"

"Wrong? It was horrible! Everybody knows that Fifth Avenue is not on the West Side!"

✓   ✓   ✓

The local chairman of the school board in a small farming community, who was also a dealer in hogs, was walking along the street when a school teacher passed by without greeting him.

"Just a moment, there!" called the chairman. "Would you be kind enough to tell me why you did not give me a courteous greeting just now —why you cannot be more respectful to the man who puts bread and butter on your table?"

"Mister Chairman, let's be fair about this," the teacher countered. "You earn your money from pigs, but do you greet them respectfully?"

✓   ✓   ✓

An untutored but wealthy merchant who yearned to be known as a cultured gentleman, arrived late at the concert one evening because his wife had taken so long to dress.

The concert had already started when they entered the hall and the husband asked the usher what part of the program was being played.

"They are playing Beethoven's Fifth Symphony," whispered the usher.

"It's all your fault," the husband complained to his wife as they took their seats. "If you hadn't taken almost two hours to dress we wouldn't have missed the first four."

✓   ✓   ✓

Simon Shapinsky from Poland was visiting his cousin Dave Jacobson in London. One day Jacobson took his guest on a sightseeing tour around the city, visiting the historic monuments and ogling the beautiful homes of the very rich.

Shapinsky, who had never dreamed that such gorgeous residences existed, exclaimed ecstatically at each mansion, "I should live in a house like this!"

In the course of the day, they passed by Buckingham Palace, but this time Shapinsky did not utter a word. He just stared glumly at the magnificent home of the royal family.

"*Nu*, why so silent?" asked cousin Dave. "Wouldn't you like to live here?"

"God forbid!" answered Shapinsky. "The cost of *mezuzahs* alone would ruin me!"

✓   ✓   ✓

For some weeks a young woman had plagued the renowned pianist, Arthur Rubinstein, to give her an audition. Finally, in hope of getting rid of her once and for all, he called her into his studio.

"Oh, if only you would consent to be my teacher, I know I could become a great concert pianist," she gushed.

"Very well," replied Rubinstein, "I will listen to you. Please be seated at the piano."

For half an hour the poor man listened in silent torture as the woman played, her notes sounding as though she were hitting the keys with an umbrella handle.

CULTURE

When the woman finished her "concert" she turned to Rubinstein and asked, "Well, what do you think?"

"I think, Madam," he said wearily, "that you should get married!"

✓   ✓   ✓

Bertha and her husband were watching a very sad play—an old-fashioned melodrama about unrequited love in which one of the sweethearts commits suicide and the other is beset with tragedy after bitter tragedy. Before the first act was over every woman in the theatre was weeping.

But Bertha's husband was unmoved. "Ridiculous!" he snorted every few minutes. At one particular scene, as the heroine lay dying in her lover's arms, and Bertha sobbed aloud, he actually laughed.

Bertha turned to him. "Look," she cried furiously through her tears, "if you don't like the play why don't you go home and at least let me enjoy myself!"

✓   ✓   ✓

Cynthia Ostrow, now teaching art in a mid-Western university, tells this funny little story about the time she went to Rome to visit the museums as part of her studies. Because there was no one to stay with her aged grandfather she insisted that he accompany her, despite his violent protests.

"You'll have a chance to see the ancient masters," she argued.

"Old Italians I can see right here in America," he insisted. But, as always, granddaughter Cynthia had her way.

In Rome, they visited the Vatican where she and the old man toured the Sistine Chapel. Cynthia pointed toward the gorgeous roof. "Grandpa, do you know that it took four whole years to get that ceiling painted?" she asked in awed tones.

"Four years!" exclaimed Grandpa. "The Pope and I must have the same landlord!"

✓   ✓   ✓

Then there's the story of the girl who desperately hoped to become an opera star, but although she had a superb voice, was unable to make the grade.

Being half Spanish and half Jewish, she could never remember whether she was Carmen or *goyim!*

✓   ✓   ✓

It is no disgrace to be born poor and it is no disgrace to die poor, but in between, what does it hurt to be rich?

✓   ✓   ✓

The Mendelsohns were perfectly contented with their housekeeper, especially when good domestic help was so difficult to find. So they were

329

chagrined to learn that the woman was about to quit her job. "I'm pregnant," she announced, "and everybody knows I don't have a husband."

But the Mendelsohn family provided a solution. "We'll adopt the baby," they told her, "and you can stay right here as always."

All went well for the next two years, when the housekeeper announced, rather shamefacedly, that she was "expecting" again.

"Rather than lose you," said the Mendelsohns, "we'll adopt this baby, too."

The following year, the housekeeper again had an appointment with the maternity ward, but so valuable was she to her employers that they adopted the third baby.

As soon as she was out of the hospital, the housekeeper approached her benefactors. "I'm quitting," she said, her voice hard with determination.

"But why?" they gasped.

"Because when I came to work for you," she snapped, "you didn't tell me I'd have to work for a family with three kids!"

✓ ✓ ✓

"Grandpa, I'm really proud of you," said the modish young lady.

"What's to be proud?" asked the old man.

"I notice that when you sneeze you've learned to put your hand in front of your mouth."

"Of course," explained Grandpa. "How else can I catch my teeth?"

✓ ✓ ✓

Phil Levy, a refugee from eastern Europe, emigrated to France where he opened a small *kosher* restaurant. The business was an overnight success and before long he became immensely wealthy, and even changed his name to Francois LeVeigh. As with all good Parisians of his standing, Francois entered politics, and soon became embroiled in a hot political controversy. Unfortunately, he became so carried away with the sound of his own voice that he overstepped the bounds of decorum and called his opponent a vile name.

His political opponent, one of the best pistol-shots in all of France, immediately challenged M. LeVeigh to a duel—and because he was the offended party it was his prerogative to choose the weapon. Naturally, he chose revolvers.

As dawn broke on the fateful morning, the opponent and his seconds were waiting for Francois at the appointed place. But no Francois. An hour later they were still waiting, and still no Francois. Finally, two hours after the agreed-upon time, a courier arrived on horseback. He handed the opponent a note:

"Sir:

A few matters of business detained me. But please don't bother waiting. If you get tired, just go ahead and shoot.
FRANCOIS LeVEIGH"

✓ ✓ ✓

CULTURE

Joey Adams: "I took my wife to the *Folies Bergère*. That's like taking a meatball to a twelve course dinner."

✓ ✓ ✓

Mama, much against her will, was persuaded to visit the Bronx Zoo so that she might absorb some of the culture of the city. Her daughter steered her to the lion house.

"That small animal," said the daughter helpfully, "is a leopard. It belongs to the feline family."

Mama nodded. "*Azoi!* And the city is taking care of it while the Felines are on vacation?"

✓ ✓ ✓

A greenhorn, just arrived from a small village near Odessa, burst into his apartment and made a beeline for the bathroom. He called to his wife, "We're going to be rich. Regular millionaires!"

His wife scurried into the bathroom. "What do you mean?"

The greenhorn pointed to the water closet. "How much is that thing costing us?"

"Why, nothing!" she exclaimed, surprised.

"Exactly," he smiled. "But downtown—I saw the sign with my very own eyes in a store window—they're selling toilet water for $3.50 a small bottle."

✓ ✓ ✓

"Daddy, were we poor when I was a little girl?" asked sixteen-year-old Ruthie.

"Honey, when we first came to this country from Rumania we were so poor we had to live in a shack. On one side was the City Dump, on the other side was the stockyards, on the west was a glue factory and on the east was a fertilizer plant."

"Gee, Daddy, why didn't you move?"

"Because, Ruthie dear," the father grinned, "we wanted to know which way the wind was blowing."

✓ ✓ ✓

Jackie came home from school one day to find his mother in a new mink coat.

"Gosh, Mom, that poor animal must have suffered terribly just so you could have a fur coat."

"Why, Jackie!" exclaimed the mother, shocked. "What kind of way is that to talk about your father?"

✓ ✓ ✓

Only in Beverly Hills: The small son of a rich movie producer was having a heated argument with the son of a wealthy director.

"My father can lick your father," yelled the producer's son.

"Oh yeah?" shouted the director's boy. "Well my analyst can lick your analyst!"

✓ ✓ ✓

Helen and Joe paid their check at the restaurant and prepared to leave when Joe noticed the dark cloud on his wife's face.

"What's with you?" Joe demanded.

"You disgraced me again," snapped Helen. "Even the waiter noticed how you gobbled your food."

"What are you talking? I didn't eat fast."

"Listen, Joe," snapped Helen, "you grabbed so fast for your dessert the echo of the soup hadn't even died down."

✓ ✓ ✓

Nothing could shake Chaim Hirsch's negative outlook on the foibles, mores and superficialities of American life. His son, thinking to divert the oldster from his obsession with the nostalgic past, one day persuaded him to visit the Aquarium. After studying the many exhibits and elbowing his way through the milling crowds, the elderly scholar pleaded that they return home. "Allright already, I've seen the Aquarium, so be happy," he grumbled.

"Weren't you excited about this magnificent place?" demanded the son.

"What's to get excited?" said the father wearily. "A flooded fish market I can always see on Hester Street."

✓ ✓ ✓

Stanley and Gertrude, a couple of *nouveaux riches,* moved from the East Bronx to Riverside Drive, and to furnish their new apartment in the style in which they planned to become accustomed, they went to an exclusive Fifth Avenue furniture salon.

The salesman, a perfumed, obsequious man, showed them an antique bedroom suite. This," he said, "is a genuine restoration. The bed, you will notice, is an authentic Louis XIV."

Stanley was all for making the purchase at once, but Gertrude eyed the length and width of the bed with misgivings, well aware of her own girth. "It's a little too small," she finally said. "Can you show us maybe a Louis XV or XVI?"

✓ ✓ ✓

Malke Meyerson had always wanted to sing opera, and now that the children were grown and she had a little money to spare she went to a voice teacher.

The teacher seated himself at the piano. "I'll play a few bars and you can accompany me," he said. "Then I'll be able to judge whether you have any talent."

Smiling, Malke agreed, and the teacher began to play an aria from *Aida*. But with her first note the musician shuddered. She emitted a screech, her voice broke on middle notes and almost shattered the windows on the highs. When he played "re" she sang "mi." When he hit "fa" she bellowed "so."

Finally he could stand it no longer. "Mrs. Meyerson," he said slowly, "why is it that when I play the white keys you sing the black keys; when I play the black keys you sing the white keys; and when I play both, you sing the cracks?"

✓   ✓   ✓

Fat and middle-aged Malke was boasting to her next-door neighbor about her earlier musical achievements. "When I was a girl," she said, "I not only sang at the Metropolitan Opera House but I was the most beautiful diva they ever had."

"You sang at the Met?" echoed the neighbor suspiciously. "What was the aria?"

"How do I know?" retorted Malke. "What am I, an architect?"

Chapter Thirty-one

Quick Wits and Taut Retorts

Not long after the destruction of the Second Temple when numberless captives had been brought to Rome in fetters, a Roman senator acquired a Jewish slave—a scholar versed in business principles and adept with figures. In a short time he had made himself so indispensable to the nobleman, and because of his caustic wit, he had virtually become one of the royal family.

One day the senator observed his slave poring over a roster of names. "What have you got there?" he inquired curiously.

"This, your Eminence, is a list of fools in your employ."

Intrigued, the senator studied the list closely and was astonished to find his name among the others. "What's the meaning of this?" he roared.

"Forgive me, your Eminence," replied the Jewish slave calmly, "but I placed your name on the fool's list only a few days ago, when you advanced credit to the Greek merchant for a thousand bags of grain."

"But he's certain to repay it," the Roman protested. "He's an honest man. When he returns to Greece and sells the grain he'll return to Rome and pay me my due."

The Jewish slave shrugged but made no reply.

"If he does return and pay for the grain, then what will you have to say?" the senator persisted stubbornly.

"In that case," answered the Jew, "I'll take your name off my list of fools and replace it with his!"

✦ ✦ ✦

"Americans are a strange breed," quipped David Ben-Gurion. "They devote one day a year to fathers and a whole week to pickles."

✦ ✦ ✦

Albert Einstein, guest of honor at an intercollegiate banquet of his peers, was describing conditions in Nazi Germany. The dean of Harvard interrupted.

"Dr. Einstein, I cannot understand how Germany, a nation that was foremost among the liberal arts and sciences, could have succumbed to the anti-intellectualism of Nazi philosophy. What in the world happened there?"

"I'll tell you what happened," replied Einstein. "The German people were imbued with three qualities: honesty, intelligence and Nazism. However, our Creator, in His wisdom, decreed that because we mortals are partly creatures of free will, a German could only possess two of the three qualities. That is why a German who is honest and also a Nazi cannot be intelligent. If he is intelligent and a Nazi, he cannot be honest. And if he is honest and intelligent, he cannot be a Nazi."

✓   ✓   ✓

A rabbi learned that a member of his congregation had played pinochle on the previous Sabbath. At his very first opportunity he confronted the gambler.

"You should be ashamed of yourself," the rabbi scolded. "Surely you know that playing cards on *Shabbes,* especially for money, is sinful."

"Yes, I know," sighed the other, "but believe me, Rabbi, I paid heavily for my sin!"

✓   ✓   ✓

A Russian Jew was arrested by the Soviet secret police when they found American matches in his possession.

When his trial came up, he told the judge, "Your Honor, it is true that I was using Capitalistic matches, but only to light our People's matches."

✓   ✓   ✓

Rabbi Meyer Malbim, the famous commentator on the Bible, was a man of wide erudition. His knowledge did not consist of talmudic lore alone, as was the case with most Orthodox rabbis of his time, but included, among other things, science and geography.

One time the sage came to Berlin on a visit, and engaged a suite in a hotel patronized chiefly by his co-religionists. As he stood in the lobby of the hostelry one evening, studying a huge map that decorated one of the walls, two "modern" Jews sat nearby and chuckled. It seemed utterly ridiculous to the two "emancipated" Jews to see an Orthodox rabbi engrossed in a map. The outwardly-appearing illiterate old man, they thought, was either pretending or else looking at it from sheer curiosity. So the pair decided to have a little fun with the patriarchal gentleman. They approached and engaged him in conversation.

"Do you know what this is?" asked one, with a knowing wink at his companion.

The old rabbi studied the two out of his shrewd, intelligent eyes. Then he countered with a question of his own: "Suppose you tell me?"

"Why, it's a map of the whole world!" came the grinning reply.

"Is Palestine here too?"

"Sure! Here it is."

"And can you see the Temple here?"

The two strangers could scarcely suppress their mirth. "The Temple is right here where the dot is," they explained.

"Then do me a favor," said the rabbi, now taking his own turn to smile. "Please go inside and tell the *shammes* I want to see him!"

✔   ✔   ✔

"Marriage," said the rabbi after the wedding ceremonies, "is like a violin. When the beautiful music is over the strings are still attached."

✔   ✔   ✔

"Rabbi, I have a ritual question to ask," said Velvel. "A real problem."

"*Nu*, what's the problem?"

"I have a hen and a rooster and one of them has to be sacrificed for our Sabbath dinner. But which will it be—the rooster or the hen? If I take the rooster, the hen raises such a tumult that the noise drives me crazy. But if I take the hen, the rooster shrieks so that my blood curdles. Tell me, what shall I do?"

The rabbi mulled the matter over for a few moments and then gave his decision. "You really have no problem," he said. "According to Jewish law you must take the hen."

"But you're forgetting the rooster," protested Velvel. "He'll scream and holler as though I had wounded him."

"So he'll scream and holler," answered the rabbi mildly. "There's a law that makes you stand there and listen?"

✔   ✔   ✔

The Grand Rabbi of Bucharest first said it:

"The division between man and woman is not as important as the multiplication."

✔   ✔   ✔

The rabbi had a penchant for hell-fire and brimstone preaching. One Sabbath, however, after an unusually critical tirade, he realized that he had gone too far.

"My friends," he went on quickly, "I did not really intend all those harsh words in my sermon for you. In reality, I was merely addressing myself. However, I am a little hard of hearing, and I may have spoken a little too loudly. So, if you happened to overhear my self-criticism— excuse me!"

✔   ✔   ✔

When Professor Mandelstam returned from the first Zionist Congress, he undertook to interest the wealthy men of Kiev in giving contributions for Palestine. He called a meeting of all the prominent men of the city, including the very wealthy Brodsky. Mandelstam proceeded to inspire his audience with the Zionist ideal, telling them how urgent it was for each to assist in building up the Holy Land.

"Do you mean, Professor, that I should sell all my land and real estate and settle in Palestine?" Brodsky asked.

"God forbid!" Mandelstam retorted. "Are you a patient in all the hospitals to which you contribute?"

🥖 🥖 🥖

David Schatz, the only Jewish inhabitant in a village not far from Warsaw, drove into the big city to make some necessary purchases. He was afraid to leave his horse alone, and addressed a respectable-looking passerby:

"*Reb Yid*, will you be good enough to help me out? Take care of my horse while I pay a brief visit to the store across the street."

"How dare you ask me to mind your horse?" cried the stranger indignantly. "Do you know who I am?"

"*Nu*, who are you?"

"I happen to be manager of the central office of the Jewish community, that's who!"

"All right, so you're the manager," said David calmly. "But if I trust you, what do you care?"

🥖 🥖 🥖

A young student prided himself on his ability to confuse the wisest of scholars. Once, when he was surrounded by friends, he sought to prove his self-asserted cleverness, so he asked the town sage, "What was the first thing Eve did when Adam came home late one night?"

"She counted his ribs," said the sage promptly.

🥖 🥖 🥖

A female officer of the Salvation Army entered a small East Side restaurant where a group of middle-aged bachelors usually dined and then stayed to play cards. The girl approached their table and held out her tambourine as a receptacle for coins.

"Won't you give something for New York's fallen women?" she coaxed.

Replied one of the bachelors, "Sorry, but I'm already giving direct."

🥖 🥖 🥖

A certain *shnorrer* of Prague so enflamed the people of his city against him because of his monumental *chutzpah*, that he decided to move to another town. But how does an unknown *shnorrer* compete against the native beggars in a strange city? Obviously he would require a different approach. After much thought, an idea occurred to him. He would grow a long, well-groomed beard and, dressed in an immaculate gabardine, he would pose as a *lamdan*.

337

In the new town, the patriarchal-looking "talmudic scholar" was at once invited to the rabbi's house for dinner. Several other dignitaries were present, and, when the *rebbetzn* had cleared away the dishes, they fell into a heated dispute over the interpretation of a difficult passage in the Talmud; one of those hair-splitting controversies so beloved of Orthodox Jews everywhere. Unable to conclude the wrangle, they turned to the newcomer for his interpretation.

The *shnorrer*, who had never even heard of the passage, thought for a moment and then answered glibly:

"I cannot blame you for asking a *lamdan* like me for his opinion. As a scholar I am very well able to answer correctly. But just suppose that you had asked this question of another *lamdan* who was not as brilliant as I? You would have humiliated him in front of everyone. Therefore, just to teach you a lesson in manners, I'm not going to tell you!"

✦ ✦ ✦

The elderly Aaron Zimmerman found it necessary to travel to the city of Vienna. He purchased a second class ticket but entered the first class compartment instead. There he remained undisturbed, contentedly smoking his pipe until the train reached the Prerau station. At that point the Archbishop of Olmütz was expected to occupy the compartment which had been reserved for him.

So important was the Archbishop that an official of the railroad personally went to the compartment to inspect it before the prince of the church arrived. But when he found the old Jew inside, fouling up the air with his unfragrant pipe, he hit the ceiling.

"Get out of here at once!" shouted the official, his anger bringing him close to apoplexy. "This compartment is reserved for the bishop."

"*Nu*, what's the commotion?" answered old Zimmerman placidly. "Who said I am not the bishop?"

✦ ✦ ✦

Speaking of bishops, the comedian, Joey Bishop, was asked why his father, a rabbi, had not changed his name, as had the son.

"He was quite right to keep his Jewish name," said Joey. "After all,. how would it sound to address him as 'Rabbi Bishop'?"

✦ ✦ ✦

Here is a classic expression of wit well-known and often repeated by the Jews of earlier decades.

Col. Robert Ingersoll, the famed agnostic, was scheduled to lecture at the Hartford Opera House. The coming event aroused widespread interest, and Mark Twain (also an agnostic, but a compassionate man) was asked if he planned to attend.

"No," replied Twain. "I understand that Ingersoll will talk about what he thinks of Moses. But I would be far more interested in hearing what Moses thinks of Ingersoll."

✓ ✓ ✓

Professor Josephus Bronstein, instructor of Jewish history at CCNY, was once invited to a prom dance by his students. Surprisingly, the ordinarily aloof instructor showed up. At the height of the festivities, the Queen of the Prom, a lovely girl who was one of his pupils, approached him. To her (and everyone else's) amazement, the scholarly professor soundly kissed her.

"Oh, my God!" gasped the surprised girl.

"Let's dispense with the titles," he grinned. "For tonight only, just call me Joe!"

✓ ✓ ✓

A priest and a rabbi, longtime friends, were discussing the oddities of their respective religions.

"Rabbi, tell me, why do you Jews persist in wearing both a *yarmulkeh* and a hat? Isn't the hat sufficient without the skull cap?"

"Now just a moment, my friend," retorted the rabbi. "Your own cardinals and bishops wear a head covering at church services. Even your Pope wears a *yarmulkeh*."

"That, dear rabbi, is symbolic of a roof over their heads. But you haven't answered my question."

"I'm developing my thesis," smiled the rabbi. "A cow in a stable has a roof over his head. We Jews want not only the roof that even a cow is entitled to, but a symbol of civilization as well—a ceiling!"

✓ ✓ ✓

Rabbi Stephen S. Wise, much in demand as a lecturer, was rarely seen in his own synagogue because of his many speaking engagements.

"How is it," he was once asked, "that your congregation doesn't fire you?"

"They can't, very well," said the rabbi with a merry twinkle in his eye. "They have to find me, first!"

✓ ✓ ✓

A *Galitzianer* grew tired of hearing his wife constantly praising the *Sephardic* Jews on her side of the family.

"I'll tell you something," he said one evening. "I have reached the conclusion that all *Sephardic* Jews are deeply religious."

"How do you figure that?" asked the wife.

"Because," he snapped, "you have convinced me that they all worship each other."

✓ ✓ ✓

Dr. Albert Einstein, at a testimonial dinner:
"The most aggravating thing about the younger generation is that I no longer belong to it!"

✓ ✓ ✓

Two women were in their back yards, and boasting about their respective home towns as they hung out the wash.
"Where I come from," bragged the first, "we girls could get beautiful pearls from almost any large oyster."
"So what?" retorted the second. "Where I come from, we girls could get expensive diamonds from any little shrimp!"

✓ ✓ ✓

An aspiring young poet came to the home of a well-known literary critic and begged him to give an opinion on his new book of poems.
Trapped in his own living room, the critic nodded glumly and after twenty tortured minutes of listening to the poorly written verses, he dozed off.
"Sir," cried the poet, "how can you pass an opinion on my poetry when you are sound asleep?"
"Believe me," answered the critic, "when I fell asleep I was definitely expressing an opinion."

✓ ✓ ✓

Here is an oldie, but a goodie!
Harry Rosenberg bought a shiny new Studebaker, but as he was too nervous to drive, his wife, Ida, took the wheel. Ida drove masterfully, going uptown on Lexington Avenue, when they reached 102nd Street—one of the steepest hills in all New York.
Immediately the Studebaker shot out from beneath them, careening wildly down the steep incline, gathering speed by the second.
"The brakes won't hold!" Ida gasped as the foot pedal went down to the floorboard. She grabbed for the emergency brake. It flopped loosely in her hand. "*Oy vay,* what'll I do!" she wailed as the car hit ninety miles per hour, completely out of control.
"Ida, for God's sake!" Harry screamed. "Hit something cheap!"

✓ ✓ ✓

"Anyone in the clothing business will agree that men are smarter than women," claimed lovely Sharon Lynn Koffman, Hollywood's youngest fashion designer. "Did you ever see a man buy a shirt that buttons in the back?"

✓ ✓ ✓

Toastmaster George Jessel listened attentively as the chairman at an Israel Bonds banquet described, in eloquent terms, the Holy Land's accomplishments in cultivating arid areas.

"For the first time since the Creation," explained the chairman, "apples are growing in many territories of the country."

Jessel, apparently, did not agree with the statement. When it came his time to speak, he asked, "Who says they never had apples? What did Adam bite into—a dill pickle?"

✓ ✓ ✓

The late Supreme Court Justice, Felix Frankfurter, had a tongue that could clip a hedge. Yet he would often be quite benign with those whose ideas differed from his own. He was once asked to explain this paradox, and he gave this historic answer:

"I am *always* tolerant with those who disagree with me. After all, they have a perfect right to their ridiculous opinions!"

✓ ✓ ✓

Dave Friedman, owner of Royal Furs, although a married man, was deeply infatuated with his secretary. But she couldn't stand the man.

Despite the continued rebuffs, he persisted with his unwanted attentions until one day she made her feelings perfectly clear.

"Whisper the three little words that will have me walking on air," he pleaded.

The secretary looked up, and then told him:

"Go hang yourself!"

✓ ✓ ✓

Kimmel went into a hardware store and asked if they sold rat poison.

"Sure!" said the clerk. "Shall I wrap it for you?"

"No!" was the retort. "I'll send the rats down here so you can feed it to them personally!"

✓ ✓ ✓

When Rabbi Harold Metzger was eighty-one years old, he was asked how he managed to maintain his health, vitality and slim figure. "You never exercise," he was told. "All you do is pore over books without giving your muscles a chance to stay in shape."

"Oh, I stretch my muscles occasionally," the rabbi chuckled. "I get all the exercise I need acting as a pallbearer for those in my congregation who exercised!"

✓ ✓ ✓

Mrs. Finkel was hanging out the wash when her gossipy neighbor approached. "I hate to tell you this," said the gossip, "but there's a rumor that your husband chases girls. And at his age, too," she clucked. "He's sixty-five, no?"

"Yes, he's sixty-five," said Mrs. Finkel. "So let him chase girls. Dogs chase cars also. But when they catch one, can they drive it?"

✓ ✓ ✓

341

Segal and Schuster had spent the evening out on the town and now Segal was beginning to worry about the reception he would get when he returned home. "My wife gave me strict orders to be back at six sharp, in time for supper," he said.

"What's the matter with you?" said Schuster. "Stop being such a coward and act like a man!"

"*Oy!*" said Segal, lifting his eyes heavenward. "Here I'm in all kinds of trouble and he wants me to do imitations."

✔   ✔   ✔

She: "You shouldn't be afraid of him. He's an ignorant savage and you're an educated, intelligent man."

He: "So what should I do? Beat him to death with my college diploma?"

✔   ✔   ✔

It was their fifth anniversary and Millie and Maxie had just returned from the movies. Millie was feeling romantic. "Will you love me when my hair has turned to silver?" she crooned.

"Why not?" Maxie grunted. "Didn't I love you through four other shades?"

✔   ✔   ✔

Levy the landlord wasn't a bad-hearted fellow, but Carl, the artist, had not paid his rent in five months, and enough is enough. So he gave the tenant an ultimatum—pay up or get out!

"You don't realize what you are doing!" Carl protested. "Why, one of these days people will pass by and look at this miserable apartment and say, 'Carl, the famous painter lived there!'"

"I got news for you," answered Levy. "If you don't pay your rent by this evening, they'll be saying it tomorrow."

✔   ✔   ✔

Grandpa, at the age of seventy-five, went to see his first football game. When he returned home, Grandma asked him what it was all about.

"It's something like insurance," the old man said. "Everybody comes to see you kick off!"

✔   ✔   ✔

A man went to a jewelry store to buy his wife a set of pearl earrings.

"You'll like these," said the jeweler, displaying an expensive set. "Guaranteed one-hundred-per-cent cultured."

"Cultured! Pultured!—Shmultured!" exploded the customer. "I want just plain pearls. Let somebody else pay for their college diploma!"

✔   ✔   ✔

Jake and his brother returned home from a double date.

"I'll bet you kissed that girl a dozen times, didn't you?" Jake teased.

"How do I know?" answered the brother. "What am I, an accountant?"

✦ ✦ ✦

It was their first date, and Jake felt the time was ripe. "Kiss me, sweetie!" he crooned.

"Don't be so fresh!" she said, drawing away. "Remember, I'm a lady!"

"Naturally!" he answered. "If I wanted a man I'd go home and kiss my grandfather!"

✦ ✦ ✦

At a tea, Darryl Zanuck, the motion picture pioneer and president of 20th Century-Fox, was discussing with a middle-aged female author the difficulty of properly casting a part in a picture.

"I want a young fellow who is exceptionally handsome," said Zanuck. "He should be tall, with beautiful eyes, and have a well-muscled body. He also should have a good sense of humor, a pleasing voice and an air of distinction. That's what I want."

"So do I!" sighed the lady.

✦ ✦ ✦

Sam: You mean to say you're married twenty-five years and your wife still looks like a newlywed?

Sid: No, I said I'm married twenty-five years and my wife still *cooks* like a newlywed!

✦ ✦ ✦

Ruthie, a romantic young teenager, was reading poetry to her grandfather, a pragmatic oldtimer. "What is so rare as a day in June?" she sighed.

"An Arab military victory," responded grandpa promptly.

Chapter Thirty-two

Judges, Lawyers and Defendants

A burglar alarm sent out its piercing wail in the dark of a December night and the police arrived just in time to collar the burglar as he was leaving the premises with a satchel full of loot. Soon he was in court, facing a grim-looking judge.

"Did you have an accomplice?" asked the magistrate.

"What's an accomplice?"

"A partner. In other words, did you commit this crime by yourself?"

"What else?" demanded the culprit. "Who can get reliable help these days?"

✓ ✓ ✓

Milton Stein was summoned to court as a witness in an important criminal trial. After he was sworn in, the prosecuting attorney asked, "Where were you on the night of August 15th?"

"I object!" yelled the defense lawyer, leaping to his feet.

"Now just a minute!" Milton interrupted before the judge could rule on the objection. "I don't mind answering. Let him ask."

Again the prosecutor asked, "Where were you on the night of August 15th?"

Once more the lawyer shouted, "I object!"

"Why are you objecting?" Milton called from the witness stand. "By me, a good citizen is supposed to answer all questions."

At this point the judge attempted to clear the situation. He addressed himself to the defense lawyer. "In view of the fact that you yourself called this witness to the stand, and knowing that he is favorably disposed toward your client, to say nothing of his willingness to answer the question, I fail to see why he should not be permitted to do so."

The defense lawyer shrugged, and the prosecuting attorney framed his question again. "For the third time, sir, where were you on the night of August 15th?"

"Who knows?" said Milton.

✓ ✓ ✓

The judge was examining Julius on his application for naturalization papers.

"Where is the seat of the Federal Government?" asked His Honor.

"In Vashington, D.C."

"Do you know what 'D.C.' stands for?"

"Soitanly," replied Julius. "De Cepital!"

🦶 🦶 🦶

A bearded, Orthodox Jew who had long since passed his allotted three-score-and-ten, was brought up before the judge on some minor civil matter.

"What business are you in?" asked the judge.

"Me, I'm a *minyan*-man," the ancient Jew replied.

"What in the world is a *minyan*-man?"

"Well, in our religion, when there are only nine men at Sabbath services, it's up to me to join them and that makes ten."

The judge was obviously puzzled. "I still don't understand. After all, when I join nine other people that too makes ten."

"Ahhh," exclaimed the old Jew with delight. "Also a *Yid!*"

🦶 🦶 🦶

A husband was suing his wife for divorce and his lawyer was determined to put her in as bad a light as possible.

"What line of work were you in before you married my client?" he asked when she was on the witness stand.

"I was a stripper in a burlesque," she answered promptly.

"Aha! And do you consider that a decent occupation for a respectable lady?"

"Well, to tell the truth, I was proud of my work in comparison to what my father did for a living."

The attorney smiled, sure now that he had already won his case. "Tell the court, please, just what it was that your father did for a living. Speak up, Madam!"

"He was a lawyer!" she snapped.

🦶 🦶 🦶

Had Goldstein been more observant he would have noticed a policeman standing in the shadows when he broke into the Zion Bakery and stole a box of *matzohs*. In a matter of minutes he found himself in the clutches of the law.

In court, Goldstein and the arresting officer stood before the bar of justice.

"Are you Goldstein, the defendant?" asked the stern judge.

The prisoner, who had never heard the legal term before, hesitated a moment before answering. "No, your honor," he finally replied, "I'm the Goldstein who stole the *matzohs!*"

🦶 🦶 🦶

A public-spirited doctor was named "Man of the Year" in his city and a banquet was tendered in his honor. As expected, he made a fine speech. However, he noted with mounting irritation that a prominent lawyer in the front row was sound asleep. To make matters worse, the man was audibly snoring.

When the doctor finished his oration the lawyer, as though on cue, suddenly awoke. Hands in his pockets, he slouched over to where the doctor was sitting, and said, "Congratulations, that was the first time I ever heard a doctor make an acceptable speech."

The doctor, knowing the other had not heard a single word, gave him an icy stare and then replied, "Congratulations to you, too. This is the first time I have ever seen a lawyer with his hands in his own pockets!"

✓   ✓   ✓

During the 1930's, Samuel Leibowitz was among the most prominent judges in New York, if not the United States. One of his friends, an inveterate *kibbitzer*, decided to have some fun with the learned barrister.

"Judge, I hate to tell you this," he said, "but a legislative committee has voted to abolish your bench."

"Who testified against me?" demanded the outraged Leibowitz.

"Well, there was Jake Zimmerman, the banker, for one."

"What!" cried Leibowitz. "Why, he's usurious. He cheats widows and orphans out of their life savings! Who else?"

"Feldman, the contractor; he voted against you also."

"That *ganeff*! He cheats the underprivileged by building slum dwellings before they even become slums. He's a disgrace to the building profession! So who else?"

The friend then mentioned a number of others who, he claimed, had testified unfavorably, while, with mounting rage, the judge denounced each as a scoundrel or worse.

Finally, the *kibbitzer* confessed that he had only been joking; that the committee, in fact, had unanimously praised him.

"Now why," sighed Judge Leibowitz, "did you go and make me say all those mean things against the finest group of men I know?"

✓   ✓   ✓

Max Pomerantz was in court to become an American citizen.

"Have you fulfilled all the requirements necessary for United States citizenship?" asked the judge.

"What else?" replied Pomerantz.

"Who was Abraham Lincoln?" queried the magistrate.

"What kind of question is that? Doesn't everybody know?"

"There are two political parties in this country. Name them."

"Parties? A working man has time to go to parties?"

"Listen, do you always have to answer a question with another question?" snapped the judge.

"Why not?"

The judge glowered. "I shall ask you one more question, and you had better answer me fully if you expect to become a citizen."

"Did I say you shouldn't ask?"

"All right," sighed the judge. "Do you solemnly swear to support the Constitution of the United States?"

"What's the matter?" answered Pomerantz promptly. "It's not enough I have to support a wife and four children? Blood, you need?"

✓　　✓　　✓

While the Jewish community may not approve of former mobster Mickey Cohen, the man does have a sense of humor.

"At first I was afraid that death in the electric chair might be painful," he reminisced, "until I realized that no one had ever complained."

✓　　✓　　✓

The magistrate of the divorce court peered down curiously as the aged couple approached the bench, their steps faltering and uncertain.

"Do you mean to say you people want a divorce?" he asked incredulously.

"What else?" replied the white-haired old man in a cracked voice.

"How old are you?" the judge demanded.

"Ninety-six."

"And you, Madam; what is your age?"

"Ninety-one, ninety-two; who knows?" answered the woman.

"Now see here, this is a lot of foolishness!" said the judge. "People your age should be able to settle your differences at home. How long have you been married?"

"Seventy years," sighed the little old man.

"Seventy years and you want a divorce?" the judge exclaimed. "Why, for heaven's sake?"

The long suffering wife looked up at the magistrate and her reply was terse. "Because, your honor, enough is enough already!"

✓　　✓　　✓

"Hello, Abe, how's the law business?"

"Don't even ask! Its' been so long since I had a client, I divorced my wife last month just so I would have a case."

✓　　✓　　✓

"What, you here again?" demanded the judge.

"It wasn't my fault," said Goldberg. "The man bought a garment and then complained I didn't give enough change. It's a lie!"

The judge shook his head. "Mr. Goldberg, last year you were in this court because a customer accused you of wrapping up a cheaper suit than he had actually ordered. Then you were brought in again for doing business

347

without a license. After that," continued the judge, reading from a thick dossier, "you had a fistfight with your competitor across the street. This year, so far, you've been here twice—and each time you have been found guilty. I wonder, Mr. Goldberg, if you realize how much trouble you are to this court?"

"Well, look who's talking!" snapped Goldberg indignantly. "I'm troubling *you*?"

✓ ✓ ✓

In his private chambers, the judge sat down heavily at his desk and faced the condemned murderer and his lawyer. "I'm sorry, but your plea for clemency looks very doubtful at this time."

"B-but," sputtered the surprised lawyer, "only a few days ago you said the governor would grant a last-minute reprieve."

"That was a few days ago," agreed the judge. "But since then the governor himself has been indicted."

✓ ✓ ✓

The young fellow had only been out of law school for two years, but his wife seemed to think that instant wealth was granted with the law degree. She nagged him constantly about their modest home furnishings. "We need a new dining room set," she complained. "We need a new rug in the living room. We need a new television set. We need . . . we need . . . we need . . . !"

"All right," said the patient hubby. "Very soon you'll have all the new furniture you want."

"Why, what happened?"

"A wealthy client came to the office today. He's suing his wife for divorce. Now just as soon as I break up *his* home, you can furnish *ours*."

✓ ✓ ✓

Joshua's married life had come to a bitter end, so he went to his older brother for advice.

"Who is the best divorce lawyer in the city?" Joshua asked.

"Well, Josh, the best of all is old man Feldman. In fact, he's unbeatable—when he's sober."

"My God!" exclaimed Joshua. "He wanted $1,000, so I told him what he could do. And he did it! Now he's representing my wife."

"Hmmm, that's bad."

"Wait a minute! You said Feldman's the best, but only when he's sober. Tell me, who's the second best?"

"Feldman," said the brother promptly—"when he's drunk!"

✓ ✓ ✓

Feinberg was the defendant in a bigamy action. The prosecutor had brought into evidence that the accused man actually married four women, so it was little wonder that he was in a cold sweat when the foreman of the jury stood up to deliver the verdict:

"We, the jury, find the defendant—not guilty!"

The judge peered down over his spectacles at Feinberg. "You are a free man," he said. "Go home to your wife."

"Thank you, your honor!" shouted the surprised and delighted Feinberg. "But tell me, which one?"

✓ ✓ ✓

A sunken-cheeked, arthritic old man of ninety-one was being sued for breach of promise by an eighteen-year-old chorus girl. The judge looked hard at the shriveled-up defendant and then fixed a gimlet eye on the girl.

"I'll hear the case," he said, "but first I want you to tell me something: What could this mummy of a man have possibly promised you?"

✓ ✓ ✓

Judge: "So you want a divorce on account of incompatibility. What seems to be the trouble—aren't your relations satisfactory?"

Wife: "Mine are wonderful, your honor. But my Hymie's relations—you never saw such *yentehs* in your life!"

✓ ✓ ✓

Henry Frankfurter went to court to change his name legally.

"What is your reason?" asked the Judge. "Frankfurter sounds like a fine name to me."

"It was my daughter's idea, Your Honor. You know how these modern girls are. They want to sound more American. So, for her sake, I thought it best to change it."

"What do you want to call yourself now?"

"Weiner," said Frankfurter.

✓ ✓ ✓

A Russian peasant lodged a complaint against his Jewish neighbor Yankel. The latter, it seems, had erected a *sukkah* for the Feast of Tabernacles and the peasant discovered that the frail structure occupied a portion of his land. The judge before whom the case was tried studied the matter carefully. His verdict stipulated that the booth must be removed by the Jew within ten days from the day of its construction.

✓ ✓ ✓

An English jurist who was about to administer the oath to the Jewish plaintiff remarked, "I assume, as a Jew, you would prefer to use the Old Testament."

"Yes, your honor."

"Bring me a copy of the Old Testament," the judge ordered the bailiff.

When the book was handed up to him, the judge examined it briefly and was startled to see the titles Matthew, Mark, Luke and John.

"I told you to bring me an Old Testament," snapped the judge.

"It's the oldest one I could find," protested the bailiff. "In fact it belonged to my grandfather."

✦   ✦   ✦

A free-thinking young attorney and a rabbi were deeply involved in a theological discussion.

"Heaven and hell, you will agree, may very well be separated by a wall," contended the lawyer. "Should this wall accidentally fall down, who, in your opinion, would rebuild it? The righteous would insist that the wicked do it; the latter would likely refuse. If this case should come up before a judge, which do you think would emerge the winner?"

"It seems to me," said the rabbi, "that any fair-minded judge would render a verdict against the wicked, since the likelihood is that the wall would crumble from the fires of hell rather than from whatever is taking place in Paradise. On the other hand," he concluded, "I realize that hell surely contains a predominance of glib-tongued attorneys and I would therefore not be surprised if they won the case."

✦   ✦   ✦

Two businessmen from Canal Street, Joe and Ben, appeared before the Jewish Court of Arbitration in New York City. The presiding officer, a rabbi, asked the litigants to state their case.

"I summoned my neighbor to this court because he is an ingrate," said Joe. "I loaned him three hundred dollars when he needed it and now he refuses to pay it back."

The rabbi turned to Ben. "And what have you to say about this?"

"It's true that I borrowed the money," Ben admitted, "but I already told him that times are hard and I couldn't repay it this month."

"Now wait a minute, Rabbi!" interrupted Joe. "That's what he said last month."

"*Nu*," answered Ben, "did I go back on my word?"

✦   ✦   ✦

A Jewish judge in Brooklyn was bitter toward the culprit who was charged with petty larceny. The latter was a Jew and the judge did not like to see a member of his religion arrested and brought to court. He therefore spoke sternly to the defendant.

"Is this your first offense? Have you stolen anything before?"

"Yes," replied the Jew.

"So this is your second offense! What did you steal the first time?" thundered the judge.

"The *afikomen* on Passover," said the Jew.

✦   ✦   ✦

JUDGES, LAWYERS AND DEFENDANTS

A Jewish woman in a small western town sued her husband for divorce. He had left her and refused to support her, she claimed. The case was presented to the judge by a Jewish attorney who concluded his petition in the following manner:

"Your Honor, this good-for-nothing husband is a most undesirable citizen. He drinks like Lot, sins like Haman, and curses like Balaam."

"The divorce is granted," said the judge, "and as for this fellow's dangerous associates, if they are ever brought into this court I will personally see to it that they are punished accordingly."

Chapter Thirty-three

Doctors and Patients

Selig Zimmerman, in his seventies, Orthodox in his religion and ultra conservative in his attitudes, began to suffer from insomnia. Hot toddies, a walk around the block, a little *schnapps*—all the home remedies—were useless. His daughter, Shirley, took him to a specialist but he was unable to help the oldtimer. As a last resort, and on the advice of the physician, she took her father to a psychiatrist who specialized in hypnotism.

"Now don't be concerned about him," the psychiatrist told Shirley. "I'll simply put him in a deep trance and the power of suggestion will do the rest. Your father's sleepless nights are a thing of the past."

"It isn't dangerous?" asked the daughter.

"Of course not! You just wait in the outer office, and when he goes under I'll call you so you can see for yourself."

Alone with his patient, the doctor turned to the old man and ordered him to lie down on the couch. "Now then," he began, "you will concentrate on nothing but my voice. It will make you very sleepy. You are already growing tired. Your eyes are getting so heavy you can hardly keep them open. Your body is relaxed. Every muscle and nerve is asleep. That's right, close your eyes. You are now fast asleep. D-e-e-e-p s-l-e-e-e-p!"

The psychiatrist studied the reclining, quiet figure for a few brief moments and then tiptoed to the outer office. He beckoned to Shirley and said softly, "You may go in now. He is sound asleep. I'll wake him in a little while and, take my professional word for it, his insomnia will be cured."

The daughter went inside and knelt beside the couch. "Papa, can you hear me?" she whispered in his ear. "Are you really asleep at last?"

Very cautiously, old man Zimmerman opened one fearful eye, and asked, "That *meshuggener*—he's still here?"

✓ ✓ ✓

It is no secret that many, if not most Jews tend to be more subjective than objective. In this heartwarming illustration which dates back to

World War I, we find that the Jewish nurse took excellent care of her patient but also felt an innate compulsion to pour out her own woes.

Wounded Yanks were beginning to return to American hospitals in the year of 1918 in ever increasing numbers, and many volunteer nurses served without pay as their contribution to the war against the Central Powers.

At the Veterans' Hospital in Long Island, during that period, a physician entered the room of a seriously wounded young man and asked the volunteer nurse, a gentile, how the patient had fared through the night.

"The patient was very restless," reported the *goyishe* nurse. "He had a temperature of 103° and could not sleep."

The next day a Jewish volunteer nurse was on duty. The physician made his usual rounds of the hospital and asked the new nurse how the patient was.

"*Oy!*" she moaned. "Did I have a night!"

✓ ✓ ✓

The history of medical charlatans goes back to the dawn of recorded history. In Russia there was a class of practitioners known as *feldshers*, or quacks. The *feldshers* never went to college, never studied anatomy, and never read books on medicine; they simply familiarized themselves with a number of nostrums and used them for all sorts of ailments.

There is the story of one such quack who himself became ill, and sent for a fellow practitioner to examine him. His comrade entered the sick room with all the dignity of a true specialist. Seating himself at the patient's bedside, he took hold of his wrist and solemnly felt his pulse.

"Now, just a minute!" cried the patient. "Cut out that nonsense! I don't blame you for pulling that stuff on a layman, but why go through that silly rigamarole with me? You know as well as I that there isn't such a thing as a pulse!"

✓ ✓ ✓

Max Eisen, the pushcart peddler from Hester Street, was suffering from abdominal disturbances so he went to see his doctor. The physician immediately diagnosed the case as stomach pains resulting from an excess of gas.

"Tell me," said the doctor, "do you suffer from breaking wind?"

"Suffer!" exclaimed Eisen, a look of ecstatic relief on his face. "From this who suffers?"

✓ ✓ ✓

Laurence Merrick, producer and director of the Princess Theatre in Hollywood, tells this one about the father of psychiatry, Sigmund Freud:

It was late at night and Dr. Freud was fast asleep when the silence

353

was shattered by a furious pounding on his door. He rushed downstairs and admitted a distraught Jewish woman.

"Doctor," she cried, "my husband fell on the floor and he's gasping for air. Please, come with me at once!"

"Lady, I'm sorry but I can't help you," Dr. Freud interrupted. "You see, I'm not a regular physician. I'm a doctor of psychiatry."

"Psychiatry?" echoed the woman. "What kind of a sickness is psychiatry?"

✓　　✓　　✓

Dr. Max Mandelstamm was the greatest Russian eye-specialist of his day, and the faculty of the University of Kiev proposed his appointment to a full professorship. The Senate of the University, however, could not agree to this appointment because the candidate was a Jew. When Dr. Mandelstamm heard of what had transpired at the meeting of the Senate, he hurriedly penned the following note to the president, and asked his furnace-tender to deliver it:

> "I respectfully recommend the bearer of this letter to the Chair of Ophthalmology at the University. He is not an eye-specialist but he answers to your requirements. He is a Christian, and has for years been my dependable janitor."

✓　　✓　　✓

Grandma Vogel had just finished celebrating her ninety-second birthday when she became ill. One of her grandchildren called the doctor.

"You're going to make me better?" Grandma Vogel asked hopefully.

The kindhearted doctor took her withered hand in his and attempted to soothe her without diminishing his professional ethics. "*Bobeh,*" he said, "when one approaches the century mark, all kinds of little ailments, aches and pains happen. You must understand, my dear, that I am a doctor, not a magician. I cannot make you any younger."

"Younger?" Grandma Vogel cried out impatiently. "Who's asking you should make me any younger? Just do me a favor and make me grow older . . . lots older!"

✓　　✓　　✓

This editor's father said it some forty-five years ago, back in 1921: "I don't mind dying of old age: Not when I consider the alternative!"

✓　　✓　　✓

The waiting room was crowded, and the doctor was anxious to examine all the patients as quickly as possible. He stalked out of his inner sanctum and pointed to a bearded little man. "You! You're next! Inside, please, and take your pants down!"

"But, Doctor . . ."

"Don't but me no buts! I'm too busy to talk. Didn't you see all those other people waiting for me? Do as you're told!"

Thoroughly cowed, the diminutive man entered the examining room, lowered his trousers as ordered, and stretched out on the table. But when the doctor completed his examination he was puzzled. "I don't seem to be able to diagnose your case," he growled. "As far as I can ascertain you are in perfect health. What were your symptoms?"

"Symptoms? Who has symptoms? I feel fine, Doctor."

"Then what the devil are you here for?"

"I'm from Temple Beth David," said the little man, adjusting his trousers. "I only came to ask you about renewing your membership."

✓ ✓ ✓

The dapper young medic was in his first year of internship but already believed he knew more than any doctor in the hospital. On this particular morning he strode into Ward E where two men were suffering from the same injury—a dislocated shoulder.

The interne examined the first man's shoulder, turning and twisting it with an impressively professional air. The poor patient screamed with the pain. Then the young doctor turned to the other man and went through the same procedure, but not a sound escaped the injured patient.

When the interne left, the first patient said to his neighbor, "Mister, I admire you. Where did you ever find the stamina to endure such pain without uttering a single cry?"

"Stamina? Who has stamina!" demanded the second man. "I just used some old-fashioned *saichel*."

"What do you mean, *saichel*?"

"After what that *shnook* did to you, do you think I was silly enough to let him touch the shoulder that was injured?"

✓ ✓ ✓

Dr. Ginsberg finished his examination, made his diagnosis, and wrote out a prescription. The patient, as soon as he finished dressing, handed the doctor two dollars.

"I'm sorry, sir, but my fee is ten, not two dollars," said the physician.

"Well, that's certainly news to me!" exclaimed the patient. "My sister-in-law told me it was only five!"

✓ ✓ ✓

For several weeks Schotz, the tippler, had been complaining of pains in his stomach. His wife, fearing he might have ulcers or worse, hounded her husband into visiting the family doctor. He returned home an hour later.

"*Nu*, what did the doctor say?" she asked.

"I got liver trouble," Schotz told her.

"Oy gevald! So what did he recommend?"

"No more drinking," Schotz sighed, his eyes cast longingly on a half-filled bottle of Mount Carmel wine. "The doctor said it was a matter of life and death."

A few minutes later, the wife returned from the kitchen where she had been preparing the evening meal and, to her horror, saw that her husband had poured himself a tumbler-full of the wine.

"Are you *meshuggeh?*" she cried. "What are you trying to do, commit suicide?"

"No, of course not," he replied mildly. "I'm just assuming I saw the doctor tomorrow instead of today!"

❧ ❧ ❧

Zvi Landau was a chronic hypochondriac, and nothing could convince him that he was not at death's door. In desperation, the local village doctor suggested that Zvi consult a specialist in the big city, so that his mind might be at rest.

A few days later, Zvi was given an exhaustive examination by the specialist. "Mr. Landau," said the big city doctor, "your illness is all in your imagination. There isn't a thing wrong with you. With your constitution you'll live to bury your mother, your father, your wife—even your children."

"Aw, Doctor," said Zvi, "you're just saying that to make me feel good!"

❧ ❧ ❧

A doctor was called to the home of a very pious, Orthodox Jew who lay gravely ill.

"I'll have to examine his throat," said the doctor to the man's wife. "Bring me a spoon!"

The woman, as Orthodox as her husband, faltered, and then asked haltingly, *"milchik* or *flaishik?"*

❧ ❧ ❧

Abe Rabinovitch finally accumulated enough money to leave Russia and emigrate to America where the rest of his family had preceded him years earlier.

The first thing he did, after his clearance through Ellis Island, was to look up his older brother. It saddened him to find his nearest relative ill. "Joseph, tell me," Abe asked gently, "what kind of sickness do you have?"

"Who knows?" answered old Joseph, shrugging. "Fancy names the doctors have for everything. All I know is that I've been in bed for three months and already it has cost me three hundred dollars."

"What!" exclaimed Abe. "Why, back in Odessa you could have been sick on that kind of money for a whole year!"

❧ ❧ ❧

DOCTORS AND PATIENTS

One day, Aaron Shulberg, the slyest *shnorrer* of them all, became ill, so he went to the most eminent and expensive specialist in all Poland. The physician examined, diagnosed and then treated the patient.

"How much do I owe you?" asked Shulberg.

"Fifty thalers."

"How much did you say? Fifty thalers? You must be crazy! Who has that much money?"

"Well, all right, make it thirty."

"Thirty thalers for a few minutes' work? It's still too dear."

"Too much? Then give me twenty."

"Ridiculous! Who walks around with twenty thalers?"

The doctor was growing more exasperated by the moment. "See here, pay me five thalers and get out! I'm tired of haggling."

"Impossible," retorted Shulberg. "You don't seem to realize I'm a poor man."

"If you can't pay five thalers," the doctor snapped, "just how much can you afford?"

"Nothing. I haven't a zloty to my name."

Now the doctor was really furious. "If you have nothing, what's the big idea coming to the most expensive doctor in the country?"

"Don't you dare shout at me!" yelled Shulberg, his face flushed with righteous indignation. "When it comes to my health, *no* doctor is too expensive!"

✔   ✔   ✔

Old man Krantz, a druggist for more than fifty years, finally retired and left the store to his young pharmacist son. Occasionally, however, he would drop in just to "keep a hand in the business." But the old man had a strict policy which greatly displeased the son—"Never let a customer walk out empty-handed."

"Pop," the younger man remonstrated, "conditions are different now. I'm a member of the State Board of Pharmacy—we have a code of ethics and standards to maintain. We sell only what is best for the customer, and never—I repeat, never!—offer substitutes just to put something in the cash register."

"Ethics-shmethics!" the old man snorted. "The Board will pay the rent if you don't make business?"

Considering the old man's attitude, it came as no surprise therefore, when he heard his father waiting on a customer while he himself nibbled on a sandwich in the back.

The customer was a middle-aged woman. "I've been coughing all day," she complained. "Do you have a good cough medicine? Anything that stops it, even for awhile, would be a relief."

Old man Krantz, not wishing to disturb his son during his lunch period, searched every shelf but could find no cough medicine. Suddenly he was seized with an inspiration. With his son peering at him from behind a

357

partition, he took a bottle of castor oil from a shelf, poured the entire contents into a glass, mixed a little fruit juice in it to help disguise the unpleasant taste, and handed it to her. "Drink it all—every drop!" he ordered.

As soon as the woman downed the concoction and paid the old druggist, the son rushed out from behind the partition and began to upbraid his father.

"Pop, for heaven's sake, how many times must I tell you—*never give substitutes!* And what was the idea giving her castor oil? That can't possibly relieve her cough."

"*Sha, sha,* don't make such a commotion," said the elder Krantz placatingly. "Castor oil is better than cough medicine." He pointed toward the street. "See her there on the corner, leaning against the lamp post? Believe me, Son, she's *afraid* to cough!"

✓ ✓ ✓

Hyman Edelson, the well-to-do grocer, was a pleasant sort of chap, but he hated to pay the asking price for anything.

One day, while eating herring, a bone became lodged in his throat. He could neither swallow nor disgorge it, and within moments he could scarcely breathe. His wife hurriedly called the family doctor, who arrived just as the patient's face was turning blue. The physician quickly removed the bone with a pair of forceps.

When Edelson recovered and was again breathing normally, he was overwhelmed with gratitude, but he cautiously asked, "How much do I owe you for this little two-minutes' work?"

The doctor was well acquainted with the grocer's miserly nature. "I'll tell you what," he said, "Just pay me half of what you would have given when the bone was still stuck in your throat."

✓ ✓ ✓

From out of the wondrous tales by Sholom Aleichem, there emerges this little gem:

Tevye, having had a stomach ache all day, decided to visit a doctor. After the examination, the physician regretfully informed the patient that he had cancer.

"*Cancer—shmancer!*" said Tevye gaily. "Who cares, just so long as I'm healthy!"

✓ ✓ ✓

There are those who will insist that the listener must be Jewish to enjoy the full flavor of the following tale, but in any event, it points up the Jewish tendency to "revert to type."

Although he himself had been deprived of the opportunity for a higher education, the wealthy Mr. Levine long ago decided that his only daughter would have all the educational and cultural advantages he had never known. So he sent her to an exclusive finishing school in Paris.

Upon her return to the United States she married and, in due course, she was taken to a maternity hospital. When her obstetrician came to find out how she was progressing she moaned langorously, *"Mon dieu! Mon dieu!"*

"Doctor—Doctor!" gasped old man Levine in alarm, "Quick, she's giving birth!"

The doctor shook his head from side to side. "Not yet," he said, almost indifferently.

An hour later, when the daughter heard the doctor coming to her bedside, she wailed elegantly, *"Sauvez moi, Docteur!"*

"Doctor—Doctor: quick, she's giving birth!" cried Levine once again, wringing his hands frantically.

"Not yet," replied the doctor, in his bored voice.

A few minutes later a piercing shriek rang through the hospital corridors. *"Oy gevald! Mama, Mama!"*

"Now!" said the doctor, grinning.

✓ ✓ ✓

There is a time for everything, as the Bible says: a time to play and a time not to play, if we may be forgiven the paraphrase.

In the reign of Franz-Joseph of Austria, the emperor had a Jewish physician of whom he was quite fond. The good doctor would call every day but there was little wrong with the royal "patient." So the monarch and the physician would invariably play a little pinochle, laughing together about the "not feeling well" alibi.

One day when the physician called, he was told that the emperor preferred not to see him this time, since he wasn't feeling well.

The doctor, who had been hearing that prelude to his daily pinochle game for several years, was astounded. "But that's impossible!" he retorted. "How can he not be feeling well when he's not feeling well?"

✓ ✓ ✓

Most Jews zealously adhere to the dictum, "Cleanliness is next to Godliness." Here is an 18th-century anecdote about one who entertained independent ideas about the subject:

The story is told of the Israelite whose foot became infected. The local village practitioner, unable to clear up the lingering problem, suggested that the patient consult a certain well known specialist in Moscow. An appointment was made, and the village Jew entered the great doctor's office at the agreed upon hour.

"Now then," said the specialist, "let's have a look at that ailing foot of yours. Take off your shoe and sock."

But when the patient did as he was told, the doctor took one look at the dirt-encrusted foot and saw, instantly, the reason for the continuing infection. "What's the matter with you?" he bellowed. "Don't you know enough to wash your feet?"

"Sure," said the patient, nodding in agreement. "That's exactly what the village doctor asked me, but I wanted to get the opinion of a specialist."

✓ ✓ ✓

Mendy Mendelson was the first patient to walk into Dr. Solomon's office on that day, two years ago, when he hung out his shingle as a psychiatrist. Mendy, it appeared, was suffering from an inferiority complex. Now it was the doctor's pleasant duty to tell the patient that all was well.

"Mr. Mendelson," the young psychiatrist began, "for the past twenty-four months we have gone through word and thought association, dream analyses, and delved deeply into your subconscious. Today, I am proud to announce, there is good news awaiting you."

"Oh, thank you, Doctor," breathed Mendy gratefully. "I no longer have an inferiority complex?"

"No, and you never did," said Dr. Solomon. "You really *are* inferior!"

✓ ✓ ✓

"Mrs. Yifnik," said the psychiatrist, "there is nothing physically wrong with your little boy. But I must tell you this: he has an Oedipus complex."

"Oedipus—shmoedipus!" snorted Mrs. Yifnik. "Just so long as he loves his mother!"

✓ ✓ ✓

Rifkin, the baker, had a flourishing business, a loving wife and well mannered children. He should have been a contented man, but he was not. Rifkin, unfortunately, was a dedicated hypochondriac. He came down with sicknesses that had yet to be invented, and those that he did select were carefully chosen so as to be within the limits of his budget.

One day, he showed up at Dr. Seligman's office in Bensonhurst. "Doctor," he began, "I don't know how to put this, but last night, at exactly two A.M., I died!"

The doctor eyed his patient closely, gathering his wits before he dared speak. "Hmmm," he finally said, "so you're dead, eh?"

"Like a pickled herring."

"What did you die of, if I may be so bold?"

"My heart, Doctor Seligman. There was a sticking pain in my chest, I couldn't breathe, and suddenly I passed away."

"Well, there's no use in treating a dead man, of course," said the physician after he had recovered his composure, "but I would like to conduct a little experiment."

"What kind of experiment?" asked Rifkin.

"You know that dead people can't bleed, don't you?"

"No! By me that's news. You don't say!"

"It's really very simple," continued the doctor warily. "When a person dies and his heart stops, as yours did, the circulation ceases. That's because the heart is no longer pumping blood."

"It makes sense. Believe me, I'm glad I have for a doctor such a smart man."

"Now, Mr. Rifkin, I'm going to prove something to you," said the doctor, his voice now firm. He leaned across the desk. "Give me your arm."

Wonderingly, Rifkin extended his bared arm and before he could withdraw it the doctor jabbed it with a pin. A drop of blood slowly welled from the wound.

The doctor watched Rifkin's reaction with intense concentration, for this little experiment would surely bring the patient to his senses. As for Rifkin, he stared at the spot of blood, his initial consternation slowly giving way to pleased surprise.

"Well, who'd have thought it, Doctor!" he exclaimed. "Dead people *do* bleed!"

✓ ✓ ✓

Doctor: "You have nothing to worry about, Mr. Epstein. You'll live to see sixty-five."

Epstein: "But, I *am* sixty-five!"

Doctor: "*Nu*, did I lie?"

✓ ✓ ✓

Mama: "To take out a five-year-old boy's appendix you're charging $300? It's too much."

Doctor: "Sorry, Madam, but that's the way the belly buttons."

✓ ✓ ✓

Dr. Charles Leibowitz, whose practice was mainly confined to New York's lower East Side, was called to the cold-water flat of a poverty-stricken peddler. The young doctor examined the patient and then prescribed medication. But in his heart of hearts he knew that the poor peddler could not afford to have the prescription filled. He noted, with rising sympathy, the absence of food in the house and the lack of even the simplest of necessities. So, unobserved, the kind physician left ten dollars on the table as he left.

The next day the peddler telephoned the doctor. "I want to thank you for leaving the ten dollars, Dr. Leibowitz," he said. "Now I can afford to call in a specialist!"

✓ ✓ ✓

'A dog's life' can be more than just a meaningful phrase, as witness this little item:

Two cocker spaniels met on the street.

One said: *"Oy,* have I got *tsorres!* I'm heading for a regular nervous breakdown."

"Why don't you consult a psychiatrist?" his pal suggested.

"I can't," moaned the first spaniel. "I'm not allowed on the couch!"

✔ ✔ ✔

Hymie Schechter had always been a little eccentric but as he grew older and his antics could no longer be tolerated at home, his family had him committed to a mental institution. But if Hymie had been a nuisance at home, the doctors soon discovered that he was the worst pest they ever had in the hospital.

The very first evening, when his supper was served, he set up a howl of protest. "I can't eat this *traifeh* food!" he yelled. "I demand *kosher* food!"

The psychiatrist in charge, feeling the therapy might be good for the patient, hired a Jewish cook—just for Hymie Schechter. On the following Friday evening, after Hymie had dined on a sumptuous meal of roast *kotchkeh,* vegetables, tea and *chaleh,* the doctor decided to check the man's progress. To his surprise, he found Hymie puffing away contentedly on a big cigar.

"Now look here, Hymie," protested the doctor, "what's the idea of breaking the Sabbath by smoking?"

"What's the matter, you got rules against it?" retorted the patient.

"It isn't that at all. First you complained because we didn't serve you *kosher* food. You said you were religious, so we hired an expensive Jewish cook, just for you. So here I find you smoking on a Friday night. You can't get away with that!"

"Doctor," countered Hymie evenly, "you're forgetting something—I'm nuts!"

✔ ✔ ✔

Old man Rubin had been confined to his bed for several months, suffering from a variety of illnesses that included ulcers, a heart murmur and diabetes. Somehow, despite his advanced age, the gifted doctor managed to pull him through, and old Rubin was now convalescing nicely.

"Well, there isn't much more I can do for you," said the doctor at his next visit. "Except for a little high blood pressure, your condition is fine. And if I were you, I wouldn't even give another thought to the blood pressure."

"Doctor, take my word for it," snapped Rubin. "If I were you I wouldn't give another thought to my high blood pressure either!"

✔ ✔ ✔

"The stork just brought you a beautiful baby boy," the nurse told a new father.

"The stork never brought this baby," declared the young man, staring at the hospital statement. "The bill is way too long."

✓ ✓ ✓

Here is another example of a "dialect" joke that carries no anti-Semitic overtones, but whose denouement results from the natural misunderstanding of poor pronunciation. This is the way Yetta Koffman of Los Angeles tells it:

Tessie Margolis had been talking strangely of late. "Having hallucinations," her children and grandchildren delicately put it. As a last resort they sent her to a psychiatrist. Lying on the couch, she insisted that ducks were keeping her up all night—it was impossible for her to sleep.

"But, Mrs. Margolis," the doctor protested, "let's be reasonable about this. You live in the middle of Flatbush; there isn't a farm within fifty miles of your house. Surely you must realize you are mistaken."

"Look, Doctor, for the lest time, I'm tellink you; all night long the ducks they're kippink me avake."

"And has anyone else complained about the quacking of these ducks?" the doctor asked gently.

Mrs. Margolis lifted her eyebrows in genuine surprise. "Kveckink? Who said ennatink about kveckink? These ducks they're bahkink!"

✓ ✓ ✓

Same lady, same problem, same doctor:

The young psychiatrist had been studying Mrs. Margolis' case for some time, and had finally arrived at a strange conclusion.

"I don't want to seem rude, Mrs. Margolis," he began somewhat hesitantly, "particularly since I know that you have had nine children and fifteen grandchildren. But—well, do you mind if I ask you an intimate question?"

"Esk!"

"Tell me, frankly, just what is your attitude toward sex?"

"I love it," beamed Mrs. Margolis. "It's the finest store on Fift Evnoo."

✓ ✓ ✓

From a patent medicine testimonial: "Since taking your tablets regularly I am another woman. Needless to say, my husband is delighted."

✓ ✓ ✓

The average Jewish mother, it is said, would rather have a doctor for a son than one in any other profession. The next best is for a daughter to marry a doctor. Here is a whimsical, one-sentence switch on the adage:

"My mother always wanted me to marry a doctor," the girl confided, "but I didn't know any doctors so I married a patient."

✓ ✓ ✓

Dr. Mortimer Saperstein, a brilliant ophthalmologist, but a chronic fault-finder, was stricken with a heart attack. His wife immediately called the local hospital, and because of his own medical standing, he was rushed to the College of Surgeons.

Almost as soon as he arrived, he started to complain. He found fault with the food, the service, the nurses and the entire administration of the College. On the tenth day, the grumpy doctor unexpectedly returned home.

His wife greeted him in pleased surprise. "How is it you're home so soon?" she asked.

True to character, he answered plaintively, "I was expelled from the College for conduct unbecoming a cardiac patient!"

✓ ✓ ✓

If there was one type of patient whom the doctor disliked more than any other, it was the kind who telephones at four in the morning with some trivial complaint that could just as well have kept until the next day. Typical was the call from Mrs. Bender at 3:30 A.M.

"Doctor, Doctor, come quick. My Izzy swallowed a pen!" she yelled into the mouthpiece.

"Pig, ball or fountain?" he muttered sleepily.

"A pen! A founting pen! My Izzy swallowed it!"

"Mrs. Bender," he said evenly, making a Herculean effort to control his temper, "my office hours begin at high noon. Until then, tell your dear dear Izzy to chew on a blotter."

"But what about the pen?"

"Until I see him tomorrow," said the doctor, "there is no valid reason I can think of why he cannot use a pencil. GOODNIGHT, MADAM!"

✓ ✓ ✓

Painless Petrovsky, the Orchard Street dentist, finished his examination of the patient's mouth. "Well, Miss Feigel," he said, "I'm afraid I'll have to extract your wisdom teeth."

"*Oy vay!*" Miss Feigel squealed, "I'd rather have a baby!"

"Look, make up your mind," snapped Painless Petrovsky, "so I can adjust the chair accordingly."

✓ ✓ ✓

Patient: "Say, what's the matter with you? You just pulled the wrong tooth!"

Dentist: "Don't get excited. I'm coming to it!"

✓ ✓ ✓

Dr. Gordon had had a long and tiring day and he was feeling rather surly. He beckoned to the last patient in the waiting room, a bearded little man with eyes as alert as a hungry sparrow's.

DOCTORS AND PATIENTS

"Well," said the doctor snappishly, "what's your trouble?"

The bewhiskered little guy raised his eyes to heaven in feigned helplessness. "How do you like that?" he intoned, elevating his brows, shoulders, elbows and palms in the time-honored gesture. "Here he studies medicine for ten years and he's asking *me* to make the diagnosis!"

✓ ✓ ✓

Then there's the quickie about the former grocery clerk who became a druggist. His first day on the job, a woman came into the store and asked for a mustard plaster.

"Sorry, Madam, we're all out of mustard plasters," he said, "but how about some nice mayonnaise instead?"

✓ ✓ ✓

The late Joe Cook, a popular comic for more than forty years, swore that this story actually occurred.

A Syracuse doctor was scheduled to speak at a convention of medics interested in anthropology. He strode on stage and addressed the five hundred physicians and researchers in the audience. "I have here a skull of the famous Indian Chief, Sitting Bull," he announced holding the skull aloft for all to see. There was a stir of interest among his colleagues as they craned forward to view the surprising object.

Now that he had the undivided attention of the audience, the doctor was loathe to lose it. He reached into his bag and withdrew another, much smaller skull. "And this," he announced, holding it high for all to see, "is the skull of the same Sitting Bull—when he was only eight years old!"

✓ ✓ ✓

Mrs. Fagin was complaining about her abdominal pains to her friend and next-door neighbor, Mrs. Bloom.

But Mrs. Bloom had a ready solution. "Do yourself a favor," she said, "and go see my son the doctor. He's not only smart but I'll talk to him he shouldn't overcharge you too much."

So Mrs. Fagin went to see young Dr. Bloom, who had hung out his shingle only two months before.

"Now, Mrs. Fagin," he said as professionally as he could, "please disrobe and lie down on this table."

Mrs. Fagin, blushing from head to toe, took her clothes off and climbed upon the table. Then the doctor began his examination; probing, squeezing, tapping and peering at every inch of her ponderous body. When he finished he told her to get dressed while he sat at his desk and wrote out a prescription.

"Look, Doctor Bloom," she said as she was leaving, "by me it isn't nice that people should stick their noses into other people's business, but let me ask you something: Does your mama know how you make a living?"

✓ ✓ ✓

Not that we want to change the subject, but ask a doctor for his definition of lox, and he'll tell you it's a herring with high blood pressure.

✓　✓　✓

"*Oy*, Doctor, did I have a rough time at Palm Beach!"
"You look fine to me. What happened?"
"A lobster bit off my toe."
"Is that so? Which one?"
"What do you mean, which one? Who knows one lobster from another?"

✓　✓　✓

A *nouveau riche* dress designer insisted on nothing but the best for himself and his family, but, like many another parvenu, he was more than inept when trying to distinguish real values.

One day his daughter was stricken with appendicitis and taken to a hospital. The surgeon approached the father to assure him that all would be well—after all, it was a routine operation.

"Good!" said the man. "But just remember—no local anaesthetic. I'm wealthy enough to afford the best. Give her something imported."

✓　✓　✓

The gardener of a mental institution, pushing a laden wheelbarrow, was accosted by one of the inmates. "What is that in your wheelbarrow?" asked the patient.

"Fertilizer."

"What are you going to do with it?"

"I'm going to spread it on my corn and tomatoes," said the gardener.

"Huh!" snorted the inmate, "And they call me crazy because I spread whipped cream on my *schmaltz* herring!"

✓　✓　✓

"Doctor, I'm really worried about my growing loss of memory," complained the patient. "I seem to forget everything a few hours later. What must I do?"

"Well, considering your condition," replied the doctor, "the first thing you must do is pay me in advance."

✓　✓　✓

The patient was clearly on the verge of a nervous breakdown, and the psychiatrist lost no time in persuading him to lie down on the couch.

"May I smoke?" asked the patient.

"Sure, go ahead." The doctor waited until the visitor was comfortable and then asked, "How many packs a day do you smoke?"

"Three."

"You must quit at once," said the doctor, his voice imperative. "And I mean now—this very minute!"

"Why?"

"Look, just give up smoking immediately."

"Is it the cigarette smoking that is making me so nervous?"

"No," snapped the doctor, "but you're burning my new couch!"

✓   ✓   ✓

An author who had labored for years over a book about the trial of Adolf Eichmann became so involved with the characters and unfolding events in his manuscript that it began to affect his mind. So he consulted a psychiatrist.

"Doctor," the novelist said, after he had explained his work of the past several years, "it has gotten to the point where I'm beginning to think that I myself am Eichmann. I even said so to a number of people."

"Well, don't be too concerned about it," replied the psychiatrist. "As soon as you finish the book the delusion will disappear. After all, it isn't too serious."

"But you don't understand," protested the author. "I live in a Jewish neighborhood!"

✓   ✓   ✓

At a fancy-shmancy Bar Mitzvah party, old man Karp was introduced to Dr. David Miller. Now Karp, a well-to-do wholesaler, did not mind paying his way through life, but he wasn't at all reticent about obtaining free advice when he could do so.

He drew the doctor aside. "Listen, Dr. Miller, I realize this isn't the best time to ask, but tell me, what should I do for pains in the stomach? Every morning, when I get up I have such *tsorres* in the *poopik* it drives me *meshuggeh*."

The doctor laid a compassionate hand on the other man's shoulder. "I'm afraid you made a mistake," he said. "I'm not a medical doctor. My doctorate is in economics."

"Oh, is that so?" answered the oldster, undaunted. "Tell me something; would you advise me to sell my General Electric and buy AT&T with the proceeds?"

✓   ✓   ✓

Dr. Jacoby, one of those oldtime physicians who really loved his work and was devoted to his profession, had so many patients who kept him up all hours of the night (and day) that he finally succumbed to the strain. He was taken away in a straitjacket to a mental institution. For three years, the poor doctor made slow but steady progress until one day he was pronounced cured.

The institution's social worker paid him a visit as he was packing his suitcase. They exchanged the usual pleasant amenities and then she said, "Doctor, I know you have an enviable reputation as a physician, but suppose you are unable to resume your practice? Frankly, I'm worried about how you will earn a livelihood."

The doctor smiled and patted the girl's arm. "Thank you for your concern, my dear," he said warmly. "I am pleased to see you are so involved in your social work, but as far as I am concerned you need have no fears. As your records will show, I am not only an M.D. but also a dentist. So I can practice orthodontics. And if that proves unprofitable, I am also an engineer. I can go to work for one of the big aircraft companies or establish my own engineering consultant firm. If that shows no possibilities, I have a Ph.D. in chemistry and I can always set up a chemical laboratory. In addition, I have a degree in pharmacy and there is nothing to prevent me from opening a drug store. So you see, young lady, you need have no worries about me. I not only am completely normal now, but I have a number of professions in which I can make a good living."

"But suppose none of them are successful," persisted the social worker.

"In that case, Madam," said the doctor, "I can always be a tea-kettle!"

✓ ✓ ✓

The time finally arrived when Jacoby was pronounced sane by the board of psychiatrists. He was scheduled to leave the institution the next morning. The inmate arose bright and early, lathered his face and, with an old-fashioned straight razor, started to shave. As he shaved, a number of people—doctors, nurses and other patients—passed by and wished him well. He returned each greeting with a cheery wave of his hand. Finally the asylum's social worker passed by. "Good-bye, Mr. Jacoby," she called, "and good luck."

He acknowledged the greeting with the usual wave of his hand, but this time, when he turned, the razor in his hand cut the cord that held up the mirror, and it fell to the floor. When he resumed his former stance to continue shaving he found himself staring at the blank wall.

"How do you like that," he moaned. "Here it is my day to get out of this place and I have to go cut my head off!"

✓ ✓ ✓

Morris Shochet was an observant Jew. When the physician ordered him to the hospital for an operation he did not forget to take along his prayer book and *tefillin*. The following morning Shochet rose early and began to put on his *tefillin*. An Irish patient in an adjoining bed looked at him with amazement.

"No wonder they say these Jews are brilliant!" he exclaimed. "That guy hasn't been in the hospital twenty-four hours and already he's taking his own blood pressure!"

✓ ✓ ✓

Let us close this chapter with the modern definition of a doctor: Someone who acts like a humanitarian and charges like a TV repairman.

Chapter Thirty-four

Political Potpourri

Although many Jews found a secret (if minuscule) pride in the presidential nomination of a half Jew, probably no other candidate received so few Jewish votes as did Barry Goldwater in the 1964 elections. American Jews, who are, generally speaking a progressive, liberal-minded group (granting the usual exceptions), thought his policies too conservative for their tastes and were suspicious of some of his associates.

It is not surprising, therefore, that many of the most devastating Goldwater jokes were conceived by Jewish comedians—and more often as not were repeated by Goldwater himself. Indeed, there never was any question that he possessed a lively wit and could laugh at himself without embarrassment. To illustrate, there is his own smiling quip that, if elected, he would re-decorate the White House in 18th Century Modern; an allusion to his suspected reactionary tendencies. As a senator, he told the story of his attempt to join an exclusive 18-hole golf club in Virginia, just across the Potomac River from the District of Columbia. When informed that club membership was only extended to gentiles, Barry retorted, "Well, I'm only half Jewish, so why can't I just play nine holes?"

But while the *goyim* laughed at his sallies they could not know that the Jews had a concomitant reason for their appreciative chuckles: Goldwater's self-deprecatory jokes, whether he realized it or not, were typically Jewish. He is, of course, a Christian; a fact which induced the intelligent and very witty Mort Sahl to make this observation: "He is the only man who could stand on the Israel border and get shot at from both sides."

One day Barry Goldwater appeared at a Republican political rally with his name inscribed on a huge banner. Following his name were the initials of his rival for the presidency, Lyndon Baines Johnson. A colleague asked why he was displaying a Goldwater-LBJ flag. "LBJ doesn't stand for the president's name," grinned the candidate. "It means 'Little Bit Jewish.' "

That he would be prone to "push the panic button" in this day of possible atomic destruction was another widespread (and unjustified) canard hurled at the Republican nominee. A Greenwich Village nightclub comedian told his audience that if elected, Goldwater's first major address as president would begin: "Ten - nine - eight - seven - six . . ."

And to anyone who might wonder what life under Goldwater would be like, the answer was, "Brief!"

Singer-comedian Dean Martin evoked chuckles with his reassuring words to his friend Sammy Davis Jr., the Negro-Jewish entertainer. "Don't worry, Sammy," consoled Dean. "If Goldwater wins, I'll buy you!"

At the height of the presidential campaign, *Time* Magazine told of a company called *Panic Productions* which released an LP recording called *I'd Rather Be Far Right Than President.* The tongue-in-cheek "report" imaginatively follows Goldwater to victory at the polls and into office, chronicling his first presidential acts. His initial moves include withdrawing United States recognition from such "Socialist" countries as Great Britain, India, Switzerland and Sweden. He ejects the correspondent of the *New York Times* from a press conference, and conducts the war on poverty with thermonuclear bombs.

There is the titillating account of a conversation between Goldwater and the then-Prime Minister of the Soviet Union, Nikita Khrushchev, said to have occurred the day after the elections.

"Hello, Nikki?" begins Goldwater. "This is Barry. I'm calling you on my—you should pardon the expression—ham radio."

"*Nu,* Goldbottle, how's by you the election?" asks Khrushchev.

"Don't even ask!"

"It's true you lost by fifty million votes?"

"Don't jump to conclusions, Nikki," snaps Goldwater. "I'm demanding a recount."

Did Goldwater appreciate a good joke, even when he was the object of ridicule? Yes; and here is one that he himself repeated with unabashed enjoyment:

Barry Goldwater is sworn in as president, and Chief Justice Earl Warren is administering the oath of office.

"Repeat after me," says the liberal Judge Warren: "I swear to protect this nation against its enemies, foreign and domestic, so help me God."

"I swear," repeats Goldwater, "to protect this nation against its enemies, foreign and domestic, so help me God . . . you're under arrest, Warren!"

✓　　　✓　　　✓

Let us go back over a century in time, for a bit of Americana that has never been taught in the classroom.

When Stephen A. Douglas was stumping the country, speaking in dozens of cities, he arrived in Springfield, Illinois, where he gave one of the most eloquent exhortations of his political career. As he spoke, he noticed that one of his most avid listeners was a tall, gangling, black-haired youth who hung on to his every word. At the close of his speech, Douglas approached the intense young man and remarked that he was quite flattered to find him so attentive.

"I know you are a great orator," said the youth, "and I am studying your speaking style because someday I will be up there on the platform debating with you."

"Well, I must say I admire your ambition," replied Douglas. "Tell me, what kind of work do you do?"

"I'm a rail-splitter."

"And what is your name, young man?"

"Abe."

"Abe what?" asked Douglas.

"Abe Goldfarb," was the answer.

✔   ✔   ✔

A priest and a rabbi were discussing politics.

"Wouldn't it be a great step toward real brotherhood if a Negro and a Jew were to run for president?" asked the priest.

"Yes," the rabbi agreed. But in a moment he visualized the possible newspaper headlines and public reaction, and he quickly added: "Just so long as they aren't running at the same time."

✔   ✔   ✔

This hoary old chestnut was popular five decades ago. It merits retelling for tomorrow's generation, dressed in modern garb.

Berman, an American spy, was ordered by the Central Intelligence Agency to cross over the Iron Curtain and make contact with another CIA spy named Shapiro. The password with which they would identify each other was, "The sun is shining."

Under the dark of the moon, a U.S. Air Force plane dropped Berman by parachute into the woods on the outskirts of Moscow. Our hero buried the parachute as he was instructed, and then skulked into the city, keeping to the shadows and moving stealthily as befits a high-class espionage agent.

He had memorized Shapiro's address but when he reached the place he found, to his chagrin, that it was a four-story apartment building. A resourceful fellow, Berman consulted the letterboxes in the hallway, where he found not one but two Shapiros listed. So he tried ringing the doorbell of the first one.

When the occupant opened the door Berman asked, "Are you Shapiro?"

"Yes, I am," said the man.

"All right, the sun is shining," said the American agent, giving the password.

"Oh, no!" the other said. "I'm Shapiro the butcher. You want Shapiro the spy—he's on the third floor!"

✔   ✔   ✔

"I'm not saying this because I was born in Russia," said Uncle Max, "but by me a peace settlement with the Soviet Union should be easy.

After all, we have nearly all of the world's cars and the Russians got all the parking spaces."

✔   ✔   ✔

A member of the *Knesset,* well known for his irascible temper and sharp tongue, became so incensed one day that he leaped from his chair and shouted, "Half of this Parliament are jackasses!"

There immediately arose angry shouts, catcalls and demands that he apologize forthwith or be ejected from the chamber.

"All right, I take it back," he grumbled. "Half of this Parliament are not jackasses!"

✔   ✔   ✔

Nikita Khrushchev, Harry Truman and Chaim Weizmann were discussing the complexities of their respective positions.

"There are two million Communist Party members in Russia," remarked Khrushchev. "That should give you an idea of my difficulties."

Said Truman: "Two million? What's two million? In the United States there are 180 million people, and I am responsible to every one of them!"

"Your job is easy compared to mine," commented Weizmann. "How would you like to be president of two-and-a-half million presidents?"

✔   ✔   ✔

At great deprivation to himself and his wife, Alex the tailor managed to send his son to Columbia University where the young man earned his master's degree in political science.

He had not been home more than two or three days after graduation when he grandly announced that henceforth he would vote Republican.

Old Alex, a Democrat ever since his arrival to the United States thirty years earlier, was aghast. "Why are you doing such a thing?" he asked.

"Because a Democratic president always surrounds himself with yes-men," the son explained. "Without opposing viewpoints we will inevitably have a one-party, yes-man government. If you were President would you want that?"

"No, that I wouldn't want," retorted the father. "By me it must show both sides of the question. I would have around me yes-men and yes-*sir* men!"

✔   ✔   ✔

One thing we can always say about Barry Goldwater: He could always see two sides to every political and social problem—conservative and ultra-conservative.

✔   ✔   ✔

Feivel, whose ignorance was exceeded only by his *chutzpah,* decided to run for local office. His brother-in-law, a professional writer, offered to prepare his first speech which was to be delivered over the radio the next evening. But Feivel, who fancied himself as something of a literary man, indignantly refused.

The following night he rushed home, breathless. "Did you hear my speech on the air?" he asked.

"Yeah, I heard it," replied the brother-in-law curtly.

"What's the matter?" asked Feivel, his face anxious. "Should I have put more fire into my speech?"

"No," snapped the brother-in-law. "You should have put more speech into the fire."

✓ ✓ ✓

Moe Mandelbaum, who had recently taken an active interest in politics, was invited to a local rally of the Socialist Party. He arrived at the hall and said to the assembled guests, "Good evening, gentlemen; so hit me already."

"Hit you! What for?" asked one of the astonished members.

"Well, last week I went to a Republican political rally," explained Mandelbaum, "and I told them I was a liberal. Right away they started to beat me. Then, just last night, I went to a Democratic meeting, and they asked me whether I was a leftist or a rightist. I thought I had learned my lesson, so this time, to play it safe, I said I was a conservative, and immediately they began to pummel me worse than the others. So here I am this evening, gentlemen. Never mind the preliminary questions—hit me already!"

✓ ✓ ✓

Avrum had somehow managed to escape from the Soviet Union and, after much hardship, settled in New York's lower East Side. He was very happy in his new-found *shtetl*, and decided he would become active in local politics so that he might better express his love and admiration for America.

At the next meeting of the Orchard Street Democratic Club, he was accepted and then asked to make a little speech to the other members. Avrum, uncertain of his constitutional rights, stammered, hesitated, and began to perspire.

"You needn't be nervous," said the district leader kindly. "Here in this great country you have freedom of speech."

"It's not that," said Avrum. "What worries me is freedom *after* speech!"

✓ ✓ ✓

Down through history there have always been those bigots who will not support a Jew for public office. Disraeli encountered one when he first ran for Parliament. When he solicited the anti-Semite's vote, the man hissed, "I would rather vote for the devil himself than vote for you."

"I understand perfectly," countered Disraeli in an even voice. "But in case your friend decides not to run, may I count on your support?"

✦　✦　✦

A few of the inhabitants of a little Polish village on the border of Russia had become enamored of Bolshevism, right after the overthrow of the Czarist regime.

The local Communists called on the one and only rabbi of the town with a request. "Rabbi, you are a man whose opinions and suggestions are held in high esteem by everyone. We respectfully ask that you preach on the evils of capitalism and the benefits of socialism."

"My friends," answered the old rabbi patiently, "I have always believed that the Socialists do not really share the wealth; they just spread the poverty around a little more. So what is there to preach?"

"What is there to preach? The capitalists own all the wealth in the world and the poor struggling workers barely earn enough to feed themselves. Do you call that fair?"

"*Nu,* what do you suggest *I* do about it?"

"Tell the people about the new system."

"I'll do what I can," sighed the rabbi, "but only on the condition that you cooperate with me."

"Anything—anything!"

"Very well," said the rabbi. "You get the capitalists to part with their wealth and I'll see to it that the workers accept!"

✦　✦　✦

Dr. Albert Einstein told of the time the late Mayor La Guardia of New York became ill with an intestinal disorder. While recuperating at Montefiore Hospital he received a resolution from the powers-that-be: "The City Council wishes you quick recovery by a vote of 19 to 12."

✦　✦　✦

Worried Father: "Rabbi, I don't know what has come over my son. A nice teen-age boy like that, and he believes in Communism."

Rabbi: "At his age there is no need for concern, my friend. When a young boy believes in Communism it only means he has a soft heart. But if he still believes in Communism when he becomes an adult it will mean he has a soft head."

✦　✦　✦

Papa arrived at Ellis Island from Russia, was accorded courteous treatment by customs and sped onward to New York where he and his fellow immigrants were given a kind welcome to our shores by American officials.

"What a wonderful country!" exclaimed Papa. "I tell you, New York has the finest politicians money can buy!"

✦　✦　✦

Izzy and Joseph were discussing international affairs.

"Today it is very fashionable for other countries to burn down our libraries, stone our embassies and jail our tourists," Izzy observed. "I ask you, Joseph, have the billions of dollars America sent overseas in Foreign Aid made us any friends?"

"Perhaps not," answered Joseph after a moment or two of thought, "but you have to admit we got a much better class of enemies."

✦ ✦ ✦

The chairman of the Communist Party of America was expounding on Marxism before a study group in New York. On and on he droned until one of the listeners fell asleep. The lecturer regarded him sternly.

"Comrade," he shouted, awakening the man, "if you must sleep, I suggest you go home."

"Now just a minute!" retorted the offender. "What do you mean, telling me to go home? I'll sleep wherever I please and I'll listen to you or not, also as I please. Just where do you think you are, Comrade—in the glorious Soviet Union?"

✦ ✦ ✦

The beloved entertainer of the Yiddish and English theatre, Molly Picon, once posed this question:

Can you imagine a woman president of the United States? The Secretary of State rushes into her office and gasps, "Madam President, the Soviets are building up their military strength in Eastern Europe, the Arabs are poised to invade Israel, and two revolutions have just started in South America."

And the lady president answers: "Please, first you'll eat, then you'll talk!"

✦ ✦ ✦

The old man, much against his will, was persuaded by his civic-minded granddaughter to attend a political lecture. The speaker was one of those intellectuals who expound lofty ideals couched in polysyllabic words and phrases.

When the oldster returned home three hours later, his granddaughter exclaimed, "Didn't he make you feel exalted?"

"No," said the grandfather, "he made me feel dumb on one end and numb on the other!"

✦ ✦ ✦

Sol and Jerry Pomerantz, two brothers, were both running for the same office. Jerry won.

"I can't understand it," complained Sol. "My campaign manager swore to me that if I gave every taxi driver a big tip and told them I was a Republican they would influence a lot of voters."

"That was lousy advice," said Jerry. "You should have given them no tip at all and told them you were a Democrat!"

✓ ✓ ✓

The minions of the Czar caught Irving Gottessoff handing out revolutionary pamphlets and the very next morning he found himself facing a firing squad. The lieutenant in charge walked over to the political prisoner, tied the blindfold and then started the fatal count: "One—ready! Two—aim! Th . . ."

He was interrupted by a shout from the condemned prisoner; "Long live the revolution! Down with the Czar!"

Aghast, the lieutenant stalked over to the victim, jerked the blindfold from his eyes, and snarled; "What the hell is the matter with you? Aren't you in enough trouble already?"

✓ ✓ ✓

Two recent immigrants had just been listening to a political speech on the radio. Now, over their glasses of tea, they were discussing the issues.

"Frankly," said one, "I never really understood all this *mishmash* about capital and labor. Do you know what it is all about?"

"Sure," answered the other. "It works like this: Suppose you were to lend me a hundred dollars. That means I take and use your capital. But when you try to collect the money from me—that's labor!"

✓ ✓ ✓

The Bolshevik court of inquiry finished its work and condemned the three political prisoners to be hanged. Before carrying out the executions the three men were invited to state their final wish.

The first prisoner, a former cossack, said, "I'd like to have a full pint of vodka." His wish was granted at once.

"I want to be inscribed as a Communist Party member," said the next prisoner, a priest in the Russian Orthodox Church. When the local commissar pressed him for his reason, he explained, "After I am hanged there will be one less scoundrel in the world."

The third victim, a Jew who was caught attempting to escape to America, requested a serving of strawberries and cream.

"I'm sorry," said the commissar, "but this is the middle of winter and there just aren't any strawberries. There won't be any until next summer."

"I'll wait," said the Jew.

✓ ✓ ✓

The presiding officer was addressing a Jew who was about to join the Communist Party in Russia.

"Comrade," said the officer, "before you are initiated into the Party you must pass an oral examination. Now then, suppose somebody died and you were bequeathed 10,000 rubles—what would you do?"

"I would give 5,000 to the Party and keep the other five for myself."

"Very good! Now suppose you had two houses?"

"I would give one to the Party and keep the other."

"Excellent! And now, supposing you had two pairs of pants?"

The candidate hesitated. "Sir," he finally stammered, "I don't think that question is fair. I happen to *have* two pairs of pants!"

Chapter Thirty-five

Jewish Parents

Part I — Yiddishe Mamas

The late Ben Bernie once related this episode about his mother's seventieth birthday. As a present, he gave her a magnum of champagne and a large tin of imported caviar. He telephoned her on the following day to inquire if she was pleased with her birthday gifts.

"Benny, I'm not complaining, believe me," she said. "The ginger ale was fine, but frankly the huckleberries tasted from herring!"

✓ ✓ ✓

Mama's daughter, Muriel, was away at college, but that did not prevent the anxious mother from indulging in her favorite pastime—matchmaking. So when wealthy Mr. Goldfarb, the plumbing contractor, mentioned that his only son and heir was unmarried, the lady brightened at once.

"Why not ask your son he should write my Muriel?" she suggested. "He could ask for her picture."

Mr. Goldfarb nodded. "A good idea. I'll ask him to write to her at the college. By the way, what's her zip code number?"

"38-24-36," beamed Mama.

✓ ✓ ✓

Mrs. Levine, her face wreathed in proud smiles, was pushing her baby-carriage along Wilshire Boulevard in Los Angeles, taking her infant daughter on her first outing. On the way she encountered a neighbor who gushed over the baby.

"What a beautiful child!" the neighbor cried.

Mrs. Levine smiled delightedly. "This is nothing," she boasted. "You should see her pictures!"

✓ ✓ ✓

Three well-to-do Yiddishe mamas, the mesdames Goldstein, Silverstein and Finkelstein, were sipping tea and boasting about their sons, each trying to outdo the others in their exaggerated praise.

"Let me I should tell you about mein Theodore," began Mrs. Goldstein. "Have I got a good son! When the snow it's snowing does mein Theodore allow I should stay here and maybe freeze to death? Not mein Theodore! Right away he's phoning the airport it should send me for two weeks to Miami. In the best hotel—The Founting Blue—he's arranging for me rooms. Not a penny it's costing his mama. That's mein Theodore!"

Mrs. Silverstein, who had been waiting somewhat impatiently for her turn, now spoke. "It's a good son, your Theodore, but listen about mein Harry. *Oy*, I could eat him up he's such a fine boy! When it's snowing and Harry is afraid I'll maybe freeze to death, mein Harry is not just phoning the airport, he's *taking* me and putting me on the plane. In Miami, instead of the Founting Blue he's leasing for me a private house on the beach. Who else, I'm asking like a lady, is so good like mein Harry?"

Now it was Mrs. Finkelstein's turn to do a little bragging. "No question, it's two nice boys you got, but me and mein Seymour we're regular buddies like you never heard. Every week he's going to a man and he's paying the man fifty dollars. For what? Just so he can lay down on a couch and talk. And what is he talking about at such fancy prices mein Seymour? *Me!*"

✓   ✓   ✓

Mrs. Ginsberg's friend from the old neighborhood paid her a visit. After Mrs. Ginsberg had pumped her dry of news it was now the friend's turn. "I hear your daughter Hannah got married. It's a good match?"

"Believe me, no girl ever got such a wonderful husband," Mrs. Ginsberg enthused. "Like a queen he treats her. In soapy water he doesn't allow she should put her hand. She's resting in bed until eleven and then on a tray the maid brings orange juice and breakfast. In the afternoon its shopping on Fifth Avenue—such clothes she buys; gorgeous! And in the evening she mets her husband for cocktails at the Ritz. For such *mazel* we can only thank God."

"And how is Raymond, your son? I hear he's married also."

Mrs. Ginsberg's face fell. "Don't even ask," she said dourly. "I only wish he had a little of Hannah's *mazel*. He married one of those fancy-shmancy girls from uptown. My poor Raymond he got a wife that won't even put her hand in soapy water she should wash a little something. To get up early she's against, so she lies in bed until eleven eating bum-bums— a maid yet she needs to bring her a noon breakfast. In the afternoon does she at least dust around the house a little? No! On Fifth Avenue she goes to buy expensive clothes. And in the evening does she sit down at the table with my Raymond they should have a *haimisheh* supper? I should live so long! She drags him off to the Ritz they should guzzle cocktails. *Oy!* What sin have I committed, God should punish me with such a daughter-in-law?"

✓   ✓   ✓

Sadie Goldsmith grew so weary of her mother's constant preachments that she "marry a rich doctor," the girl decided to get away from it all by joining the Peace Corps. After two years in the Congo she married a seven foot Watusi and returned to the Bronx with her ebony husband.

Mama Goldsmith took one look at the towering African in his loin cloth, feathers and pierced nose, and moaned; *"Oy*, Sadie, I said a *rich* doctor, not a *witch* doctor!"

✦ ✦ ✦

Grandma took little Marvin and Melvin with her to the corner drug store to buy them a soda. They were walking along the street, two chubby hands clutched in Grandma's, when the *rebbetzn* approached, *"Aye*, such lovely boys," she crooned. "Tell me, how old are they?"

"The doctor is four," explained Grandma, "and the lawyer is six."

✦ ✦ ✦

"My Morty went to Las Vegas on business and while he was there he gambled a little," boasted Mama Litvak.

"So what's to be proud?" asked her neighbor. "In Las Vegas nobody wins."

"Listen, my Morty did fine," retorted Mrs. Litvak. "He told me himself he went there in a five thousand dollar Cadillac, but do you know what he came back in?—A sixty-five thousand dollar Greyhound!"

✦ ✦ ✦

Mama was expecting company for *Shabbes* so she borrowed her son's car to do some Friday morning shopping.

A few hours later, the car now loaded with groceries, Mama made a sudden right turn and almost collided with a motorcycle cop. The policeman ordered her to pull over to the curb and angrily demanded her reason for the sudden turn. "Don't you know that a signal is necessary?" he stormed.

"Signal? Who needs a signal?" asked Mama, round-eyed. "I always turn off here!"

✦ ✦ ✦

It was the Day of Atonement and Mama had just returned from the synagogue, when her eyes rested on some chicken bones on the kitchen table. Her son, a husky chap of eighteen was lounging on the sofa, reading a magazine. He seemed far too contented to have been fasting.

"Morris," she said sternly, pointing to the chicken bones, "you ate on Yom Kippur. How could you do such a thing?"

"Now don't start accusing me, Mama," protested the youth. "I haven't eaten a thing, and I can prove it!"

"So prove!"

Wordlessly, Morris opened the refrigerator, extracted half a roast chicken, five hamburgers and half of a pumpernickel, all of which he devoured, washing it down with almost a quart of soda.

"See, Mama, what did I tell you," he exulted. "If I had eaten that chicken on the table do you think I'd be hungry enough to eat all this again so soon?"

✦ ✦ ✦

The rabbi smiled down fondly at the little boy. "And what did you get for Chanukah?" he asked.

"Just a little blue chair," grumbled the four-year-old, "but it's no good."

"What's the matter with it?"

"It has a big hole in the bottom!"

✦ ✦ ✦

The young man was reading the evening paper when he noticed an interesting item. "Mama," he said, "it says here that the world is getting smaller."

"That I don't believe," answered Mama tartly.

"But here it is, in black and white!"

"All right, so if the world is getting smaller why is it taking your Papa longer to get home each night?"

✦ ✦ ✦

Shirley: "Mama, what I told you yesterday about my boyfriend was in strict confidence. But you had to blab it all over the neighborhood. The trouble with you is that you can't keep a secret."

Mama: "What do you mean, I can't keep a secret? It's those big-mouths I tell it to who can't!"

✦ ✦ ✦

Little Sammy made an innocent but questionable remark about the Pope of Rome.

"You shouldn't talk like that, Sameleh," his mother admonished. "I'm sure the Pope is a fine man with a nice wife and children in the country someplace."

✦ ✦ ✦

Benjamin, the grocer, bristled through his beard as he read a newspaper account of a street demonstration in which his son was photographed picketing a super-market.

"Why does he do these things?" old Benjamin exploded.

"*Sha, sha!*" his wife said soothingly.

"I won't *sha!* Last week he carried a sign we should get out of the

381

war in Vietnam. A few days ago he's walking up and down with a sign for the New Left Party. Yesterday he's picketing at the university the professors should get a bigger minimum wage. Today he's arrested for walking around with scab signs in front of the super-market. Is this why we raised our son?"

"Please, Benny, leave him be," urged Mama. "It's the only exercise the poor boy gets."

✓ ✓ ✓

Mama checked into a hotel and the desk clerk called out, "Page boy!" The boy appeared at once and carried her luggage upstairs to her room.

Later, after a shopping tour, Mama returned to the hotel with several bulky packages. She went to the desk clerk and asked:

"Mister, would you be so kind to call again the page *goy?*"

✓ ✓ ✓

A mother gave her son two neckties as a going-away present when he left to attend the university. When he returned home from his vacation he wore one of the ties to demonstrate his appreciation for the gift.

The mother took one look at the necktie and asked anxiously, "What's the matter? The other one you didn't like?"

✓ ✓ ✓

Mama had to go to court to settle an estate.

"How old are you, Madam?" asked the judge.

"Forty-one."

"Now just a moment! I recall that you were here in this very court seven years ago and you gave me the same age."

"Your Honor," said Mama primly, "I am not the kind of person I should give every time a different answer."

✓ ✓ ✓

Mama was about to take a train trip to Chicago where her nephew was to become Bar Mitzvah, and she dolled up for the occasion. After a short subway ride from her apartment in Flatbush she entered Pennsylvania Station in all her finery, clutching her suitcase.

A porter approached and tipped his hat. "Red Cap, Ma'am?" he asked.

"What are you talking?" demanded Mama, offended. "A red cap with this brown coat and beige suit?"

✓ ✓ ✓

Mrs. Abramovitch had only recently arrived from Europe and was living with her married son. On her first weekend she learned that company was expected for Sunday. Not wishing to be an idle dependent in her new home she urged her son to allow her to cook the dinner.

"Very well, Mama," said the son. "Suppose you dress the chicken."

Mama's eyes grew wide and round. She sidled into the kitchen and whispered to her daughter-in-law: "Tell me something; how do you make a blouse for a chicken?"

✓　　✓　　✓

Mama was speaking on the telephone:

"Hello, Miriam? How's by you the gas pains? That's good! Listen, Miriam, by my daughter yesterday something wonderful happened. You never in your life heard such *mazel*. She goes to a party and who should become interested in her but a chiropodist. What do you mean, what's a chiropodist? A regular foot specialist, that's what! Why am I so excited? Why shouldn't I be excited? With my daughter's corns on both feet, already there's a physical attraction!"

✓　　✓　　✓

A prosperous son gave his mother a color television set for her birthday.

"How do you like the new color TV?" he asked.

"Marvelous!" she enthused. "Especially when the color matches my drapes!"

✓　　✓　　✓

It is sometimes impossible to predict the reaction of a doting Jewish mother. Here is a case in point:

When Oscar Levant, the famed piano virtuoso and entertainer, telephoned his mother and informed her that he had proposed to his sweetheart and she had accepted, his mother answered, "All right, Oscar; good! I'm glad to hear it. But did you practice piano today?"

✓　　✓　　✓

From the stage play, *A Family Affair,* comes this delightful misunderstanding:

Mama Finkel is taking a course in current events at the local Adult Education Center. Her teacher asks, "What do you think of Red China?"

"Red China?" echoes Mama Finkel brightly. "It's all right—but not on a yellow tablecloth!"

✓　　✓　　✓

A worried mother cautioned her small son, on their first visit to Disneyland: "Now I'm warning you, Mendel, hold tight to my hand. If you get lost don't come crying to me."

✓　　✓　　✓

The best advertiser is a Jewish mother. Take the case of the Yiddishe Mama and her grown son who went to Coney Island. The son, who was a physician and should have known better, went swimming too soon after eating, and almost at once was in distress. The mother saw him struggling in the water. Frantically she ran along the beach, wringing her hands and shrieking at the top of her voice: "Help! Somebody, please help! My son, the Park Avenue doctor, he's drowning!"

✓ ✓ ✓

The transit companies in various cities issue a weekly pass or commutation ticket which, for two or three dollars, permits the holder to ride the buses all week without extra payment of fares.

Comedian Alan King tells of the time his family lived next door to the McCarthy family. One day, his mother, Minnie, borrowed her neighbor Mary's commutation ticket.

"When that Prussian-background man in uniform, the conductor, looked at Minnie and saw the name 'Mary McCarthy' on the pass book he demanded that Mama sign her name on the open-blank RR ticket," Alan King said.

"Mama looked at him and huffed: 'I'm sorry, General, but on Saturdays I never write!' "

✓ ✓ ✓

The art of ego deflation is highly developed among the Jewish people. Without obvious insult, and more often as not with gentle innuendo made more palatable with a dash of humor and a pinch of bluntness, the boaster is eased back to reality. Here is another illustration by columnist Dorothy H. Rochmis:

When the late Moss Hart bought a yacht and a captain's outfit he invited his mother up to see the new, swanky vessel. She was awed by the magnificence of the boat. Then Moss, extremely proud of himself, asked, "Well, Mama, now what do you think of your son, the captain?"

"I'll tell you, Mosseleh," she answered sagely; "By you, you're a captain. By me you're a captain. By Papa you're a captain. But, let me ask you, by *captains* are you a captain?"

✓ ✓ ✓

A little boy heard an announcement on the radio and rushed into the kitchen where his mother was preparing dinner.

"Mama—Mama! Can I go out and watch the eclipse?"

"All right," she answered, "but don't get too close!"

✓ ✓ ✓

The stewardess on the Israeli airline went to the microphone and her voice resounded in the loudspeakers: "Good evening, ladies and gentlemen. We are flying at 21,000 feet, destination New York and we should arrive on time. Your stewardesses are Mrs. Goldie Kaplan and Mrs. Sadie Kaminsky, and, of course, my son, the pilot."

✓ ✓ ✓

The Schoenbergers, paupers all their lives, hit the Irish Sweepstakes and won a hundred thousand dollars. They invested the money in real estate but when they started to dig a foundation they struck oil. Now they were multi-millionaires. A few years later they were visited by an old neighborhood crony from Orchard Street. He was too overwhelmed to do more than gasp at the opulence now enjoyed by the Schoenbergers, but just as he was leaving he saw a butler pushing young Harold, the son, in a wheel chair.

"What's the matter with your boy?" asked the friend. "I didn't know he was crippled. Can't he walk?"

"Of course he can walk," answered Mrs. Schoenberger with some show of asperity. "But, *Gott sie dank!*—he doesn't have to."

✔   ✔   ✔

Mama: "How much please it costs to send a telegram?"
Clerk: "Where to, Madam?"
Mama: "To my son, the medical student."

Part II — Yiddishe Papas

We hear much of Yiddishe Mamas, bless them, but Yiddishe Papas are just as distinctive, endearing, pragmatic and wise. Consider this anecdote, for example:

A Yiddishe Papa took his small son to the public baths for the first time. Following his father's instructions, the boy jumped into the cold pool and in a moment began to shiver, his teeth chattering like castenets and his lips blue. "*Oy*, Papa, *Oy!*" he wailed.

The father then led his son to the dressing room and rubbed him down briskly with a towel until the little boy tingled pleasantly. He was now quite warm. "Aahh, Papa—a-a-h-h-h-!!" the lad purred contentedly.

"My son," the father said quietly, "do you know the difference between a cold bath and a sin?"

"No, Papa. What?"

"Well, when you jumped into the cold pool you first hollered '*Oy!*' Then you said 'Aahh!' But when you commit a sin you first say 'Aahh,' and then you holler '*Oy!*'"

✔   ✔   ✔

A prosperous wholesale furrier in New York received a telegram from his son who was in his first year at Harvard University. But the furrier, wealthy and successful though he was, had never learned to read English. So, as usual, his secretary read the cablegram aloud to him.

Now the secretary was in a disagreeable mood and she read the few words in an unpleasant and demanding tone: "In need of money. Shoes run down. Very cold here without new coat. Can't afford school books. Not enough to eat."

When the secretary finished reading the telegram in her disagreeable, petulant and demanding voice, the father roared, "Why, that impudent scoundrel! Who does he think he's talking to? How dare he address his own father so disrespectfully? Not a penny will he get from me. Let him first learn some manners!"

That night, at the dinner table, he thought of the telegram and withdrew it from his pocket. "Read this, Mama," he said testily. "Did you ever think our Yankeleh would be so rude?"

But when the boy's mother read the same words her maternal instincts were immediately aroused and her heart melted like *schmaltz* in a hot pan.

"Maybe you didn't understand our Yankeleh," she said gently. "Let me read it to you."

"*Nu*, so read!"

"In need of money," she read, her throat constricting with a motherly sob. "Shoes run down," she continued in a voice that would have softened a stone. "Very cold here," she read further, her voice conjuring up pictures of their Yankeleh shivering in his underwear and cowering in a blizzard. When she came to the phrase "Not enough to eat," and her eyes swept their table which was richly laden with food, her Yiddishe Mama's heart broke completely and she wept.

"Well, that's different," grumbled the father as he reached for his checkbook. "Now at least he's asking like a gentleman!"

✓ ✓ ✓

Mama and Papa were discussing a suitable birthday present for their young son. Said Mama: "A little boy should have a dog, he should be a well-rounded personality like in the psychology books." Papa agreed, and the next day he went to a pet shop to make the purchase.

"Mister, have I got a special dog for you!" enthused the proprietor. He quickly selected an alert-looking cocker spaniel from a litter of other puppies.

"What kind of dog is this?" asked Papa.

"He's a little cocker."

"That's all I need around the house," muttered Papa. "What's so special about him?"

"I'll tell you what's so special," said the store owner. "You throw a stick into the water and this dog will not only fetch the stick and bring it back to you, but he does it by walking on the surface of the water."

"Then keep the mutt—I don't want him!" said Papa.

"Maybe you didn't hear me. I said he walks on water."

"I heard you. But who needs a dog that's too stupid to learn how to swim?"

✓ ✓ ✓

Papa was an immigrant who had never had the advantages of a higher education. As might be expected, he married a college graduate—a regular intellectual. They became involved, one night, in a mild argument about the origin of creation.

Said the intellectual Mama: "I accept the universe as it is."

"*Nu*," countered Papa, "and if you didn't . . . ?"

✓   ✓   ✓

"I can't marry Marvin. I prefer a man who makes things—like that nice Mr. Kaplan who makes half-a-million a year!"

✓   ✓   ✓

"Whaddyamean, I don't make good money? My salary runs to four figures . . . my wife and three daughters!"

✓   ✓   ✓

Father: "I don't know what to do about my son. He can't play pinochle."

Rabbi: "That's something to be concerned about?"

Father: "Of course! He insists on playing anyway."

✓   ✓   ✓

"When I was a boy in the old country we knew the value of a ruble," complained Papa. "But the younger generation here in America is different. The other day I gave my daughter one of those tiny compact cars for her eighteenth birthday. 'Now you have something to go shopping in,' I told her."

"So she went shopping—for a bigger car."

✓   ✓   ✓

Twelve-year-old Sidney labored for many days to build a chair for his father, and finally, on Chanukah, he presented it as a gift. But when the boy's father sat on the chair he found that the seat was far too high.

"Oh, Dad," cried Sidney in disappointment, "I made the chair too high!"

"No you didn't," said his father gently; "it's just that the table is too low."

✓   ✓   ✓

A father grew tired of listening to his married son's complaints about his nagging wife. "Don't complain to me about the girl," grumbled the father. "You should have asked for my opinion before you married her, like any respectable Jewish son."

"Did you consult me for my opinion when you got married?" snapped the wrought-up son.

"Now see here, don't get so fresh with your own father!" roared the

387

older man. "Who needed to ask for your advice? When I got married it was to your mother. But look what you did—you went and married a perfect stranger!"

✓ ✓ ✓

Most Jewish fathers know better than to interfere in the domestic problems affecting their married children. One elderly father solved the problem in his own unique fashion.

He was having dinner at the home of his daughter and son-in-law when the young couple became involved in a violent argument. In the heat of anger the girl called her husband a naughty name and, without thinking —almost a reflex action—the young man slapped her.

The father's face turned red and then it turned pale. Then, without warning, he leaned across the table and gave his daughter a resounding slap on the other cheek.

The girl was too astonished to utter a word, but the youth, instantly sorry for striking the girl he really loved, rose up, furious. "Now listen," he shouted, "father or no father, how dare you slap my wife?"

"By me we're even," said the older man calmly. "You strike my daughter, I'll hit your wife!"

✓ ✓ ✓

Teen-age Marvin had just bought a battered old car for twenty-five dollars. It was in such bad condition that even the auto wreckers had refused to buy it. Nevertheless, Marvin, who never owned a car before, was quite proud of his new possession. On the first day, he insisted on washing the crumpled, dented, rusted jalopy.

His father, who was watching the laundry operation with a caustic smile, finally commented:

"Marvin, into your business I want you to know I'm not sticking my nose, but after you finish washing that thing, maybe you better iron it also!"

✓ ✓ ✓

A father and son were discussing the younger man's stormy marriage. "No matter what I say or do, she finds fault," grumbled the son. "I guess we're just incompatible."

"The fancy word I don't know," responded the father, "but to me it seems you and your wife never had a meeting of the minds. Now take me and your mama, for example. When I first married her we had a meeting of the minds right away. I agreed to turn over to her every week my salary, and she agreed to accept."

✓ ✓ ✓

Mama and Papa Weiss were entertaining a neighboring couple. "Our daughter," said Mama Weiss proudly, "is now in the dungarees and loafers stage."

"Yeah," muttered Papa Weiss, "she wears dungarees and dates loafers."

✔   ✔   ✔

Feival and Kaminsky, two old friends, had not seen each other for many years, so when they accidentally met on the street one day, they went to a coffee house to talk over times gone by.

"Feival," said Kaminsky over their third cup of coffee, "I have happy news for you. I just married off my oldest daughter to a fine man—a dentist."

"Wonderful—wonderful!" enthused Feival. "But a dentist? You must have had to give a substantial dowry to get such a son-in-law."

"Don't ask! I had to sell my business, mortgage the house and give them all my savings. Now they live in a mansion. It's so fancy they won't even let me come near the place."

"You're a lucky man," sighed Kaminsky. "I only hope when I marry off my daughter I should have such *mazel!*"

✔   ✔   ✔

Every ethnic group has its quota of unsavory characters and Jews are no exception. Jack "Legs" Diamond passed along his reputation as a gangster when he was cut down by machine gun bullets in the "Roaring Twenties," but his single legacy to humor remains:

When Jack ("Jake" to his family) approached the Bar Mitzvah age, his proud father was at a loss as to a suitable gift. So he consulted his son's Hebrew teacher. (Yes, the mobster came from a fine, respectable family.)

"Well, Mr. Diamond," said the instructor, "I can think of no better Bar Mitzvah present than an encyclopedia."

"What!" cried Mr. Diamond, outraged. "God forbid, he'd get himself killed in all this heavy traffic. Let him walk, like other thirteen-year-old boys!"

✔   ✔   ✔

Sometimes it requires a rude, even brutal shock, to awaken us to our own shortcomings. This ancient tale provides the example.

Many, many years ago there lived a rich man who had such confidence in his beloved son that he gave him all his money and property. But soon the ungrateful young wretch began to neglect his good-hearted father. He treated the older man shamefully and finally sent him away from the very house that he himself had once owned. Sadly, the father went to live among the beggars of the city. Meanwhile, the son married, and in the course of time his wife bore him a son of his own.

One day, twenty years later, the old man, clad in tatters, met his grandson and asked him to beg his father to give him a cloak. It was cold and he shivered in his ancient bones. After much pleading, the father

389

grudgingly sent his son to the attic and told him to select the oldest, cheapest cloak he could find. The boy found the cloak, but before bringing it downstairs, he took a pair of scissors and cut the garment in half. Then he took the two halves to his father and presented one of them to him.

"Why did you cut the cloak?" demanded the father. "And why are you giving me one of the halves?"

"That part of the cloak, Father," the young man answered slowly, "is for you when *you* grow old!"

✓   ✓   ✓

"Our kids grow up before we know it," commented the late Eddie Cantor wistfully. "Just today my youngest daughter got her first pair of long pants."

✓   ✓   ✓

Max Baer, the only Jewish heavyweight boxing chamption of the world, told this story to your editor only a few days before his untimely death of a heart attack in Los Angeles.

I was only eleven or twelve when I had a fight with an older, much bigger boy, Max reminisced. That night, when Pop came home from work, he asked about my black eye and then scolded me for fighting.

"But, Pop," I said defensively, "I was only hitting back. He started up. I don't start up with guys bigger'n me."

"*Nu*, so why doesn't he start up with me?" asked Pop in the traditional, if illogical, Jewish idiom.

"Okay, have it your own way," I said, resigning from the argument. "But tell me, why don't *I* start up with you?"

✓   ✓   ✓

A young man returned home after attending a fancy-shmancy party. At once his father perceived that his son was in a foul humor.

"What's with you?" asked the father. "You didn't like the party?"

"I guess I just wasn't born to be an aristocrat," the young man grumbled. "I met a nice girl there, but when I left her at her apartment all she did was raise her hand for me to kiss. Can you imagine! Me, a hand-kisser?"

"Why not?" asked the father tolerantly. "After all, you got to start someplace."

✓   ✓   ✓

Columnist David Schwartz told this one in the *California Jewish Voice*:

A Jewish boy was in love with a girl of another faith. The boy's father was against the marriage but the son married her anyway.

The son was employed in his father's store and on the Sabbath following the honeymoon, the bridegroom failed to show up at the place of business. He explained to his father that his wife would not allow him to work on *Shabbes*.

"Aha!" exclaimed the father. "Didn't I warn you not to marry her?"

✦ ✦ ✦

A father was lecturing his Bar Mitzvah-age son on the advantages of thrift. "A fool and his money are soon parted," he said, quoting the old adage.

"I guess you're right, Dad," answered the boy. "But tell me, how did the fool and his money ever get together in the first place?"

✦ ✦ ✦

Son: "Dad, what was your ambition when you were a little boy?"

Father: "To wear long pants. I got my wish, too. There isn't another man in America who wears his pants longer than I do."

✦ ✦ ✦

The proud papa stood over his boy's cradle and said, "I'm going to give you all the things I never had—girls!"

✦ ✦ ✦

Mama, Papa and little Isidor were at the supper table.

"Papa," asked Isidor, "what's the difference between a husband and a bachelor?"

Papa winked at Mama, and in a solemn voice he answered his son, "A bachelor, Isidor, is a man who comes to work every morning from a different direction."

✦ ✦ ✦

"Young man, I do want my daughter to marry," said the father, "but whoever marries her will need a lot of money."

"Sir," the would-be groom answered, "you're talking to the right man. Nobody needs a lot of money more than I do."

✦ ✦ ✦

Eternal Triangle: Mama ordered her small son to take the garbage out.

"No!" said the boy sullenly.

"How dare you disobey your mother?" roared Papa. "Are you any better than your father?"

✦ ✦ ✦

Sammy was supposed to bring his girl home to meet his parents but that afternoon his mother was rushed to the hospital with a gallstone attack. Sammy brought his lady love home anyway to meet his father. When the mother returned from the hospital she asked her husband: "You met the girl?"

391

"I met her," said the father without enthusiasm.

"You didn't take to her—I can tell. What is she like?"

"Well, put it this way," said the father, "she's kind of in-between the Queen of Sheba and Camille—sort of a *Shlemiel*."

✔   ✔   ✔

"Dad, how is it that you and Mom get along so well? I certainly don't get along that well with my wife."

"Well, Son, it's all a question of dividing the responsibilities of marriage. The man handles his part, the woman takes care of her duties. The important thing is that the wife should be in charge of the household necessities while the husband looks after the more important things."

"I've tried, Dad, but our marriage is still shaky. How do you work it?"

"Well, as I said, we divide the responsibilities. Your mother worries about the gas and electric bills, the rent, the food, the children and grandchildren; and I worry about the more important things—the war in Vietnam, the Suez Canal, the national budget, the first landing on Mars . . . !"

✔   ✔   ✔

The girl's father saw her smooching with her boyfriend on the front porch. For a good five minutes they kissed before she finally said "good night" and entered the house. The father met her in the living room and indignantly asked, "How many times did you kiss that boy?"

"How should I know, Daddy?" countered the daughter. "You raised me to be a housewife, not an accountant."

✔   ✔   ✔

Papa called at the General Delivery window of the local post office. The clerk glanced through the mail and held up a parcel. "I don't know whether this package is for you or not. The name is obliterated."

"No, that's not my name," said Papa. "It's Shapiro."

✔   ✔   ✔

It was a tranquil evening at home. The little boy was doing his homework and his father was reading the evening paper. The boy came across two words whose meanings were not clear to him. "Dad," he asked, "what's the difference between 'anger' and 'exasperation?'"

"Well," answered the father, "it is really a matter of semantics. Let me show you an example so you won't forget it."

The father then went to the telephone and dialed a number at random. To the man who answered the phone, he said, "Hello, is Hymie there?"

"Mister," the man answered, "there's no Hymie here! Why don't you look up the number before you dial?"

The father turned to his son. "See?" he pointed out, "that man wasn't really angry with our call. But he was exasperated. Now we'll call him again and see what happens."

He dialed the same number. "Hello," said the father calmly, "is Hymie there?"

"Now look here!" came the heated reply, "you just called this number and I told you there's no Hymie here! You have a lot of nerve calling again. You better look up the right number or call Information. I'm sick of you!" The receiver slammed down hard.

Once again the father addressed his son. "Now I'll show you the difference between the kind of exasperation our unknown friend displayed, and true anger. For the third time he dialed the man's number and when the voice at the other end of the line bellowed a violent "HELLO!" the father calmly said:

"Hello, this is Hymie. Any calls for me?"

✦   ✦   ✦

Son: "Pop, why can't we have wall-to-wall carpets like other people?"

Father: "Listen, when I was your age we were lucky to have wall-to-wall floors!"

✦   ✦   ✦

A sharp-looking man sidled up to David Katzenelson's pushcart and picked up a pair of scissors which he began to examine closely. He finally decided to buy it and put his hand in his pocket to take out the money. At that point David's twelve-year-old son ran up to his father.

"*Tateh!*" cried the boy in Yiddish.

"Quiet!" snapped the father. "Not a word out of you!"

"But *Tateh!*"

"I told you to keep quiet," cried the father, more sternly than before.

By this time the transaction was completed and the shifty-eyed customer had left the pushcart.

"*Tateh*, why did you stop me?" the little boy complained. "I wanted to tell you that the man put another pair of scissors into his pocket. I saw him."

"Don't worry about it, Son, I saw him too," said David. "But I charged him extra."

"You charged him for *two* pairs?"

"No, my son. For three!"

✦   ✦   ✦

It was Father's Day on the campus and Dave Philipson was uneasy. His Dad, an immigrant with a wealth of kindness and a poverty of manners, was scheduled to have dinner at the fraternity house. But as the dinner progressed, Dave's fears were stilled; his father's table manners were impeccable. At the last, however, the old man poured some tea into his saucer and blew upon it.

"Dad, for heaven's sake; why are you doing that?" hissed the son, crestfallen.

"What kind of question is that for a college boy to ask?" cried the surprised father. "I'm cooling off the tea—what else?"

Chapter Thirty-six

High Finance

The story is told of Harry Berman who had a flourishing ladies' wear store on 14th Street and Second Avenue, during the mid-1920's. Successful as he was, however, Harry was always in debt because of his wife's extravagances.

One day, when he was on the verge of utter financial ruin, he went to the Bank of The United States and borrowed $3,000. The loan was granted so quickly and easily that he wondered why he had not thought of it before. But when the note fell due, Harry was unable to repay the money. So he went to another bank, The First National, and borrowed enough to pay off the first one. Six months later this note, too, became payable, and as Harry's wife was still spending more than he earned, he found it necessary to go to the Chase National Bank. When that loan became due and payable he went to the Corn Exchange Bank, and from there to several others, always paying off one to satisfy the other. Soon he ran out of banks and started the cycle all over again. Now, a number of institutions were pressing him for payment at the same time. The day of reckoning was close at hand.

Inevitably he received a sharp reminder from one of the banks requesting immediate payment. Harry showed up at the bank early the next morning and confronted the manager in his office.

"Look here," he said indignantly, "nasty letters like this nobody needs. What am I, your servant that I should run around from one bank to another making payments? From now on you can just pay each other and stop bothering me!"

＊　　＊　　＊

A poor carpenter from Bensonhurst once built a small cottage all by himself and sold it at a profit. With the proceeds he bought more material and built two houses. One sold at a profit and the other at a loss. With the proceeds he bought still more material and built four houses, and sold one at a profit and three at a loss. With the proceeds he bought material again and built eight houses, all of which he sold at a loss.

From that time on, although he was known as a big-time builder, he never made a profit on his houses, but kept borrowing more and more money from the various building and loan associations. Finally he was called in by the president of the biggest lending institution. "Tell me, how do you expect to continue in business when you constantly operate at a loss?" the official asked.

"It's easy," explained the builder. "The new houses give me just enough collateral to borrow additional money so I can keep on building."

"But sooner or later all this must come to an end. Your collateral may drop below the amount of money you need. You can't always be this lucky."

"Why not?" retorted the builder. "With the help of God I might suddenly drop dead right in the middle of my biggest loss!"

✓ ✓ ✓

As an aftermath of the Wall Street crash of 1929, the Bank of The United States closed its doors, defaulting on refunds to thousands of depositors. This was prior to the establishment of the Federal Deposit Insurance Act, and the public had no recourse whatever.

Among those who waited in line all night for the bank to open in the forlorn hope of retrieving even part of their savings was Goldfarb the peddler. He was actually next in line and was about to enter the bank when the doors were slammed in his face. "The bank's funds are exhausted—there will be no further payments," said a voice over the loudspeaker.

Goldfarb turned sadly to the uniformed guard at the entrance. "You can go home now," he sighed. "My forty-three dollars and nine cents is gone. What's there to guard?"

✓ ✓ ✓

Friedman learned about a tiny piece of worthless land, not more than a few feet square, that was for sale. It adjoined the city dump and he could buy it for only $75.00. So he went to his brother-in-law and borrowed that amount, promising to repay the loan in a year.

With the land now his, Friedman scouted the dump, found various items which he stocked on his property and was soon selling the items to junk dealers. He bought a larger piece of property and sold it at a profit. With the proceeds he built a couple of duplex houses and immediately sold them, too. Now, only six months from the time he had borrowed the initial $75, he was worth $100,000.

Then Friedman got an option on a large suburban tract, and tripled his money. Next he bought into a huge housing development. On the very last day of the eleventh month since he had started his junk business, he invested every penny he had, somewhere in the neighborhood of twelve million dollars, in a fifty-story office building. The assessed value of the structure was one hundred million. But just two hours after all the papers were signed and he took possession, an earthquake erupted and the office building came tumbling down in ruins.

His year was up. Sadly, he went to his brother-in-law. "I'm sorry, Max," he apologized, "but I guess I'm not much of a businessman. I just lost your whole seventy-five dollars!"

✓ ✓ ✓

Leo and Becky Gordon had eked out a bare subsistence in their general dry goods store for three decades so that their son, Milton, might have the advantages of a higher education. Now, to their joy, Milton had returned from the university with a degree in economics, determined to help his father put the store on a paying basis.

To Milton's consternation, he quickly discovered that his Dad kept few records. There was no bookkeeping system, nor were records of sales or purchases anywhere in evidence. Neither old man Leo nor his wife had the slightest idea of modern store management. The son was aghast.

"Now look, Dad," he protested, "this is no way to run a business. First of all, you need an accountant."

The old man beamed at Milton's display of knowledge. "Fine! Anything you say."

In due course an accountant was employed, but a few days later Leo received the bad news. "You haven't a dime," the new accountant told him. "You're bankrupt. Had you kept proper records you'd have known this yourself, long ago."

That night, at the dinner table, Becky could not help but notice Leo's downcast expression. "What's the matter?" she asked.

"Becky, the accountant says we're bankrupt," he told her, a muffled sob in his throat.

Her heart went out to him in quick sympathy. After all, they had been married for almost thirty-five years. She laid a gentle hand on his arm. "You're making from a mountain a molehill," she said. "We always managed there should be *eppes* in the house to eat, yes? The rent it was always paid, yes? The money for Milton's college education was raised, yes?"

"But things are different now," Leo moaned.

"What's different?" Becky demanded. "The store? No! The merchandise? No! The customers? No! I'll tell you what's different—the accountant! By me the answer is no problem. To get back on a paying basis, fire the accountant!"

✓ ✓ ✓

The minister of the local Methodist Church was in a quandary. His committee had voted to replace the present building with a new church, at a cost of $61,000. The members of his congregation, through direct contributions, tithes, raffles, suppers and bazaars had only managed to raise $40,500. Clearly it would be necessary to seek additional capital elsewhere. So the minister and his deacons canvassed all areas of the city.

The minister, himself, chose the Lower East Side area of New York as his territory. He was making the rounds on Hester Street when he came to the shop of an Orthodox Jew.

"Look," protested the wizened Israelite when the problem was put to him, "you can't expect an observant Jew to contribute to a Christian church when my own synagogue is also in need."

The minister turned to leave, but the old patriarch called him back. "On second thought," he said, "let me ask you something; does it cost anything to tear down the old building before you start the new one?"

"Of course! We must pay the contractor for the demolition."

"In that case," answered the Orthodox Jew, "I really can't give anything for the new building, but here is fifty dollars to tear down the present church!"

✓ ✓ ✓

Hirshkovitch, the barrel-maker of Yekaterinoslav, fancied himself as something of an economist. One evening, at the supper table, his brother-in-law asked him to explain the monetary system of Russia.

"The first thing to remember," explained Hirshkovitch, "is that there is only one large gold coin in the whole country, and it is constantly changing hands. This process is called 'circulation.' "

"Now wait a minute!" protested the brother-in-law. "That just isn't so! I myself once saw two gold pieces at the same time."

"Don't be such a *shlemiel*!" retorted Hirshkovitch. "What you saw was an optical illusion, created by the speed of the circulation!"

✓ ✓ ✓

An imaginative member of a Chicago finance company sent the following letter to one of his delinquent accounts:

> "Dear Mr. Levy:
> After checking our records, we note that we have done more for you than your own mother did. We carried you for fifteen months."

✓ ✓ ✓

Paul Pincus, sole owner of Paul's Pretty Panties Corp., decided to expand his manufacturing plant. His ready cash was tied up in inventory and running expenses, so he went to a bank for a loan.

"How much do you need?" asked the banker.

"Fifty thousand should do nicely."

"Hmmm. That's a lot of money. I'll have to ask for some collateral. Tell me, how many panties do you have in stock?"

"At least 100,000 pairs."

The banker mulled the matter over in his mind for a few moments,

398

conferred with one of his associates, and then nodded. "That should be satisfactory. Just fill out these forms and you can have the money."

Grumbling impatiently at the close questioning and paper work, Pincus did as he was told. He took the $50,000 check, used it for the intended business purposes, and within three months he returned to the bank.

"Here's your money back, paid in full, and with interest," he said to the same banker. "This has been a good panties season."

"You needn't pay it back this quickly," the banker assured him.

"I don't mind. Actually, I doubled my money."

"Well, I'm delighted to hear it. Listen, now that you have so much extra money, why not place it on deposit here?"

The manufacturer looked the banker straight in the eye. "I thought of it," he confessed. "But there are two requirements."

"What do you mean?"

"First, it will be necessary for you to visit my office and fill out a few forms."

The banker gritted his teeth, but agreed.

"Next, you will have to answer one question: How many pairs of panties do *you* have in stock?"

✓   ✓   ✓

A poor milliner rushed home and joyfully exclaimed to his wife, "Freida, I'm on the verge of becoming a very wealthy man!"

"What makes you think you're going to be so rich all of a sudden?"

"Because when I was bargaining for material at the jobbing house this morning, the man, even though he knew I haven't got a dime, already started calling me *momzer!*"

✓   ✓   ✓

The youth was telling his fiancée about his family background. "Papa lost everything in the '29 Wall Street crash."

"You mean he was a big banker?" the girl asked, surprised.

"No, not that. A ruined financier jumped out of the thirty-fifth story window of the Securities Building and landed on Papa's pushcart."

✓   ✓   ✓

Zeitlin the cloak-and-suiter had a rare opportunity to buy 20,000 silk linings at a fraction of their true worth. But, alas, every penny he owned was tied up in the business—and business was especially poor that season. The bank, he knew, would not lend him a dime without adequate collateral so he decided to ask his brother-in-law for a loan.

"Herb, I have a chance to make a killing on silk linings," he began abruptly. "All I need is twelve hundred—a short term loan."

"*Azoi,*" murmured Herb, reading his newspaper.

Zeitlin waited a full minute, but when no further comment was forthcoming he repeated the request. "I need a loan of twelve hundred dollars."

"Azoi," said the brother-in-law again, still absorbed in his paper.

Another minute passed without further comment, and Zeitlin boiling at Herb's silence, shouted indignantly, "What's the matter with you? Are you deaf? At least you owe me an answer."

Deliberately, Herb folded his paper and faced Zeitlin. "You're right, I do owe you an answer, and let's keep it that way. Better I should owe you an answer than you should owe me twelve hundred dollars."

✓ ✓ ✓

Isaac and Leah had lived on the East Side for fifty years, ever since they emigrated to the United States as newlyweds. In the course of time their little dry goods store flourished, and they added furs, jewelry and expensive perfumes to their stock and built one of the most profitable enterprises in the neighborhood.

Came the day when they decided to branch out—to enter the big world of the *goyim*. They told their banker of their desire. "A big department store—the best in New York. Money is no object."

The banker soon found the one store in the city that fitted their requirements and their swollen purse—Macy's. An appointment was made with Macy's board of directors, and Isaac and Leah were escorted around the huge department store by none other than Mr. Macy himself. When they had finished their tour of inspection Isaac seemed quite satisfied and was just about to write a check for five million dollars as a deposit when Leah ran over to him and tugged at his sleeve.

"Isaac, don't buy!" she whispered urgently.

"Why not?" he asked in surprise.

"You didn't notice? The store doesn't have an apartment in the back."

✓ ✓ ✓

Shmuel the tailor came to America from a little Russian town. He could not read or write English but he opened a shop and began to prosper. In time he went to the bank and opened up an account. Unable to write, he signed his name by making two crosses on the bank documents in lieu of his signature.

As the years rolled by, he prospered still further. He sold his tailor shop, went into the cloak-and-suit business and then into the manufacture of piece-goods. Again he went to the bank, this time to open up a new account to handle his expanded business. But, instead of signing two crosses, he signed three.

"Why three crosses instead of two?" asked the bank president.

"Oh, you know how women are," muttered Shmuel. "My wife got fancy-shmancy these last few days. Now she wants I should take a middle name!"

✓ ✓ ✓

The infallibility of the economic laws of supply and demand may have been popularized by the American tycoons of the 19th and 20th

400

centuries, but their principles were well known to the Jews of an earlier age. Witness this example by Jacob Richman in *Laughs from Jewish Lore*, published in 1910.

Many of the great rabbis of Russia, up to the end of the 19th century, were noted for their lack of interest in worldly matters, and their utter contempt for (or ignorance of) the material things of life.

Nathan Sokolow, the celebrated Hebrew journalist and Zionist, related the story of the rabbi who settled a case, and was handed ten rubles by the two litigants as compensation for his trouble, as was customary in those days. The venerable man looked at the bills rather curiously and asked what they were.

"This," explained the erstwhile opponents, "is money."

"What's money?" asked the godly one.

"It's a medium of exchange," explained the two laymen. "With money one does business, builds houses and so forth and so on."

"What does a rabbi need with business and houses?" demanded the holy man.

"*Nu*, you don't want the money, give it to the *rebbetzn*," said one of the practical men.

"And what, if I may be so bold, will she do with it?"

"What a question! She can buy fish, meat, potatoes, shoes, clothes, or anything else she chooses."

"Oh, is that so?" exclaimed the sage, brightening up. "In that case, maybe you better let me have a little more!"

✓   ✓   ✓

A merchant, notorious as a poor payer, was arguing with his wholesaler over the price of a bolt of cloth. For a half hour they haggled and scolded until only a penny separated them.

"Let me ask you a question," said the exasperated wholesaler. "We're old friends and I know you well enough to realize I'll have a long wait for my money. In fact I might not get paid at all. So why do you haggle like this, especially for a measly cent?"

"Because I like you," said the merchant. "The lower I can get the cost, the less you'll lose when I don't pay!"

✓   ✓   ✓

Korn borrowed a thousand dollars from his friend Kahn, promising to repay him in a week. And he did, much to Kahn's surprise. A few days later, again needing funds, he borrowed another thousand, agreeing to pay it back within a week. Once more he kept his word.

Not long after, Korn asked for another thousand, but this time Kahn refused. "Enough is enough!" he said tersely. "Twice already you fooled me—three times is asking too much!"

✓   ✓   ✓

It was a beautiful summer's day in Gotham. Jack and Leo, owners of Mini Bottom Creations, had spent a frustrating morning in a vain attempt to borrow $25,000 so they could get started on the next season's line of apparel. But they simply did not have the necessary collateral for a loan of that size. Now it was lunch time and they hadn't raised a dime.

"Look, Jack, instead of eating at the Greasy Fresser like we always do, let's take a walk in the park. Maybe the fresh air will give us an idea," suggested Leo.

Well and good! The partners strolled the paths of Central Park until they came to the lake, where rowboats are offered for hire by the hour. The exercise, they thought, would energize their thinking processes, so they decided to take turns at the oars. But when they reached the middle of the lake, the boat suddenly began to leak. In the panic and pandemonium that followed they overturned the boat. Both were struggling in the water, Jack swimming strongly, but Leo clinging for dear life to the prow.

"Jack! Jack! Save me! I can't swim!" yelled Leo in terror.

"Don't let go!" shouted Jack. "I'm going for help. Can you float alone?"

Sputtering and choking in the water, Leo gasped, "Idiot! If I could float a loan would I be here?"

♪   ♪   ♪

Jake: "Sorry, Phil, but I can't accept this check."

Phil: "What do you mean, you can't accept my check? I have more than enough in the bank to cover it. Don't you trust me?"

Jake: "Sure I trust you. It's your bank I don't trust."

Phil: "You must have had a bad experience."

Jake: I did. For awhile my checks were coming back marked 'no funds.' Then I got a check back marked 'no bank.' "

♪   ♪   ♪

Skip this one if you've heard it: Rubin is making a fortune selling theft insurance—for people who steal.

♪   ♪   ♪

Another shortie: Kolinsky, the furrier, is making a fortune. He crossed a fox with a mink and got a fink.

♪   ♪   ♪

"I'm sorry, Mort, but I can't marry you," said Edna. "The man I marry must be rich. I want a little happiness out of life."

"But Edna, money doesn't necessarily bring happiness," Mort protested. "Take Rockefeller. He has a hundred and fifty million dollars. Is he any happier than Henry Ford who only has a hundred and forty-nine million?"

♪   ♪   ♪

The last time Rose saw her brother, two years ago, he was down at the heels. His suit was threadbare, his shirt collar and cuffs were frayed, and he was emaciated. Now, to her immense surprise, he was expensively attired, sleek and fat, and drove a custom Cadillac. "How did you get so rich?" she exclaimed.

"My partner and I formed a corporation and won a government contract," the brother explained.

"How could you form a company? You didn't have a dime."

"My partner put in the money—fifty thousand dollars. I contributed the experience."

"You must have done very well."

"I sure did, Rose. When we dissolved the company last month, I had the fifty thousand and he had the experience."

✓ ✓ ✓

A wealthy Los Angeles contractor was lecturing one of his employees on the value of thrift and hard work. "When I left New York for this city," he said, "I arrived here with only fifty cents in my pocket. But did I go around sniveling about poverty? Not me!"

"You mean you invested the fifty cents wisely?"

"I certainly did! I used it to wire my father for more money!"

✓ ✓ ✓

Sidney worked for a law firm named "Button, Button, Button and Button." One day he arrived at the offices and noticed that the sign on the door had been changed to "Button, Button, Button and Zipper."

"Hey, what happened around here?" he asked the secretary.

"A company shake-up," said the girl. "They felt that the old name was too old-fashioned."

✓ ✓ ✓

An American manufacturer was showing a prospective customer from the Soviet Union through his plant. When the noon whistle blew and thousands of men scurried away for lunch, the visitor was aghast. "They're all escaping!" he cried.

"Don't worry," the manufacturer said, smiling. "They'll come back."

The visitor looked at him skeptically, but when the starting whistle blew again, the men, of course, returned to their jobs.

Later in the day the manufacturer broached the subject of business. "Now," he said, "about those machines you were interested in buying . . ."

"Never mind the machines," interrupted the Soviet customer, "how much do you want for that whistle?"

✓ ✓ ✓

"I would hate to be an American businessman," said the Soviet Consul. "If he does wrong he is arrested. And if he does right he's taxed."

✓ ✓ ✓

When the Bureau of Internal Revenue installed its new computers to detect suspicious tax returns, one of the first to be ensnared was Moe Moskowitz, president of Knickerbocker Leather Novelty Company. He was summarily ordered to report at the Bureau's New York office with copies, receipts and statements to prove his many deductions.

Moskowitz appeared the next day as directed, and spread his "proof" on the desk—bits and scraps of paper on which were scribbled a jumble of meaningless hieroglyphics, shorthand notes and diagrams.

"This is no good," said the inspector. "If you want to be credited with all those deductions you'll have to show me actual receipts, invoices, inventory lists, income and proven expenditures."

"Listen," Moskowitz exploded, "that kind of information I don't even tell mine partner!"

✓   ✓   ✓

As was their custom for the past thirty years, Ralph and Miriam went to sleep early, but the wife quickly discerned that her husband was greatly worried about something. He kept turning from side to side, muttering, and grinding his teeth.

"What is it, Ralph?" she asked. "Why don't you go to sleep?"

"I can't," said Ralph in an anguished voice. "You remember that two thousand dollars I borrowed from your brother last year? Well, the note is due tomorrow and I haven't got a penny. You know that brother of yours—he's liable to sue."

"Look, Ralph, just worrying about it isn't going to solve anything," said Miriam reasonably. "Why not get dressed and go over to his house? Maybe he'll give you an extension of time. Take my advice, see him right now—he's not so bad."

So Ralph got out of bed, put on his clothes and, at three o'clock in the morning he reached his brother-in-law's house. After much pounding on the door, he finally awakened the man and was admitted. "I'm sorry to bother you at this hour, but I simply can't pay you your two thousand dollars tomorrow," Ralph explained apologetically. "I was worrying about it so much I couldn't sleep."

"Did you have to come here at this hour to tell me that?" cried the brother-in-law. "Now *I* won't be able to sleep."

✓   ✓   ✓

A Jewish agent was connected with an insurance firm whose heads were all staunch Catholics. The Jew did exceptionally well and all agreed that he was worthy of becoming a member of the firm. The Jew's religion, however, was a serious obstacle, since the heads of the company did not believe it wise to have a non-Catholic as an official of the firm. After some debate, they decided to call in a leading priest to convert the Jewish insurance agent.

On the appointed day the agent and the priest met in a private office.

Finally, after they had been closeted for two hours, the two emerged.

The president of the firm addressed the priest: "Well, Father, did you succeed in converting the Jew?"

"No, I didn't," replied the priest, "but he did sell me a ten thousand dollar policy."

* * *

Mr. Salzberg answered the phone.

"This is the cashier at the Bowery Savings Bank," said the voice at the other end of the line. "We find that you are overdrawn on your account by five hundred dollars."

"*Nu,* so I'm overdrawn! What are you going to do, sue me?"

"But, sir . . . !"

"Just a minute!" Salzberg interrupted. "Do me a favor and tell me how I stood last month."

The cashier consulted the bank records and then answered, "Last month you had twelve thousand in your account."

"All right," snapped Salzberg, "did I call *you* last month?"

Chapter Thirty-seven

Low Finance

The season was over and the inventory disclosed that ten pairs of summer slacks remained unsold. The slacks were priced at $10 each, and Abe Margolies, the manufacturer, would have gladly accepted less for them, but who wants summer slacks in October?

Margolies, however, hadn't spent a lifetime in the business for nothing. The man had *saichel*! Smiling to himself, he shipped the ten pairs of slacks to an out-of-town retailer who was not exactly famous for his honesty, and in a separate letter he wrote that he was sending him *nine* pairs of slacks at $10.00 per pair. The dishonest retailer, he was sure, would be unable to resist the temptation of obtaining ten pairs and having to pay for only nine. Naturally, the consignee would be expected to keep the merchandise and send him a check for $$90.00, a sum Margolies considered more than satisfactory for out-of-season goods.

But he received the shock of his life when he received the following communication from the wily retailer:

Dear Sir:
I have examined the nine pairs of slacks you shipped to me and found them perfectly satisfactory as to price and quality.
However, because the season is over, I am returning the merchandise to you.

In the package that came back there were only nine pairs of slacks.

✓ ✓ ✓

Fishman had been a tailor all his life, as had his father and grandfather before him. Now his son was about to enter the business world, but unlike his *mishpocheh*, he had no desire to continue the tailoring line. Despite his father's entreaties, the youth insisted on becoming a shoemaker, so he went to another town and set up shop.

A few years later, while visiting his father in the old home town, he reminded the elder Fishman of their initial argument.

LOW FINANCE

Papa Fishman grumbled: "I still think you should have been a tailor like the rest of the family."

"Papa, believe me, I should thank God three times a day for refusing to become a tailor."

"Why so?"

"Because in the tailoring business I would have starved to death. Do you realize that in the three years since I opened my shoe-repair shop, not a single customer has ever asked me to make even one pair of pants?"

✐   ✐   ✐

Mendel bought a gorgeous necklace of matched pearls for his wife. He intended to present it to her that night, but at lunchtime he showed it to his friend Berel.

"How much did it cost you?" asked Berel, his eyes glittering with admiration and envy.

"A cool thousand."

"It's beautiful. Look, sell it to me for twelve hundred. Then we'll both be happy. I'll have the pearls and you make two hundred easy profit."

Mendel quickly agreed. After all, two hundred is two hundred. But he began to think of the pleasure his loving wife might have derived from the necklace. So he went to Berel's shop and appealed to him: "Listen, my friend, I want that necklace back. Sell it to me and I'll give you fifteen hundred dollars—cold cash!" Berel, not at all averse to making a fast three hundred, gladly handed over the pearls.

But Mendel never found an opportunity to present the gift to his wife. He showed the necklace to his partner who promptly offered two thousand dollars for it. Naturally, he sold it.

The next morning, Berel telephoned, offering eighteen hundred for the necklace.

"Sorry, Berel, but I already sold it to my partner for two thousand," Mendel explained.

"Wha-a-a-t!" cried Berel furiously. "You blunderer! You idiot! *Shlemiel!* How could you do such a thing? From that pearl necklace we were both making such a good living!"

✐   ✐   ✐

Melvin came to visit his brother-in-law, Louie.

"The last time I was here," Melvin reminisced, "you told me you were starting a fool-proof business. So how goes it?"

"Better you don't ask," muttered Louis despondently.

"Why, what happened?"

"You remember how I figured out the perfect guarantee against failure? Well, I followed my own advice and opened up a *kosher* delicatessen, because, after all, people have to eat. But then I realized that people also have to die, so in the back of the store I conducted an undertaking parlor. In that way I had them as customers whether they lived or died."

"*Nu?*"

"I made an important discovery, Melvin. In this town we Jews neither live nor die. We just suffer!"

✓   ✓   ✓

The salesman from Pechter's Baking Company was making a pest of himself as he tried to induce the grocer to carry his line of baked goods.

"Look, against you I don't have a thing; against Pechter's I have nothing, but I'm carrying now more bread than I can sell. Please, do me a favor and don't bother me. Go away!"

But the salesman persisted. "You have a large Jewish following and they're sure to buy Pechter's bread in preference to all those *goyishe* breads you keep on the shelves." He then launched into another long eulogy about his rye and pumpernickel until the grocer, now thoroughly aroused over the other's aggressiveness, grabbed him by the collar and threw him out into the street.

The salesman picked himself up, dusted himself off, took out his salesbook, and re-entered the store.

"What just happened was in connection with our bread," he told the grocer. "So how are you fixed for our other baked goods? We have a wonderful line of rolls, buns, cakes, cookies, crackers . . ."

✓   ✓   ✓

Benny Leonard, the famous boxing champion, was in Los Angeles, training for his next bout. Finding that he needed more shirts, he wired his haberdasher in New York to ship a dozen silk shirts to his California training camp. The next day he received an answering telegram from his supplier that read: "Cannot ship your shirts until last ones are paid for."

Leonard wired back at once: "Unable to wait that long. Cancel order!"

✓   ✓   ✓

Abba and Gideon, two *landsleit* who had not seen each other since they emigrated to this country several years earlier, happened to meet in front of New York's *Forverts* Building.

"Hello, Gideon, how's by you?" greeted Abba.

"I can't complain," said Gideon.

"In that case, do me a favor. Lend me a few dollars."

"What are you talking? I hardly know you anymore."

Abba shook his head mournfully. "I just can't understand this country. Back in Poland nobody would lend me money because they knew me. Here in America nobody will lend me a penny because they *don't* know me."

✓   ✓   ✓

LOW FINANCE

Jack Karp, Eighth Avenue furrier, had no time for his usual leisurely lunch, so he decided to have a quick snack at the Busy Bee Businessman's Brunchroom, next door. Inside, he spotted Al Weinberg who owed him $300, a sum Weinberg had borrowed over a year before. Now Karp was a kindhearted man who hated to press a debtor for payment, but he did want to remind the man of the overdue loan as delicately as possible. So he went to the other's table and greeted him cordially.

"Hello, Weinberg, I'm glad to see you. How's the wife? The kiddies are OK? You're in good health, I hope?"

"Look, Mr. Karp," retorted Weinberg, "be reasonable. Do *I* get paid by anyone?"

✹ ✹ ✹

Oldtimers swear that this is a true anecdote.

An eager young man solicited the advice of the late Bernard Baruch, at the turn of the century. Although a young man himself, Baruch had already become a financial tycoon.

"Tell me, is there any sure and certain way to make a million dollars?" asked the youth.

"Yes, one," replied Baruch. "All you need do is buy a million bags of flour at a dollar a bag and then sell them for two dollars a bag."*

✹ ✹ ✹

A man bought some material and went to see a tailor. "Have I enough goods here for a suit?" he asked.

The tailor put his yardstick to the material and measured it. "No," he said. "It will never do. There just isn't enough."

So the man went to the tailor shop across the street. He too measured the goods carefully. "Yes, there's enough," he told the customer.

When the man called for his suit he was amazed to see that the tailor's little boy was wearing a suit made out of the same material as his own.

"See here," he said to the tailor, "can you tell me why the tailor across the street said there wasn't enough material, and yet you not only made me a suit out of it but had enough left over to make a suit for your boy?"

"Well," replied the tailor, "for me the material was enough, but for the other tailor it would never do. He has *two* boys!"

✹ ✹ ✹

Phil Fine, owner of Fine's Fashionable Footwear, a store on LaSalle, in Chicago's Loop, was a notoriously poor payer. There was scarcely a

---

* (In itself, the above is an amusing story, but Baruch did not know that the young man, although he grinned at the sally, had taken him seriously. And so it was that August Hecker went on to start the mighty Hecker's Flour Mills, at one time the largest company of its kind in the world.)

manufacturer or jobber to whom he did not owe money. It wasn't that business was bad—the man just hated to pay his bills.

One morning he telephoned Schneider, one of his suppliers, and asked for another consignment of merchandise.

"You already owe me for three months," Schneider protested.

"I'll pay up the whole bill next month," Fine solemnly promised.

"W-e-l-l, just this one more time."

"You won't regret it. Thanks."

"To tell you the truth, Mr. Fine, I wish I had a hundred customers like you. I'd be much better off."

"Now you're making fun of me," said Fine. "You know I'm a slow payer."

"No, I'm not making fun of you at all. I really would be better off with a hundred customers like you. The trouble is, I have *two* hundred."

✓ ✓ ✓

Jay Perlmutter, of the Bon Ton, met his friend Max Goldstein of the House of Nine.

"Max," Perlmutter asked, "how is it that I advertised strapless evening gowns and topless bathing suits and did only so-so business while you had a store full of women with your ad?"

"Because I used a little *Yiddishe saichel*," grinned Max. "The strapless evening gowns I advertised as gownless evening straps, and the topless bathing suits I advertised as seat covers!"

✓ ✓ ✓

Jacobson, owner of the largest department store in town, was afflicted with a lazy nephew—a good-for-nothing loafer with big ideas and small talent. One day the nephew came to see him about a job.

"What kind of position do you want?" asked the uncle. "Can you clerk behind the counter?"

"Oh, come now, Uncle," said the boy loftily. "That's beneath my dignity."

"Then how about office work? Can you type or keep books?"

"Nothing like that, I assure you."

"Well, can you dress windows?"

"No!"

"For heaven's sake, what *can* you do?"

"I'm glad you asked me that, Uncle," the nephew said eagerly. "You see, I'm the executive type. I don't want to sound conceited but, as long as you asked, I think you should hire me as your business advisor."

"Very well!" the uncle snapped, slamming his fist on the table. "Now give me your first piece of advice. How the hell do I get rid of you?"

✓ ✓ ✓

LOW FINANCE

Two Jews, strangers to each other, met on a bench in Central Park. They introduced themselves and were soon deep in conversation.

"My family has no regard for me at all," complained one. "The way they spend my money you'd think I was Rothschild himself. Believe me, nobody gives me anything. I live by the sweat of my brow and suffer plenty to earn a living."

"I know how you feel," said the other sympathetically. "I also live from sweat, but at least it's not my own, *Gott sie dank.*"

"Not from your own sweat?" exclaimed the first Jew indignantly. "What are you, a capitalist? Do you exploit the workers so you can live off their honest sweat?"

"God forbid!" cried the other fervently. "Do I look like a capitalist? I work in a Turkish bath!"

❡ ❡ ❡

Sam applied for a job at Gotham Frocks as a cutter. He filled out an application and handed it to Mr. Perlberg, the owner. Perlberg studied the application for a few minutes and then asked, "Why did you quit your job at Rubin and Rabinowitz? You didn't give a reason on the application."

"They were always fighting," explained Sam. "How can anyone do his work with such conditions."

"Fighting, you say?"

"Yeah, all the time. When Rubin wasn't fighting with me, Rabinowitz was."

❡ ❡ ❡

Jake picked up the phone and called his friend. "Hello, Milt? Say, I heard you bought a restaurant."

"That's right."

"It's true your refrigeration stopped in the middle of the night and all the food spoiled?"

"It's true."

"And the Board of Health closed you down for a week?"

"Yeah."

"So you had to borrow another $3,000 from the bank to get everything straightened out?"

"Exactly."

"And now you're back in business?"

"Well, it looks like you have all the information."

"Yeah," said Jake, "but this is the first time I'm hearing all the details."

❡ ❡ ❡

Sidney: "How's the dry goods business?"

Melvin: "It couldn't be worse! Even my customers who never pay their bills have stopped coming!"

❡ ❡ ❡

America isn't the only land where salesmen meet and share a few hours of conviviality. Take, for example, the traveling salesman from Lithuania. Hailing from a small town, he was totally unfamiliar with world affairs, so when he found himself on a train in Germany with the famous Count von Bismarck sitting next to him, he had no idea of the man's importance.

"How do you do," said the salesman politely. "I am traveling for Litvak and Gronsky—woolens. You too look like a traveling salesman. May I ask the name of your concern?"

Bismarck found the situation vastly amusing and decided to play along with the courteous, friendly salesman.

"I travel for Kaiser and Reich," said Bismarck, suppressing a grin.

"Say, those names sound familiar!" exclaimed the Lithuanian. "Jewish boys?"

ヶ   ヶ   ヶ

Sid and Mort, two poor brothers in New York, were parted when Sid was drafted into the Korean War. Upon Sid's military discharge he settled in California, somehow wangled his way into the motion picture industry, and before long made a fortune as a big producer. He sent for his brother Mort and proudly showed him around his newly-purchased mansion in Bel Aire.

"You'll never guess how much I paid for this place," boasted Sid. "In fact, I had to protect my investment by taking out insurance; fire, burglary and earthquake."

Mort was genuinely astonished. "Fire and burglary I can understand," he gasped, "but how do you start an earthquake?"

ヶ   ヶ   ヶ

"Mr. Scharf, when are you going to pay me for that last shipment of silks?"

"How should I know? What am I, a fortune teller?"

ヶ   ヶ   ヶ

Mark Hellinger, the late, famous New York columnist and Hollywood writer, was bitten by the newspaper bug at an early age. He would run into his father's place of business shouting, "Stop the presses—stop the presses!"

His father finally threw him out of the tailor shop.

ヶ   ヶ   ヶ

Sokolow, a notorious *shnorrer*, approached Finsteryahr and asked for a loan of twenty dollars. "I swear, I'll pay it back in a week," implored Sokolow, voicing the same oath he had been giving for the past twenty years.

After some hesitation, Finsteryahr, against his better judgment, handed him ten dollars.

"Hey!" protested Sokolow, "I asked you for twenty."

Finsteryahr shrugged. "Look at it this way," he explained philosophically. "You lose ten and I lose ten!"

✓ ✓ ✓

Friedman the clothier was distressed at the haggard appearance of his partner Weinberg who suffered from insomnia.

"Look, my friend, I know you went to the most expensive doctors," said Friedman, "but I'll bet you never tried the simplest remedy of all."

"What's the remedy?"

"Counting sheep."

"All right," said Weinberg, "what can I lose? Tonight I'll give it 'a try."

But the next morning, Weinberg was even more haggard than ever. "I didn't sleep a wink again last night," he mumbled.

"Did you do like I said?" asked Friedman.

"Sure I did," said Weinberg wearily. "But something terrible happened. I counted sheep up to 50,000. Then I sheared the sheep and in a little while I made up 50,000 coats. Then all of a sudden I was faced with an awful problem, and I was tearing my hair all night: *where could I get 50,000 linings?*"

✓ ✓ ✓

Winkelman the furrier was walking on cloud nine. He was sure that he had figured out a way to make millions. He crossed a mink with a gorilla, sure that he would now have a cheaper, longer-lasting fur. But when he saw the results of his experiment he was plunged into the depths of despair.

The pockets were too low and the sleeves too long.

✓ ✓ ✓

"I can give you a real bargain in this piece of property," said the real estate agent. "It's a beautiful house. Even has a sunken living room—the plumbing leaks!"

✓ ✓ ✓

A wholesale tailor was bemoaning the cruel fates. Here it was July and he was stuck with a big inventory of winter coats.

"Stop worrying so," consoled his wife. "Those heavy winter coats are better than money in the bank."

"What are you talking?" asked the cut-and-trim man.

"Well, for one thing," explained the wife, "money, everyone is out to steal from you."

✓ ✓ ✓

A big ad in the newspapers announced a sale of two $75 suits for the price of one. The next morning there was a block-long line outside of the store, waiting for the doors to open. The prospective customers guarded their places carefully so that others might not sneak in ahead of them.

About nine o'clock a man walked to the very head of the line, but the early-comers seized him and threw him into the gutter. He rose to his feet, brushed himself off, and again tried to crash the front of the huge line. Once more he was pushed into the street, accompanied by rude comments concerning his ancestry. For the third time he attempted to get to the front of the line, and this time they beat him up and threw him, bleeding, into the street.

The man picked himself up and walked away. "If that's the kind of *shlemiels* they are," he muttered, "I won't open the store!"

*   *   *

Lincoln freed the slaves, but there are some bosses in the garment district who have yet to hear the glad tidings. Worst among the modern Simon Legrees was Moe Offenberg, of Paris Fashions. He hired a cutter right after Labor Day, but in a very short while he called the new employee into his office.

"I want to know something," he said, glowering. "Why is it that you have been here for a whole week, yet already you are behind in your work a whole month?"

*   *   *

Offenberg's secretary got married so he called the New York Employment Office for a new girl. She was gorgeous, bewitching, intoxicating. Offenberg could feel the faint tuggings of his long-forgotten youth. He wanted to hire her, but as a last-minute precautionary measure he re-read her application and then called her former employer.

"How long did she work for you?" asked Offenberg.

"Oh, about two days," said the party on the other end of the line.

"What?" cried Offenberg. "She says right here on her application that she was with you for over three years!"

"Yes," sighed the former boss, "that's quite true!"

*   *   *

A man walked into the tailor shop on Rivington Street to get his suit pressed.

"That will be two dollars," said the tailor.

"Two dollars!" cried the customer, outraged. "Why, back in Minsk I could get my suit pressed for twenty-five cents!"

"That I believe," said the tailor coolly, "but look at the fare!"

*   *   *

LOW FINANCE

Eisenstein was sure he had written the most saleable article a magazine would ever be fortunate enough to publish. He sent it off to the *Saturday Evening Post,* confidently expecting a substantial check by return mail.

When the editor opened the envelope and scrutinized the title page, "How To Make Your Own Free Mink Coat," he was immediately intrigued. Then he read the opening sentence; "First catch ninety-six minks . . ."

✦   ✦   ✦

"What! Me go into partnership with that phoney? He has absolutely nothing! And if you'll excuse me for saying so, he has very little of that!"

✦   ✦   ✦

"Say, whom are you calling a pauper? I want you to know I have all the money I'll ever need for the rest of my life . . . provided I drop dead this minute!"

✦   ✦   ✦

Mrs. Baum went to the local department store to open a charge account. The manager questioned her closely about her financial status.

"Do you and your husband live within your income?" he asked.

"Heavens no!" exclaimed Mrs. Baum. "We have all we can do to live within our credit!"

✦   ✦   ✦

The difference between the *shlemiel* and the *shlimazl* is accentuated in the business world. When a *shlemiel* receives a check for a hundred dollars he loses it. When that luckless fellow known as a *shlimazl* receives a check for a hundred dollars, the only one who can cash it is the man to whom he owes ninety-nine dollars.

✦   ✦   ✦

Meyer needed $2,500 for a business venture so he went to the bank to arrange a loan. The credit manager approved the application and handed him the money, to be repaid in twelve months. As Meyer rose to leave, the credit manager observed, "We were glad to let you have the $2,500. Remember, it will be due in a year."

"Allright already, you'll get your money!" growled Meyer. "Stop hounding me!"

✦   ✦   ✦

Bemelmann needed a temporary loan so he went to his friend for the money. "Listen, I can use $300 for six months," he said. "I'll pay you six per cent interest."

"How much did you say? I'm a little deaf in my left ear."

"Three hundred dollars."

"I still can't hear. You better tell me again in my other ear."

Bemelmann shouted in the man's right ear: "I need $5,000."

"Mister," said the friend, "go back to my $100 ear."

✓ ✓ ✓

An Orthodox rabbi took a leisurely walk one Sabbath afternoon and came upon a man urging people into his store. The rabbi recognized him at once as a member of his congregation.

"Shmuel," admonished the rabbi sadly, "you should know better than to work on *Shabbes*."

"But I must get rid of these suits," said the merchant. "They're last year's models and I'm selling them at 50% discount."

"But you're not supposed to do business on *Shabbes!*"

"Business!" retorted Shmuel. "I'm selling these suits for less than what they cost me! You call that a business?"

✓ ✓ ✓

For two decades Grossman the bagel man was a familiar sight on Orchard Street. All day long, year in and year out, he called, "Bagels, fresh bagels—below cost!" Whenever he made a sale he would dip into his basket, hand the customer the bagels and mutter piteously, "I'm losing money."

One day a stranger approached. "Look, if you are losing money with every sale, why don't you quit?"

"Quit?" echoed Grossman, peering at the man as though he were insane. "Then tell me, how will I make a living?"

✓ ✓ ✓

Papa Sol Benson was discussing the careers of his four sons with a friend.

"My oldest son just graduated from medical school," he said, a touch of pride in his voice. The second oldest wants to be an engineer; he's in his second year at M.I.T. The third wants to be a successful merchant and he's studying business administration. As to my youngest, he is very spiritual. I think he wants to be a rabbi."

"A rabbi!" cried the neighbor, aghast. "What kind of a business is that for a Jew?"

✓ ✓ ✓

Sam and his partner Ike were unable to decipher the invoice for merchandise which had been sent from New York. The document stated: One dozen sweaters $28; ditto $34; ditto $40; ditto $46.

"What are these dittoes?" Sam and Ike asked each other. They refused to open the cases to ascertain the nature of these mysterious articles

416

because they feared the wholesaler would not accept the rejected merchandise. The partners resolved that Sam should go to New York and obtain first-hand information on the subject of "dittoes." Two days later Sam returned from the metropolis.

"Well, did you find out?" asked Ike.

"I certainly did," replied Sam. "I found out that I am an ass and that you are ditto!"

✓ ✓ ✓

Finkel was in need of a new suit, so he went to see his old *landsman* Kaminsky who had a clothing store on Canal Street.

After they had exchanged greetings, Kaminsky got down to business. "Since we are such longtime friends I am going to give you a real bargain," he began. "Now here's a suit in the latest style and the best quality money can buy. On Fifth Avenue the same suit is selling for a hundred dollars. But I'm not going to ask you a hundred dollars for it. I'm not going to ask you ninety-five. I'm not even going to ask you eighty. Just give me seventy-five and the suit is yours."

"My friend, I don't want you to lose money on this sale just because we are *landsleit*," countered Finkel. "I'm not going to offer you twenty-five dollars for the suit. I'm not going to offer thirty-five. I'm not even going to offer you forty. Here is fifty, take it or leave it."

"Sold!" cried Kaminsky.

✓ ✓ ✓

Old man Schwartz was about to take his son into the business. The boy was a college graduate who had majored in business administration, so the father-son enterprise looked bright. The son was particularly pleased when, on his first day, he noted that crowds of people came in and bought almost everything that was offered for sale by the elder Schwartz.

At the end of the day, however, the new junior partner went over the books and was dismayed to see that his father had been selling everything below his own cost.

"No wonder you're so busy!" exclaimed the son. "How do you expect to make a living?"

"I made enough to send you to college, didn't I?"

"But I don't understand! How do you earn a profit?"

"Easy," said the father. "At the end of each month I juggle the books!"

✓ ✓ ✓

Willie Johnson invited his little Jewish friend, Izzie, to attend the Sunday School class at the local Baptist Church. The subject for that day was "love," and in order to arouse the interest of her pupils, the teacher offered a prize of twenty-five cents to the child whose answers were most correct.

417

"Whom does our religion teach us to love above all others?" the teacher asked, opening the class discussion.

"Our mothers," said a little girl.

"Our fathers," said Willie Johnson.

The teacher shook her head. "It is true that our religion teaches us to love our parents," she said, "but there is one other whom we must love even more."

"George Washington?" asked one of the boys.

"Abraham Lincoln!"

The Jewish boy raised his hand. "I know the answer," he said. "You mean Jesus Christ."

"Correct!" exclaimed the teacher. "Step forward and get your twenty-five cents. What's your name?"

"Izzie Eisenstein."

"Aren't you Jewish?"

"Yes, ma'am."

"Why, I think it is marvelous that even a Jewish boy knows we must love Jesus above everybody else. How did you happen to think of it, young man?"

"Well, lady, actually I thought of Moses," muttered Izzie, pocketing the twenty-five cents, "but business is business!"

Chapter Thirty-eight

Only in America

Leonard considered himself quite an authority on philosophical and theological subjects. One evening he became involved in a discussion with his rabbi, a truly learned man.

"It is my contention," expounded Leonard, "that we humans are creatures of destiny rather than free will. In fact, choice plays no part in our existence; it is all a matter of fate."

"But that belief was discredited long ago," protested the rabbi. "Except for a small minority of our people, we believe in free will as opposed to predestination."

"I can prove that my theory is the right one," answered Leonard. "What happened to me personally is a good example."

"*Nu*, what happened?"

"I was walking along Tremont Avenue, not thinking of anything in particular, when all of a sudden I experienced an overwhelming urge to walk into the Second National Bank. There was no denying that inner compulsion, so I went inside. There, behind each window, sat a man with huge stacks of money, busily counting. Now, Rabbi, this is important: I cannot explain what supernatural force compelled me to enter that bank. I only knew that I was tingling from head to toe; my blood raced through my veins. Then, all at once I knew—something wonderful was about to happen. Destiny was upon me!"

Leonard paused to collect his thoughts.

"Yes, yes; go on!" the rabbi urged.

"Well, I innately felt that my rendezvous with fate had arrived, but I also knew that everything depended on two little words which the man at the window might utter; two simple words which might well relieve me of all my burdens and bring me lifelong contentment." Leonard shrugged, his face now bitter. "But did the man at the window say those two words? No! It was not ordained that he should."

The rabbi was absolutely fascinated. "Don't keep me in suspense!" he cried. "Tell me, what were the two words he could have said that would have changed your life?"

"He could have said," replied the fatalist, "Leonard, *take!*"

✓   ✓   ✓

419

Freud was right, as Mollie Berson learned to her sorrow. Our unconscious thoughts are sometimes revealed despite all conscious efforts to keep them hidden.

Mollie was not only a very pretty girl, as were all the Berson girls, but she had more than her share of ambition. It was her dream to marry a millionaire, though she herself came from a poor immigrant family.

One day, at a party, she was introduced to a handsome, well-groomed man. "Mollie, this is Jack Rothschild, the banker," purred her girl friend. Mollie did not need to be told that this stranger was the wealthy scion of the famous family. She became completely flustered.

"Pardon me," she gasped, "but how much did you say your name was?"

✦   ✦   ✦

One evening, Mollie was expecting a gentleman caller—a fellow she had never seen, although she had been introduced to him on the telephone by her brother. When she finally admitted him to her apartment he turned out to be a nice enough young man with one outstanding feature—his nose. And what a noble, majestic nose that man had! Mollie had to exert all her will power to avoid staring at it.

After the usual halting conversation between two people who are just getting acquainted, she invited him to have a glass of tea and some chopped liver. She poured the tea and then reached for the sugar bowl.

"Do you take one or two lumps in your nose?" she asked.

✦   ✦   ✦

The Zionist Organization of America (ZOA) was sponsoring an important rally for Israel Bonds, to be followed by a sumptuous banquet and dancing in the Gold Room of Miami's swankiest hotel. The *schnapps* was flowing freely and everyone was in—let us say—"high spirits."

On the dance floor, one tipsy couple came too close to another, and one man stepped on the other lady's foot.

"Mister," said the other man, also swaying, "you stepped on my wife's foot. I demand an immediate apology!"

"Apologize? Why should I apologize?" retorted the other belligerently, glaring through an alcoholic fog.

"Okay, then put up your dukes!" cried the first man, assuming what he thought looked like a fighting stance.

"Now wait a minute; to fight nobody needs," protested the other man, backing off. "I stepped on your wife's foot? All right, here is my wife. If it will make you happy, step on *her* foot!"

✦   ✦   ✦

Two traveling salesmen met. It was the slack season and both were short of funds, so they decided to save expenses by renting a small room with a single bed. But the bed was so narrow they simply could not sleep. In fact, they did not even have enough room to move an arm or a leg.

After an hour or so of lying completely immobile, one of them got up and crawled out of bed.

"What's the matter?" asked the other salesman. "Are you leaving so soon?"

"I'll be right back," answered the first man. "I just wanted to turn over on my other side."

✦ ✦ ✦

A traveling salesman arose early after spending his first night at a run-down hotel in a small town. He went to the desk and slammed a bill on the counter. "I'm checking out," he growled.

"What's the matter, didn't you sleep well?" asked the clerk.

"No!"

"What kept you awake?"

"Frankly, I found a dead bed-bug on the sheet."

"You mean to tell me that a harmless dead bed-bug could keep you up all night?"

"Yes, that's exactly what I mean to tell you!" snarled the guest. "All his friends and relations came to the funeral."

✦ ✦ ✦

A haggard guest checked out of the dilapidated hotel very early in the morning. The sleepy-eyed desk clerk accepted the room key and said, "Goodbye, sir. I hope you slept well last night."

"I slept like a log, if you must know," snapped the departing guest. "But your poor bed-bugs—they were up all night!"

✦ ✦ ✦

The rich cloak-and-suiter checked into the lavish Fontainebleau Hotel and lived royally for two weeks. During his stay, however, he had not given the bellhop a single tip, and naturally the boy grew apprehensive. His wealthy guest might leave without giving him any gratuity at all. So he decided to use a subtle reminder.

"I hope, sir," he said courteously, "that when you check out you won't forget me."

"Certainly not," answered the cloak-and-suiter. "Give me your address and I'll write to you once in a while."

✦ ✦ ✦

It was ten minutes until six, and Berger the salesman, his temper frayed, was exhausted. Methodically he began to cover the merchandise for the night when in walked a lady customer. "Damn!" muttered Berger beneath his breath.

"I'd like to see something in nightgowns," she said brightly.

He reached for a box on the shelf and spread several samples on the counter.

"These aren't exactly the color I wanted," she told him after inspecting the goods.

He suppressed his irritation, mounted a ladder and brought down three boxes of nighties. The customer went through all three, strewing the contents all across the expanse of the counter, examining, feeling for texture, and holding them up against her body for size. She shook her head. "The colors are all right," she said, "but I wanted a little more lace on the bottom."

It was now long past six and Berger was fuming inwardly. Scarcely able to suppress his irritation, he burrowed under the counter and found another box of nightgowns. "Here are some in your color and with more lace," he almost hissed.

But when the lady examined them she again shook her head. "These won't do at all. But don't let it bother you, sir. I wasn't planning to buy anything anyway. I was just out looking for my sister-in-law."

Berger glanced at the clock, took in the wild disarray of the merchandise strewn from one end of the counter to the other, and clenched his teeth. "Madam, I'll make you a present of a whole dozen nightgowns —absolutely free—if you'll answer just one question."

"Why, of course! What's the question?"

"If you were just looking for your sister-in-law, tell me, what made you think you'd ever find her in one of those boxes?"

*   *   *

It happened during the great blackout of November, 1965, when the electric circuits went dead from Canada to as far south as Baltimore. New York was especially hit, with not a light in evidence anywhere.

Max was in his Brooklyn apartment, screwing a light bulb into the socket, when suddenly the power failed. His wife jumped up, ran over to the window, and saw that all New York was in pitch-black darkness.

"Max," she wailed, "now look what you did!"

*   *   *

Grandpa took his first taxi ride in America way back in 1924. As the cab careened along the narrow, pushcart-laden streets of the lower East Side, Grandpa grew increasingly nervous. He had told the driver he did not want to be late for his granddaughter's *bas mitzvah*, but now he regretted it.

"Mister," he pleaded, "slow down a little. I'm not in that much a hurry."

"You said you didn't want to be late," the driver reminded him.

"Look, my friend," said Grandpa, "better I should be a little late down here than too early up there."

*   *   *

ONLY IN AMERICA

An illiterate shoemaker who had been poor all his life, inherited several million dollars from a distant relative he never even knew he had. Immediately he was besieged with requests from various charitable organizations.

One of these requests came from the Jewish Home for the Aged, and the shoemaker, a kindhearted man, felt that this was truly a worthy cause. However, he wanted to see for himself where his money was going.

The superintendent of the Home welcomed the now-rich shoemaker and conducted him personally through the building and grounds. He showed the prospective donor the comfortable reading room where the oldsters sat contentedly reading or watching television. He showed him the clean dining room, the neat bedrooms and even the garden where other oldtimers sunned themselves on benches or strolled among the shrubbery.

"Everything is fine," said the shoemaker. "I have no objection to making a large donation, but I want to ask you something. What for do you need all these old people cluttering up the place?"

✔   ✔   ✔

When the former Lord Mayor of Dublin, Robert Briscoe, an Orthodox Jew, visited the United States in 1965, several delightful anecdotes were quoted about him. At a banquet in Los Angeles, Briscoe remarked, "A Chinese restaurant just opened in Dublin. I would like to take your President Johnson there some day. It will be the first time a Protestant was invited by a Jew to a Chinese restaurant in Ireland."

The Irish-Jewish mayor was also worldwide sales representative for several brands of native whiskeys, including "Irish Mist." (Leave it to a *Yiddishe* mayor.) Commented Briscoe, " 'Irish Mist' is *kosher* because it is made of wild bee honey instead of sugar, and it is not matured in a sherry cask. So if you want something different for a change, try a genuine *kosher* Irish cocktail."

Finally, with a twinkle in his eye, Briscoe concluded, "You may not believe it, but in Ireland the leprechauns are now known as lepre-Cohens!"

✔   ✔   ✔

Boss: "How many times do I have to tell you to stop arguing with the customers? You should know our policy by now: the customer is always right."

Clerk: "You don't understand, sir. This customer was arguing that he was wrong!"

✔   ✔   ✔

A male customer, clearly embarrassed to be seen in the bra and pantie section of the department store, approached the saleslady.

"I want to give my wife a Chanukah present," he said shyly.

"What did you have in mind?" asked the understanding woman.

"A brassiere."

"Certainly. What bust?"

"What are you talking about?" exclaimed the husband. "Nothing bust! The old one just wore out."

✓ ✓ ✓

A young *shaigetz* had no alternative but to meet his Jewish sweetheart in the lobby of a department store because her Orthodox father would not allow him in the house.

The boy and girl met one evening in the usual place. "I saw your father on the street today," said the youth, "but he didn't see me."

"Yes, I know," answered the girl. "He told me."

✓ ✓ ✓

Jake and Joe were partners in a small tavern. By all accounts they should have been making good money, as they enjoyed a large clientele, but somehow, business was poor.

"I can't understand it," said Jake. "After all, we always add half water to every drink we serve. On top of that we always add more drinks to the bill than the customer actually ordered. So how can we be losing money?"

"I think I have the answer," said Joe thoughtfully. "We never add water to those drinks that we sneak in on the bill."

✓ ✓ ✓

Papa: "I hope you liked that new boy you went out with last night. He comes from a fine Jewish family and has a good future. Frankly, he'd make a good husband."

Daughter: "To tell the truth, Papa, I had to slap his face last night."

Papa: "What! You mean he got fresh?"

Daughter: "No, I thought he was dead!"

✓ ✓ ✓

Lou Katz borrowed a hundred dollars from his former partner, Davidov, with the written promise that he would repay the loan in six months. That was more than a year ago. Now, Davidov would wait no longer. "You'll pay me tomorrow—in full—or we go to court!" he threatened.

Squeeze blood out of a turnip? All night he walked the floor, cudgeling his brain for a way out of the dilemma. Back and forth he paced—endlessly—like a caged animal.

"Louie!" his wife finally called when the dawn began to break. "Haven't you been to bed yet? Come to sleep this minute!"

"Who can sleep?" he moaned. "If I don't pay Davidov his hundred dollars in the morning he'll sue. That's all I need—I should sit in the penitentiary for ten years."

"Look, Louie, don't be a fool," she scolded. "It's Davidov's money, no? So come to bed. Let *him* walk the floor!"

ᐟ   ᐟ   ᐟ

America is still the land of opportunity. A man can start out as a bricklayer and wind up as a contractor—if he doesn't mind the financial sacrifice!

ᐟ   ᐟ   ᐟ

It was stifling hot on Orchard Street, so Mrs. Yifnif decided to buy a fan. At a pushcart she rummaged through every fan the peddler had for sale, examining them for strength, texture and appearance, bending and weighing them in her hand, trying to make up her mind as to which one she would buy.

"Wrap me up this penny fan," she finally said.

"Penny fans we don't wrap up," the disgusted peddler told her. "Take it like it is."

But the next day, first thing in the morning, Mrs. Yifnif returned to the pushcart, her face grim. "Give me back my money!" she demanded, showing him the tattered remains of the fan she had purchased the day before.

"How much did you pay for the fan?" asked the peddler.

"A penny."

"How did you use the fan?"

"What do you mean, how did I use it? I waved it in front of my face, what else?"

"Lady, that's what you're supposed to do with a nickel fan," cried the peddler. "With a penny fan you hold it still in front of your face and wave your head!"

ᐟ   ᐟ   ᐟ

Although Benson was hard-pressed for money, he was paying off an accumulation of bills regularly each month. One day his wife announced that she had just purchased a new fur coat.

"*Gevald!*" he moaned. "Everytime it looks like I'm going to make ends meet, you have to go and move the ends!"

ᐟ   ᐟ   ᐟ

A man was strolling along Second Avenue one day when a beggar sidled up to him and pleaded, "Mister, please, can you spare a nickel for a cup of coffee?"

"But coffee is a dime now."

The beggar looked at him haughtily and replied, "So who buys retail?"

ᐟ   ᐟ   ᐟ

Sam Spiegel was boasting about his new secretary.

"She isn't the fastest typist in the world but she can erase fifty words a minute!"

✦ ✦ ✦

The assimilation of the American Jew into the general social structure was already being parodied at the turn of the century, as illustrated in this gentle admonition:

Avrum Davidovitch went into a bookstore and asked for a gold-stamped, Morocco leather-bound copy of the Talmud.

"We haven't anything so expensive in stock right now," said the clerk, "but we can order one for you if you would care to come back in a few days."

"Well, all right," answered Davidovitch somewhat uncertainly, "but I can't wait too long. It's a Christmas present!"

✦ ✦ ✦

Al Berger, who was sometimes careless about his personal hygiene, registered with his wife at a summer resort. He awakened early the next morning, only to find that his wife had already dressed and gone downstairs for breakfast. He met her in the dining room a few minutes later.

"Al, did you take a bath before you came downstairs?" she asked anxiously.

"Of course not!" was the astonished reply. "Why? Is there one missing?"

✦ ✦ ✦

The real estate agent was intent on making a sale to the wealthy jeweler. It was an expensive summer house in Newburgh-on-the-Hudson.

"Just look how ideal the location is," rhapsodized the agent. "Right on the bank of the river. Two steps from the back door and you're in the water, ready for a nice swim. Or you can go fishing—right from the porch. You like boating? There's a little pier right at your doorstep. Believe me, mister, it's perfect."

"W-e-l-l-," the jeweler said doubtfully, "one thing worries me. Suppose the river overflows its banks?"

"So what?" answered the agent smoothly. "How could that possibly affect your house? It's so far from the river!"

✦ ✦ ✦

A European rabbi spent his last cent for passage to America. He secured a position in East New York where he rented a small house for himself, his wife and children, but the salary he was about to receive was far too small for the support of his family. However, it occurred to him that he might balance his budget on the fees earned from marriage ceremonies. June, he had heard, was a popular month for weddings in this country.

But the whole month of June passed without a single ceremony. It was well into July before the first young man and his fiancée came to be united in wedlock. Promptly, the rabbi got out the canopy, extracted a bottle of red wine from his meagre stores, and proceeded with the business of making them man and wife.

When the ceremony was over, the bridegroom, apparently a workman, judging by his blue shirt and denim pants, furtively drew the rabbi aside. "I'm sorry, but I can't afford to pay you for your services," he said apologetically. "However, if you'll take me down to the basement I'll show you how to fix the meter so that as long as you live you'll never have to pay a gas bill again!"

✦   ✦   ✦

"If you really loved me you'd buy me a nice mink," she pouted.

"All right, I'll buy you a mink if it's that important to you," he grumbled, "but only on one condition."

"Condition? What kind of condition?"

"You have to keep its cage clean!"

✦   ✦   ✦

A former New Yorker who had lived in Los Angeles for the past ten years, returned to the East for a brief visit with his relatives.

"Is California as beautiful as we've heard?" asked a cousin.

"It's a regular Paradise," enthused the adopted Californian.

"And is it true that in Los Angeles you have sunshine 365 days a year?"

"It's not only true," he answered loyally, "but take my word for it, that's a conservative estimate!"

✦   ✦   ✦

Joseph Schildkraut, star of the Yiddish theatre, once commented: "My wife and I have a perfect arrangement when we go for a ride in our new car. I sit at the wheel and she drives in an advisory capacity."

✦   ✦   ✦

The lady of the house went into the kitchen for a snack and was surprised to see the maid standing, eating her lunch.

"What kind of way is that to eat, with your plate on top of the refrigerator?" the lady asked. "You'll enjoy your meal better if you sit down."

"What, in such dusty chairs?" the maid snapped. "They haven't been cleaned in a month!"

✦   ✦   ✦

When Moe landed on Ellis Island, after a long journey from his native Lithuania, he was met by a representative of the Immigrant's Relocation Association of New York. Moe had planned to settle in New York with his *tanteh*, but the Association agent convinced him that he would find it much easier to earn a living in a small town, rather than in the metropolis. Moe reluctantly agreed, and in a few days found himself in Pocatello, Idaho.

After finding a place to live, he asked a policeman about a local synagogue, but the officer merely shrugged. He asked if there were any Jewish families in Pocatello, but was answered with a blank stare. In desperation, he went to the main intersection of town, and, there in the center of the street, he shouted as loudly as he could, *"Gevald! Men shlogt Yidden!"* ("Help! Jews are being beaten!")

Immediately a trio of Jews sped toward him. "Where? Where?" they cried.

"Who knows?" replied the immigrant. "Poland—Hungary—Russia maybe. I just wanted to know whether anybody here gave a damn!"

✓ ✓ ✓

Inflation: What used to cost five dollars to buy now costs ten dollars to repair.

✓ ✓ ✓

It is customary in Orthodox synagogues to auction off the honor of reading a portion of the Torah during the holiday services.

One Yom Kippur, Feldman took his Irish neighbor with him so that he might witness the services in a local synagogue. For an hour the son of Erin sat spellbound, watching attentively as the solemn and awe-inspiring service unfolded. Finally there came a lull and the selling of ritual honors began.

"Twenty dollars for *maftir*," cried the sexton.

"Thirty dollars," came a bid from Feldman.

"I bid sixty!" yelled the Irishman.

Feldman grasped his neighbor's arm. "What are you doing?" he hissed. "Have you lost your mind?"

"Nothing of the sort!" responded the Irishman. "I've known you a long time, Feldman. If you offer thirty dollars it must be worth at least a hundred!"

✓ ✓ ✓

Paul Muni, famed actor of the Yiddish and American stage and cinema, bought his wife a new car. Asked how she liked it, he replied, "She loves to drive! My wife now has 250 horses that can take her through ten city streets of solid concrete, from our house to the supermarket, and then all the way back home, in a two-ton vehicle, just to transport four ounces of pastrami."

✓ ✓ ✓

ONLY IN AMERICA

A landlord had just finished collecting the rents from the tenants in his apartment house. He was on his way home when suddenly he noticed that his wallet was missing. The loss of all his money was a stunning blow and, in his despair, he began to sob. He was still weeping as he entered his house.

"What's the matter?" exclaimed his wife.

"My money is gone," he cried. "I believe I put it in my inside coat pocket."

"Did you look in your pants pockets?"

"Yes, the money isn't there either."

"How about the side pocket of your jacket. Did you look there?"

"Of course not!" he said irritably. "Do you want me to lose the last bit of hope I have left?"

✓   ✓   ✓

"I'll never forget the time my wife, Ida, went for her driver's test," reminisced the late Eddie Cantor. "She got three tickets—just on the written part!"

✓   ✓   ✓

Manny and Jack were invited to a lecture on hypnotism. Manny volunteered to become a subject.

"And now," said the hypnotist, "I will put this man into such a deep trance that he will forget his entire past."

"*Oy vay!* Don't do that, Mister," shouted Jack from the audience. "He owes me a fortune!"

✓   ✓   ✓

An old man, recently arrived from Europe, was perceptibly growing deaf. His granddaughter insisted that he get a hearing aid.

"Who needs a hearing aid?" he protested. "In this country I hear more already than I can understand."

✓   ✓   ✓

It may be true that we Jews are part of a patriarchal social complex, but that wasn't the case in Sarah's family—she insisted on buying one of those cars with a bed in the back, over her husband's vehement objections.

On the first day of the purchase she was returning home from a shopping tour when she was stopped by a policeman and given a ticket for a minor traffic violation. Her husband noticed the glum expression on her face the moment she entered the house. "What's the matter, Sarah? You look mad."

"I got a ticket," she snapped.

"What for?" he asked maliciously. "Dirty sheets?"

✓   ✓   ✓

When Hawaii was officially declared as the nation's fiftieth state, the bright youngster read the news to his grandfather. "Grandpa," cried the boy, "we're bringing Hawaii into the Union!"

"That I don't believe," contradicted the old man. "How can they ever get that big island over here?"

✓ ✓ ✓

Rubin the typesetter was emerging from the *Forverts* Building after a hard day's work when a man rushed up to him and struck him a stinging blow. Picking himself up from the sidewalk he yelled, "Bum! Loafer! How dare you hit me?"

The other was immediately contrite. "I'm very sorry," he apologized. "It's all a mistake. I thought you were Feival, the butcher."

"So what if I were Feival? You don't have to hit a man so hard you should maybe break his backbone. You call that a nice thing to do?"

"Now hold on!" exploded the stranger. "You're sticking up for a man you don't even know. Take my advice and keep your big nose out of Feival's business!"

✓ ✓ ✓

On February 2nd, 1915, Sol Jaffe passed through Ellis Island and was cast upon the teeming, highly competitive streets of New York's lower East Side. In the Ukraine he had driven a team of mules but here in Manhattan nobody wanted a mule driver. Nor were the streets paved with gold, as he had heard in his little village; and rich American widows did not besiege him, begging on bended knees to marry—also as he had been led to believe back home.

While he was making the employment rounds one day, he heard about an opening for the position of *shammes* in the Utica Avenue Synagogue. A subway train whisked him there in short order, and soon he was conferring in Yiddish with the Temple's president.

"Before we get too involved," said the official, "tell me, can you read and write English?"

"No, not a word—not even my name," the immigrant answered truthfully.

"In that case, Mr. Jaffe, I'm sorry, but this isn't a Ukrainian village. In a big city like New York a *shammes* must be able to read and write."

With a sinking heart, the dejected newcomer returned to the lower East Side on Orchard Street, and for a year or two eked out a miserable existence. But as he learned the rudiments of merchandising and became somewhat familiar with the English language, his fortunes gradually took a turn for the better, until, one day, he opened a little dry-goods store. The store prospered and he opened another, and then still another. Soon he owned a chain of retail outlets. In time he built one of the largest department stores in the United States.

One day he decided to manufacture a line of garments under his own private label, so he went to the president of his bank and asked about the possibility of borrowing a million dollars.

"Why, of course; anything you need, Mr. Jaffe," the banker said, in the manner of all bankers to the rich but never to the poor. "But why borrow the money? You have ten times that amount on deposit. Just write your own check for the million."

Jaffee hesitated, obviously embarrassed. "I-I can't read or write," he stammered. "I didn't know I had that much money in my account. But I'll put my 'x' on the check where I'm supposed to sign my name."

The banker was thunderstruck. "Mr. Jaffe, you're a genius! If you were able to make such a tremendous success of your life without any formal learning, just think what you might have become if you knew how to read and write English!"

"I know exactly what I would have been," sighed Jaffe nostalgically; "the *shammes* of the Utica Avenue Synagogue!"

✓ ✓ ✓

"When I was a boy," the late Jewish movie star Jeff Chandler once remarked, "we were so poor in our house we were never sure whether to wash with the soap or eat it."

✓ ✓ ✓

A sports-minded young fellow was reminiscing about the time he first met and fell in love with his wife.

"We were introduced in 1963," he said with growing enthusiasm. "That was the year the Dodgers took the Yanks for four straight in the World Series, and one of our boys, Sandy Koufax, became the most outstanding Jewish athlete since Samson!"

✓ ✓ ✓

Bill Koffman, West Coast humorist, tells about the cloak-and-suiter who was persuaded to play his very first game of golf.

"Fore!" called the man at the next hole.

"Three-ninety-eight!" yelled the garment man from force of habit.

✓ ✓ ✓

Grandpa Levi had not been in America long, but though he was unable to accustom himself to the strange *goyishe* ways, he was inordinately proud of the Americanization of Joey, his grandson.

One day Joey burst into the house, his eyes shining with excitement. "The Dodgers won the World Series!" he shouted.

"*Azoi!*" said Grandpa. "Is that good or bad for the Jews?"

✓ ✓ ✓

Ask former judge Aaron Stern of Peekskill, New York, the strangest traffic alibi he ever heard and he'll tell you this one:

"It was a busy Friday afternoon during the height of the tourist season in the Catskills. I was presiding at court, rather bored with the varied and sometimes wild excuses given by the defendants. Suddenly the rear doors flew open and in walked a determined motorcycle cop and a protesting civilian."

"This man," testified the officer, "was driving sixty miles an hour on the wrong side of the highway."

"Couldn't you see the white dividing line?" I asked.

"Sure I saw it," retorted the offender. "But I thought it was sour cream!"

✓   ✓   ✓

It was the first day of *Pesach,* a lovely spring morning in Chicago. In his car, a sports-minded young rabbi sped along the Outer Drive, anxious to arrive at the synagogue in plenty of time for the Passover services. But as he drove by the South Side Country Club he was seized with an overwhelming urge to play a few rounds of golf. "What will it hurt?" he thought. "I have an hour or so before I'll be needed at the temple." Of course, it was an act of sacrilege, but no one in his congregation was anywhere near the golf course and it was highly unlikely he would be found out. Somewhat guiltily he went into the locker room, selected some clubs and then strolled out to the green where he teed up a ball and began to enjoy himself.

But his every action had been observed. High above, the patriarch Abraham had seen the rabbi swerve from the straight and narrow, and he phoned God who lived in a nearby exclusive section of heaven. "I don't want to seem like a busybody, Boss, but as God is my witness I just saw a rabbi playing golf—and here it is *Pesach,* too."

"Don't call me 'Boss,' " said God testily, "and stop taking my name in vain. I know all about that rabbi. You think I need secondhand information? You leave that rabbi to me. I'll punish him good."

Meanwhile the rabbi was enjoying himself immensely. He took careful aim, hit the ball squarely and it rolled into the cup on the other end of the fairway—a beautiful hole in one.

The patriarch Abraham roared in righteous anger. Grabbing the phone he voiced his indignation to God. "What kind of punishment do you call this?" he cried. "Here a rabbi plays golf on *Pesach* when he should be in *shul* with his congregation, and what do you do? You actually reward him with a hole in *one!*"

When God answered, his voice was infinitely patient: *"Nu, zogt mir,* Abe, who can he tell?"

✓   ✓   ✓

Jake gave lengthy and explicit instructions to Yossilov the barber. When the haircut was finished, Yossilov held up a mirror so Jake could see the results, from sides and rear.

"It's satisfactory?" asked Yossilov.

"Not quite," answered Jake. "Make it a little longer in the back."

✓ ✓ ✓

Skip this one: A bank robber opened the safe with his toes. He just wanted to drive the fingerprint specialists out of their minds.

✓ ✓ ✓

Two musicians, old friends who played the New York Bar Mitzvah and wedding circuit, were hired to play a swanky engagement at the I. J. Fox mansion.

"Hey, Moish," whispered the first musician, between numbers, "see that gorgeous doll in the corner? She just got to America from some little town in Israel. Let's show her the difference between right and wrong."

"Okay," agreed Moish. "You teach her what's right."

✓ ✓ ✓

Girlfriend: "Honey, what happened to your nice Morris chair?"

Boyfriend: "Morris took it back."

✓ ✓ ✓

"Rabbi, I want an honest opinion from you. Is it really a sin to play pinochle on *Shabbes*?"

"The way you do, it's a crime to play pinochle any day!"

✓ ✓ ✓

It's silly, but let's tell it anyway.

Stanley was enjoying a leisurely Sunday at the Bronx Zoo when a perfect stranger ran up to him, slapped him on the back and joyfully cried, "Pat O'Brien, as I live and breathe! Last time I saw you, you had red hair, were a foot taller and worked for Mulligan's Tavern over in Red Hook!"

"Mister," said Stanley in his reserved, dignified manner: "I have never been taller than I am now, since I was seventeen years old. I never had red hair—it has always been brown. I never worked for Mulligan— I'm a tailor, and have been for fifteen years. And my name is certainly not Pat O'Brien, it's Stanley Leibowitz."

"Well, well," exclaimed the stranger, undaunted. "So you changed your religion too, eh?"

✓ ✓ ✓

"Darling," he whispered passionately, "do you remember the other night when I kissed you for ten whole minutes?"

"Oh, yes, yes!" she breathed ecstatically. "I remember! How can I ever forget?"

"Well, by any chance did you happen to find a pivot tooth?"

✓ ✓ ✓

The New Yorker was in the nation's capital to complain about some legislation. He faced his Jewish senator and demanded to know what he had been doing for his constituency.

"I'll have you know that my nose has been to the grindstone for two years in your behalf," said the senator, defensively.

The voter took one long look at the senator's schnozzle and muttered, "Boy, it must have been a beaut when you started!"

✓ ✓ ✓

Herb Singer, successful manufacturing furrier of New York, recently opened a branch plant in Los Angeles. One morning he received an urgent call that demanded his immediate presence at his new West Coast offices. Herb picked up the phone and called the airport for the next flight to California.

"I'm sorry," said the reservations clerk, "but all flights are booked until tomorrow. Would you care to wait at the airport in case someone cancels?"

"No, I wouldn't," snapped Herb, whose temper had a short fuse.

"Well, in that case . . ."

"Look, don't well me cases," interrupted Herb. "Do you know who the president of your airline happens to be?"

"Why, yes," said the clerk nervously. "Mr. Aloysius McClellan."

"And do you usually tell Mr. McClellan that he can't get a reservation?"

"No, sir," said the clerk, close to fainting.

"Well, Mr. McClellan can't make the next flight, so save me his seat!"

✓ ✓ ✓

"The difference between a conversationalist and an orator can be clearly defined," said the professor to his class of English students. "Let me elucidate:

"If you meet a man and ask him the sum of two and two, and he answers 'four,' he is, in all probability a conversationalist.

"But if you ask another man the same question and he replies, 'When in the course of human events it becomes necessary to take the second numeral and superimpose it upon the figure two, then I say unto you, and I say it without fear of successful contradiction, that the consequential result amounts to four'—*that*, dear students, is an orator!"

✓ ✓ ✓

The new cars being made in Israel have many outstanding features found in no other cars in the world. Of course, they have a few minor drawbacks, too. The exhaust smells from *schmaltz*, and on *Shabbes*, the owner must hire a *goy* to turn on the headlights. But the Israeli cars get very good mileage: thirty-eight miles to the gallon. Not gasoline—chicken soup!

✓ ✓ ✓

ONLY IN AMERICA

Radnitz had been in this country for only a few days when he saw a revolving door for the first time. He watched, thunderstruck, as a line of people swung into the building. Finally, during a lull in the traffic, he gathered his courage and tried the revolving door himself. Out he came, back on the sidewalk. Again he pushed his way through, raced around once or twice and, as before, emerged on the sidewalk where he had started.

He was trying to figure out this strange phenomenon when a bearded old Jew pushed his way into the building. In a moment a clean-faced young man emerged.

Radnitz gasped in disbelief, then in bewilderment. He clutched at the man's arm. "Mister, tell me something before I go crazy! How did you ever manage to shave so fast?"

1 1 1

Aleph: "Are you going to preach at the new synagogue?"
Baiz: "N-n-n-no. The r-r-rabbi said I w-was t-t-too f-f-f-fat!"

1 1 1

One evening not too long ago, an immigrant Jew and his wife who had lived all their lives in a remote Russian village, arrived in New York harbor. As the ship passed lower Manhattan, everybody on deck was impressed with the countless lights which dotted the various skyscrapers. The many coastal vessels that plied back and forth were also well illuminated and the harbor lights added to the brilliance.

"America is not stingy about light," remarked the wife.

"No, and that's what puzzles me," said her husband. "With all this light in the Port of New York, why do they make such a big *aye-aye-aye* about Columbus discovering America?"

1 1 1

Abe Cohen had only one son. He had high ambitions for the lad and gave him the best education that money could buy. Mr. Cohen realized, however, that since both he and his wife were of foreign origin and spoke with a decided accent, the boy was at a disadvantage. He could not learn to pronounce English correctly at home. A friend gave Mr. Cohen some sound advice. He suggested that the father take the boy to New Haven where a professor at Yale would be glad to take him into his home at the right price. There the boy's accent would improve marvelously.

Mr. Cohen carried out the friend's suggestion and took the boy to New Haven where he found a professor who consented to look after him. But the father was warned not to come to see his son for a whole year.

"It will require that length of time for the youngster to lose his foreign accent," said the professor, "and nothing should be done to impair his chance of learning English correctly."

435

At the end of the year Mr. Cohen rushed down to New Haven. "How is my son doing?" he asked.

"D'un't esk," said the Yale professor. "His spich is poifict!"

✓ ✓ ✓

A shabbily-dressed immigrant Jew was strolling leisurely along lower Broadway admiring the numerous tall buildings. Arriving at the Singer Building he walked across the street to study the high tower. Suddenly, his back began to itch and unconsciously he scratched himself against the wall.

An Americanized Jew happened to pass by and, noticing the antics of his co-religionist, he grew incensed. "Mister," he rasped, "when members of our religion make such unsightly spectacles of themselves it reflects on all of us. Aren't you ashamed of yourself? Don't you realize this is Broadway?"

"What do you expect me to do?" demanded the immigrant. "If it itches me on Broadway should I go scratch myself on Hester Street?"

Chapter Thirty-nine

Signs of the Times

A newcomer to the East Side was attracted by a sign in the window of a tailor shop:

> My Name Is Fink
> What Do You Think
> I Press Clothes For Nothing

The new arrival hurried home, gathered up his three suits and brought them back to the tailor. A few days later he called for his clothes, admired the work and then started for the door without paying.

"Mister, you didn't pay me," called the tailor.

"Pay you? What are you talking? I read your sign before I brought in my clothes."

"You didn't read the sign right, then," retorted the tailor. "Here is how you should read it: My name is Fink; what do you think, I press clothes for nothing?"

✦ ✦ ✦

Nancy Sinatra, daughter of the famous entertainer, Frank, reported a sign on a Hollywood delicatessen parodying Shakespeare's words of wisdom:

What Foods These Morsels Be

✦ ✦ ✦

Billboard on the roof of Gold's Auto Body Repair Shop:

May We Have the Next Dents?

✦ ✦ ✦

Herschel Bloom had not lived in America very long and his knowledge of English was rather limited. When Easter arrived he heard his devout Christian neighbors repeatedly intone, "Christ has risen! Christ has risen!"

At first he did not grasp the meaning of the phrase, but after some reflection he thought he finally understood.

That Easter Sunday, when his pious neighbors were on their way to church, they could not help but notice the large new sign in Bloom's store window:

Christ Has Risen—But Our Prices Remain the Same

✔   ✔   ✔

One boss put a sign on the wall of his office that discouraged 90% of the job-seekers. It read:

If You Consider Work a Pleasure—
You Can Have a Lot of Fun Around Here

✔   ✔   ✔

The late Polly Adler, author of "A House Is Not a Home," once contemplated using this sign in her "establishment":

It's a Business Doing Pleasure With You

✔   ✔   ✔

In the year of 1911, a dentist who billed himself as "Painless Parker," built himself the largest practice in New York. He charged fifty cents to extract a tooth, and as a pain-killer he used cocaine—the granddaddy of the novocaine which did not come into use until many years later. "Painless Parker" was located at Atlantic and Fourth avenues, in Brooklyn, near the Long Island Railroad, but his patients flocked to him from every borough in New York.

Other dentists also were beginning to use cocaine but few advertised "painless extractions" as blatantly as did Parker. One of the competing (and resentful) dentists, Dr. Mortimer Seligman, who had an office on Bronx Park South, grew so weary of patients who would ask if he was "painless" that he finally put this sign on the wall of his reception room:

I Am Not Painless—
Every Time a Patient Bites my Finger
I Holler OY!

✔   ✔   ✔

At Berman's Shoe Store in Beverly Hills:

Come In and Have a Fit

✔   ✔   ✔

Seymour and Harry Kaplan, two brothers, had retail stores next door to each other in the Bronx. Seymour ran a delicatessen, Harry a book shop.

One day Harry put a big red sign in his window announcing the current best-selling novel, "All This and Heaven Too." Not to be outdone, Seymour put this sign in his own window:

All This and Herring Too

✔   ✔   ✔

Hirschfeld, who opened the Old London Men's Shop in Detroit, picked a very poor location for the new store. Six months later he decided to close the place before he went bankrupt. This is the notice he placed in his window:

Opened By Mistake

✓ ✓ ✓

On a fruit stand in New York's Spanish Harlem:

Se Habla Yiddish

✓ ✓ ✓

Sid Blumberg, president of Commercial Rubbish Company, mounted a poster on his collection truck reading:

Satisfaction Guaranteed or Double Your Garbage Back

✓ ✓ ✓

The Jewish sense of humor crops out on signs in affluent as well as in poor neighborhoods—laughter is no respecter of social status. In an exclusive Beverly Hills area, studded with expensive nightclubs, and featuring nightly entertainment by prominent Hollywood and Broadway personalities, there is a tiny delicatessen.

One busy Saturday night the restaurant to the left of the little delicatessen displayed a sign reading "Frank Sinatra Appearing Nightly On Our Stage." The club on the right immediately installed a sign of their own: "George Jessel Appearing Nightly On Our Podium."

Not to be outdone, the little delicatessen between these two giants, soon had a sign in its own window:

Sam Feldman Appearing Nightly on Our Cash Register

✓ ✓ ✓

Contractors also have a funny-bone. Billposted in a half-completed building in Brownsville, where the alarm system had not yet been installed, were these instructions:

In Case of Fire
Run into the Hall and Holler

✓ ✓ ✓

In the personnel office of Hellman and Stein Fashions:

Your Salary Raise Becomes Effective as Soon as You Do

✓ ✓ ✓

An Israeli fly, hearing about the wonders of America, smuggled himself aboard a Zim ocean liner bound for the United States. His first day in New York he learned all about bigotry in this democracy when he buzzed past a sign in a hardware store window, reading: *Special! The New, More Powerful Insecticide, Guaranteed to Kill Instantly!*"

"*Vay is mir*," he observed sadly, "there's a lot of anti-Semitism in this country!"

✓   ✓   ✓

This neatly painted sign on a Newark synagogue:

Not Everybody Believes in God—
But God Believes in Everybody

✓   ✓   ✓

In the window of the Los Angeles travel agency owned by George Jessel and George Raft:

Please Go Away

✓   ✓   ✓

There is an Italian-Jewish restaurant in Philadelphia with this sign proudly displayed on the marquis:

The Kosher Noshtra

✓   ✓   ✓

The Crown Car Wash in Los Angeles has this sign out front:

Drive in, and Give Us the Latest Dirt

✓   ✓   ✓

In a little railroad station outside of Kiev, an attendant stalked over to a Jew who was placidly puffing away on a home-made cigarette.

"What's the matter with you, can't you read?" snapped the attendant, pointing to a sign directly over the offender's head.

"Yes, I can read," replied the Jew. "It says *Fine for Smoking*. All right, I agree!"

✓   ✓   ✓

In Visalia, California, reported actress Sally Winn, the Reliable Shoe Store was sold and the new owner named it Acme Shoes. This sign proclaimed the change of name:

Acme Shoes—Formerly Reliable

✓   ✓   ✓

Here is a notice tacked to the door of a Long Island haberdasher:

Let's Play Store—You Be the Customer

✓   ✓   ✓

SIGNS OF THE TIMES

Arnstein, a recently-retired insurance executive in Bucks County, Pennsylvania, had a penchant for complete privacy. To make sure he would not be annoyed by intruders he got a vicious dog and then put up this double-threat sign:

Beware of Dog
Survivors Will Be Prosecuted

⚡ ⚡ ⚡

In the window of the hip delicatessen on West Sixth Street in Greenwich Village:

Daddy-O Hot Pastrami Sandwiches
Made Like While You Wait, Man!

⚡ ⚡ ⚡

Walter Winchell reported this one on a West 56th Street coal and kerosene dealer's sign:

Fuel's Paradise

⚡ ⚡ ⚡

On the outside bulletin board of a reform temple in Miami:

Come Early and Get a Back Seat

⚡ ⚡ ⚡

The following sign is translated from the Yiddish. It appeared in the window of Herzog's Dairy and Bakery store, on Houston Street, in New York:

"We are not saying that milk grows hair,
but have you ever seen a bald-headed cat?"

⚡ ⚡ ⚡

Among the earlier "sign" jokes, the one about Otto Kahn evoked laughter in the mid-1920's.

The noted financier was being chauffeured to his office one day when his eye caught a tailor's shop displaying the proud sign, *Max Kahn, Cousin of Otto Kahn.* Enraged, the banker stopped the car, roared into the store and ordered non-relative Max to take the sign down forthwith. "Yes, sir," said Max timidly.

The next day, Kahn drove by again and was greeted with a new sign:

Max Kahn, Formerly Cousin of Otto Kahn

⚡ ⚡ ⚡

Sign on top of the cash register in Goldie Stein's Beauty Shoppe:

Just Married!
Please Count Your Change Carefully!

⚡ ⚡ ⚡

441

In the window of Jake's Delicatessen and Diner, on Chicago's South Side:

Customers Who Think Our Waiters Are Rude
Should See Our Manager

✓　✓　✓

Mike Saltzman operated a popular milkshake bar near the University of California at Los Angeles. Business was so flourishing that, to handle the overflow trade, he opened another milk bar across the street. On opening day, this sign proclaimed the expansion:

The Udder Place

✓　✓　✓

Safety Week was off to a bad start when these immortal words were displayed in the window of the Fairfax Delicatessen in Los Angeles:

Closed! Chef Burned His Hand
On a Hot Girdle

✓　✓　✓

In a Staten Island supermarket, above a crate of neatly stacked bananas:

Please Don't Tear Us Apart—We Grew Up Together

✓　✓　✓

A fish dealer on Intervale Avenue in the Bronx, put out a sign reading *Fresh Fish Sold Here.*

Soon a customer came into the store and pointed to the message. "Why did you put the word 'fresh' in your sign?" she asked in surprise. "It's understood your fish are fresh—or do they stink?"

"No, of course not!" said the fish dealer. Hurriedly he painted out the offending word.

A little while later another customer came in and commented, "What for do you need the word 'here' on your sign? Where else would you be selling fish, for heaven's sake!"

"You're right," agreed the fish dealer, painting out the word 'here.'

After an hour or so, another customer complained: "Sold? What do you mean, 'Sold'? Surely you haven't been giving away any of your fish!"

"Indeed not!" agreed the dealer, and he painted out the word 'sold.'

Finally, an old lady wearing a head kerchief, hobbled in. She saw the sign and croaked in a high, thin voice, " 'Fish?' You don't have to advertise your fish! Believe me, you can smell them a mile away!"

The fish dealer heaved a deep sigh, picked up his brush, and painted out the last word, 'fish.'

✓　✓　✓

SIGNS OF THE TIMES

For twenty years, Goldstein and Karp operated a prosperous dry goods store in a Jewish neighborhood. But gradually the area changed so that the local inhabitants were now predominantly Irish. Business began to fall off, and the two Jewish merchants grew more and more concerned. They wracked their brains for a solution.

"I have an idea," said Goldstein. "One of us should change his name to something Irish. Then maybe the new people will come to our store."

"A good plan," agreed Karp. "I'll call myself McGillicuddy from now on."

So they put up a new sign, *"Goldstein and McGillicuddy,"* and sure enough, business picked up almost immediately.

"Look," said Goldstein, "if one Irish name helps us that much, maybe we had better drop the 'Goldstein' too."

So they took down the old sign and put up another: *"McGillicuddy and McGillicuddy."*

Now they were even more prosperous than before.

One day a customer entered the store and asked to speak to McGillicuddy.

"Which one do you want?" asked the office girl. "The Goldstein McGillicuddy or the Karp McGillicuddy?"

✓   ✓   ✓

A policeman stalked over to where Benny was lying on the grass, reading a book.

"Hey, you!" the cop demanded loudly, "ain't you never been in a park before?"

Benny looked up, perplexed. "What's the matter, officer?"

"Can't you see that sign, *Keep Off the Grass?*"

"Well, yes, I saw the sign" Benny admitted, "but it doesn't say 'positively!' "

✓   ✓   ✓

A new tenant in the Empire State Building noticed a sign on one of the doors: *Goldberg, Goldfarb, Ginsberg and O'Grady—Attorneys.*

His sense of curiosity overcoming his manners, the new tenant button-holed the building superintendent. "Not that I want to stick my nose into other people's business," he said, pointing to the sign, "but tell me something; how did O'Grady get in there?"

"Easy," explained the superintendent. "He put up the money!"

✓   ✓   ✓

Sign in a pet shop:

Attention, Cat Lovers! Save Money!
Feed your cats lox. Instead of cream they'll drink water!

✓   ✓   ✓

A man was strolling idly along Pitkin Avenue when he saw a sign in the window of a store that had been converted into an office: *Brooklyn Lonely Hearts Club For Ladies Who Care.*

Intrigued, he walked inside and there, on the wall, he read another sign: *For Every Lovesick Man There Are Ten Lovesick Women.*

The astonished guy walked over to the desk and, pointing to the announcement, he crooned, "Tell me, Lady, how long is that offer good for?"

✓ ✓ ✓

"Madam," the manager of the Yid'l Lonely Hearts Club said severely, "you have no cause for complaint. Our sign distinctly said *'guy,'* not *'goy.'*"

✓ ✓ ✓

In the toy section of a large department store:

Attention All Kids! Get Your Own H-Bomb Kit!
Be First on Your Block to Rule the World!

✓ ✓ ✓

On the wall of Krasnoff's grocery store in Milwaukee:

I Am Sure Your Check is Good,
But I Just Don't Trust Your Bank

✓ ✓ ✓

Fred Rosenberg, owner of the "Top-O-Marquis" on Hollywood's famed Sunset Strip, evoked grins with this lively announcement:

Of Course We Serve Knives with Our Steaks!
How Else Can You Butter the Bread?

✓ ✓ ✓

Sign on a Reform Temple in Baton Rouge:

Come This Friday—Avoid the Passover Rush

✓ ✓ ✓

A plaque in a Manhattan lawyer's office:

For the Woman Who has Everything—A Divorce!

✓ ✓ ✓

Posted at the entrance to a cemetery:

Due to a Strike
Grave-digging Will Be Done by a Skeleton Crew

✓ ✓ ✓

In the window of Alpertson's Antique Store in Chicago:

Best Prices Paid for Old Furniture and Junk
—Genuine Antiques Sold Here—

Glossary

Glossary

(Definition: A Collection of Glosses)
by
Dorothy H. Rochmis

Gloss, according to Webster (master of glosses) is a noun meaning "an interpretation, as of marginal or interlinear words; a note of explanation; loosely, a running commentary."

The ensuing, then, is a collection of glosses which may serve to introduce (or clarify) certain Yiddishisms which are contained in some of the stories in this book.

There are many different pronunciations in Yiddish, just as there are in English. Some say "pittehr" and some say "pootehr" for the Yiddish word meaning butter, just as some say "cahm" and others say "cawm" for the English word which is spelled "calm." But the literate word has, in any language, only one accepted spelling.

Since Yiddish is a phonetic language, that accepted spelling (as authenticated by the Yiddish Scientific Institute in New York City) becomes the accepted pronunciation. In other words, your mother might have said "pittehr" when she wanted butter, but if she were writing the word, and writing it correctly, she'd have spelled out "pootehr" and—it therefore follows—if she read what she wrote, she would pronounce it "pootehr." But then again, you know how Jewish mothers are! She'd probably refuse to read her own handwriting.

Anyway, to further enhance your enjoyment and understanding of this anthology, here is our collection of "glosses"!

✓   ✓   ✓

AFIKOMEN: This is a Hebrew word (many of them have crept into Yiddish) which means dessert. It is most familiarly known as those pieces of *matzoh* which are hidden during the Passover *seder* and which are to be eaten at the end of the meal. The children wait for this moment all during the *seder*, since the head of the house rewards the finder with tender more negotiable than *matzoh*.

ALEPH-BAIZ: Of course, everything starts with the ABC. In Yiddish, however, the first three letters of the alphabet are: *aleph, baiz, gimmel*. Since that's a bit cumbersome, everyone always refers to the Yiddish-Hebrew alphabet as "The Aleph-Baiz."

ALTEH: Old one (when speaking of a woman). It's *altehr* when speaking of an old man. And, to complicate matters, *alteh* is used as the plural as in *alteh shich*, meaning "old shoes." That "ch" in "shich" is not pronounced like the "ch" in "chosen people" but is a sound that starts deep in the throat as if you wanted to clear out a bone or a crumb that's stuck there. Or, in other words, like the "ch" in the German "*ach*, mein Gott."

APIKOYRES: A heretic, a free-thinker, a tongue-in-cheeker. A skeptic.

AZOI: This is a type of comment similar to the Japanese "Ah-so!" and its connotation is: "Really!" or "You don't say!" But it can also be used to indicate "This is how"—as in: *Azoi dertzailt men a vitz?* which means: This is how one tells a joke? (Yes, the word *vitz* means "joke.")

BACHURIM (Sing. *BACHUREI*): In old Europe (and as used in this encyclopedia) the word refers to students attending a Yeshivah, or talmudic college. In modern usage, *bachurim* also means young men.

BAGEL: A hard roll shaped in the form of a ring, resembling a doughnut; the dough is boiled and then baked. Highly recommended split and spread with cream cheese and lox.

BALEGOLEH: A coachman, a wagoner. One who carts goods or passengers.

BAR MITZVAH: The literal meaning is "son of the commandment." It is a religious ceremony at which time the Jewish lad of thirteen becomes a member of and assumes his inherent responsibilities to the Jewish community.

BAS MITZVAH (BATH MITZVAH): Ceremony held in the temple, usually on Friday night, to admit formally as an adult of the Jewish community, a girl of thirteen.

BIMAH: A dais or platform in the center of the synagogue where the Torah is read.

BLINTZES: Cheese, kasha (groats) or berries rolled in thin dough and fried in fat. The French would call them "crèpes suzettes." There is no singular form for the word *blintzes*, because who eats just one?

BOBEH: Grandmother. It should be noted that *bobeh myseh* literally means a grandmother's story, but actually it refers to a story that's a complete fabrication—in the realm of a fairy tale or a lie.

BORSCHT: This is a soup made either of beets or cabbage. The beet *borscht* may be eaten hot or cold, with or without sour cream. The cabbage *borscht* is served hot—very, very hot, and is especially good with pumpernickel bread.

GLOSSARY

BRIS: Covenant; the act and ceremony of circumcision, usually performed on the eighth day after the birth of the boy.

CHALEH: Rich white bread usually associated with Sabbath or holy day feasts. In our "affluent society" however, *chaleh* may be eaten at any time.

CHANUKAH: Holiday commemorating the victory of the Maccabees in the year 165 B.C.E. It is celebrated for eight days beginning on the 25th day of the month of Kislev. One of its traditions is the lighting of candles for eight days as a reminder of the miracle of the cruse of oil which burned for eight days instead of one. It is a festival most popular with children who enjoy lighting the candles, receiving traditional gifts of money (*Chanukah gelt*) and playing appropriate games, especially the *dreidel* which is a top with four Hebrew letters: *Nun, Gimmel, Hay* and *Shin*. These letters stand for *Nes Gadol Hayah Sham* or "A great miracle happened there." Chanukah marks what was probably the first struggle for religious freedom in history.

CHASSENEH: Wedding. Jewish weddings were always, even in the poorest families, unforgettable events, accompanied by much hoo-hah. And why not? Anyone who remained unmarried was obviously a misfit in the Jewish order of things.

CHASSID (pl. *CHASSIDIM*; adj. *CHASSIDIC*): The word itself means "pious." In actual reference it is a follower or member of the Chassidic movement which was founded by Israel Baal Shem Tov in the 18th century. While Chassidism has lost its significance as a mass movement, it is still practiced by numerous small groups—some as close as the Williamsburg section of Brooklyn, New York.

CHAZAN: A Cantor.

CHEDER (*HEDER*): Jewish parochial school for the teaching of the bible, Hebrew, history, prayers, etc., in the Jewish liturgy.

CHOCHEM: Both of these "ch's" are pronounced in that same, deep, dry clearing of the throat indicated earlier. (See *Alteh*.) *Chochem* is a wise man or sage, or when used sarcastically, a "wise guy."

CHOLLILEH: God forbid!

CHOZZER: Pig; glutton.

CHRAIN: Horseradish.

CHUTZPAH: Impudence; unmitigated nerve.

DIASPORA: Exile; dispersion of Jews after the conquest of Palestine by the Romans in 70 A.D. Also called "Galuth" or more commonly, in Yiddish, as *Golos*, referring to the collective lands of Jewish dispersion.

EFSHER: Perhaps.
EPPES: Something.

449

FAHRSHTAY: Understand. The noun is *fahrshtand,* and somehow it means more than "understanding." There's a Jewish thumb in *fahrshtand* which lends concepts like intuition, knowledge and *Yiddishe kop*—meaning, of course, a Jewish head. Do you *fahrshtay?*

FARFEL: Small pellets of crumbs, made of dough, matzoh or noodles, as part of Jewish cookery.

FARGESSEN: Forgotten. The phrase *shoin fargessen* means "already forgotten."

FARSHTUNKENEH: Stinking.

FAST OF GEDALIAH: Gedaliah, the prince appointed by the king of Babylonia as governor of Judah after the destruction of the First Temple, was assassinated by Jewish zealots. Thereafter many of the Jews who had escaped Babylonian captivity, settled in Egypt. Gedaliah's assassination was considered a national calamity and the event is still commemorated by Orthodox Jews on the third day of Tishre, as *Tzom Gedaliah* (the Fast of Gedaliah).

FEH: Exclamation of distaste or disgust.

FLANKEN: This is a cut of meat which, in these ecumenical days, one can even buy in a *goyishe* butcher shop. It is usually boiled and is great with *chrain* (and by this time you know that is horseradish, don't you?).

FLAISHIK: Pertaining to meat; meat dishes.

FORVERTS: Forward; progress. Name of a Yiddish daily newspaper.

GABBAI: Synagogue manager or trustee.

GALITZIANER: A Jew from Galicia. But it means more than that. Among the "Litvaks" (Jews from Lithuania) a "Galitzianer" is a no-goodnik, an illiterate, almost a *shaigetz.* And, of course, among the Galitzianer, a Litvak is a no-goodnik, an illiterate, etc. There is much esprit de corps among the Galitzianer about the Galitzianer and among the Litvaks about the Litvaks. And never the twain shall meet.

GANEFF: Thief. Transliterationists also spell this word *goniff.* But either way, he's still a thief.

GANTSEH: Whole.

GAON: Genius; outstanding scholar. Title was originally given to the chief of the rabbinical academy in Babylon from the end of the sixth century to the eleventh century, and to some extent even later. *Gaon* is a title meaning "excellency" and is applied in common usage to a person of outstanding originality and talmudic scholarship.

GEFILTE FISH: Stuffed fish seasoned with spices, usually served as a separate course in the Sabbath meal. Originally, house-wives would actually stuff the skins of the fish with the body of the fish which they had scooped out, fileted and chopped up fine with various spices. But our modern housewife awoke one Friday morning and asked herself, "What's so important about the skin of the fish?" And when she could find no logical, meaningful or traditional answer, she promptly discarded the skin, formed the filling into servable portions and dropped them into the broth in which they simmered quite contentedly.

GEMARA: In Yiddish, this is pronounced *Gemoreh*. It is part of the Talmud which deals with the interpretation and discussion of the law as presented in the Mishna.

GEVALD: Help!

GIMMEL: Third letter of the Hebrew-Yiddish alphabet. Corresponds to the English letter "g" as in *"Gevald!"*

GOY (pl. GOYIM): Gentile.

GRIBBEN: When the Jewish housewife renders chicken fat, she puts small bits of the chicken's skin into the pan along with the fat. When the fat is rendered, these bits of chicken skin are removed and drained so that they are crisp and, oh, so delicious! The rendered chicken fat is called *schmaltz*. (See our "gloss" below.)

GROSCHEN: A silver coin whose value, around the turn of the century, was about two cents. It is now the 10-pfennig piece. In Austria, a *groschen* is a minor bronze coin worth 1/100 schilling.

GUT GEZOGT: Well said.

HAIMISHEH: Homey; homelike; comfortably undemanding.

HAMANTASHEN: This is a pastry designed especially for Purim, shaped into a triangle, like Haman's three-cornered hat. The dough is filled with either a prune paste, a cheese filling or poppy-seeds.

HELZEL: Neck of a bird. In Jewish cookery, *helzel* refers to the neck-skin of a fowl (goose, chicken, duck) and its stuffing, consisting of meal, egg, spices, etc.

HERR: This is a German word meaning "mister" or "sir."

HOCKFLAISH: *Hock* means "chop" and *flaish* means "meat" and together they spell "chopped meat" or what we know so well as "hamburger."

INGELEH: Little boy. A boy is an *ingel* (and a girl is a *maidel*) but when you put the "eh" at the end of the word, it's so much more tender and diminutive.

KADDISH: The mourner's prayer after the death of a close relative, usually after the death of a parent. The son who recites the prayer after the death of his parent is also called the "kaddish."

KAFTAN: Long black coat worn by East European Jews.

KASHA: Groats (buckwheat).

KATCHKEH: Duck.

KIBITZER: Spectator at a card game who gives uninvited advice; one who jokes and chitchats while others are trying to work.

KICHEL: Cookie.

KINDERLACH: Plural of *kind* (child) is *kinder*, but when you want to speak of the *kinder* with special tenderness, you call them *kinderlach*.

KISHKEH. Stuffed intestine. On some menus, this is listed as "derma."

KNAIDLACH (sing. *KNAIDEL*): Matzoh-balls.

KNISHES (sing. *KNISH*): Filled patties or dumplings, often made of rolled dough.

KOHEN: A priest; a member of the priestly tribe (Levi). When translated into surnames, all Cohens, Kahns, and even Kagans and Cogans stem from that kingly title. How did the Kagan and Cogan get in there? Well, the Russian "h" is the equivalent of the English or Latin "g" and the Russian Jews spelled their names wrong to the questioning immigration authorities, substituting the "g" for the "h" . . . which most assuredly is a fascinating part of the history of the Jews in America.

KOL NIDRE: A solemn prayer that ushers in the Day of Atonement on Yom Kippur eve.

KOPEK: (Russian). A copper coin; the 100th part of a ruble.

KOSHER: Food prepared according to Jewish ritual law. Relates to the slaughter of animals, preparation of food and dietary regulations. The Jewish dietary laws which are based on biblical and rabbinical ordinances are as old as the Jewish people themselves and have had a great influence on Jewish life. These laws distinguish between foods which are *kosher* (permissible) and *traif* (forbidden).

KREPLACH: Dough filled with meat and boiled. The Chinese call them won ton and the Italians have a version which they call ravioli.

KUGEL: Noodle or bread pudding usually cooked with raisins.

LAMDEN: Erudite scholar.

LANDSMAN (pl. *LANDSLEIT*): Countryman.

LATKES: Chanukah is the time for this delicious edible. It is made of raw potatoes which are grated (thus, all properly made *latkes* contain a bit of mama's scraped knuckles), onion, egg and seasoning, all mixed thoroughly and fried like all good pancakes should be fried. The singular is *latkeh*, but have you ever heard of anybody eating just one? It's as impossible as eating a single potato chip.

LIEBEH: Loved one, or love affair.

LITVAK: Lithuanian Jew.

MAFTIR: One who reads the weekly selection of the Prophets after the reading of the Torah.

GLOSSARY

MAGGID: Preacher; orator.

MALACH—HAMOVES: Ghost; angel of death.

MAMENYU: In that inimitable manner of the Jews, the diminutive for Mama has the Russian-Polish *nyu* added as a suffix to become the very endearing *mamenyu*. Similarly *tateh* (father) becomes *tatehnyu*. And when *mamenyu* raises her eyes to the ceiling and moans, *"Tatehnyu"* (note the capitalized "T"), she is, of course, addressing God whom she also frequently refers to as *"Gottenyu."*

MATZOH: Unleavened bread eaten during Passover (Pesach) in commemoration of the exodus of the Jews from Egypt.

MAZEL: Luck.

MAZEL TOV: Good luck.

MEGILLAH: Scroll; the Book of Esther read during Purim. But it is used freely in Yiddish to indicate a long and complicated story.

MELAMED: Teacher, usually at the elementary grades level.

MENTSCH (MENTSH): One who is, or is considered to be, more than an ordinary human being. Hence the familiar admonition: "Be a *mentsch!*"

MESHUGGEH: Crazy, insane, nuts.

MESHUGGENER (fem. and pl. *MESHUGGENEH*): Someone who is *meshuggeh,* i.e. crazy, insane, et (without) al.

MEZUZAH: A small metal or wooden case with a strip of parchment placed therein on which are inscribed twenty-two lines from Deuteronomy (6:4-9 and 11:13-21) dealing with the Jew's obligation to love God and obey His commandments. The reverse side of this parchment bears the name *Shaddai* (Almighty), which is visible when the parchment is folded and placed in the case. This case is attached to the right (as one enters) doorpost of the house and of each room used for living purposes. Actually the word *mezuzah* literally means "doorpost."

MIDRASH: This is a Hebrew term meaning "investigation" or "study," and applies to a special type of broad interpretation of the biblical text. These are devotional and ethical in character and illustrate the literal text of the Bible and its allegories.

MIKVEH: Ritual bath; indoor bath or pool for ritual purification.

MILCHIK: Dairy; pertaining to dairy foods, to the cooking utensils in which they are prepared and to the dishes and cutlery used in serving them.

MINCHEH: Afternoon devotional prayers.

MINYON: Quorum of ten males required before public religious services may begin.

MISAH MESHUNAH: Literally this means "a strange death." Actually it is used to suggest a fit, not unlike apoplexy.

MISHPOCHEH: Family, relatives.

MITZVAH: Divine commandment; good deed. It is the Hebrew term for

453

a religious and moral obligation. In tradition all commandments, statutes, teachings and observances are *mitzvahs*.

MOHEL: Circumciser.

MOMZER: Bastard. This is not a nice word, and is used only when there has been a good deal of provocation.

MOSER (pl. *MOSRIM*): An informer; a tattler.

MUZHIK (*MOUJIK*): A Russian peasant.

NEBACH: An exclamation usually used to connote pity. Some just say "tsk-tsk!" and shake their heads sorrowfully. On the other hand, there are some whom we label a *"nebach"*—usually because they are so pitifully unendowed.

NU: This is a most versatile non-word. It can be used to nudge someone into action. It is also used to connote "well?" or "so?" or "so what?" and "what about it?" and so on.

NUDNIK: A bore. Best illustrated thusly: A *nudnik* is a person who, when asked how he is, really tells you exactly how he is.

OY: An exclamation denoting either pain or surprise, and sometimes even rapture. It all depends on the inflection—and, of course, on how many *"oy's"* you say, sigh or scream: *Oy, oy!* or *oy, oy, oy!* and occasionally even five or six *oy, oy's*.

OY VAY: You already know what *oy* means. When you add *vay* to it, you are adding "woe." And if you hear an over-protective mother exclaim: *"Oy vay iz mir!"* she is saying, "Oh woe unto me!" and is probably rushing her mischievous young one to the sink to stop his nose-bleed.

PARNES (*Russian*): Representative of a community.

PASKUDNIAK: This isn't a nice word and is used about a person who is not very nice. While the root of the word might come from the word "nausea," a person who is called a *paskudniak* is not only a nauseating individual but, in plain English, a louse.

PASSOVER (*PESACH*): The spring festival which commemorates the deliverance of the Jews from their bondage in Egypt. It lasts eight days, beginning with the 15th of Nisan (March-April). It is a time when only Passover foods are eaten (*matzoh* and such) and only on special Passover dishes.

POOPIK: Technically, this means a belly button or navel. But it is used freely in Yiddish to denote something small and insignificant, and is even personalized when the individual referred to is called "Moishe Poopik" or "Moishe Pippik" and as such it means "Mr. Nobody."

PORETZ: a Polish squire. A gentile all-rightnik.

GLOSSARY

PURIM: Festival of Lots, marking the deliverance of the Jews from Haman's plot to exterminate them (Book of Esther). Celebrated on the 14th and 15th day of Adar (March). Children enjoy Purim carnivals when they can dress up like their heroes, Ahasuerus or Mordechai, or like the villain of the piece, Haman. Adults may have "beauty contests" in which the lovely Queen Esther is selected. *Hamantashen* are eaten.

REB: Teacher; title given to a learned or respected man. It is also used as the equivalent of "mister."

REBBE: Teacher; title given to a learned man. Usually referred to a Chassidic leader—but there are so few around these days that *rebbe* remains "teacher."

REBBENYU: This is a term of endearment for a rabbi, something like saying: "Rabbi dear."

REBBETZN: Wife of a rabbi; wife of a teacher; wife of a Chassidic leader; and usually the backbone, materialistically speaking, of the un-wordly rabbi, teacher and/or Chassidic leader.

ROSH HASHONAH: This means "beginning of the year." It is a Fall holiday celebrating the beginning of the Jewish New Year and, on the Hebrew calendar, that makes it the 1st of Tishri (in September).

RUBLE: Silver coin of Russia. Valued at 51¢ during the Czarist regime.

SAICHEL: Good common sense; good judgment.

SCHMALTZ: Usually chicken or goose fat which has been rendered. It has been freely adapted into the English language, particularly in show business parlance, to denote anything well-larded with corny sentiment. *Schmaltz* is delicious when spread on a piece of pumpernickel bread and lightly salted.

SCHNAPPS: Whiskey, or any strong liquor. The "aperitif" was very popular among Jewish families who could afford it—only it was called a *schnapps*.

SCHNOOK (SHNOOK): An unimportant or stupid person. A dope.

SEDER: The Passover Eve ritual during which the *Haggadah* is read, recounting the liberation of the Jews from Egyptian bondage. The *seder* is a gala family event during which the patriarch sits on a well-cushioned "throne" and leads the *Haggadah* reading. The *seder* is held on the first night of Passover and is repeated on the second night, except by Reform Jews who have eliminated the second *seder*.

SE'UDAH: Festive meal.

SHABBES: The Sabbath; i.e. from sundown Friday to sundown Saturday.

SHADCHAN: A marriage broker; professional matchmaker. On the other hand, there is a natural-born *shadchan* in every family—because in every family there is someone who just loves to "arrange" things.

455

SHAIGETZ: A gentile; a *goy*; it is even applied sometimes to a Jew who is ignorant of Jewish customs or Judaism in general.

SHAMMES: The sexton of a synagogue.

SHAYNER: A good-looker (when referred to a man or a masculine noun). When you want to refer to the feminine gender, you say *shayneh*.

SHEKEL: This word has become part of the English language—so why don't you look it up in Webster's?

SHEVUOS (*SHEVUOTH*): Holiday commemorating the giving of the Torah to Moses. Feast of Weeks; Pentecost.

SHIKKER: Drunkard.

SHIKSE: The feminine of *shaigetz* (see above).

SHLEMIEL: He's very much like the *shlimazl*, except that he is also clumsy, inept, and a dolt.

SHLEPPER: This is the noun taken from the verb *shlep* which means "to pull or drag." When used as a noun, it is quite unflattering and means someone who just drags along without ever achieving anything. When used about a woman, it conjures up a total picture of someone whose slip is showing, whose hair is bedraggled and whose nose is running.

SHLIMAZL: Someone who always manages to run head first into hard luck. He just can't help it, poor luckless oaf.

SHMATTEH: Rag. The complaining wife will often weep that that's all she has to wear. If she steps all over her husband, he becomes a *shmatteh*.

SHNOR: To beg.

SHNORRER: One who begs. Frequently, competition among *shnorrers* was so keen that it became a contest of wit, brass and resourcefulness to wheedle money from others. When it was forthcoming it was accepted as if it were the *shnorrer's* right. But then, isn't that the road to success in every business? Even *shnorring*?

SHOFAR: The ram's horn which is blown on Rosh Hashonah as part of the ritual.

SHOICHET: Ritual slaughterer.

SHOLEM ALEICHEM: A greeting meaning, "Peace be unto you." It is also the pseudonym of Sholem Rabinowitch, the foremost Yiddish humorist and satirist who enjoyed much popularity in his lifetime. When he died in 1916, in New York, his funeral was attended by 150,000 people. Most recently, the smash hit, *Fiddler on the Roof*, was fashioned from his stories about Tevya the Dairyman.

SHREI: Yell.

SHTETL: Small town, village or hamlet. (Doesn't "*ham*let" sound too *goyish* to use in connection with *shtetl*?)

SHUL: Synagogue or school.

SIMCHAS TORAH (*SIMHATH TORAH, SIMCHATH TORAH*): Jewish festival that is joyously celebrated on the last day of *Sukkoth,* marking the annual completion of the reading of the Torah.

STREIMEL: A fur hat worn by Chassidim.

SUKKAH: Booth; a wooden construction covered with branches, used during Sukkos, the autumn harvest holiday which is celebrated for seven days (nine, if you include Shemini Atzereth and Simchas Torah), starting with the 15th day of Tishri. It commemorates the fact that the Jews lived in booths or tents during their wanderings in the desert.

TALLIS: Prayer shawl.

TALMUD TORAH: Hebrew school for children.

TANTEH: Aunt. This is an international word. It is the same in French, German and many other languages. But the *tanteh,* in *Yiddish,* is next of kin, certainly, to a Jewish mother (like which there is no other).

TATEH: Father, papa, daddy.

TEFILLIN: Phylacteries. Leather cases containing quotations from the Pentateuch, worn by Jews on the forehead and on the left arm during morning prayers.

THALER: Any of various large silver coins of the former German states, and Austria; a dollar.

TORAH: The teachings; the Law; the Old Testament. The entire body of Jewish wisdom. The Five Books of Moses. Pentateuch.

TRAIF: Food which, according to dietary laws, is impure; unfit for consumption. Or, to put it another way, not *kosher.*

TSADDIK: Literally, this means "the just." It is used to indicate someone with saintlike qualities; a Chassidic leader; a righteous one.

TSIMMIS: A sweet dish in which carrots and prunes are mixed with honey and several other ingredients. It is eaten as a side-dish.

TSORRES: Troubles; miseries.

TUCHUS: Rear end (of a person).

VAY IZ MIR: Woe is me! (See above for *oy* and *oy vay.*)

VAYN: Cry.

YARMULKEH: Skull cap worn by religious Jews, in order to have the head covered at all times.

YENTEH: Someone who sticks her nose into everyone else's business; a busybody; a gossip and tattle-tale. And Jews, being the wits they are, sometimes give the one they are calling "*yenteh*" a surname: Yenteh Tellabendeh. The surname does little else than rhyme with *yenteh.*

YESHIVAH: Rabbinical academy; talmudic college.

YICHES: Lineage; pedigree; status gained through scholarship, through money in the family, or a combination of both.

YISHUVNIK: *Yishuv* means community. The *nik* added to *Yishuv* refers to someone who lives in the community.

YOM KIPPUR: Day of Atonement. The most solemn of all Jewish holidays, during which time one abstains from all food and drink for twenty-four hours.

ZEMLIAK (ZEMLYAK): A Russian word meaning countryman.

ZHID: This is a Russian word meaning "Jew" and, as the Russians used it, it was pejorative.

ZLOTY: Large silver Polish coin. 100 groschy equalled 1 zloty.